Choosing to Smile

To Arlene
Ronald says you are most
definitely a cancer THRIVER!
Keep on shining!
Love,
Glenda.

Choosing to Smile

Keep smiling!

Julie Houlker

Michelle Rickaby

Glenda Standeven

Choosing to Smile Publications
Chilliwack, BC

Choosing to Smile Publications
P. O. Box 2372
Sardis Station Main
Chilliwack, BC V2R 1A7
Canada
www.choosingtosmile.com

Printed in Canada

ISBN 978-1-9865227-0-3

FIRST EDITION
15 14 13 12 11 10 09 10 9 8 7 6 5 4 3 2 1

Designer: Detta Penna
Copyeditors: Wendy McClelland and Detta Penna
Proofreader: Sarah Nermo

Cover photo and author photos: Karen Massier

This book is dedicated to every person
who is choosing to smile after facing any of life's adversities
and to those who may one day have to choose…

Contents

Prologue

The four women stood among the stacks, inhaling the familiar smell that can only be found in old book stores. Each woman was inexplicably drawn to the books that spoke to them and today all four were drawn to the inspirational section. What led these four women to this particular point in time? What coincidences and challenges had created this circle of friendship that couldn't be broken? Life has a way of unfolding the way it should, although not necessarily the way we want. Michelle, Julie, Glenda, and Bonnie decided that their stories needed to be told because they are like so many others — ordinary, yet extraordinary. They are friends who have chosen to smile through all the adversities life has given them. Here is the story of three of the four women in the book store... the fourth remains to be told.

Left to right: Michelle Rickaby, Bonnie Holmes, Glenda Standeven, and Julie Houlker.

Introduction

The book you are about to read is not just another cancer story. It doesn't begin with cancer and it doesn't end with cancer. This is the story of three ordinary women who decided to do the extraordinary. They started a global movement for people who are choosing to smile, despite the adversities they faced in the past, or are still facing today. Every minute of every day, people around the world are faced with universal struggles such as illness, divorce, the death of a loved one, financial concerns, addictions, and many other obstacles, but how we cope with these challenges is a choice. We can live with bitterness, disappointment, and regret, or we can choose to smile as each hardship we encounter along the way becomes a lesson in appreciation.

In the following pages, you will meet Glenda. Her story is filled with laughter and love amid the many memorable moments of her life as a small town girl with big dreams. Glenda's story revolves around friendships and family; tragedies and triumphs. Throughout her story, Glenda reveals that she is a woman who chooses to smile even when life turns out surprisingly different than the way she'd imagined it would.

You will meet Michelle; soft-spoken with an inner strength and determination that belies her freckles and twinkling eyes. Michelle is a woman who went from a high school dropout to earning a degree and working in a university. Her story of achievement is told with humbleness and modesty because, to Michelle, her story is not extraordinary. It is simply the story of her life.

You will meet Julie; a petite, porcelain-skinned English woman with the heart of an adventurer. Julie is blessed with the gift of "stubborn determination" which allows her to overcome whatever hurdle is placed in front of her. Following her journey from a small English village to becoming an international traveller, wife, mother, grandmother, and an author, Julie's story of loving, and living with extraordinary passion, reaffirms that anything is possible, if you believe.

You will meet their families and become part of the circle of their lives. The gift of friendship resonates in all three womens' journeys. You may see your own life stories woven throughout this book. Each of us has a piece of Glenda, Michelle, and Julie inside. We cannot help but be destined for great things when we have the heart of a survivor, the gift of friendship, and are choosing to smile.

Glenda's Story

I remember sitting cross-legged on the sundeck of our North Vancouver home with a group of neighborhood kids. I was the centre of attention, regaling them with horror stories invented about my recent surgery. Barely five years old and already a consummate storyteller, I had just returned from the hospital where I'd had my tonsils removed. The truth was, I didn't remember anything about the operation except eating Jell-O® and ice cream and looking through the bars of my hospital crib at the little blonde boy in the bed beside mine. It's funny and just a little ironic that one of my earliest memories is of being in a hospital. I don't remember the pain, I don't remember the doctors; I do remember the cute little boy. I guess that's how I've always lived my life; I try to block out anything bad and focus on the good instead. It drives my three sisters crazy that I recall very little of anything unpleasant about my childhood but why would I? I grew up in a wonderful state of self-induced family bliss. If I do recall any minor upheavals, I try to come away with a lesson learned. I attempt to see every rotten thing in life as an opportunity to grow. That is easy to say but not always easy to do.

I am the third oldest in a family of four girls and two boys. That makes me a middle child, which explains a lot. I had a brother, Sylvan, two years older than me, who died as a baby. I'm glad to put his name in this book because sometimes I think the family has forgotten him. Mom and Dad never really talked about Sylvan, but I feel an odd connection with my big brother even though I never met him. When I was a little girl, I found a photo of him in his tiny little coffin and I remember thinking that he looked like a doll sleeping. That single photo made him real to me. I don't know what happened to the picture, but Mom probably has it tucked away in a box somewhere. Knowing I had a big brother looking out for me from heaven helped me through some tough times. I knew he was in heaven because that's where all "good" Catholics go. Sylvan had been baptized before he died and, no matter what anyone else said, I was sure Sylvan shot straight to heaven without having to do time in purgatory. I knew he hadn't committed any sins. He was my personal angel, although he wouldn't be my last.

Mom had us two years apart. The rhythm method obviously worked well for my parents. My sister Sylvia came first in 1951; Sylvan in 1953; I was born in 1955; Lorrie in 1957; Corrine (we all call her Beanie) in 1959; and then suddenly the rhythm method failed. My wonderful little brother, Jimmy, came along as an unplanned, unexpected and unabashed miracle in 1960. He and my sister were just 16 months apart and he was the joy of all our lives. Well, most of the time. He was such a gorgeous little boy; we all adored him. For all the love and attention his big sisters showered on him you'd think he would be spoiled rotten but he wasn't. He had a gentle soul and a heart as big as a house.

Jimmy was only two years old when we left North Vancouver in 1962. We moved to the small town of Yarrow, about 60 miles (100 kilometers) from the North Vancouver home where I was born. It may as well have been another country though. We went from city kids to country kids in the span of an hour.

My dad was unusually hard on my little brother. Dad figured Jimmy would end up being a sissy because he was growing up in a house full of girls. That couldn't have been further from the truth. Jimmy took on the "man of the house" role as if he'd been born to it. He was always the little fixer when our dad was away, and he was away a lot. Dad worked for BC Hydro (the power company) and spent long stretches away from home. Mom was fiercely independent and I think she actually resented it when dad came home and took over. With dad away so often, mom didn't always have the time to keep a watchful eye on us around the clock, and we took advantage of our extra freedom in many ways.

For example, I first kissed a boy when I was five or maybe even younger. We were living in Lynn Valley, North Vancouver, BC. It was largely undeveloped back then. I remember going to play in the empty field up the road on a clear, cold winter day. My big sister, Sylvia, pulled me there on a sled and we went sledding for hours. While I waited my turn, Danny Hanson kissed me. Danny was the boy next door and was just a year or two older than me. That sweet little kiss warmed me and I never felt cold all afternoon while we played. I didn't want to leave even when Sylvia said it was time to go but then I cried all the way home because I was freezing. I never felt the cold when I was playing with Danny. I wonder if he remembers that first kiss. For a while, I loved Danny Hanson but then he did something so horrible I could never forgive him and I was glad we moved away soon after "the incident."

I'm sure Danny and his brothers were all involved but I distinctly remember Danny being one of the culprits on that warm spring day. He and one of his older brothers had caught a snake. Unlike some girls, I didn't have a problem with snakes. I liked them. I liked the way they felt and I liked the way they would wrap themselves around your arm and let you carry them anywhere. That sunny day in North Vancouver, Danny and his brothers had caught a big — and I mean BIG — garter snake. They stretched it across the sidewalk and it reached from one side to the other. I remember being fascinated because it was so big and fat. I'm not sure which of those boys picked up the first big rock, but nobody stopped him. I couldn't believe that he was going to hurt the snake. The snake had done nothing wrong.

I watched in disbelief as he dropped the big rock dead center on the snake and the snake's body seemed to explode. Pieces of the snake flew everywhere. I think that was how I learned garter snakes give birth to live babies. The little snakes became projectiles. A piece of snake, or maybe one of its babies, hit my cheek and I remember screaming and crying at the same time. It was one of the most horrific things I've ever seen and one of the cruelest acts I've ever witnessed. I hated boys for a long time and never forgave Danny for being part of that sadistic act. I was only a child but I knew it was so very wrong to hurt an innocent creature — even a snake.

Those two events still stand out vividly in my memory even to this day. The first kiss was the best and the snake was the worst. It's just a little odd that both memories should involve the same boy.

I also remember the lovely couple who lived on the other side of our house in North Vancouver. They were English and they let me come over to visit. They didn't have children, so maybe I filled a void somehow. They had quite a lovely rock collection. I'd been taught that it's a sin to covet your neighbor's stuff and I was pretty sure that meant his rocks too, but oh how I coveted those rocks. They were shot through with silver — probably mica — but I thought they were the most amazing things I'd ever seen and I wanted them. I was five or six years old. I knew stealing was a sin, but I didn't care. I had to have those rocks. So I took them. With unabashed pride I showed the rocks to my mother and when she asked me where I found them I told her without a moment's hesitation that I had found them under a tree. She made me show her where, and I marched down the road to a big tree and pointed confidently at the base and lied. She believed me!

I couldn't quite grasp the scope of the event but I knew I was onto something. I could get away with a crime and not be punished. In retrospect, I'm surprised I didn't become a kleptomaniac or a criminal because that lie came remarkably easily. I feel guilty for this act even to this day. When I made my first confession at church, years after my theft, I confessed my "sin" and the priest told me that the only way I could be forgiven was to return the rocks. We had already moved to Yarrow, an hour drive away from where the "crime" had occurred years earlier. I decided I was either going to go to hell at that point or I could just get rid of the evidence. I threw the rocks away and decided that confession was stupid, and so was the priest for coming up with such a ridiculous suggestion. I decided I'd take the matter up with God when we met. I still feel that way! I've got quite a list of things to go over with Him when we meet, or IF we meet, because according to some staunch believers I'm way past redemption.

Possibly the best thing my parents did for us was to move us from North Vancouver to that four-acre hobby farm in Yarrow, even though it was tough to go from a private Catholic school to a mostly Mennonite community school. On my first day of classes at my new school in grade one, I remember feeling like a Martian when I made the sign of the cross after our morning prayer. The kids looked at me as if I was some kind of weirdo. That night I talked to mom about it and she said it would be okay not to make the sign of the cross. Luckily for me, Miss White, my grade one teacher, was Catholic, and she would say the rosary with me and a couple of other Catholic kids at the end of the day so I didn't feel completely out of my element.

Our life in Yarrow was idyllic. We had unlimited freedom. We rode our bikes everywhere. We stayed out till dark without a worry. Mom never knew exactly where we were but she believed we were safe and generally just a front porch holler away. We had four acres to roam around on and neighborhood kids to play with every day. We had chores — lots of them — but there was always time to play. I was happy...really happy. I had good friends and, as siblings go, I had pretty good ones. When I was 14, my sister Sylvia moved to Edmonton after her graduation. When she left home, I suddenly became

Family portrait 1965: From left, Sylvia, Glenda, Dad Barney, Lorrie, Jimmy, Mom Carol, and Beanie (Corrine).

the older sister, a role I wasn't very comfortable with. I tried hard to be a good role model but I was too busy getting into trouble. It was definitely a simpler time to grow up than nowadays, but if mom had known what we were really up to, she would never have let us out of her sight!

Growing up in farm country, there were large families and plenty of kids to play with. Kathy moved to Yarrow when I was in grade three. She lived just down the road and was the opposite of the good little Mennonite girl. Kathy was what the teachers called "bad," because she questioned their authority. Some of the teachers warned my parents not to let me associate with "that new girl," which only made me want to play with her all the more. We lived five houses away from each other and made an instant connection. Our mothers became friends and so did we. She spoke German, which made her seem intelligent and exotic to me. Even though many of my school friends were Mennonite, not many of them spoke German. I loved the way she laughed, and I loved the way she didn't care what anyone else thought about her. That first summer together, she and I built sturdy rafts and amazing underground forts; we smoked stolen cigarettes in the barn and built tunnels in the hay. I have no idea why we never set a barn on fire. We confided in each other and shared our hopes and dreams. She was going to be a writer and I was going to be a TV reporter.

In September, we were thrilled to discover that we were in a grade four/five split class together. For the entire school year and an amazing summer afterwards we were inseparable, but the following September, she moved on to grade six and I went on to grade five. I think she found me too tame and, being a whole year younger, the age difference had caught up to us at last. We stayed friends, but our friendship circles widened to include other people. (Note: Kathy eventually chose a life filled with travel and adventure. Her wild side led her to serving time in a women's prison and the HIV virus, but also eventually to an amazing career as a counselor with vast life experiences to draw from. She was, and still is, a remarkable person.)

It seems unlikely to have such strong memories of my youth, but good friendships make lasting impressions. I'm funny about friendships. I choose them wisely; nurture and treasure them. I guess I choose friends who value friendships the same way I do because many of the friends I made in school are still my friends today.

Shelly came into my life in grade five and quickly replaced Kathy in the top spot on my friendship pole. Her family moved to Yarrow from Lloydminster, Alberta, and our parents became good friends. At first, I thought I wanted to be friends with her because her older brother loved snakes as much as I did, and was the most handsome boy I'd ever seen. I soon realized that Shelly was more like a sister to me, in some ways than my own were, and we became inseparable. I taught her how to kiss boys, climb trees, smoke cigarettes, and build forts. Where I led, Shelly bravely followed. When we first met, I thought she was shy, quiet, blonde, and beautiful. She was the perfect daughter — obedient, hard-working, intelligent and just plain good — everyone loved her. It used to upset Shelly when my mom would openly measure us against each other. Mom would say, "Why can't you be more like Shelly? She cleans her room and vacuums the house without being told. Shelly is such a good helper." At first I felt inadequate when my mom compared me to Shelly, but I hated housework more, so I learned to let my mom's criticism roll off me. It was an ability that would serve me well with my mom in later years. It really is quite amazing to see how life's lessons unfold when you examine them after-the-fact.

Shelly quickly lost her shyness. We were both outgoing and fun-loving. I remember in grade five we lip-synched a song — Teen Angel — in front of our class. It was a very brave thing to do back then because most of the kids were Mennonite and singing and dancing was frowned upon. That song broke the ice. Every lunch hour we'd go over to a friend's house beside the school, listen to music and dance. We learned The Swim, The Pony, and Twisted our lunch time away. I loved dancing and singing. Music became a wonderful release for me. Even today, I sing constantly — completely off-key, but with unabashed joy and abandon.

Shelly and I were soul sisters. When she moved away to a nearby town, we still kept in touch even though we didn't see each other very often. I missed her terribly at school but in grade seven I met Paula K. She was a fast talking, intelligent Ukrainian girl. We were both tomboys and clicked right away. When we introduced our parents to each other they clicked too. Our dads used to enjoy drinking together, and our mothers would complain about them. In school, Paula and I competed with each other for top student and top athlete. We both loved public speaking and somewhere there's a faded newspaper clipping of Paula K. and me standing on a stage with the girl who won the contest that year. We did everything together. When she moved away to Australia in grade nine, we promised each other that as soon as I graduated, I'd come to see her. I planned to work every summer and on weekends during the school year as soon as I got my driver's license. I would save every nickel I could and join her for a wild time in Australia in four years. When the two of us made plans we seldom deviated, but four years was a long way off and anything could happen. When Paula K. moved away in grade nine, my friendship circle continued to expand.

From kindergarten to graduation, I have to admit that school was mostly fun for me; the only subjects I struggled with were grade 11 academic math and French. When I realized I needed both these subjects to go to university I decided to change to a business/clerical program instead. I changed schools in my senior year to attend one that offered a semester system. I would be able to complete two years in one and still graduate with my peers.

At my new school, I was happy to reconnect with Shelly. She was still the same beautiful, warm, outgoing person I remembered, and it was great to resume our friendship. Those childhood bonds still held, and we spent a lot of time together in our senior year. Shelly introduced me to her friend Paula-Marie, a beautiful girl with light brown hair that hung down to her knees, and we also became good friends. She was painfully shy. The three of us found school was easy and we'd often skip classes.In those days, as long as we maintained an A average, many of our teachers let us cut class. It was an added incentive to do well!

Mom and dad encouraged all of us to work hard both in and out of school. We had jobs from the time we were old enough to start picking fruit and vegetables. I hated working in the fields, so I lied about my age and worked in a jam cannery, until they found out I was only 14. They told me to go home until I was legally old enough to work there. It was a relief to be let go because it was a horrible job. We had to stand at the conveyor belt picking out rotten berries and bugs. One girl wouldn't touch spiders; one wouldn't touch slugs; another one wouldn't pick out the earwigs; I was at the end of the belt and was expected to pick out anything they missed. Guess what? I wouldn't pick them out either! They probably would have fired me eventually even if I was old enough to work there. I can't eat raspberry jam to this day.

My sisters Sylvia, Lorrie, and Beanie started dating quite young and they had a lot more boyfriends at an earlier age than I did. Although I think I more than made up for the slow start in later years. As a matter of fact, my younger sister, Lorrie, introduced me to Lawrence, my first serious boyfriend, when I was in grade 11. Lorrie was much more precocious than I, and she travelled with a popular and wild bunch of kids who were into all the things our parents warned us about. When I first met Lawrence, I thought he was incredibly gorgeous, with long, blonde wavy hair. I couldn't believe he was attracted to a plain Jane like me. I was tall and skinny, with crooked teeth but a great set of "knockers." Lawrence may have had something to do with me wanting to switch my grad program and change schools for my grad year. He lived closer to the semester system school and we could skip out at lunch hour to get into all sorts of wonderful trouble. (I'm so glad I'm writing this after my own kids have graduated! My kids think I was an angel, and up until now, I've been happy to oblige them with that little fantasy.)

I was happy when I turned 16, because I was finally old enough to drive a car and get a decent job. Every weekend I worked as an usher at the local Paramount Theatre. It was a great job to have during school. I couldn't believe how lucky I was to find work that allowed me to see all the new movies, and earn money at the same time. The

Lawrence and Glenda skipping school at the river.

only downside was that I had to watch some movies more than once and when a movie was held over I'd cringe. I watched *A Clockwork Orange* 27 times! Lawrence would often come in to keep me company and we spent lots of time together, kissing in the balcony on slow nights. Hmmm, I wonder if the projectionist may have enjoyed our show more than the one on the screen!

Lawrence gave me an engagement ring on my 17th birthday which I dutifully accepted out a sense of guilt and obligation. Being the good Catholic girl that I was, I thought I had to marry him because he was my first love. Lawrence, who was two years older than I and already finished high school, sometimes went out of town to work. When he left, I found that I liked being single and happily discovered the joy of dating even though I was supposed to be engaged to Lawrence. When he came home from working away we would pick up where we left off and he was none the wiser. It seems that my Catholic guilt only went so far after all!

Choosing to Smile

One night I had to drive my sister, Lorrie, to work at the theatre. Lawrence was in town and I was going to go out with him for a few hours while she was at work. Dad told me not to take the freeway, but we were late and I knew it would be faster, so I ignored his advice. I drove past the turnoff for the long way to town and headed to the freeway. I should have known that my dad was right, and I should have listened to him, but I was stubborn and figured he was just being paranoid. I'd driven on the freeway many times and wasn't in the least bit nervous. We were only a couple blocks away from home when we saw headlights on the road ahead. It was winter, and it was dark early, so it was hard to gauge how fast the approaching car was traveling. By the time I realized the drunk was driving in reverse on our side of the road, it was too late to avoid him. I hit the brakes and tried to swerve but he swerved the same way and we ended up in a head-on collision. My car was a mess but fortunately, neither of us was seriously hurt. My sister's head cracked the windshield when she slammed into it but she didn't have a concussion or a cut. I rammed my right leg into the dashboard and my hip and knee were sore for weeks. I never did regain full range of motion. We called dad and he was at the accident site in minutes. Instead of yelling at me for disobeying him, he wrapped both of us in his big arms and said, "The car can be replaced, my girls, but you can't." I never forgot that lesson: kids need love the most when they deserve it the least. Unfortunately, I didn't know enough to put the lesson into practice until I had children of my own.

The summer I was 17 and my little brother was 12, I had an opportunity to practice the "love" lesson my dad had taught me the night of my car accident. I was enjoying a relaxing soak in the bathtub when I heard shouts and screams coming from the yard. Mom wasn't home and she'd left me in charge. I jumped out of the tub, wrapped a towel around myself and ran onto the deck. I saw my brother standing by our old blue Plymouth with tears on his face. My sisters were screaming and crying. At first I couldn't figure out what they were crying about until I saw my dog's back legs sticking out from underneath the car. Jimmy had tried to drive and, without checking, backed the car over the dog sleeping in the shade under the car. Jimmy was crying but I didn't care. I started to cry too, and screamed at him, "What were you thinking? How could you! Poor Lady! My poor dog! How could you be so stupid? You've killed her!" Suddenly, there was a movement from under the car. Lady's tail started wagging when she heard my voice. Miraculously, Lady wasn't badly hurt but I missed a chance to be forgiving and I still feel bad about screaming at my little brother when he obviously felt bad enough already. Jimmy taught me a lesson that day too — don't add salt to any wound. When someone is already in pain, there's no need to make them feel worse by pointing out the obvious. I just wish I had remembered that he needed my love the most when he deserved it the least. How I wish I had hugged him hard and said, "Jimmy, it was an accident. I know you didn't mean to hurt her." It's one of those missed opportunities for graciousness that still haunts me today.

I felt like I was the ugly duckling of our family. In my eyes, my sisters were perfect and gorgeous. I had an underbite and crooked teeth. When I look at old pictures, I have to admit it wasn't as bad as I remember it being.. I just always thought that my sisters were more beautiful than I was, so if I couldn't be as beautiful, I was going to be smarter. I read voraciously anywhere and anytime I could; I'd sneak away to the bathroom after supper and read a book. My sisters would sometimes — but not always — get tired of waiting for me to do the dishes, and would do them for me. Mom and dad both encouraged me to read. I read under the blankets with a flashlight long after I was supposed to be asleep. Consequently, I became a nighthawk and still am. Many times my mom would have to shake me awake in the morning. I would miss the bus or be late for school on a regular basis. I still don't do mornings very well.

Some of my favorite times were spent in the kitchen with my family. We'd snap at each other with wet towels — or have wonderful food fights. One time, Lorrie threatened me with the plastic ketchup bottle and, as she was taking aim, I smacked her arm up and away. A neat strip of ketchup flew across the ceiling. No amount of scrubbing can clean those old pressed cardboard tiles. They just crumble after awhile. We prayed our mom wouldn't notice, and for a long time she didn't, but when she did — we all clammed up and nobody would take the blame. There was a certain unity in being sisters. We didn't often tattle on each other although we certainly could have and probably should have on more than one occasion.

My sister Lorrie tells about how I made paper airplanes and put pins on the end to throw at her. She still has both eyes, so either she's exaggerating or I was a really bad shot. Probably both! I do remember making nasty weapons out of bobby pins that would snap hard enough to leave a welt. I also remember making stink bombs with empty ball-point pens, a bobby pin, and a wooden sulfur-tipped match. I'd let them go in class and pretend one of the boys did it. They never suspected a girl of being so naughty. I was a master spit-baller in school too. I'd chew up a wad of paper and blow it through a straw at the ceiling above someone's head and wait for it to drop on them, or sometimes just shoot directly at the back of their head. I never got caught at school for all the mischief I got into but my sister Lorrie did. I don't remember what her crime was, but knowing Lorrie, she probably talked back to the teacher and she wouldn't apologize if she thought she was right. They took her into the office and hit her with the strap. She never cried. Made not a sound. She just slowly started to rebel instead.

Sylvia, the oldest, was the mother hen to all of us. She would hoard candies in the top drawer of her dresser and would dole them out to us whenever we got in trouble. Those candies were always the bright side of getting a spanking with mom's wooden spoon. I remember getting spanked but I don't remember why. I also remember hiding mom's wooden spoons in my bedroom cubby hole—a long narrow closet that ran under the rafters. When we finally moved away from that old farm house, we must have found five wooden spoons in there!

My two younger sisters, Lorrie and Beanie, formed a tight bond when Sylvia moved away after graduation. It was them versus me most of the time, or at least that's how it felt. I would walk in on them as they were whispering together and they'd stop sharing whatever secrets they were telling in case I might overhear. With Sylvia gone, I was the dreaded older sister.

Sylvia was 19 when she married Ray, her high-school sweetheart, and Lorrie and I were her reluctant bridesmaids. Lorrie was horrified because not only did we have to wear long, yellow empire-waist dresses, but she had to wear an extremely padded bra to fill out the dress properly. Mom and dad wouldn't let Lorrie's hippie boyfriend come to the reception, but I think Lorrie was secretly happy because she didn't want him to see her dressed like a "girl." We were far more comfortable in jeans. Lorrie taught me how to dress inappropriately in jeans that dragged on the ground. She and my younger sister, Beanie, were both good at sewing and made skimpy halter tops out of every scrap of fabric they could find — and sometimes those scraps were pretty small! There wasn't an ounce of fat on any of us. When I look back at how incredibly fit and healthy we all were, I'm forever grateful for growing up on that farm and my mom's good cooking. Damn, sometimes I would sure like to turn back the clock!

We didn't have a lot of money but we did know how to have fun. I was particularly good at inventing games. In those days we could legally (and easily) buy firecrackers every October around Halloween. We'd always buy enough to last us throughout the year. One of our favorite games was "Chicken Cow Pie," where I'd load up a fresh cow pie with a string of firecrackers and a bunch of us would stand in a circle with our backs to the steaming pile of cow poop. I'd light the fuse and see who would stay the longest without running away and risk getting plastered with cow dung! The winner was often either very lucky or very poop-splattered, which made the game so much more interesting! Kids nowadays just don't know how to have fun.

Growing up with a house full of girls and one little brother wasn't all fun and games though. I shared a room with Sylvia for years. We loved each other but fought a lot. She was a neat freak and I wasn't! I remember one occasion when Sylvia took the fight to a whole new level. I was reading a good book at the time and, no matter how many times she told me to get busy and clean my side of the room, I wasn't planning to do any work until I finished reading. Finally, she was so fed up she picked up the closest thing at hand and hit me with it. Unfortunately, it was one of her bras. I remember how mad she was because all I did was laugh at her and say that it didn't hurt, because it was padded. Of course, that only increased her annoyance but there was no way I could stop laughing at that point. Sylvia had a lot of patience with me but she would invariably have to beg mom to make me clean up my side of the room, and I would reluctantly stuff things into my closet or under the bed. We shared a bedroom until she moved away. At 14, I finally had my own space, and I thought it was heaven. I could be as messy as I wanted and no one could nag me to clean up "my side" of the room.

Although I loved having my own room, I hated to sleep alone. Even after Sylvia moved out, I would often sneak into Lorrie's room so I wouldn't have to sleep by myself. I would read a book for hours and, as long as I scratched her head until she fell asleep, she put up with me sleeping in her bed with the light on until the wee hours. She was just a little afraid to sleep alone too, because we both believed our old farmhouse in Yarrow was haunted. Lorrie often said that she saw strange creatures at night. Of course I thought she was dreaming, but one night, my youngest sister Beanie and I stayed up later than usual to finish watching a movie. It wasn't a scary movie or anything — I can't even recall what we were watching — but we both headed off to bed after everyone else, including mom and dad, was asleep. She went to her small bedroom at the end of the long upstairs hallway, and I crawled into bed with Lorrie in her room.

We followed a bedtime ritual every night. We must have sounded just like the The Waltons, because we'd never go to bed without saying, "G'night Beanie, love you."

"G'night Glenda, love you."

"G'night Mom, love you. G'night Dad, love you." and so on until everyone had received more than enough "love you"s and mom would have to holler at us to "knock it off and get to sleep!"

That night, Beanie and I whispered our goodnights so we wouldn't wake anyone up and turned out the lights. A few minutes later, I heard her walking around in her room. I knew it was Beanie, because I could hear the papers on her floor crunching when she stepped on them. She was an amazing artist and her floor was always littered with works in progress. I couldn't understand what she was doing walking around when we were supposed to be asleep, so I whispered to her, "Beanie, what are you doing? You're going to get us in trouble — you're supposed to be asleep!"

The hair on the back of my neck stood straight up when, after a long pause, she whispered back, "Glenda, it's not me!"

I screamed, "Dad! Somebody's in Beanie's room! Dad! Come

quick!" In mere seconds dad flipped on the hall light and bolted upstairs ready to beat off the intruder, but when the lights went on there was nobody there. Not a soul — not a cat, not a dog, not a mouse. Beanie swears to this day that she watched a man walk down the hallway, silhouetted against the street light shining through the hall window, and come straight into her room. She said he was wearing a tall black hat and had on a black cape. She pulled the covers over her head and she was so scared she could hardly breathe. When I called out to her she mustered up the courage to answer back to tell me that she wasn't walking around her room.

We slept three in a bed for weeks! Dad tried to convince us it had been the cat walking around, but I knew what I'd heard and it was no pussyfooted cat — it was heavy footsteps in the dead of night — every child's nightmare! Years later, Sylvia told us about seeing the same dark silhouette coming down the hall when she occupied that same room just prior to her wedding. She didn't tell us about it then, but she remembers it vividly, even now in her fifties. Who or what it was we haven't a clue, but it makes for a good ghost story!

My dad taught me how to change oil and fix flat tires. He taught me how to fish. He made each of us feel special. I always felt a strong connection to my dad because he encouraged me to follow my dreams. Mom was more practical. Dad was a dreamer and mom was a realist. It was probably a good thing she was practical or we could have ended up being flat broke depending on the failure or success of my dad's many schemes and dreams. Mom made sure dad never spent more on his dreams than we could afford. She would put her foot down if his schemes and inventions would cost more than she was comfortable spending, and dad always seemed to respect her decisions. We would never be rich, but we would never go hungry either.

I could do no wrong in my dad's eyes; even when he caught my sister Lorrie and I in a screaming fist fight with each other. Lorrie and I had been duly warned to knock it off by mom several times already, but we ignored her. Finally, dad was sent to settle things once and for all. Lorrie and I both heard him coming and when he flung the bedroom door open, we froze in mid-swing as my giant of a dad ducked to get through the doorway. He looked madder than I'd ever seen him and he whipped his belt off through its loops with a threatening zing; folded it in half and snapped it like a thunder clap. A normal person would have wet her pants, but I've never been accused of being normal. Instead, I started to giggle. Before dad could help himself, he started laughing too, and the fight dissolved into a wonderful fit of laughter all around much to mom's dismay.

My dad was my hero. Apparently he drank too much, but I never noticed. He would come home from long stints away at work and bring wonderful surprises for us. Once, he brought us a hamster, but somehow it got lost inside his pick-up truck. Weeks later, when the weather turned chilly, he turned the heater on in his truck and blew out bits of fur and maggots. Sadly, the missing hamster was found too late. Dad had a devil of a time trying to get rid of the smell, and from then on would avoid turning on the heater until it was absolutely necessary.

Dad would sometimes come home late at night after working out of town for weeks with BC Hydro. We wouldn't know until the next morning that he had arrived, and all five of his happy kids would pounce on mom and dad's bed for a cuddle and airplane rides on dad's strong arms. Poor mom and dad; they must have dreaded our invasion of their privacy. Dad was 6'5" and the most handsome man I'd ever seen. He had amazing green eyes which I am happy to say he also gave to me.

Choosing to Smile

Mom worked far too hard on the little four-acre hobby farm. She grew all our vegetables and made bread from scratch. We had chickens for eggs and, when they stopped laying, mom would do the butchering herself, with our help to do the plucking. I'll never forget the awful smell of boiled feathers and blood. It was hard work, but mom didn't complain. She loved working in her garden and our house was always in happy disarray until dad was scheduled to come home. Then we'd all pitch in and "bull-doze" which is what mom called a major housework blitz. We'd vacuum, dust the furniture, wash and wax the floors, clean our rooms (which I hated!) and put away the laundry. Mom would put our clothes in piles on the stairs. Sylvia, the oldest, had the top stair; mine was next; and so on down the line to little Jimmy. We were each expected to put our clothes away neatly. I usually just stepped over all the piles hoping that someone would do it for me. I really hated working in the house and would much rather have been building forts outside or working in the barn.

Dad adored my mom. She didn't always return the adoration. He'd sidle up behind her while she was cooking, wrap his arms around her, and nuzzle her neck. For his attentions he'd usually get whacked with the wooden spoon she was using to stir our supper. We all thought it was funny and he'd never give up trying to sneak a snuggle. I think we inherited dad's love of showing affection and all of us girls are very "touchy-feely" — rubbing each other's shoulders, scratching heads and backs or massaging feet. Mom hates it when we do that — she calls us a bunch of monkeys. I often wonder what drew mom and dad together in the first place because they were such opposites. Watching mom and dad interact helped me to make up my mind to marry someone who enjoyed cuddling as much as I did.

My childhood is a wonderful collage of happy memories. I remember dad taking me fishing and mom coaching our ball team to victory. I remember building rafts and forts, climbing trees, burying our dead pets (and any other dead animals we happened to find) in a little pet cemetery complete with crosses made out of old sticks and twine. We picked berries and beans every summer. We worked hard doing our chores but we always had time for fun. Looking back, I'm glad I was a tomboy. I did things many girls wouldn't have dared to do.

I loved to ride horses. When dad showed up from one of his longer trips away from home with not one, but TWO horses, we were all ecstatic. Big Red was supposed to be Sylvia's horse and Pepper, the pony, was to be mine, but we all shared. Pepper was a Shetland/Welsh mix with a wicked sense of humor but he could run faster than Red, the quarterhorse. I loved to go fast so Pepper suited me just fine. One day, my little sister Beanie was riding Pepper and the bad-tempered pony decided he wasn't willing to be ridden that day. She managed to get him to the end of the field and then all hell broke loose when she turned him back towards home. That pony took off like a bullet with Beanie bouncing on his back. She was hanging on for dear life, screaming like a banshee, as Pepper gave her a wild ride almost to the fence. Unfortunately, it had been raining heavily for awhile and there was a huge puddle of water just beside the barn. It was almost like a small lake, knee-deep at the centre, and Pepper headed straight to the middle of it. With a sudden jolt, Beanie came to a butt-crunching stop in the middle of the pond when Pepper decided to stop and roll with Beanie still in the saddle. Beanie sat for a split second and then let loose the most ear-shattering scream I've ever heard. I've never laughed as hard as I did that day to see Beanie leap from the saddle into the puddle, and Pepper roll — saddle and all — in the mucky water. That pony had a mind of his own, and if he didn't want someone to ride him he'd find a way to get them off. He even figured out that he could just fit under the sour cherry tree branch but any hapless rider on his back would be swept off! We had lots of adventures on those two horses and whatever dad paid for them was more than worth it.

One summer day I was hanging out with some neighborhood kids. We would often stop somewhere along the road and steal whatever fruit happened to be in season from someone's field or garden. We never thought of it as being "wrong" or "bad" we just did it because we were hungry. No one ever stopped us or caught us until that day in Mrs. Mac's orchard. We were hungry, so we decided to raid an apple tree. We were busy, sitting in the trees, happily munching apples, when Mrs. Mac came out of her house. "You children get down here now!" She had a wonderful English accent and it was hard for me to gauge just how mad she really was because her voice sounded so lovely to me. In the back of my mind I was thinking I just might end up in trouble if she told my parents but we dutifully climbed down and prepared to be chastised. She ordered the lot of us into her kitchen, and I was sure she was going to call our parents. Instead, she served us all cookies and milk. It was the best thing she could have done because from then on, Mrs. Mac's trees were off limits to all the marauding neighborhood kids. She had a bumper crop every year because she chose to befriend us instead of punish us. She said anytime we were hungry we could stop and have a bite to eat and she meant it. Mrs. Mac taught me that it is generally best to find a way to turn your enemies into allies and I have applied her tactics more than a few times in my life.

I think Mrs. Mac may have been a catalyst for me. In that one simple act, she showed me how to turn a negative into a positive. My sisters might say I became a master manipulator but I prefer the term master mediator. For example, one day when Sylvia wasn't home and our parents were out, we broke the rules and were playing catch in the house and of course we smashed a window. We knew we'd be punished and that meant either the wooden spoon or kneeling in a corner, which none of us enjoyed. I told my siblings to bring their piggy banks and line them up on the kitchen counter. I wrote mom and dad a note:

Glenda's Story

Dear mom and dad,
We are very sorry we broke the kitchen window. We hope there is enough money in our piggy banks to pay for it. Don't bother looking for us. We ran away because we don't want to be in trouble. We will miss you very much. Love, your children

I ushered them all upstairs to hide under my bed until mom and dad came home. The first thing they did was call for us, but of course we didn't answer. Our parents read the note and started to laugh, which was the sign I was waiting for. They called for us to come out and the four of us lined up sheepishly in the kitchen in front of them. Mom and dad said they knew it was an accident and appreciated the honesty we'd shown in owning up to the crime we'd committed. I've realized over the years that when I mess up it's generally better to admit I've made a mistake rather than try and bluff my way out of it. Taking responsibility and having a sense of humor are both tools that have served me well.

I ended up graduating from Chilliwack Senior Secondary School in 1973 with honors from the Commercial/Clerical Program. It wasn't what I wanted to do, but it was easy and I was more interested in having fun with my friends than furthering my education. When my kids read this they'll be having a fit because I pushed them so hard to do well in school and work hard because they would regret not going to university.

I don't really regret it though, not going to university. I've had a wonderful and interesting life. In September 1973, I headed off to visit my childhood girlfriend, Paula, who was still living in Australia

Graduation 1973.

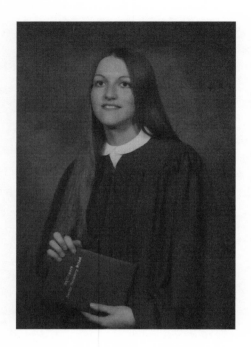

and still waiting for me to come and visit. I had just turned 18 and was ready to see the world. Lawrence and I were still engaged but I really wanted a break from our serious relationship. Paula and I had written many letters to each other over the years and, true to my word, when I graduated I packed my suitcases (a set of luggage was my graduation gift from my parents) and went to Australia to visit her. I had saved enough for a one-way ticket. I never thought too much about how I'd get back home if I didn't like it there.

When I arrived at the Sydney airport, it was hot and humid. My dress was clinging to me and I immediately regretted wearing pantyhose. My plane had arrived two hours early and no one was there to meet me. My first time away from home, and I'm standing in a huge airport, half a world away, without a clue about what to do. I decided to take a cab to Paula's and surprise her. I knew I was entirely out of my element when the cab driver held the driver's side door open for me. He must have thought I was an idiot when I said, "You can't be serious — there's no way I'm driving!" Nobody told me they drive on the "other" side of the road in Australia but I was jet lagged, and looked at the driver as if he was crazy — much the same way that he was looking at me!

Paula was surprised when I came knocking on her door unannounced and two hours early, but not nearly as surprised as I was. She had neglected to tell me that she was the only girl living in a house with five men! I was expected to share a room with a gorgeous Sydney soccer player. I hadn't realized how sheltered I'd been until I arrived in Sydney to live in a crazy house filled with crazy beer-drinking Australians. I lived there about three weeks until Paula and I found a place of our own overlooking Coogee Beach in Sydney. Paula and I both found great paying jobs in a food factory and, if I hadn't been so young and homesick, I probably would have stayed. But I worked harder than ever before in my life, to earn enough to buy a ticket home in time for Christmas. The thought of eating turkey sandwiches on the beach on Christmas day just didn't seem right. I missed my family and, believe it or not, I missed winter.

I grew up a lot over the four months I lived in Australia. The men were gorgeous and flirtatious but I never slept with any of them. I stayed true to my fiancé (stupid girl!) and came home four months later with a gorgeous tan just in time for Christmas, and 25 pounds heavier than when I left. I ate and drank my way through Sydney. I learned how to guzzle beer faster than most men, and discovered that by winning, I never had to buy a beer. Being naturally frugal, I honed my talent, and even today, when properly motivated and really thirsty, I can pound back a beer with gusto, much to the amazement of my children and husband! For the next two years I worked at a bank and continued to date Lawrence, although by then I knew I wasn't in love with him enough to marry him. When my sister Lorrie graduated in

1975, we took off for a three-week vacation in Hawaii, and I discovered the joy of disco dancing! I can't remember if the legal drinking age was 18 but then they never questioned us in any of the nightclubs. We slept on the beach all day and danced all night. Ironically, one day when we were taking a shortcut through a local hotel lobby to get to our favorite beach spot we bumped into a couple from Chilliwack. She and I had graduated together, and they were just leaving to go back home to Chilliwack. I noticed her husband Rick, slim and tanned, standing quietly to the side while we three girls chatted animatedly about how wonderful it was in Hawaii. Years later, after his divorce, Rick would joke that he fell in love with me that first day when he saw me in my pink bikini. I wonder what his ex-wife will think if she reads this!

Lorrie and I loved Hawaii. We made a pact to go back home to Canada, pack up our suitcases, leave Chilliwack, find great jobs, save every penny possible, and in one year we would return to Hawaii to live. Like I said, once I set a goal, I don't often deviate from the path. So, when I was 20, my 18-year-old sister and I moved away from home together. We had no destination in mind, but we figured we'd just drive until some town caught our interest. I give my mom and dad credit for giving us the freedom to be adventurers.

After returning from our Hawaiian vacation, we said goodbye to our family and headed east. We had no idea where we'd end up, but we decided to stop in Calgary to visit our aunt and uncle at the end of our first day on the road. We loved Calgary. The drinking age was 18 and it was a booming oil town with lots of rich men. Lawrence was still clinging to the idea of marriage even though he was back home. I mailed the ring back to him with a Dear John letter. He mailed it back to me asking me to keep it "just in case" I changed my mind someday. I knew I wouldn't change my mind and our five-year relationship was finally over for good.

I started dating late, compared to my sisters, but I made up for a slow start by doing a lot of dating in my twenties. Lorrie and I rented a small, one-bedroom apartment together in Calgary and we had a pact — whenever we had a date we'd order the biggest meal on the menu and bring half of it home in order to save grocery money. We were very frugal and we both dated a lot! Our plan was to work at least six days a week for one year, save every penny and then move to Hawaii for as long as our money would last. We figured we could easily live in Waikiki for a couple of months without working if we worked hard now and kept to our budget. My sister Lorrie and I had a lot of fun living and working in Calgary that year before we went back to Hawaii. We both found jobs working in a sports bar where we met and dated a lot of professional athletes. Lorrie ended up falling in love with a very handsome older man but I was happy being single. I wasn't looking for a serious relationship. I loved working in the club where I made some amazing friends and had some wild times. I remember one night in particular partying with my girlfriend Cindy, who managed the bar. We were there on our night off celebrating her divorce and our table was crammed with people we knew along with people we didn't know who were just attracted to a good party. A man with gorgeous blue eyes was sitting beside me, buying me drinks and providing lively conversation. He said his name was David. We hit it off and I thought I'd introduce my new friend to Cindy, who was sitting down a few chairs from me. When I said, "Cindy, I want you to meet my new friend, David." She looked aghast and said, "Glenda, I know who he is!" This seemed odd to me because we knew most of the same people but I shrugged it off and didn't realize until later when I asked his last name — Clayton-Thomas. He was the lead singer with the famous band "Blood, Sweat and Tears." He invited me to a party at his hotel — his band had the entire top floor of the hotel booked just for them. This story would be a lot more interesting if I had had the courage to go to the party, but I'd heard too many stories about groupie girls and had no desire to find out if the stories were true. He said he'd leave tickets for me for the concert the next night but I had already made other plans, so we ended up never seeing each other again. I'm sure to him I would have been just an interesting interlude on another road trip but, as it is, he's become an interesting side-line to my life story.

Lorrie and I lived in that tiny apartment in Calgary for a year. She continued to date her older man, but we never let go of our plan to move to Hawaii. I worked at the sports bar and at The Bank of Montreal, saving every dime possible while still having fun and enjoying being single. By 1976, my older sister, Sylvia, had already been married for five years to Ray, her high school sweetheart; Lorrie at 19 was in a committed relationship with the handsome older man; Beanie, at 17 and in grade 12, was already engaged; and, at 16, my 6'4" gorgeous little brother Jimmy was breaking hearts wherever he went even though he was only in grade 11.

I'll never forget when Lorrie and I quit our jobs in Calgary and set off for Hawaii in October, 1976. It was an amazing and wonderful time in paradise. We ended up exceeding our goals and lived a totally self-absorbed life style for three glorious months in a brand-new, beautiful, one-bedroom, fully furnished apartment, just a block from the beach in Waikiki. Nobody told us that it was totally unreasonable for two young ladies in their twenties to undertake such an ambitious adventure and I've come to realize that if nobody tells you that something is impossible then anything is possible.

We'd never been away from our family for Christmas but nei-

Lorrie, Jimmy and Glenda standing on the lanai when he first arrived in Hawaii.

ther of us wanted to leave Hawaii, either, so we suggested that the entire family join us for a vacation, which they readily agreed to do. Mom, dad, Beanie and Jimmy settled into our little one-bedroom apartment — we gave mom and dad our bedroom and the rest of us slept on the lanai, the couch, or the floor. My married sister and her husband rented a hotel room right across the street from our apartment. We could actually step out our doors and wave at each other! It was wonderful, and it was the first year we broke the tradition of having Christmas and presents at home. We hung candy-canes on our table lamp in place of a tree, and we drew names for Christmas instead of buying gifts for everyone. Dad drew my name and I was so glad because he bought me a huge suitcase which I really needed to haul three months worth of living in Hawaii back to Canada. I wish I had cherished that Christmas a little more because it would prove to be the last one our entire family would ever spend together.

We left Hawaii before the end of the year. Lorrie flew back to Calgary to spend New Year's Eve with her boyfriend and they were engaged shortly afterwards. Beanie, who was finishing grade 12 in Chilliwack, was also engaged, so my two little sisters decided to have a double wedding in August. I flew back to Chilliwack with the rest of my family to spend New Year's with them but decided to return to Calgary to find a new job and a place of my own in the New Year. I rented a little basement suite just a block away from where Lorrie was living with her fiancé, Jim. I found a job as an office manager during the day and took a second job as a waitress in the evenings. It was a hectic schedule, but I still had time to play softball, date a wide array of men, and have plenty of fun. When Lorrie returned to Calgary from Hawaii, she took a job as a cocktail waitress in a lounge. As fate would have it, the bartender there was also from Chilliwack. Brady was tall, long-haired, and handsome, with a booming laugh and wild moustache. Lorrie introduced us and we immediately hit it off.

It wasn't long before Brady and I became exclusive. Gradually his belongings found their way into my basement apartment and by August, 1977, we were practically living together although he kept his own apartment. I was very grateful that he was there the night I got the hysterical phone call from Lorrie. It was August 16 in the early morning hours and nothing could have prepared me for the words I was about to hear.

"Glenda, get over here now! Jim's not home, and I need you now. Jimmy is dead!"

I remember being confused because her fiancé's name was Jim and our brother's name was Jimmy. It didn't make sense. Neither of them could be dead. That wasn't possible. Lorrie and Beanie were having a double wedding in four days. We were supposed to be driving back to BC the next day together. Jim was at his stag party in Calgary. Jimmy was supposed to be safe and sound in his bed at home in BC. How could either of them be dead? Yet, the hysteria in Lorrie's voice reached through the phone and I remember screaming and crying,

No! Not Jimmy, not our little brother! You're wrong! You're lying! No! But the anguish in Lorrie's voice told me it was true.

Dad had called her first with the news because he thought Jim would be there to support her and they would then be able to share the tragic news with me. Dad didn't know that Lorrie would be alone that night. She was hysterical in her grief. Brady held me in his arms as I sobbed so hard I thought I would die from the sense of loss flooding through me. The phone rang again. Lorrie sounded even more frantic than the first time she called. Jim was still out celebrating at his stag and she couldn't reach him. She was sobbing uncontrollably. Brady helped me get dressed and somehow I made my way over to Lorrie's apartment. Lorrie and I collapsed in each other's arms and sobbed in disbelief until Jim arrived home from his stag — shocked into sobriety by the news.

Somehow we got a flight home early the next morning. I kept thinking, "This has to be a mistake. They have to be wrong. He's only sixteen. Nobody dies when they're sixteen. Jimmy is too tall — too strong — too handsome — too kind — too special — he can't be gone." On the plane, Lorrie and I went from moments of silence and quiet tears to hiccupping sobs and disbelief. We shared our best memories of Jimmy and continued to hope that it was all a big mistake and everything would be fine; our family would still be whole and we could celebrate the double wedding as scheduled on August 20... four short days away.

We found out that the day before, Jimmy had been asked to be the designated driver for Beanie's fiancé's stag party. His job was to drive anyone home who had too much to drink. He had been working at his job catching chickens since 3:00 AM but he was young and figured he could handle putting in a 24-hour shift. They'd planned the stag on my sister's birthday, August 15. She would go out with her friends to celebrate her 18th birthday and her fiancé would have his stag party.

Choosing to Smile

It seemed ironic that she was old enough to get married but wasn't old enough to legally go to the bar for a drink. The party was winding down and it looked as if his only passenger would be Beanie's fiancé's younger brother. Jimmy took the back road home and probably was going too fast along the winding road. He lost control of the truck and it slammed into a telephone pole. Our little brother was killed instantly. His passenger was thrown from the vehicle and, although injured badly enough to have his spleen removed, he would live.

It was too late to cancel the weddings. Out-of-town guests were arriving for a wedding, but soon the word spread that they would also be attending a funeral. Jimmy died one day after Beanie's eighteenth birthday — he was sixteen and a half. He was buried on August 18, my twenty-second birthday. The church was packed. I remember walking up to his casket and looking down at his waxen face and his folded grease-stained hands. How many motors had those young hands tinkered with? How could this young man with so much promise be gone? His hair was neatly combed and I remember thinking it didn't look anything like him. This shell wasn't my Jimmy. The body was there but Jimmy wasn't. I knew then it was real. He was gone. Ray, my sister Sylvia's husband, held me up as my knees buckled under me.

I remember wishing Brady had been able to come with me to hold me but he couldn't afford to take time off from work. A huge wave of sadness rolled over me and for the first time in my life I understood what it felt like to experience the dark depths of grief.

Just two days after burying our little brother, my two younger sisters wore their lovely white dresses and walked down a red-carpeted aisle in a double wedding ceremony attended by over 500 people. The same people who had attended a funeral two days earlier in another church now tried to pretend to feel joy and happiness at the union between two mismatched couples. Beanie married a man seven years her senior and Lorrie married a man about 20 years older than she was. Both marriages would eventually end in divorce, which to me seemed inevitable after such a tragic start. I remember curling up inside a cement playground pipe during the wedding reception. I could hear music and laughter and I thought, "How can life go on as if nothing has happened? How can people smile? How can the sun rise and set as if nothing tragic has occurred?" Ironically, Sylvia was almost six months pregnant with her first child; the first grandchild for mom and dad. This was supposed to be the happiest of times for all of us but everything just felt wrong now. It was my first encounter with death and loss and grief. I didn't know how to handle it and I didn't think I could ever smile or be happy again.

After the funeral and the weddings, I went back to Calgary feeling numb, and went into a strange state where I appeared normal on the outside but was completely shattered inside. Brady tried to comfort me, but he didn't know how. I would wake myself up sobbing into my pillow and reach for him to comfort me but he couldn't. I kept wondering if Jimmy knew that I thought he was wonderful. I couldn't remember if I had told him I loved him and it was killing me. I tried hard to recall our last words to each other but I couldn't. I felt myself dying of grief a little more each day until one night, about a month and a half after his death, as I cried myself to sleep, I realized I didn't want to wake up to this pain anymore. I just wanted to sleep forever. That night I had a dream.

A beautiful woman came to me and said she would take me to see Jimmy. She was dressed all in white, glowing with an inner light. I felt she was like a sister to me and I trusted her completely. She took me up through an amazing beam of light that reminded me of transporters in some hi-tech space movie. We stopped at what seemed to be a waiting room. I wanted to keep going through the light but she said that this was as far as I was allowed to go, and Jimmy would come to me here. I was so excited when Jimmy appeared — we hugged each other tight and it felt so real. We laughed and talked and I told him how much I loved and missed him. He said he knew that. He looked at me and said, "You've got to tell mom to stop crying so much. Tell her I'm with her more than she knows. When she hears the bird calling — she'll know which one — she'll know it's my way of saying hello. Tell everyone that I'm okay. I miss you guys too, but there's so much to do here. I'm on a level learning patience. Please tell everyone that I'm okay and remember, when you need me, I'll always be there. I won't be there for everyday little things but when you really, truly need me, I'll always be there." I remember wondering what on earth he meant by all that. Being raised a Catholic I was taught that heaven was eternal rest. The idea of it being a busy place of further learning never occurred to me but I remembered his message word for word. We hugged goodbye and I was escorted back down the beam of light by the beautiful guardian. I woke up for the first time since my brother's death feeling a tremendous sense of closure and peace. The dream had felt so real. Finally, there were tears of happiness on my pillow instead of sadness. I knew exactly what I needed to do.

I gave a month's notice at both my jobs and on my apartment. I told Brady I was going home to help my parents through their grief.

Brady still had his own apartment and I left knowing it was the right thing to do. I left him the big TV I had bought just a few months earlier. Instead, I took a huge plush toy that he had won for me at the Calgary Stampede fair — it was a white buffalo and it rode beside me in the passenger seat on the long trip home. If I hadn't been so senti-mental about keeping the white buffalo, my big TV would have been sitting there in its place. It was a decision that possibly saved my life. I jumped in my car which was loaded to the rafters with all my worldly possessions packed inside.

On November 1, 1977, I headed back to Chilliwack. It was a beautiful warm Chinook weather day in Calgary. It was so warm I hadn't even bothered to wear any socks. I slipped into a light sweater and a pair of clogs and jumped behind the wheel of my loaded car. I had my bicycle tied to the roof rack and had even packed all my jars of canning into the back seat of my little yellow Maverick. I headed home with a sense of purpose and Jimmy's message ringing in my ears "Tell mom to stop crying so much... when you really, truly need me, I'll always be there."

The drive home from Calgary, Alberta to our hometown of Chilliwack, BC would take me through the beautiful Rocky Moun-tains. But as beautiful as they were, these mountains could become dangerous very quickly if the weather turned ugly.

Around Field, BC, I hit the first snowstorm of the year. It was a whiteout. I could barely see the road in front of me and the pave-ment was like a skating rink. There wasn't another car on the road. I thought that I would go as far as Golden and just get a hotel room for the night until the storm blew over. Suddenly, I heard my brother's voice as if he were sitting right beside me. "Fasten your seatbelt!" It was a command not a request.

I looked around in surprise as if to make sure there wasn't some-one else in the car with me. I was definitely alone but I wasn't the least bit afraid. I reached over my shoulder and pulled the seatbelt across my lap. It clicked into place and I gripped the wheel with both hands. I spoke out loud, "Okay Jimmy. But whatever happens, you better be looking after me because mom can't handle both of us going!" I'd no sooner said the words than the car began to slide off the edge of the road to the right as I was attempting to drive up a small hill in the blinding blizzard. I lifted my hands from the wheel to cover my face as I felt the car slip over the embankment and begin to roll sideways. The snow seemed to muffle the sound of crunching metal and breaking glass. I don't know how many times the car rolled but I found myself hanging upside down inside what had been my beautiful little yellow Maverick. It came to rest at the bottom of the embankment with its wheels spinning in the air and smoke pouring from the engine. I looked up at the steep bank of snow out my driver's side window and realized with surprise that the window wasn't broken. I was suspended upside down by my seat belt. Something red and sticky was covering my head and shoulders. A jar of canned tomatoes had broken and the contents had spilled all over me. I didn't feel injured but the smoke was beginning to worry me. I'd seen enough TV movies where cars exploded after they went over embankments and I felt a sense of urgency to get out. I unrolled the window and yelled, "Help! Please, someone help me!" I felt a little foolish after I called for help, because I realized that there was no possible way for anyone to hear me, let alone see me. The tire tracks were already being covered by the pounding snow. If I was going to get out, I had to do it by myself. I reached over and undid my seatbelt. I suppose I fell onto the roof but I don't remember. I crawled through the open driver's window and made my way up the embankment in the snow. Somehow I'd managed to lose my right shoe and was climbing with one bare foot digging into the hill. I don't remember feeling cold, just determined to get to the top. When I reached the snow-covered road, I looked down at my car and it seemed so far away. The bicycle had come off the roof rack on the first roll and lay in a bent, snow-covered heap in the path the tumbling car had cleared. The car's wheels were still slowly turning — I didn't notice if the motor was still running or not but I do remember thinking, "Oh my poor car!"

I stood on the road, with my bare right foot raised in the air — I was feeling the cold now. I was hopping up and down waving my arms at invisible traffic — trying to flag down a car — but nobody was out in weather like this. The road was empty — not a car in sight. I heard myself say, "Help! Oh God, somebody please help!" and suddenly a pickup truck appeared at the top of the hill headed towards me. I frantically waved my arms for them to stop but they kept on driving right past me. I couldn't believe they wouldn't rescue me and it took a moment for me to realize that the roads were so slippery that they couldn't stop. The truck finally managed to roll to a stop at the bottom of the hill and the driver jumped out of his vehicle and ran towards me through the driving snow.

"Are you alright? Are you okay?" He was staring at me and it took me a second to realize what I must look like standing in the middle of the road in a pounding snowstorm covered from head to toe in tomatoes with one foot bare and only one shoe on!

I pointed down the embankment at the slowly spinning tires of my car and said, "I'm okay. But look at my poor car!" He asked if anyone else was in the car and when I said I was alone, he breathed a sigh of relief. He helped me into his warm truck beside his worried wife and they insisted on taking me to the hospital. I guess they didn't believe it was really just tomatoes covering me. They explained that it was just luck that they were out in such bad weather. They were on their way to visit friends and were heading back home because the weather had turned bad so quickly. There was a turnaround point just ahead that they were going to use. Not a single vehicle had come along after them.

I told him I'd left my purse in the car and it had my medical card inside. He graciously volunteered to make his way down to my car to try and retrieve my purse and my missing shoe. When he returned to the truck with my purse and my clog he was as white as the snow. Even in my state of shock I realized something was wrong. He shook his head in disbelief and asked, "How did you get out of that car?" I explained that I'd crawled through the driver's side window. He just shook his head and said, "There's no way you could have gotten out that window. I couldn't get into your car. I had to lie down in the snow and try and reach my hand through to grab your purse and shoe off the roof. I could barely get my arm into that car so there's no way you could have gotten out. It's just a miracle, that's what it is. I've seen accidents on this road every winter but I've never seen anything like this before."

He and his wife were like angels to me that day. They took me to the hospital. I was checked over and released. My angels, Mr. and Mrs. Clarke — I'll never forget them — waited for me at the hospital. They took me home to their mobile home and allowed me to shower and clean off the tomatoes. They washed and dried my dirty clothes; fed me and warmed me. I was a complete stranger to them but even as I write these words I feel their kindness envelop me. Sometimes God sends earth angels to do his work and they were that and more that day. I had called my mom from the hospital. Lorrie was home visiting and waiting for me to arrive. I lied and told them that, because of the snow storm, I had decided to leave my car in Golden with some friends and take a bus the rest of the way home. I gave them the Clarke's phone number in case they needed to reach me. Mom believed me, but Lorrie knew right away that I was lying. Mom said, "Oh honey, I'm so glad you're such a careful driver — I never have to worry about you!" I had to bite my cheek to keep from laughing.

The Clarkes were amazing. After I got cleaned up, they loaded a bunch of empty boxes into their truck and drove me to the nearby auto wreckers where my car had been towed. The Clarkes had called to report the accident while I was in the hospital getting checked out and had asked for the car to be towed.. When I walked into the office and explained to the man behind the big desk that I was there to unload my car he just stared at me.

"You mean to tell me you were in that car and now you're walking into my office without a scratch on you?" He shook his head in disbelief. He waggled his finger at me and said, "Come with me, young lady." It had stopped snowing, and he walked me through the lot filled with rows of mangled and rusting shells to my car. My beautiful little yellow Maverick was practically unrecognizable. The passenger side was squashed flat to the dashboard. If I had that huge TV sitting in the passenger seat instead of the soft, white plush stuffed buffalo it very likely would have killed me, either by rolling on top of me, or exploding into a million pieces as the car was flipping. The roof of the car over the driver's side was hardly crushed at all. It was as if an invisible hand had held the roof up over my head. Every window was shattered except for the driver's side window. It was in perfect condition. Every part of the car was squashed except for the driver's seat. Any passengers would most certainly have been killed but as it was, I had been alone, except for my brother's voice commanding me to do up my seat belt.

When I met my mom and my sister at the bus depot I told mom what had happened and how Jimmy's voice—and the message he gave me in my dream—that he'd be there when we really, truly needed him—had saved my life. Mom's face softened as she said, "It was Jimmy's time to go. It wasn't yours." She was struck with the sudden realization and acceptance that each of us comes into this world for a specific amount of time and nothing can change that. It's all about living the time we have no matter how short or long that time might be. Jimmy packed a lot of living into his short 16 years. Somebody "upstairs" obviously thought I still had a lot more living to do!

The dream I had, and (miraculously) surviving a terrible accident did more than help me cope with the devastating loss of my baby brother — they helped me to reshape my entire belief structure and I became more questioning of matters of faith that, in my opinion, didn't make sense. I would believe only the parts that resonated with truth in me and began exploring other religions and philosophies. To me, the idea of death being a time of eternal rest had always seemed like a tragic and horrible end to living. Surprisingly, Jimmy had described heaven as a place to continue learning and growing which seemed much more appealing to me and a much more likely way to please God than an eternity of being idle.

I told mom all about my dream visit with Jimmy and what he had asked me to tell her. She broke down and cried. She admitted she had been doing a lot of crying in privacy, away from anyone who could have comforted her. She also knew exactly what bird I was talking about, although the message had seemed rather cryptic to me. Apparently, Jimmy had gotten into the habit of standing on the deck and whistling to imitate the unusual call of a local bird and the bird would answer him with a return call. The very next day when Mom stepped onto the sundeck the bird began to call and she was instantly comforted.

When I felt that mom and dad were okay and would be able to get through their grief together, I returned to Calgary and Brady. We moved to Fort McMurray, a booming oil town in northern Alberta, to be near my newlywed little sister, Beanie.

In Fort McMurray I worked two jobs — again. I worked days in one lounge and nights in another. Brady couldn't seem to find steady work, so I was the main bread winner. He enjoyed coming to the bars and visiting with people while I worked. I didn't mind — I was in love and he always had a way of making me laugh whenever I got mad. We'd been together almost two years. One evening as we sat cuddled on the couch watching TV a cute commercial with a kitten flashed across the screen. I made some comment about how nice it would be to have a cat someday. He didn't hesitate. He just blurted out, "What are you talking about? We're not getting a cat! If we get a cat we might as well get married!"

I was shocked. I asked him where he saw our relationship going, and he said he was just taking it day by day. I was 23 years old; living with a man that I had assumed intended to marry me. I'd never lived with a man before, but in my mind it was almost the same as being married. Obviously what we had here was a failure to communicate. During that brief conversation, I realized that I didn't want to waste my time with him anymore. Leaving Brady was surprisingly easy. Jimmy's death had taught me that time was far too precious. I stood up, walked into the bedroom, and started packing my clothes. Within a week I had quit both my jobs and left Brady and most of my belongings behind in Fort McMurray. I returned back to the family home in Yarrow. It was perfect timing. Mom wanted to go with dad to live on Vancouver Island where he was working and they needed someone they trusted to housesit. I worked at a local nightclub four nights a week and enrolled in a six-month hairdressing and beautician course. It seemed that it would be an interesting skill to learn and I could still work nights and attend school during the day. It was ideal for me. I began dating again. Nothing serious — just lots of fun. I was dating a cop who liked to pull me over just for a hello and a kiss, but at the same time, I was dating other guys too. I loved working at the nightclub. I made great money in tips and I felt like I was getting paid to be the hostess at a party where I knew all the guests. I reconnected with some old friends and made some new ones. There was nobody who I was really serious about and I was just enjoying my life immensely as the summer of 1978 drifted by in a blurry haze of tequila, parties, work, and school. I would work long hours at the nightclub and often didn't roll into my driveway until 3:00 AM or later and then have to be at school by 8:00 AM. I was tired but doing well with my classes. I found hairdressing to be a creative outlet for me.

Every weekend that I worked at the nightclub, a group of local guys would come in eager to spend their money and flirt with the waitresses. One guy in particular was very attentive. His name was Rick. He remembered me from when we'd met briefly in Hawaii. He had been there vacationing with his wife. He was now divorced, but he was far from my type. I was into disco and he was into country. He wore a cowboy hat and pointed-toe cowboy boots and boot cut jeans. He was much shorter than I was, but there weren't many men taller than me when I slipped into my 4-inch spiked heels and turned 5'9" into a quick 6'1"! But Rick was persistent. Every night, he stood at the same spot, leaning against the railing, ordering rye and Cokes, and tipping me well. Every night he'd ask me to go out for a coffee with him after work, and every night I'd laugh and smile, and turn him down. But one night he asked me out a little differently than any of the other times, "Glenda, if you don't go out with me for a coffee after work tonight, I'm never going to ask you again … and you don't know what you're missing!"

My mind flashed back to an empty headed pro-football player I dated once with a perfect outside package, and I looked at Rick, with his gorgeous blue eyes, his sincere sweet smile, and his engaging sense of humor, and I said, "Okay — I'll go" … I don't know who was more surprised by those words, him or me. We went to a favorite after-hours coffee place and talked till closing — he invited me over to the house he and a buddy were renting together and we talked until he suggested I stay the night. Ah ha! He was just like most men after all — interested in one thing — getting the girl into the sack. But he said he would be happy to sleep on the couch and let me have his bed — he just didn't want me to drive home tired and late and risk an accident. I had that first little flutter, and figured I may have just met a sincerely nice guy. I declined his offer and I drove home to Yarrow that night with a smile on my face, but Rick's invitation was open. I figured that if I took him up on it I would avoid the half-hour drive home after work and have an extra half-hour of sleep in the morning. That added up to an extra hour of sleep if I stayed at his place. It seemed like a practical solution because I wasn't shy, and I was certainly uninhibited.

Rick and I continued to date for another month. It was great. He didn't have to sleep on the couch like he offered because I knew he'd keep his word and sleep on his side of the big bed. I could sleep alongside this very nice man who never made any move to touch me and I wasn't sure if the relationship would ever move beyond the friendship stage. I was getting more sleep now that I didn't have to drive the extra half-hour to and from Yarrow after work.

I'd always found that most guys were pushy and eager to move past the hand-holding phase of a relationship but Rick never rushed me. He let our relationship unfold slowly and comfortably. I began to wonder if there was something wrong with me because he never reached for me during the night. He was always a complete gentleman. I would wear a half slip to bed pulled up over my breasts and it was obvious that I didn't have any tan lines. He seemed more than a little intrigued when I told him I liked to tan naked on our private deck in Yarrow but he remained a perfect gentleman. One Sunday we drove out to Yarrow and spent a lovely day together working in the yard. I had almost a half acre of lawn to mow and flower beds to weed since I was housesitting for my parents in lieu of paying rent. Rick was a big help and I think I decided then that any guy willing to work that hard to help a girl he wasn't even having sex with just might be worth keeping, but I wasn't quite ready to make a commitment yet.

Rick was driving a logging truck and he took me for a ride one day. I was scared out of my wits when I looked out my window at the steep mountain dropoffs as we wound our way up rough roads. On the way down, with a full load of logs, Rick explained that on the steep downgrade sometimes the brakes get too hot and they fail. He said, "So, if I tell you to JUMP, don't ask me to repeat myself, because you'll be talking to my lunch bucket!" I honestly didn't know if he was serious or joking but I held onto the door handle just in case.

I loved Rick's colorful language. He described a treacherous mountain road as "being steeper than the back of God's head." He and his logging friends made up their own words and described severely dangerous driving conditions as being extremely "sevagerous." He described a foggy trip through the Fraser Canyon and painted a perfect picture for me by describing it "as if you're driving inside a milk bottle." On a cloudy moonless night I could imagine the inky blackness better when he described it as being "darker than the inside of a cow." When he described what it was like driving through a particularly bad snowstorm, he said the "snowflakes were as big as bunnies" and I pictured the huge white fluff balls of snow falling from the sky. That first summer when we were dating, he pulled his heavy work boots off his sweaty feet at the end of a long hot day; and he made me laugh when he exclaimed, "Whew, now that could bring a tear to a glass eye!" Rick did something for me that most men didn't. He knew how to make me laugh and over the following weeks we eased into a relationship without me even realizing it was happening.

The first time I made love with Rick wasn't rockets and fireworks. He was at my house and, instead of driving all the way back to Chilliwack, he spent the night. We had slept in the same bed many times before without having sex but at some point during the night we reached for each other and made love as if we'd loved each other for a long time. There was no awkward groping. No nervousness or shyness. It was a comfortable feeling — as if we were meant to be together. It just felt right. I remember being surprised that we got along so well in and out of bed. We were so different. I was tall and well-built; he was slim and short (okay, to be perfectly honest, he was downright skinny and a good two inches shorter than I); I loved to read; he loved to watch TV; I loved to dance and he obliged me; but we both loved to laugh and talk and make love. We had so much fun together and I'd never laughed with a man the way I laughed with Rick. He made everything fun. Over the next few weeks we started spending all our free time together and I couldn't think of anyone else. That's why the phone call took me by surprise.

It was 3:00 AM and Rick had been staying with me in the big Yarrow farmhouse. He was on early shift, driving a logging truck, and I was happily kissing him goodbye and cuddling at the door as he was trying to leave. With his arms wrapped around me, I grabbed the phone and said, "Hello!" with a smile in my voice as if I'd been awake for hours. I don't know who or what I was expecting — for a second I forgot what time it was and that the only calls that come at that time of the night are bad news. It was my ex-boyfriend, Brady. I told him I'd call him back in a few minutes. Rick left for work with a troubled look on his normally smiling face.

Brady wanted me back. He was flying out the next day to see me and talk about it. I had spent almost two years with this man. Once upon a time, I loved him. Did I owe him another chance to get it right? Maybe. My mom and dad were coming home the next day as well. I was glad, because I needed some parental advice. The only trouble was that my mom and dad believed in letting us make our own mistakes and never interfered in any of our decisions. All they wanted was for me to be happy, whatever the hell that meant!

I cried when I told Rick that I felt I owed Brady a second chance. Rick hugged me tight and said that he understood, but not to expect him to wait for me. He wished me luck and I cried my eyes out as he drove away. It seemed as if I was letting the best thing in my life drive away but I felt obligated to give a two-year relationship another chance over the short amount of time I'd spent having fun and laughing with Rick.

When I saw Brady, I wondered if I'd made a horrible mistake but was too proud to admit it. Brady hugged me hard and told me how much he missed me and realized he wanted to marry me. He said we could have as many cats as I wanted, as long as I came back. I felt numb inside and ached with losing Rick. Brady and I sat on the sundeck trying to work things out. All I could think about was that this was the deck where Rick and I had enjoyed sunny afternoons together, and I was leaving it to go back to Fort McMurray with Brady. The phone rang and interrupted our conversation. It was Rick. There were no cell phones back then. He'd been at work, driving down the road in his logging truck with a full load of logs on, when he felt compelled to talk to me. He'd pulled into a convenience store and used their pay phone to call. I left Brady sitting on the deck and cradled the phone to my cheek as Rick said the sweetest words I'd ever heard. "Go to Fort McMurray and figure it out. I'll be here when you get back." I knew then that I could go with Brady to find closure because I had something worthwhile to come back to.

When we arrived in Fort McMurray, I knew I wanted to leave. It didn't feel like I was coming home. It felt wrong. I didn't belong there — I belonged with Rick. Every word felt strained. Every action felt forced. Every caress made me feel sick inside. I stayed one week. Long enough to pack up a few more of the possessions that I'd so hastily left the first time and said goodbye to Brady for good. I drove all the way from Fort McMurray to Chilliwack with a smile on my face — eager to see and be with Rick again.

We picked up where we left off. Rick never asked about that

Glenda's Story

July 17, 1982—Perfectly matched!

week with Brady, and I never talked about it either. We left it in the past and carried on with our future.

We moved to Williams Lake together in 1980. We bought a little mobile home and paid cash for it. We fixed it up and turned it into a home. Ironically, a cat adopted us shortly after we bought it. Apparently someone had moved on and left it behind. Everything was perfect. We bought dirt bikes and went riding in the hills behind our park every weekend. Friends of ours had a ski-boat and we both learned how to water-ski. I cut hair for Rick's logging buddies and enjoyed staying home working on our house and knitting sweaters for my family and friends. It was idyllic and, in the summer of 1981 on Stampede Weekend, Rick and I got bleary eyed drunk together with a bunch of friends who suggested it was time the two of us got married. Rick and I looked at each other and shrugged. I said, "Okay — let's do it a year from now — everybody mark your calendars for July, 1982!" And that was how we got engaged. It was hardly romantic, and it was hardly a proposal, but it worked for us.

On July 17, 1982, we were married at the Carmen United Church in Sardis, BC. Close to 300 people attended, and it was one of the best nights of my life. My three sisters and my friend Paula-

Marie were my bridesmaids and three of Rick's buddies from Williams Lake, along with Ray, Sylvia's husband, were our groomsmen. Sylvia and Ray's son, Ryan, who was born the year Jimmy died, was our ring-bearer. I was tanned, tall, healthy, and so very happy to marry Rick who was still short, slim, and funny and the man I wanted to spend the rest of my life with. I wore ballet slippers and Rick wore tall shoes. In our wedding photos we look perfectly matched for each other because we were.

We left Williams Lake to return to Chilliwack during the recession of 1983. We were ready to start a family, and had been having fun for the past few months trying to get pregnant. In April, we bought a big house. It needed a lot of work, but we were young and my family was close at hand to help us fix it up. It was exciting to own our own home. Rick and I and our cat stayed in a tiny trailer at my mom and dad's house in Yarrow while we worked to make our dated 1950s house a home. I worked on it every day while Rick went to work and we renovated together every weekend. One day in early June, when Rick and I were painting the master bedroom, he looked at me with the paintbrush in my hand, and we made love in our half-painted bedroom. It was spontaneous and perfect. I just knew I would become pregnant and in that instant our first child was conceived in complete love and anticipation of a wonderful life together. I dreamed our baby was a beautiful, blonde, curly haired, blue-eyed boy with a smile that would melt your heart. I waited eagerly to see if my dream was right.

That summer it was unbearably hot in our upstairs bedroom, so we decided to sleep in the unfinished basement where it was nice and cool. We were the picture of contentment on that old hide-a-bed. I had the cat curled up beside me on my side of the bed; our little dog, Sam, that Lorrie had given us, was snoring softly on the floor beside my husband. I was peacefully sleeping when a gentle tickle across my shoulders woke me. I smiled and sighed contentedly enjoying my husband's soft caress. The sense of peace that filled me was short-lived when I realized that my husband and I were spooning which meant he had one arm wrapped tightly around my waist and the other arm was nestled under my pillow. My eyes widened in fear. If both his arms were around me then what was he using to tickle my shoulders? A rush of terror hit me as the realization flooded through me. It had to be a spider.

Now, most marriages have an unspoken balance to them. One spouse washes dishes while one dries; one will change a dirty diaper while the other gags in the bathroom; one spouse is terrified of spiders and the other one kills them. We, unfortunately, didn't quite have the entire balance thing working for us because we both detest those freakishly fast, horribly huge, wolf spiders!

As soon as I realized what was running across my shoulder, I started screaming. I ripped the sheet off me and sent the cat bouncing off the bed as I hit the floor running to turn on the light. Apparently screaming is contagious because Rick leapt out of bed on his side, swearing like a truck driver. He stepped on the dog and she started howling right along with us. Meanwhile I was frantically trying to reach the light switch when I stubbed my toe on the bed so now I was screaming in both terror and pain. Finally, hopping on one foot, I managed to reach the light. Mere seconds passed but it seemed a lot longer. I turned around, and there was my hubby, standing by the bed, legs splayed, chest heaving, fist clenched, and eight hairy legs hanging out between his fingers! My hero! He felt that spider skitter across his chest at the precise moment I started screaming. He nabbed it in his bare hand and he squished it. It was at that moment that I knew I would stay with that man till death did us part; however, I wasn't willing to spend another minute in the basement, even with him, so I headed up the stairs to our steamy bedroom, lifted the blinds, opened the window wide and made the best of trying to sleep in a bedroom that felt more like an oven. But there weren't any spiders there so I was happy.

Around 7:30 the next morning I was snoring away when the bedroom door burst open and Rick leaped into the room with a chainsaw in his hands at full throttle! My eyes flew open and scenes from the Texas Chainsaw Massacre flashed through my mind. At this point I was wondering, "How well do I really know this guy?" I leapt out of bed and was ready for "fight or flight" even though all I was wearing was my birthday suit! Rick calmly shut off the saw, smiled and said, "Oh, did I scare you?"

My heart was pounding and my chest was heaving, "Uh, yeah!" "I just thought I'd cut a hole in the wall for an air conditioner so we can sleep comfortably up here." The smile on his face was pure evil but it was ever so much better than being massacred.

There was no way I was going back to sleep after that rude awakening, so I decided to make the bed. Rick was standing at the bedroom door with a big grin on his face, watching me. We didn't know for sure that I was expecting and I certainly didn't look pregnant except maybe my breasts were a little bigger than normal. I admit I was vain and didn't mind Rick looking at me naked. I'm thinking, "This 27-year-old birthday suit must be fitting me pretty fine because he hasn't taken his eyes off me!"

Suddenly Rick said, "Gee honey, you're awfully brave. Aren't you afraid our neighbour Bob will see you?" We lived in a three-level split and the bedrooms are on the top floor so the only way for Bob to see into our bedroom would be if he was standing on the roof of his house. I turned to look out the window and, sure enough, there was Bob on the roof of his house, happily cleaning his chimney! I dropped to the floor like an anchor while Rick stood there laughing until tears rolled down his face. I rolled over to the window reached up, pulled the blind shut and spent the next twenty-four years trying to avoid our neighbour Bob. Our marriage has been full of laughter and surprises (not to mention a wonderful air conditioned bedroom) but I don't recommend the use of spiders, chainsaws, or voyeurism to keep a marriage interesting.

Shortly after the chainsaw incident, I went to visit my sister Beanie, who had moved from Fort McMurray to Port Hardy on Vancouver Island with her husband. She was due to have her first baby and I hoped that she would go into labour while I was there. I hadn't been to the doctor yet to confirm that I was pregnant but I told Beanie I thought I very well could be, so we bought a home pregnancy test. We laughed and cried with joy when the test came back positive. I was really pregnant and she was the first to know. I had to go home before she had her baby but I bought a pair of tiny baby shoes and wrapped them up to give to Rick. He met me at the ferry and I couldn't wait to give him his present. We sat in the truck together as he opened his gift, and at first, he didn't understand the significance of the tiny shoes, until he saw my tears of happiness and the huge smile on my face. He gave a whoop of pure joy and we laughed and cried together over how absolutely perfect our lives were.

That summer I attended my ten-year grad reunion proudly wearing a maternity dress that I didn't really need to be wearing yet. Shelly, my friend from grade five, was there wearing a maternity dress as well. She was expecting her second child. We marveled at how fast the years had flown; we celebrated our wonderful lives and our beautiful, but barely bulging, baby bellies.

I was five months pregnant when I went into the hospital delivery room with my friend Shelly and took photos of her giving birth to her son. She used self-hypnosis and a modified Leboyer method for her delivery, which was incredibly relaxed, focused, and peaceful. I knew that's how I wanted this special child of ours to come into the world too, so I practiced the self-hypnosis techniques and got special permission to use the modified Leboyer method in Chilliwack General Hospital for the first time. Our child would be born under soft lights, surrounded by calm voices, and be immediately placed in a warm tub of water to ease the transition from the womb into the world. I planned the perfect delivery and visualized it every night before falling asleep. I felt wonderful and confident that this birth would be perfect.

Pregnancy suited me. I felt so good while I was pregnant that I even enrolled in a reflexology course. Reflexology uses an acupressure technique applied to specific points on your feet that correspond to every part of your body. This wonderful procedure creates a deep sense of relaxation. In this relaxed state the body is believed to heal faster. It made perfect sense to me so I signed up for the first level and trained with The Canadian Institute of Reflexology. I loved it. Now, I could not only do someone's hair, but I could also do their feet. My grandmother, who had survived breast cancer for more than thirty-five years, used to say that my reflexology treatments were better than any medicine. She may have been right because she lived to a robust 95 years of age! I gave my dad a reflexology session and noticed that he winced when I applied pressure to the area of the foot that related to the prostate. I suggested he talk to his doctor about getting a prostate exam.

I felt wonderful while I was pregnant right up until the very end. The baby was late. I was as big as a house and was having trouble sleeping. The phone would ring a million times a day every day past the February 28 due date. I dreaded picking up the phone to answer the same question again, "No, no baby yet." Finally, I decided that this baby was in no hurry to be born so Rick and I went visiting after dinner on March 6, 1984. We went to see his grandmother and grandfather for cake and tea. I felt an odd settling sensation and a few cramps but they didn't hurt so I ignored them. We came home and got ready for bed but the cramps started to come at regular intervals. Could this be it? No, it didn't hurt very much and there was no big gush of water as I'd been told to expect. Still, the contractions were coming every five minutes. Rick and I decided I should probably go to the hospital just in case. But first, I wanted to put on my make-up and curl my hair. I wanted to look good when this child saw his mom for the first time!

We only lived three minutes away from the hospital, so I decided to phone my parents and let them know that we were on our way. I remember talking to my mom on the phone in between putting my hair in hot rollers and saying, "Oh, wait a second mom, here comes another contraction!" and I'd breathe through it using the same self-hypnosis relaxation technique my friend Shelly had used for her delivery.

Mom said, "Oh honey, if you can talk so calmly you're a long way from having that baby but dad and I will come in now anyway and meet you at the hospital. I'll let your sisters know you're on your way in."

Rick and I checked into the hospital at 11:00 PM, on March 6, 1984. At midnight, my parents and sisters were in the waiting room preparing for an allnight baby waiting vigil and at fifteen minutes after midnight I said to Rick, "I don't think I can do 16 hours of this. I feel like I have to push already." Rick called for the doctor who, according to the instructions I'd been going over with her for the last few months, turned down the lights, brought out the baby bath, spoke in a soft voice, and helped me to deliver my baby exactly the way I'd imagined. At 12:34 am. our beautiful, blonde, curly haired, blue-eyed baby boy was born looking exactly the way he did in my dream. Kevin (which means kind and gentle) James (after my brother, Jimmy) Standeven came into our lives as an eagerly anticipated and very much loved precious gift from God. Our lives couldn't have been more perfect.

One night, about four weeks after Kevin was born, I woke up at 3:00 AM when I heard him fussing. It was my favorite time to be with him. There were no interruptions. The house was quiet. I sat in the rocking chair in his bedroom with the lamp dimmed, rocking my beautiful baby slowly as he nursed contentedly. I was suddenly hit with a wave of nostalgia so intense and deep that tears filled my eyes and rolled down my cheeks. I was flooded with a feeling of infinite awe and became acutely aware of the expanding circle of life I was now holding in my arms. There was no way that life could possibly get any better than it was at this precise moment in time. I stroked my baby's cheek and marveled as he nursed. His huge blue eyes seemed to see me with all the wisdom, innocence, trust, and love of the ages behind them. He pulled his head away from my breast and he smiled so sweetly at me that I felt I was going to burst with the love that filled me. Incredibly, in that instant, life seemed immeasurably better than I had ever dreamed possible.

The summer of 1985 I turned thirty and Kevin was almost eighteen months old. He was a joyous toddler. He started walking at nine months and talking at a year. He laughed easily and rarely misbehaved. I loved being a mom and turning thirty wasn't in the least bit traumatic for me. Time passed happily enough and it seemed Kevin skipped the Terrible Twos entirely, and instead spent his days making me and everyone who saw him smile. He was a born entertainer. We bought him a little harmonica that he practically slept with. He'd stand on a chair or a footstool; tap his little foot and shout, "One, two, three! Hit it, boys!" and we'd all clap as he blew a lot of noise on that little mouth organ.

He was stubbornly honest. If I was in another room he would come and ask if he could have a candy from the bowl. Most kids would have just helped themselves, but the idea of taking something without

Kevin first playing his harmonica on Christmas morning.

asking never occurred to him. When he was about 3 years old, I gave him permission to be bad for the entire day. I said he could slam doors, yell, stamp his feet, talk back, take treats without asking — anything he wanted to do, just to be naughty for a change. He thought it over carefully, and then said, "Mommy, if it's okay with you, I think I'd just rather be good." He was an amazing little person.

We had so much fun together. One day, I was feeding Kevin some chocolate custard and he was practically jumping out of his high chair trying to get more of it. He was bouncing up and down as I was trying to get the spoon into his mouth. Before we knew it we had custard everywhere. He had it smeared all over his face and was happily painting it on the tray of his chair with his hands. We were both laughing, and suddenly he reached out and clasped my cheeks in both of his chubby, chocolate-covered hands so that we were both now covered in pudding. I scooped some onto my finger and plopped it on his nose; he took some on his finger and did the same to me; we were so busy laughing that we hadn't heard the front door open. My girlfriend Paula-Marie (now known as "auntie PoPo"), stood open-mouthed behind us, watching in disbelief as we immersed ourselves in a full-out food fight. We'd been caught.

Kevin was polite beyond a parent's expectations. When we went to a restaurant he would wait patiently for his food. People would often stop at the table and compliment him on his fine manners. Other kids would crawl under the table or scream for their meals but Kevin always sat patiently—coloring or chatting. When the waitress came to take our order, she would invariably ask me what he would like, and I'd always turn to Kevin. He would look at her with his big blue eyes, and order exactly what he wanted. He didn't care for soda pop so whenever they would ask him what kind of pop he would like he'd just smile sweetly and say, "I would like water, please." More than one waitress brought him an extra scoop of ice cream for his dessert! People just seemed to fall in love with his charming demeanor. I don't think it was anything in particular that his father and I did to make him that way, it was just the way he was wired.

Any time Kevin did something wrong, I would try not to make him feel worse. For example, one day he spilled a glass of milk on the floor, and he started to cry. The adage, "Don't cry over spilled milk" came to mind, but he was too young to understand that expression. I knew it was an accident, I tried to remember the lesson I learned when my brother ran over my dog: never make someone feel worse than they already do when they know they did something wrong. I took the jug of milk and poured some more on the floor. I said, "It's only milk, son. We can easily clean it up. It was an accident. You didn't do it on purpose. You'll never be punished for an accident." We spent the next fifteen minutes finger-painting with the spilled milk on the floor. It's one of my favorite memories.

Kevin was always mature beyond his years. On a trip to the park, I asked him if he would like to go down the slide. He counted the 10 steps up and looked at the steep pitch of the steel slide and shook his head. "No thanks, mom. A kid could get hurt on that." They don't put slides like that in parks anymore, but I was amused at his good sense.

Kevin was extremely easy to raise. One day, he left his bike in the middle of the driveway and we had to move it or run over it. He knew it was supposed to be put away in the garage when he finished riding. As much as I hated to punish him, I knew he had to have some consequence for being careless with his belongings. I said, "Kevin, you know you're always supposed to put your bike away when you're finished riding. What do you think your punishment should be?" In my mind I was thinking I should probably not let him ride for the rest of the day but Kevin, bless his little heart, looked at me with those big loving eyes and said that he should probably not be allowed to ride his bike, and no TV, and no friends over for a week. He was always much harder on himself than we ever would have been. We decided we would always let him choose his own punishment after that. Kevin and I were close; closer than he was to his dad because Rick worked long hours driving a logging truck. Working 12-hour days, six days a week, wasn't unusual during logging season. Still, Rick was a good dad and a good provider. We laughed a lot together. It didn't matter how bad his day had been, he would always come through the door whistling. We worked on our house in every spare minute we had. Painting and remodelling projects kept us busy, and we were a good team. I came up with the ideas and Rick would willingly put them into action. Rick and my dad would often work side-by-side during our bigger home renovations. Dad was a handyman and Rick was always willing to learn.

In July, 1986, Rick and I celebrated our fourth anniversary. We were doing well. I had enrolled in an oil-painting class and discovered that, even though I wasn't very gifted, I loved to paint. The first picture I made was from a card I'd found of a beautiful daffodil on a bright blue background. I loved the rich contrast between the yellow and the blue and had no idea when I painted it that it was the symbol of hope for the Canadian Cancer Society. We also had no idea our marriage would soon be put to the test by the very disease the daffodil represented.

I was almost 32 and the trouble started simply. I was physically fit, and very active and healthy but for some reason I was having trouble sleeping on my right side. It felt as though something sharp was poking me in the hip. I increased my physical activity level, thinking I needed more exercise, but the exercise seemed to make it worse. I went to my chiropractor to see if something was being pinched. He was very skilled and had helped me avoid any back pain with my first pregnancy.

Rick and I were thinking of having another child soon. Kevin was almost three years old, and we thought four or five years between kids would be perfect. I didn't want to get pregnant while having hip problems, so I hoped Dr. Clark would be able to help. After my third visit he suggested that I should see my family doctor and ask for x-rays because my hip didn't seem to be moving the way it should.

My family doctor reassured me. "It's probably bursitis. Nothing serious. Try some physiotherapy. Take some medication. It should settle down. We'll take an x-ray if it doesn't get better in a couple of weeks." It didn't get better.

Subsequent x-rays revealed that the head of my femur was deteriorating. A small piece of bone had actually fragmented off the ball of my femur and that's what was causing the sharp pain I was feeling. I was sent to a local surgeon who assured me, from looking at my x-rays, that I needed a simple hip replacement. It might possibly be a tumor, but the word "cancer" never entered the conversation. I recalled the head-on collision I'd had when I was 18. I injured my hip when my right leg was jammed into the dashboard of the car. My right hip had never been as flexible as my left since that accident but it had never really hurt until now. I wasn't worried. The doctor explained the procedure. It was simple. He'd done hundreds of hip replacements in his time. Granted, they were generally on people much older than I was, but he made it sound like no big deal. I was relieved and content to stay in that happy place in my mind. I dropped by Paula-Marie's house after talking to the surgeon, and told her what the doctor said. She looked at me and just said, "Shit." And for some reason that scared me more than any words the surgeon had spoken.

My aunt was a registered nurse working in Vancouver. My mom wasted no time in calling her to get her opinion on my diagnosis. My aunt insisted that I not let anyone touch my leg until she had arranged for me to see a specialist in Vancouver. My doctor agreed to the second opinion and before I knew it I was headed off to Vancouver. I saw no reason for Rick to take the day off from work, so Kevin and I jumped into our old car on a cool, late-March afternoon to go to the specialist. Kevin had turned three that month, and he loved car rides. I was limping a little but otherwise feeling pretty good.

The specialist took one look at my x-rays and made a quick phone call. He gave me the address of another doctor he wanted me to see right away. I went. The next doctor looked at my x-rays and made a call to a third specialist. This was the one that scared me. He was a tumor specialist. With an increasing sense of fear and trepidation, I drove the short distance to see him. In one day, I had been to see three different specialists. Kevin was getting tired and so was I. The third doctor looked at the x-rays and told me that I needed to start using crutches immediately. I was not allowed to put any weight on my leg. He wanted to schedule a needle biopsy for as soon as I could make arrangements with my family to care for Kevin. I think if I hadn't had Kevin with me he would have admitted me to the hospital on the spot. I rented a pair of crutches from the pharmacy in the lobby of his office. Kevin thought they were pretty cool. I thought it was pretty scary, but I forced a smile to keep my fear from showing.

To top off the worrisome day, my car was acting up. It kept sputtering. I was trying to keep Kevin occupied playing I Spy on the way home, but my mind was racing. I was scared. All three doctors had seemed overly concerned about what they were seeing in the x-rays. I just wanted to get home, let my husband hold me, and reassure me that I'd be okay. Suddenly, with a final sputter, the car died. I pulled over to the shoulder of the freeway and let the car roll to a stop. I tried to restart it but it wouldn't even turn over. I put on my four-way flashers thinking that somebody would stop. I got out of the car and raised the hood. I stood on the crutches beside my car. It was getting dark. Kevin was tired and hungry. We were miles from home. Ten minutes passed. It seemed like an hour and nobody had stopped to help. I figured if we started walking someone with a kind heart might be willing to pick up a small child and a woman on crutches.

I wrapped a scarf around Kevin's neck and told him we were going on an adventure walk. We often went for night time walks at home to see the animals that came to the river near our house at twilight. Kevin always looked forward to "adventure walks" so he started out happily enough.

Car after car zoomed past. Kevin wanted me to carry him. He was tired. My hip was aching. I didn't know how I could carry him and use the crutches too. I managed to hold his finger as we walked along in the falling darkness. The doctor had told me that under no circumstance should I carry anything heavy, and to keep all weight completely off my right leg. I hadn't expected to be facing circumstances like this so soon. Kevin started to cry and, quietly, grateful for the dark, so did I. I said a silent prayer for help. I was just thinking that the two of us must make a pretty sorry sight and I was grateful when someone else finally thought so too. A small sports car pulled off the road just ahead of us. The driver had seen my stalled car back along the side of the freeway. When he saw us walking, he and his girlfriend figured we might need a ride. I nodded. She climbed into the small back seat and buckled Kevin in beside her. It was a tiny car and I was too tall to fit back there. Kevin was just happy to be somewhere warm and within minutes he was sound asleep. I was grateful for the dark so they couldn't see that I'd been crying, but when they asked me why I was on crutches it was as if a dam burst inside me.

I sobbed as I explained what I'd been through that day. I sobbed as the reality of what the doctors had seen in my x-rays sank in. It was a tumor. It could quite possibly be cancer. I was scared. They listened in silence, and the woman cried along with me. I asked them if they could please drop me at a phone booth on the highway so I could call my husband to come and pick us up, but they wouldn't hear of it. They drove us to our front door. Again, I was visited by earth angels when I needed them most.

Rick was sitting in the living room waiting and watching for us to come home. He was surprised to see us climb out of a little sports car. I hadn't been able to call him to tell him what happened. I thanked my "earth angels" for their kindness and they drove away. Rick met us at the door, took one look at my face, and held me in his arms until I stopped shaking. I felt safe there. Together we could face whatever the biopsy would reveal.

I went into the hospital for a needle biopsy. It was routine for everyone but me. When the surgeon, Dr. Morton, came into my room to tell us the biopsy results, I remember thinking it was kind of sweet the way that he looked everywhere except at me. He cleared his throat awkwardly. "The biopsy indicates that it is cancer." He said he was sorry.

The tumor was a type that would not respond to chemotherapy or radiation. Surgery was my only option at this point. He would set up an appointment with the best bone surgeon in the business. He probably said a lot more but I stopped hearing him the moment he said the word "cancer." I wanted my husband to be with me, but I was alone when Dr. Morton delivered the verdict. I lay on my hospital bed after Dr. Morton left, thinking that this couldn't possibly be happening. The tears rolled down my face and I hugged the pillow to my chest, fiercely willing myself not to cry out loud. How could I have cancer? I didn't drink a lot; I didn't smoke; I ate healthy meals; I exercised regularly; I was fit and trim. What more could I have done? Nothing. It really wasn't my fault. Shit happens.

The next few weeks went by in a blurry haze of CT scans and doctor appointments. When Rick took me to UBC (University of British Columbia's medical center) for an MRI (Magnetic Resonance Imaging) scan, my hip was so sore that I couldn't lie on my back with my legs straight. I went into the imaging tunnel with strict instructions that if I moved they'd have to start the procedure all over again. I started praying. Quietly at first, so that no one could hear me, I began saying the rosary over and over. My hip was throbbing and it felt like it was on fire. The pain was excruciating and tears started rolling down my face. I desperately needed to move my leg to relieve the pain but the thought of having to repeat the procedure kept me lying still. My prayers grew louder until finally I was shouting them out as loud as I could in an effort to distract me from my pain. I don't know how many Hail Mary's I went through, but it didn't work, and I begged them to stop. I cried all the way home because not only was I disappointed that I couldn't have the procedure completed, I was disappointed that my prayers didn't work. In hindsight, I should have taken a double dose of pain pills first, and it was stupid of them not to give me something ahead of time to relax me. Maybe prayers are only good if common sense is applied first.

Soon afterwards, I sat in a room before a medical panel at the cancer agency pretending to listen as they discussed the best way to proceed. The truth was that I had mentally removed myself from the room. My body was planted firmly in the chair, but my mind was somewhere else, wondering who they could possibly be discussing, because it couldn't be me. I couldn't have cancer. I'm only 32. I'm only 32. I'm only 32. Those words repeated in my head as the panel of specialists discussed my case as if I were actually there and hearing the words they were saying. I saw their heads nod in agreement. My treatment was decided.

Dr. B. was wonderful. He was optimistic that he could remove the tumor that had destroyed almost the entire head of my femur. The CT scans showed that the tumor appeared to be encapsulated on the ball of my femur, but they would remove a section of my pelvis and replace it with pelvic bone that was harvested from donor cadavers. I heard that Dr. B. had started the bone bank himself and was well-respected in the medical field. The diseased ball of my femur would be removed and replaced as in a standard, titanium, hip-replacement surgery. Amputation was never mentioned.

I remember going for that first surgery on April 29, 1987, thinking that everything would be okay. Somehow, it would be okay. Rick held my hand until they wheeled me through the surgical doors. I don't remember falling asleep; I don't remember anything except waking up in the recovery room with a familiar face hovering over me.

"Hi, Glenda. You probably don't remember me, but my name is Kathy. We went to school together in Chilliwack. I'm your recovery nurse."

I tried to smile but instead I projectile-vomited all over my old friend Kathy from high school. Welcome to the world of recovery after an anesthetic. It didn't matter how many times I apologized, I still felt mortified, so I closed my eyes again and when I opened them Rick was stroking my hand with a concerned smile fixed on his face.

"Hi, honey," he paused as if searching for the right words and then just sort of sighed. "The bad news is they found more tumors than the CT scan revealed. The doctor said it looked like grains of rice scattered throughout your pelvic area. They removed all of it and hollowed out the head of your femur. They reattached the muscle with a plate and screws. They couldn't decide if the new tumor was malignant or benign, so they've sent it away to be looked at, but the good news is, you still have all your own body parts." He seemed relieved, so I smiled and pretended I was too. Thank God I didn't throw up on him as well.

The surgery seemed to take a lot out of me. I was tired and thin. My hip hurt and I wasn't allowed to put any weight on my leg until the hip bone regenerated. I used a wheelchair and crutches to get around. My sister Beanie and her family were now living in North Vancouver and I went to stay with her for a couple of weeks until my stitches could be removed. Kevin stayed with my parents. Rick stayed in our Chilliwack home and continued working and looking after our pets. I've tried very hard to block those two weeks out of my mind because what I went through next should never have happened. Unfortunately, my vanity stepped up front and centre, and I didn't tell anyone that I hadn't had a bowel movement for over a week after the surgery. Heaven forbid I would EVER talk about my bodily functions to anyone — not even my doctor was privy to that info. I just kept making trips to the bathroom and attempting to poop, but all the pain pills and lack of exercise had blocked me up. It felt like I was trying to pass a football. Finally, after ten days of agony, I confessed my dilemma to my sister. She rushed me down to the emergency room, where they discovered that I was impacted and needed a procedure done which they referred to as "the bomb." It was a special enema designed to blast through obstructions in a timely and very efficient manner. They did the procedure while I lay on the hospital bed writhing in agony. They'd barely finished before it started to work. I grabbed my crutches and zoomed as fast as I could to the emergency room's bathroom. I barely made it before the bomb exploded. Unfortunately, I hadn't quite made it onto the toilet! There was shit from one side of the bathroom to the other. I've never in my life felt such relief and embarrassment simultaneously. The humbling memory of throwing up on my friend Kathy in the recovery room paled in comparison to the magnitude of this event. God bless my little sister, because she cleaned me up in the emergency room shower and hosed down the bathroom walls at the same time. Now, that is love!

When the stitches were removed, I went home to my husband and our son. Little Kevin wasn't impressed with the mommy who couldn't wrestle or play like she used to, and frankly neither was I. The two weeks we waited for the biopsy results were the longest of my life. Finally, Dr. B. called to announce with unabashed delight that the overwhelming consensus of all the labs that had examined the strange rice-like tumor said that it was benign. Benign. What a beautiful word that is. Benign. I repeated it back to him and he assured me that was what he said. Non-malignant. The first needle biopsy must have been wrong. Praise God and Hallelujah — now we could get busy and build up that damaged leg so Kevin could finally get that little brother or sister he was asking for!

It's hard to recall the first few months after that wonderful diagnosis of benign. I spent it doing physiotherapy at home and at the hospital. Trying to regain the strength in my hip took a lot of effort, but I knew that it was going to be worth it when we could finally add to our family. Gradually my leg grew stronger. I could get around with just a cane. I thought it looked quite stylish, actually. Rick and I were ready to have another child but something was concerning me. Over the original needle biopsy site, the one that had come back with a diagnosis of cancer, a lump was growing. The doctors seemed to be of one mind — it was scar tissue — nothing to worry about. But the scar tissue was growing rapidly, and I was worrying no matter how much I tried not to. My leg had stopped improving and it was beginning to hurt again. Finally, I took my concerns to my family doctor. She sent me back to the specialist for another biopsy but this time I asked him to remove the entire lump. I wanted the scar tissue removed, and I knew a needle biopsy wouldn't do that. It was important to me to get it all out. I waited for the biopsy results with a sense of foreboding while everyone else reassured me that it was nothing to be worried about.

A friend called me and told me that a faith healer was coming to her church and she wondered if I would like to go. At that point I was willing to try anything, so I went to the service. It was strange, but I did feel the pain ease as I surrounded myself with people praying. Some would say it was the power of positive thinking, and some would say it was the power of prayer. I just know it was powerful. But at home, in the quiet and dark of night, the fear and pain came crashing back on me. I badly wanted to be better just to make my family and friends happy. They were all praying and worrying so much for me. But I kept asking myself, "What if it's cancer?" People with cancer die. I felt the unfairness of it all. I was too young to die, and had too much to live for. During the day, I wore a happy and optimistic face for my family and friends, but the fear, the pain and the dark thoughts always came creeping back at night.

In December, 1987, after the biopsy, I attended my mother's surprise birthday party. She was 64. I've seen pictures of the celebration but I don't remember anything about it. They say I wrote something wonderful and read it in honor of the occasion, but the biopsy had hurt a lot more than I let on, and I had masked it with pain medication. I was in a wheelchair. I wasn't allowed to walk on my leg, but I've seen pictures of me 'dancing' in my chair with my cousin on the dance floor, so I'm sure I was putting on a good front to hide all the fear and pain I was holding inside. That seems to be something many cancer patients do. I would do everything in my power to ease the worry and concern I saw on the faces of the people I loved and, if that meant choosing to smile when I felt like crying, then that's what I would do. It's hard to feel bad when you're smiling.

The pain after the biopsy was enough to make me resort to pain pills again. One night, after trying to fall asleep and not succeeding, I reluctantly took my pain medication and had the most amazing dream.

I dreamed I was 83 years old. A voice said, "This is your life on two legs." I turned around and, as if I were watching a movie, I saw my life unfold. I relived my past adventures and the birth of Kevin and, surprisingly, experienced the birth of another son; I grew old with Rick and raised our two lovely boys. It was a nice life. I remember the word 'fluffy' came to mind. It was a strange feeling to see a movie about your life, and to realize at the end that you are profoundly disappointed.

"What? That's it? That's all there was? Well, that was hardly a life that mattered!" as I said these words, the voice spoke to me again. I couldn't see who was speaking but I felt the presence all around me.

"This is your life on one leg."

Again I watched as my life unfolded, but this time I saw myself with one leg as I again gave birth to our second son; I saw myself helping other cancer patients and amputees; speaking to classrooms full of children; appearing on TV and radio programs; writing books; traveling; raising our two boys and growing old with my husband. It wasn't easy. It was so much harder than that 'fluffy' life on two legs. Every time I fell down there were strong arms there to pick me up. At the end of my life I remember sighing in complete contentment and saying, "Now that was a life worth living. That was truly a life that mattered."

Again the voice spoke to me and this time I heard five small words that would forever change my life. "This choice I give you."

I woke up, reached for my journal and immediately wrote, "After the dream I had last night, I know I am going to lose my leg, and it's going to be okay."

I didn't tell anyone about the dream. I worried that they would think I had given up believing everything would be okay, and also because I wasn't ready to share the magic of that revelation. It was a special gift from God to be allowed a glimpse into my future. That dream would give me the courage and strength to get through all the pain of the coming days, weeks, months, and years. Still, everyone around me hoped and prayed that the biopsy report would come back with that magical word 'benign' written on it. In my heart I knew that it wouldn't but that everything would still be 'okay.'

On Tuesday, December 22, 1987, I sat in the doctor's office waiting for the biopsy results. Dr. B. came in looking so somber it almost made me laugh. He sat down across from me. Rick stood behind me with his hands on my shoulders. I knew what Dr. B. was going to say but I still needed to hear the words.

"May I talk to you as if you were my wife?" Well, he was young and good-looking. I certainly wasn't going to say no to that! He gently placed his hand on my knee, looked me in the eye, and said, "Honey, it's cancer. If you don't have this operation you'll die."

I nodded my head and said, "When do you want to do it?"

He looked at me as if he thought I hadn't heard him correctly so he elaborated "By operation, I mean amputation."

Again, I nodded and said, "Yes, but I was wondering when you wanted to do it."

Poor Dr. B. I'm sure he thought I'd taken one little blue pill too many so he explained it even further. "By amputation, I mean we need to surgically remove your entire right leg including your hip and pelvis. This type of cancer moves quickly to the lungs and won't respond to chemotherapy or radiation. You need to have the operation right away. I'd like to do the surgery tomorrow or the day after." I could feel my husband's grip tighten on my shoulders and I knew he was swallowing hard to keep the lump from rising in his throat.

Dr. B. wanted to do this life-changing surgery just two days before Christmas but again I nodded. "I understand. It sure sounds like you're not giving me much chance of having another Christmas." He sort of shrugged and sighed at the same time. I could tell he hated giving this sort of news to patients. Perhaps I should have told him about my dream. I was okay with the amputation, but I didn't want to share the reason why. I thought they might think I was giving up or just being silly and unrealistic. The dream was the special talisman that would get me safely through the worst of the days to come.

I tried my best to explain. "Dr. B., I really want one last Christmas and New Year's with two legs to spend with my family; Rick and I have a wedding to go to right after New Year and I want one last night of dancing on two legs with my husband; I am also hosting a baby shower for my girlfriend, Paula-Marie, so it looks like I will be free on January 6. Would that date work for you?"

Dr. B. looked a little surprised but he nodded, "Yes that will work." And so my surgery was set for January 6, 1988. I was thirty-two and a half years old.

I'm glad I chose to postpone the surgery date. The two weeks before my operation were filled with living and loving. Rick and I had a wonderful Christmas with our families; we danced with abandon at the wedding — I put my cane away for the night, popped an extra pain pill and refused to acknowledge the ache in my hip. The baby shower for my friend Paula-Marie was a huge success, as we celebrated the miracle of life with a deeper appreciation because of my illness. By the time January 5, 1988, arrived I was as ready as I could be to face the future on one leg.

The day before my surgery, I was admitted to the hospital. My entire family stayed long past visiting hours. None of them could quite believe what was about to happen to me. I told them about how I'd read somewhere that some religions believe that if you leave this world without all your body parts in one place you'll be reincarnated in the next life without those pieces. I laughed, and said, "Wouldn't it be awful if that were true — one lifetime on one leg is enough for me!" But I secretly wondered what they would do with my leg afterwards. It was a big piece of me to throw away.

The nurse eventually came in and made everyone go home for the night. I found myself alone for the first time that day. I looked down at my two perfectly pedicured feet. I had pampered myself with a pedicure a few days before coming to the hospital. I guess I wanted my leg to feel loved and appreciated. I didn't want to sleep. I wanted to dance and run up and down the hallway one last time but instead I lay in my hospital bed quietly massaging my leg. A lovely young nurse came into my room and saw me rubbing my leg. "Are you in pain?"

"Not really. I'm just saying goodbye."

The poor nurse broke into tears and left the room sobbing, "It's not fair. It's just not fair."

I guess nobody told her that not much in life is fair — it's just life. I was simply saying goodbye to an old friend I'd known and pretty much taken for granted for the past thirty-two and a half years; a friend I had loved, but who was now putting my life at risk. I was willing to let go.

The morning of my surgery mom, dad, Rick, and Kevin were at the hospital. Everyone hugged me goodbye. My dad held my son in his arms, and I was reassured by the love of my family. Rick walked beside the bed, holding my hand until they pushed me through the surgery doors. They all looked worried, but I felt the calm assurance of my dream giving me strength.

The surgery took eight hours and many units of donor blood. They removed my entire leg, hip, and pelvis on the right side. Dr. B. did an amazing job of reshaping what was left after the surgery into a cute little half-butt for me but I wasn't in any shape to appreciate his workmanship for several weeks afterwards. I officially became what is known as a right hemipelvectomy amputee. The amputated leg was sent off to pathology to make sure that the margins were clear and no cancer was left in what remained of my body.

Three days later, the pathologist had completed his tests and determined that Dr. B. had successfully removed the leg leaving clear margins. In my mind, that meant that the cancer was entirely taken away from me with the removal of my leg, hip, and pelvis. I was relieved but still couldn't help wondering what they would do with such a big chunk of my body now that the tests were completed. I needn't have worried. My sister, Beanie, had been listening to my story about reincarnation and she had called the hospital and asked for the leg to be released when the tests were finished. She sent a cab over to pick up the leg which was neatly wrapped in a black body bag. The unsuspecting cab driver delivered his package to the crematorium. When it arrived, someone from the funeral home called my sister and said, "The leg has arrived, but can you tell us when we can expect the rest of the body?"

My sister laughed and replied, "I'm hoping it won't be for at least another 50 years!"

She presented me with the neatly boxed remains of my leg when I came home from the hospital and we laughed together when she told me the story. I don't know if she will ever understand how much this act of kindness meant to me. I still have the box of ashes tucked away; patiently waiting for the rest of me to join it someday. Just in case …

Beanie dealt with my cancer in a take charge way. She visited me practically every day in the hospital. She went to the library and researched everything there was available on my type of cancer. Whereas I had the confidence of my dream to reassure me that I would be okay, Beanie had the confidence of cold hard facts and the voices of experience from other people. All my sisters were amazing, and so supportive through my illness and recovery. However, Ray, Sylvia's husband, refused to believe I would lose my leg. Right up until the day of my surgery, he believed they had made a mistake and I would be okay. For a while he could hardly bear to look at me after the surgery. He didn't show his emotions easily. I think my cancer diagnosis hurt him almost as much as the pain he felt when my brother Jimmy had died in the car accident.

My dad also tried so hard to be brave for me but one night, before my surgery, I accidentally discovered how he was really feeling. I had gone to lie down in my parents bedroom. We'd had my last big Christmas celebration "on two legs" at their house. I was tired, so I sneaked away for a few minutes of quiet time. The phone rang, and dad escaped to his bedroom to chat with his sister in relative peace and quiet away from the rest of the noisy family. He didn't turn on the light and he didn't realize I was lying on his bed trying to rest. He sat in a chair with his back to me, and talked frankly to his sister. "You know, Glenda's cancer is harder on Carol and me than when Jimmy died. She's disappearing before our eyes and there's nothing we can do. I feel so helpless."

Dad finished his conversation and hung up the phone without ever realizing that I'd overheard him. I was stunned. It never occurred to me that they were struggling so much with this. To me, I was okay. I knew how I felt and I knew that I was going to live but they didn't know that. It was the first time I realized that my illness wasn't just happening to me — it was profoundly affecting everyone around me as well.

Later, my stoic mom told me how she cried when she first saw me after the surgery. Apparently she held on to my dad and said, "I didn't know they would take so much of her away." Cancer affects entire families, not just the patient.

What my dream had not revealed, for which I am very grateful, was the amount of pain I would be in when I woke up. I don't remember going to the recovery ward. I don't remember coming out of the anesthesia. I do remember waking up at some point, looking down at my bed and seeing the outline of one leg under the sheet. I thought it looked so odd because I could still feel my leg there and the pain was excruciating. How could something that wasn't there be hurting so much? Nobody had warned me about phantom pain. Nobody had told me that the pain of losing my leg would be 100 times worse than the pain it had been causing me before. I thought I was going to die. I would have welcomed it at that point. They gave me morphine to dull the throbbing emanating from a leg that wasn't there. The combination of pain and morphine made me nauseous, and the drugs caused me to hallucinate. My husband told me afterward, that I kept asking him to "please get rid of all the spiders on the wall." As you may remember, I hate spiders, so this hallucination would have terrified me. Thank God I don't remember it. On the third day after my surgery I do remember telling them to please stop the morphine. Even though I grew up in the 70s I never did like drugs. I hated not knowing how I was really feeling, but when the pain came crashing in on me I needed help. They switched me over to Demerol, which I tolerated much better than the morphine.

Rick, bless him, was there when I opened my eyes first thing in the morning and when I finally closed them at night. My husband did things for me that no man should have to do for his partner. He bathed me, emptied my bedpan, and, when I somehow managed to get my period right on schedule through the trauma, he even helped me change the tampon. The nursing staff was amazed at his level of dedication and very appreciative of all his help. At intervals during the day, he'd slip away for some welcome relief from caring for me. I saw a side of him I never would have seen if it hadn't been for the cancer. I discovered that he was made of strong stuff. Many marriages dissolve when the wife becomes ill, but ours grew stronger. Some men run, because they can't accept the fact that they can't "fix" the problem. I think that men traditionally feel that their role is to make things right and if they can't fix what's "broken" then it's better to walk — or run — away. They don't realize that we don't need "fixing" when we have cancer — we just need loving. Rick took over and I gratefully accepted his care. Cancer allowed me the opportunity to see the inner strength in my husband and for that I'm thankful.

Rick would rub the bed where my leg used to be just to humour me when I complained that it was hurting. I knew the leg was gone, yet somehow just having him rub the empty spot on my bed made me feel better. I drew strength from him every day, and am grateful that he was strong enough to see me through my surgery and recovery. When I asked him how he could love me when I was no longer the woman he married, he was puzzled by the question. He assumed I understood. I cried when he explained, "Glen, I married you for the person you are on the inside, not the outside package." I never loved him more than I did at that moment.

My mom would come in to visit, but sitting in my private hospital room drove her crazy. She had never learned to sit quietly and hold someone's hand. Mom always felt that she had to "do" something, so she would change the water in the flower vases; organize my cards; pull off wilted or dying flowers; fluff my pillows; brush my hair; and find a myriad of other little chores to keep herself busy. By the time she went home I was exhausted just from watching her putter around my room.

Glenda's Story

I loved to have my hair brushed, but it was getting quite oily and I wasn't up to having it washed yet. My aunt, the nurse who had insisted I get a second opinion, decided my long hair would look better slicked back and put into a pony tail until I was ready to have it washed. Unfortunately, a pony tail isn't very comfortable to lie on so, being resourceful and far too helpful, my aunt put it into two pony tails — one on either side of my head so I looked remarkably like an Afghan hound. Even in a fuzzy, drug-induced haze, I knew I looked ridiculous and prayed no visitors would come that day. It's funny that no matter how sick I was feeling on the inside, I still wanted to look good on the outside.

A week after surgery, a doctor came into my room and told me that there was no way I could ever use a prosthetic leg. I had lost three joints plus the pelvic floor on the right side. There was no hope of ever having a leg that would work. He did a distressing pantomime of how I would lurch when I walked, if I tried to use a prosthesis. I stuck my chin out at him and said, "Maybe you would walk that way but I most certainly won't!"

He shrugged and said, "Well, maybe reverse psychology will work for you." With that, he turned and left the room. I never saw him again. I don't remember his name but I do remember that I collapsed in Rick's arms and sobbed the minute he left my room. I had set my hopes on having an artificial leg so I would look normal. I knew he was probably right but, despite my reassuring dream, I wasn't ready to accept the fact that I would never have two legs again.

I had many visitors while I was in Vancouver General Hospital. I know because I had them sign a big piece of posterboard taped to the wall. I was so drugged up that I couldn't always remember who had been in to see me, so the poster helped me to remember. All the cards and flowers were constant reminders of how many people were praying for me and sending me get well wishes. One special visitor was a gorgeous lady who arrived wearing a tailored white linen suit and a big smile. My doctor had asked her to come visit me. She stood in the doorway looking so confident and beautiful. I remember thinking she looked like an angel. At first I didn't notice that she had only one leg and was using crutches. I found out later that Dianna was a hemipelvectomy amputee as well, and only used crutches. She never used a prosthesis, and she gave me a much-needed boost of confidence when I needed it the most. I was clinging to the future hope that my dream had given me, and Dianna was a welcome sign that my life was going to get better and the pain would pass someday. I just didn't know when that day would be. I prayed it would be soon.

Two weeks after my surgery, I was discharged from the hospital. Rick took me to see a pain specialist on the way home to get me onto a strict regimen of pain control. I hated taking the pills, but the pain was unbearable. I can only describe it as feeling like someone was poking me with an electric cattle prod, along with sporadic bouts of having the worst rope burn, accompanied by a feeling of popcorn being popped underneath your skin. Every time I stood up, the blood rushed into the amputated stump area and throbbed as if it would explode. I desperately needed help managing the pain. The receptionist was busy working behind the tall counter and didn't see us come in. She looked up to see Rick and I both standing in front of her desk. I told her my name and she looked surprised. Without thinking she blurted, "Oh, I was expecting a cripple." Rick and I looked at each other in stunned disbelief and didn't know what to say. "Just walk this way." She stood up to point me in the right direction.

And, of course, I started to laugh. "If I could walk that way I wouldn't be here," I grimaced.

By this time I had come around to her side of the counter, when she saw me walking on one leg with my crutches, she looked as if she wanted to throw up. She was horrified to have made such an inappropriate comment in a doctor's office where patients of all abilities and disabilities are seen. She tried to explain to us that "You just looked so *normal* standing there." Apparently she was used to seeing patients arrive from the hospital in wheelchairs. I have to admit that I enjoyed seeing her squirm just a little. I'm sure she never made such a comment again.

Rick, Kevin, and I moved in with my parents while I recovered from the surgery. Kevin had his own little room there and Rick and I slept in the other spare bedroom. Dad had rigged up an amazing heavy steel contraption that went above and across my bed. To it, he welded a triangular bar grip on a chain. It was just like the device I had used in the hospital to help me turn onto my side and get out of bed. I was in constant pain but every now and then, just for a second or two, there would be no pain. I clung to those seconds and lived for them. One day my mom came in and asked me if I wanted anything. I said, "Yeah, have you got a spare leg?" and I started to giggle. Mom was shocked at first, but then she saw the humour in it and started to laugh too. Before I knew it, tears were rolling down our cheeks and I realized that for the entire time that we had been laughing, I hadn't felt the unbearable phantom pains. It felt so good to laugh but there weren't many opportunities for laughter when the pain was so overwhelming.

My girlfriend, Paula K, who I'd lived with in Australia, had gone into the hospital in Abbotsford to have a hysterectomy. I was only three weeks out of surgery myself but I wanted to see her. I figured if I fell, or hurt myself, what better place to be than in a hospital when it happened, so I talked my mom into driving me to see my friend. I was in agony, but I took my pain pills and bravely walked through the hospital lobby wearing a long fur coat to keep me warm. The visit went well and I felt reassured that I had made my first outing and hadn't had anything bad happen. It was hot in the hospital, and I'd taken my coat off in Paula's room. As we were about to leave I slipped back into my coat but I didn't button it up. As I walked through the lobby on the way out it was obvious to anyone who looked that I only had one leg under my skirt. I had prepared myself to accept looks of curiosity, sympathy, empathy, or even surprise or distaste, but I could never have prepared myself for what happened next.

As I slowly crutched through the lobby I passed curious onlookers and gave them all brave smiles if I caught their eye. Most people smiled back, which reassured me. As I passed the 'kid zone' I noticed two young children, about 6 years old, playing with toys on the floor. They both looked up at me with big eyes. I smiled. The little boy's mouth gaped and he pointed a finger at me. "Look everybody! That lady only has one leg! Isn't that funny?" And both of those little buggers laughed big booming belly laughs as only kids can.

It seemed everyone in the lobby turned to look at me. I suddenly became a bug under a microscope. My face felt both frozen and hot at the same time. I was shocked and embarrassed. I put my head down and rushed through the lobby ahead of my mom to the car. The instant I collapsed on the seat, I burst into tears. I had prepared myself for every possible reaction from people, but I had never in my wildest dreams expected anyone to laugh at me or think that losing a leg was funny. Mom tried to tell me that they didn't know any better; they were just kids. But I couldn't get over the fact that anyone, no matter what age, would ever think a disability was *funny*. In that very instant, I resolved to go to schools and talk to children about what it's like to be different. In the more than two decades since my surgery, I have never had anyone else—of any age—react like that to my amputation. I think I was meant to be in that lobby at that precise moment in time to allow me to find the resolve and commitment to go to schools and begin speaking to kids. Their laughter provided the impetus to begin my speaking career.

Glenda's Story

We were with my parents for a full month after my surgery. Kevin was quieter than I remembered, but I was so busy trying to work through my own pain and healing that I was grateful for the peace. I didn't realize that every day my parents were telling him he had to be good because his mommy was sick. I slept in the spare room with Rick but I was afraid to let him touch me. I was afraid that making love would feel different with one leg and no pelvis on that side. I was afraid Rick would be repulsed by the way my new body looked but he was patient and so very gentle. About six weeks after my surgery, we made love for the first time, and it was wonderful. I cried with relief as he held me in his arms and told me that I was beautiful, and he didn't care if I lost both legs as long as I was there to love. It was such a relief to know that he still loved me, even though my body was no longer the one I thought he fell in love with. I hadn't realized that he fell for all of me, not just the outside package. What a remarkable man!

I was lying on the couch in the sun room at my parent's home soaking up the mid-February sunshine when the phone rang. Paula-Marie's cheerful voice greeted me. "Hi, Auntie Glenda!" At first I didn't understand why she would be calling me "auntie," but when she explained that she was calling from the hospital I broke into a huge grin. She had just given birth to her son, Jordan. I couldn't stop smiling. She had been told that she very likely couldn't ever have children, and here she was holding the little miracle in her arms. I guess the doctors aren't always right.

About a month and a half after my surgery, I was admitted to GF Strong Rehabilitation Centre in Vancouver. I was supposed to learn how to use forearm crutches, master the use of a wheelchair, be fitted for an artificial leg, and learn to live as a disabled person in an able-bodied world. Kevin would continue to stay with my mom and dad while Rick went back to work and stayed at our house in Chilliwack during the week.

On my GF Strong therapists' shoulders prior to leaving the centre.

I had recorded several bedtime stories for Kevin and plenty of "I love you" messages as well. I made a calendar so that he could put an X across each day until the weekend when he would come to visit me at GF Strong. I would eventually be allowed to come home on weekends, but for now I was expected to stay there and get well. Everyone tried to help Kevin through what had to be a very tough time, but we didn't always do what was right. Kevin was a sensitive child. He adored me and I adored him but suddenly he was being told that he had to be a good boy *now* because his mommy needed him to be her helper. People meant well. My parents meant well. I was their little girl too, and they were looking out for me. I was unaware of the demands for "good behavior" that were being put on my little boy. I can only imagine the pressure and strain that he was under trying to sort through all the turmoil of his young emotions amid the fear of losing his mom.

I remember the exact moment when I realized that I may have

lost my leg but not necessarily my sense of humor. At GF Strong, I was determined to learn to use a prosthetic leg and walk again. My first day there, I was in a wheelchair wheeling myself into the gymnasium with a little lap blanket over me — trying to hide the fact that I only had one leg. That was a dumb thing to do, since the only really able-bodied people there were the staff members. It was reassuring to wheel into the big gymnasium and be surrounded by other people with disabilities. I felt safe there. Off to one side of the gym there was a group of therapists — holding clip boards and laughing together. I thought, "What a perfect place to get well!" I wheeled over to those wonderfully happy people and asked them, "What's so funny first thing on a Monday morning?"

They didn't even look down to see who was asking the question; they just wiped the tears of laughter from their eyes and said, "We just can't wait to meet the amputee whose last name is…STAND EVEN!"

I paused, unsure of what to do or say. "Um… that would be me!" The fact that I was right there made them laugh even harder, and I soon saw the irony of my last name and began to laugh right along with them. I may have lost my leg at Vancouver General Hospital but I most definitely found my sense of humor at GF Strong. When I told Rick this story he suggested I change my first name to "Eileen" and we both laughed until we were breathless. His sense of humour is apparently as warped as mine. No wonder I loved him.

What an experience GF Strong was. I was fitted for an artificial leg that was heavy and clumsy, but I was determined to learn to use it. Both with the leg on and with the leg off, I learned how to use forearm crutches to walk and climb stairs; to walk uphill and downhill; to fall down without getting hurt; to get up from the floor; to get in and out of a car; to drive a car with a left foot gas pedal; to climb through a window and use a fire-escape; to play ping-pong and volleyball.

I learned to be confident and competitive. I learned that having one leg limited me only if I allowed it.

My friends and family visited me often. One of my high school friends, Andrea Jeffries, had a little boy, Andrew, who had been born with multiple birth defects. He spent a lot of time at Vancouver Children's Hospital which was next door to GF Strong. Baby Andrew looked like an angel with huge brown eyes and a ready smile. Sadly, he didn't live past his third birthday, but his illness allowed Andrea and me to spend lots of time together sharing our hopes and fears. Andrew's smile stayed with me long after he was gone. With all his disabilities, I marveled at the strength of the spirit that allowed such a beautiful child to smile through it all.

One of my therapists became a very good friend. Elaine taught me how to go shopping (on one leg) and use escalators at the mall. It was so much fun. She gave me a book called *Creative Visualization* by Shakti Gawain, and these techniques helped me to manage my pain. It was a bit of a revelation to read a book written by someone who saw God the way I did, and I blessed Elaine for sharing it with me.

I took relaxation classes at GF Strong and learned self-hypnosis techniques to help fight the phantom pain I was still experiencing after my surgery. I had lost a lot of weight because I couldn't eat. Food had no appeal. I was exercising from 8 in the morning till 4 in the afternoon, five days a week, trying to build my strength and rebuild my health. I was physically fit but when I stepped on the scale and realized I'd gone from 128 pounds immediately following my surgery to 105 pounds after three months at GF Strong, I knew I was in trouble. I looked like a stick. I certainly blew the "big boned" theory out of the water! I crutched over to the grocery store close to the rehab centre and bought myself two chocolate bars and a doughnut. I was determined to regain some of the weight I'd lost. (For the next 20 years I have steadily gained five pounds a year. Doesn't sound like much until you do the math! The first ten or fifteen years after losing my leg I felt that I looked pretty darn good but after that I felt that I just looked fat. I'm still struggling to get the extra weight off but Rick continues to say he loves the "me" inside, so pass the cake, please!).

At GF Strong I learned that it was okay to be different. One night, a bunch of us went to the nearby pub for drinks. My sister Lorrie and my girlfriend Shelly were visiting that night, so we all walked, rolled, and crutched our way over to the nearby pub. We may have overindulged because on the way home, one of the guys tipped out of his wheelchair when he rolled off the sidewalk and into the landscaped gardens along the walk. I knew we were in trouble when I realized that, aside from Lorrie and Shelly, I was the most able-bodied person in our group! Somehow we managed to get the laughing, drunken, paraplegic back into his chair and back on the right side of the sidewalk. Then, one of the guys decided he really had to pee after having had one too many beers. We weren't anywhere near a bathroom, but he nonchalantly wheeled over to a big oak tree and lifted his pant leg to reveal a plastic bag strapped to his leg with a catheter hose attached to it. He deftly emptied the contents of the bag against the side of the tree and re-strapped the bag to his leg. We were all laughing so hard the tears were rolling down our faces. Maybe you had to be there... or maybe you just had to be drunk and/or disabled.

The phantom pain was still excruciating but I was finding that exercise was helping me to feel stronger and more in control. I noticed I was most pain free when I was exercising the most. I desperately wanted to get off the pain medications. Many amputees suffer such severe phantom pains that they easily and quickly become addicted to strong pain killers. I didn't want that to happen to me, so one weekend I decided to stay at GF Strong and go off my pain medication. I wanted to be near doctors and nurses in case I couldn't handle the cold-turkey withdrawal, and I didn't want to expose my family to the intense mood swings that can accompany withdrawal. I came down with a high fever and felt really sick. My liver function test came back as abnormal, but within a few days I felt fine again, and we chalked it up to withdrawal symptoms. I didn't realize that there could be other reasons for my liver function test to be abnormal.

While I was at GF Strong getting well again, Kevin was busy with his grandparents, learning to read and attending kindergarten at Yarrow Elementary. He had turned four in March, but was light-years ahead of other kids his age. He was already reading, making up and printing little stories, and easily doing math at a grade two level. He knew words like *photosynthesis* and *zooplankton*, and could tell you exactly what those words meant. He couldn't say L words though, which I found extremely cute. Ls came out sounding like Ys. For example, the word *look* became *yook,* and he sounded like he had a thick Bronx accent. My dad worked on pronuciation with him every day while I was in GF Strong.

When I came home, dad announced that Kevin had something he wanted to say to me. Very slowly, deliberately, and carefully, my little boy said, "Look at the lovely lady." His little tongue flicked and curled around every L in the sentence and he just beamed with pride. I hugged him hard while my dad's eyes turned moist.

Kevin was determined to bring me to his Yarrow school for "show and tell" with my new artificial leg. Unfortunately, the doctor at Vancouver General hospital had been right. The leg wasn't com-fortable or practical, but it became a great "show and tell" piece to use with kids of all ages. With a great deal of effort, I had Kevin lug my heavy artificial leg into the classroom while I crutched along ahead of him. I delivered my first classroom talk to a very well-behaved group of kindergarten students and introduced them to "Peggy," as we had affectionately nicknamed my prosthetic leg. I felt an odd sense of déjà vu the first time I stood in front of the class on my crutches. The dream of how my life would be on one leg was unfolding already. I couldn't help wondering if everything I'd seen in my dream would come true. Time would tell.

After I finished at GF Strong in May, 1988, Rick and I enrolled together in a wonderful weekend program to learn meditation and visualization techniques. The HOPE (Help Ourselves Positively Everyday) Cancer Wellness Centre was run by a brain cancer survivor, Claude Dosdall. He had written a book (with Joanne Broatch) called *My God I Thought You'd Died* (Seal Books, 1986). It was just what we needed to teach us how to focus our energy on my getting well again. When we came home, we decided to start a support group for other cancer patients and share some of the wonderful meditation skills we'd learned at the workshop. We opened our home once a week to an eclectic mix of cancer patients. We shared books like *Getting Well Again* by O. Carl Simonton, James Creighton, and Stephanie Matthews Simonton (Bantam, 1992). We talked while having tea and always ended our sessions with a healing meditation.

Unfortunately, the very Christian town of Chilliwack wasn't quite ready for meditation yet. I started getting weird phone calls from devout churchgoers saying that if I practiced meditation, I could no longer be a Christian. They said that they would pray for me, and hoped that I would realize the sin I was committing. It was too much stress for Rick and me so, after a few months of trying unsuccessfully to ignore the harassment, we reluctantly called quits to the group. My faith had seen me through my illness, surgery and recovery, but I wasn't yet up to a battle to justify my beliefs. I continued to use meditation and visualization to help me through my painful recovery and stayed in touch with the new friends I'd made at our home cancer support group.

During one of my regular check-ups with Dr. B., we discussed the possibility of my getting pregnant. He explained that it would be difficult for someone with only half a pelvis but it could be done. He suggested I wait for ten years, to determine that the cancer was well and truly gone, before attempting to get pregnant. After the ten year mark, he said Rick and I could break out the champagne. I told him that I felt that 42 was too old for me to have another baby. He sighed and said, "Okay, then, let's compromise, and say you wait for five years?"

I smiled back at him and, remembering my dream, said, "Okay, but how about we wait for two?" He just shook his head and grinned.

The pain was bearable most days, or maybe I was just getting used to it. Every day I would push myself a little harder, and a little further. In April, the weather turned nice and Rick went out to do some yard work, so I joined him. He brought out a little stool for me and I took a lawn edger to see if I could use it with one foot if I sat on the stool. Before I knew it, I had edged our entire yard. That night, I was physically exhausted, and as I eased my aching body into a hot bath, I was struck with the realization that the bath water felt amazing. It was one of the most profound experiences I'd ever had. I was suddenly struck with another epiphany. If I hadn't been in so much pain, this would have been another bath like thousands of others in the past. Pain makes you appreciate the little things in life. It sounds so simple, but the revelation brought tears of appreciation to my eyes as I lay in a tub of hot water, feeling the pain in every muscle easing away.

On June 11, 1988, just a little over five months after my surgery, I found myself wearing a gorgeous, lacy, teal-colored dress that cost me more than my own wedding gown had. I was walking down a red-carpeted aisle on my crutches with a handsome man by my side. My friend Paula K. was getting married to a man I had gone to high school with. She had asked me to be her matron of honor at their wedding. I never dreamed I'd be walking down the aisle wearing an artificial leg and using

Dancing with my dad.

crutches on her special day, but after having had cancer, I was just happy to be there at all. That night I danced, a little stiff-legged to be sure, but I danced nonetheless, with my husband, my son, and my dad. In every photo I have a big grin on my face! Kevin seemed happy too, that night, but underneath his cherub smile something was wrong.

Our little boy was having problems adjusting to a one-legged mom. He didn't seem to be the same happy kid I'd left at my parents' house six months ago. He didn't want to cuddle anymore. He didn't want to listen to me. He was disobedient for the first time in his four short years. I was willing to overlook his behavior and chalk it up to the trauma of being separated from me for so long. I was willing to give him time to come back to me as the wonderful and loving child I remembered, but one day, shortly after Paula's wedding, he pushed me down the stairs. Maybe he was impatient because I was too slow in making my way down ahead of him on my crutches, but my little boy *pushed* me and I lost my balance.

Luckily, I wasn't hurt, but Rick saw him do it and he snapped. He grabbed Kevin by the arm and pulled him into his bedroom. He spanked him hard on the bottom. I don't know who was more surprised, Kevin, or me, by Rick's reaction. I knew Rick was protecting me and yet he'd never raised a hand to Kevin before. I stepped between them, sat down on the floor, and pulled Kevin into my arms. I asked Rick to leave the room. Kevin angrily tried to squirm away but I wouldn't let him go. I held him until he collapsed into sobs in my arms asking me, "Why did daddy hurt me?" I cried just as hard as Kevin did and I knew our family needed help. I made a call that very day.

A child psychologist came to our house that same week. She talked with Rick and me, but mainly she talked with Kevin. Within one hour, she knew exactly what was wrong with my little boy. Everyone had been telling him, "Be a good boy. Your mommy is sick and she needs you to look after her now."

The psychologist explained it simply. "Basically, Kevin is firing you before you quit." Apparently, the thought of losing the mom he loved was too much for him to bear, so, to make the pain of loss easier, he chose to separate himself from me emotionally, before I did it physically. The remedy was simple. The psychologist suggested that I prove to him that I was still capable of looking after him and being his mom. He and I needed to go on a vacation together.

I made immediate plans for us to go to Victoria and stay with my old school friend Shelly and her family for a week. I called a cab to take us to the bus depot. I wanted this to be an adventure, and a cab ride was something we had never done together before. My mom and dad came to the house to see us off. They wanted to drive us to the ferry but I said no. I wanted to prove my independence as much to them as I did to myself and Kevin. They were worried sick about me going away. I'd only been home from GF Strong for a few weeks. I put "Peggy" on in an effort to look as normal as I could to all the strangers we would meet along the way. Walking with a heavy prosthesis was much slower and quite uncomfortable, but I figured Kevin had enough to deal with without having his disabled mom stand out in a crowd. As Kevin and I walked towards the cab my

Glenda's Story

Kevin and Glenda on the ferry to Victoria.

mom instinctively said, "Now, be a good boy and look after your mom!"

Before I could say anything little Kevin turned to her and shouted, "I'm just a little kid! Who's going to look after me?" I was so proud of him for finally speaking out about how he really felt. I turned to my parents and said, "I know you love me, but I am *his* mother. I will look after him. I will always look after him. There is nothing wrong with me and I don't need a child to take care of me. We'll see you in a week." With that, Kevin and I began to rebuild our mother/son relationship the way it was meant to be.

We had an amazing week together in Victoria. We rode the bus and took the ferry over to Vancouver Island. We went sightseeing and spent time with Shelly, her husband, and her kids. We went to a wonderful street dance, and Kevin and I happily danced together. Gradually, over the course of the week, Kevin learned to be a little boy again and trust that his mommy was looking after him. When we returned to Chilliwack a week later, I had my wonderful loving child back again. I made sure that I told him several times a day that

I was the only mom he had, and reassured him that it was my job to look after him. Rick never raised a hand to him again, but our son still remembers the only spanking he ever got in his life.

Kevin and I spent lots of time together after that. We continued to go for 'adventure walks' at night to see the raccoons and bats that would come to the river to drink and hunt for food. We'd spend time reading together or building forts in the living room. That first summer after losing my leg, I took Kevin to the waterslides. Even though I only had one leg I thought I looked pretty good in a bathing suit. I was thinner, and, other than having only one leg, I was in better shape than I'd ever been in my life. We either went down the small slides together or I would wait at the bottom of the chute to catch him when he came out the end. It was a little tricky to maneuver Kevin and my crutches at the same time but the slides were small and we managed. It was a lot of fun, and neither of us paid much attention to the curious glances we occasionally got from others, but that was about to change.

Kevin was still young, so whenever we needed to use the washroom, we went into the ladies change room together. He stood outside the bathroom stall patiently waiting for me to finish and chatted happily with me through the closed door. A busload of Indian tourists wearing colorful saris arrived, and they piled into the change room. They all seemed to be talking at once. As I emerged from the bathroom on my crutches wearing my bikini with the short little wraparound skirt attached, the talking stopped completely. The change room grew uncomfortably silent as they all turned to stare at me with their mouths agape. I pretended not to notice and crutched over to the sink to wash my hands and tidy my hair. Kevin pressed himself up against my leg and looked up at me. In a stage whisper, he said, "Mom, everybody is staring."

Not wanting to be embarrassed into a sudden departure, I deliberately fiddled some more with my hair and said, "Yes, I noticed that. What do you think they're looking at?"

With the innocence of youth and the blindness of love, he replied, "Beats me, but let's get the heck out of here!" Yes, my wonderful son was well and truly back.

Rick joined us on another trip to the waterslides that summer of 1988. The three of us stood in line at the top of the slides. Kevin was being very brave and wanted to go down the steepest slide with his dad. I would go down first and wait in the pool at the bottom of the slides to watch for Kevin and Rick. I would crutch to the top of the slides and an attendant would carry my crutches down for me so I could slide without having to hold my crutches. I could hardly wait to see the expression on my little boy's face when he and his dad would shoot off the end of the biggest slide. As we stood in line at the top waiting for our turn, I noticed a little boy about five years old was staring at me. Finally, he just had to state the obvious, "Hey lady. You only got one leg! Where's your other leg?"

I looked down where my leg should be and with mock horror said, "Oh no! It was here a minute ago!"

Bless that child's heart, because without hesitation, he reached his little hand out and placed it on top of mine. With deep concern, he said, "Don't worry lady. I'll help you find it." He spent the rest of the afternoon with a mask and snorkel searching the splash pools for my missing leg. Ya gotta love kids.

Adults aren't always as forthright. They sometimes steal sideways glances or avoid eye contact. Rick and I noticed that after my surgery, people who used to stop and chat with us at the mall would often just say a quick hello and be on their way. They didn't know what to say or how to act and felt badly for me. On one occasion, we'd made dinner plans with old friends who hadn't seen me since my surgery. We had a lovely time with good food and good company at the best restaurant in town. Towards the end of the dinner, one of the men leaned over to me and said, "I'm so happy you're still you. I was so afraid you'd be different." I determined early on that in order to make people comfortable around me I needed to be comfortable in my own skin. I made an extra effort to smile even when I was hurting; I made sure I never left the house without my hair and make-up done; and I made an effort to be visible by volunteering at school and in the community every chance I could.

In March of 1989, I enrolled in a learn-to-ski clinic at the ski resort at Whistler Mountain for people with disabilities. Some of my physiotherapists from GF Strong were going to be instructors there and I knew it would be fun. I had to get my doctor's approval to attend the training and I went into his office full of excitement to get the paperwork signed. As he looked over the papers, his brow creased into a worried frown and his mouth puckered around the edges. He said, "I don't think this is such a good idea for someone with your disability. What would you do if you fell down?"

I immediately threw my crutches to the floor and I dropped to the ground at his feet. In an instant, I bounced back up again. "If I fall, I'll just get back up." He signed the papers.

I loved skiing. It felt wonderful to glide down the hills without hopping. It was such a sense of freedom to be able to go as fast as I wanted, and feel the thrill of passing able-bodied slower skiers. I took to skiing like a duck to water and I skied much better on one leg than I ever did on two. It was hilarious to see the looks on able-bodied skiers when all of us disabled skiers hit the slopes. Most of us were missing a limb and learning to use outriggers which are special poles with little skis attached. The majority of us were not wearing prostheses, but one below-knee amputee was learning to ski using his artificial limb. We just about died laughing when he hit a snow bank and left his prosthetic leg sitting, neatly attached to his ski, as he and his good leg

Learning to ski—March, 1989.

continued down the slope. People practically fell off the chairlift when they saw a leg stuck in the snow below them.

Rick, Kevin, and I often went skiing together over the next two years. Rick had a hard time keeping up to his one-legged wife, and would be content to let me fly on my own while he entertained Kevin on the bunny slope. Learning to ski was a very liberating act of independence for me as a disabled person. I highly recommend it!

In March 1990, I entered the BC Winter Games and won two silver medals in the slalom and giant slalom competitions. Does it matter that there were only two of us in that category? I was just thrilled to be there racing down Apex Mountain near Penticton, BC, as my parents, Kevin, my friend Shelly from grade five, and her two kids cheered me on. I thought that standing on the podium to receive my medals was one of the best moments of my life.

August of 1989 was a wonderful month. I turned 34, and my husband and family had planned a big surprise party for me. I love surprises, so when I found a note in my husband's lunchbox confirming a reservation for my birthday dinner at our favorite restaurant, I was really upset. I put the note back and determined to act surprised when the day rolled around. My actual birthday was on Friday but Rick said he had made plans for us on the Saturday, and I wasn't allowed to ask him questions. Well, I'd already seen the note, so I didn't have to ask questions. I knew what he had planned. He said, "But first, we have to go out to your mom and dad's for a visit." I figured we were just going to pick them up and go to the restaurant, so I played along. I didn't want him to know I'd found out about the fancy dinner party. When we pulled up to my mom and dad's house, I didn't notice anything out of the ordinary. I didn't clue in until we walked into the back yard and I saw all my friends and family gathered in the field behind my parents' home. I was shocked. Everyone had parked their cars down the road in the school parking lot. Rick had cleverly planted the note in his lunchbox to throw me off the party trail! He knew I would find it when I packed his lunch and his plan had worked perfectly.

Practically everyone I ever knew was there: my therapists from GF Strong, new friends, old elementary and high school friends, relatives from near and far; they had all come together to celebrate my birthday with me. It was absolutely amazing, but it was about to be even more incredible as Rick pointed to the sky and said, "Honey, look at that plane!" An airplane was circling overhead and I watched in disbelief as three skydivers jumped from the plane. I hadn't noticed the big red target lying on the grass and I watched as their chutes opened and they circled and swayed gracefully towards the earth. Much to everyone's delight, they landed right on target in the back yard. The first skydiver to land unclipped his chute and walked over to me where I was standing in amazement with my dad and Rick.

Glenda's Story

"Are you the birthday girl?" I nodded. He held out his hand and presented me with a small, beautifully wrapped gift box. Inside was a gorgeous pair of gold earrings from Rick, the whole delivery arranged by my sister Lorrie and her new husband. I really do love surprises.

In the first year after my surgery I had to go to Vancouver General Hospital every three months for a CT scan and lung x-ray. My mom would look after Kevin while we were gone and he always looked forward to grandma's cookies and long, leisurely walks to the river to throw rocks in the water.

My dad drove me there because he didn't want me to go alone. We had wonderful long talks and I'm so grateful that we had that special time together. By the end of the second year, I noticed dad and I generally had to stop once or twice during the hour-long drive for dad to go to the bathroom. The doctor said it was nothing serious and that he could strengthen his bladder control by starting and stopping his urine flow when he was peeing. I gently reminded dad what my reflexology session had revealed about his prostate, and asked him if he had spoken with his doctor about it, but dad's doctor didn't believe in reflexology.

Doctor B. continued to be kind and caring. By the time I would arrive home from my tests at VGH there would be a message waiting for me to announce that the scan and lung x-rays were all clear. He knew everyone in the family would be holding their breaths until the results were in. Even though I had "my dream" to strengthen me, I still felt better hearing the good news from Dr. B. every three months. After the first year, I had to go only every six months for a check-up and when I arrived home after my two-year "all-clear" exam, Rick and I "celebrated" the good news without a condom. It had taken almost six months of trying before I got pregnant with Kevin so I was sure we would have to wait at least that long now that I was older and had been through such a life-altering surgery. We both looked forward to trying to get pregnant! I silently wondered how long it would take for the next part of my dream to come true.

I had gone for my two year check-up in late January, 1990. Rick and I continued to "celebrate" through the month of February. In March, we took a one-week trip to Disneyland for Kevin's sixth birthday. I love roller coasters, and we were enjoying the wonderful rides, but on one of them I suddenly felt ill. I had to close my eyes to keep from throwing up as the simulator took us through an asteroid belt in outer space. I couldn't believe that a daredevil like me would suddenly be sick on such a relatively tame ride. I chalked it up to motion sickness. When we returned from Disneyland, I had the BC Winter Games to look forward to, so I didn't pay much attention to the calendar. I first realized my period was late when I had just won the two silver medals at Apex Mountain. I bought a home pregnancy kit. Rick and I held our breath waiting for the results to show on the stick. We were overjoyed but also a little overwhelmed when the test was positive. It had happened so fast. Later that week, my doctor confirmed it. I was pregnant.

Rick and I could hardly contain our excitement. My due date was at the end of November. We waited until our family Easter celebration to tell everyone the good news. Instead of cooking a big meal at my parents' home, we broke tradition and opted to go out to our favorite Chinese restaurant for dinner with the whole family. Rick and I were beaming when we announced that Kevin was finally going to be a big brother. There were a lot of smiling faces congratulating us, except for one. My mom leaned over to me, put her hand on top of mine, and said, "Now honey, don't get too excited. It's early and anything can happen."

I looked at her in disbelief and replied, "Mom, if it's okay with you, I'd rather be really excited until something bad happens." She looked at me with a surprised look on her face as if that thought had never occurred to her. I just couldn't imagine living my life waiting for something bad to happen rather than living and loving life for each joyous moment.

The pregnancy was remarkable simply because there weren't very many documented natural births like it. Hemipelvectomy surgeries aren't common and hemipelvectomy pregnancies are even rarer. I was a little concerned about how I would carry the baby to term because I only had half a pelvis but my concerns were diminished by the dream image I had of delivering a healthy baby boy.

My sister Lorrie called shortly after we announced the news that I was pregnant. A friend of hers had seen a TV show about a place in Oklahoma that was making legs for people with amputations as high up as mine. She gave me their number and I called the Sabolich Prosthetic Research Center right away. They sent me a video of an amputee like me who was using one of their legs and yes, they could adapt one for pregnancy with no problem. The leg would cost about $20,000 Canadian. The ball began to roll.

Before I knew it, I was petitioning our government to send me to Oklahoma. I was to be accompanied by a local prosthetist who would bring the amazing soft silicone prosthetic technique that the Sabolich Center had created back to Canada. Amazingly, our government agreed to fund a major portion of the cost of the leg. I've never known the wheels of politics to turn so quickly. My health insurance would cover the remainder but we still had to come up with hotel and living expenses. The Canadian Cancer Society heard about me and they sent a local committee to my house to present me with a check for $300 to help with the hotel and meals. Mom and dad gave us $200 and Rick and I emptied our savings for the rest. A Vancouver TV station interviewed me and my story appeared on TV and in local newspapers. I flew to Oklahoma at the end of April. I was already almost three months pregnant.

In Oklahoma, I met my prosthetist, Tony van der Waarde, who designed a lightweight leg to be worn throughout my pregnancy. He was incredibly skilled at his job as well as kind. He treated me like a member of his family. I attended church with his family on Mother's Day and shared a wonderful home-cooked meal afterwards where I was witness to the most amazing hail storm I'd ever seen. The stones were easily as big as golf-balls. Afterwards, Tony dropped me back at my hotel. As I settled down to watch TV, a tornado-warning message flashed across the screen. While the wind howled around the building, I waited out the storm; hunkered down in the bathtub as they instructed us to do on the news channel. I was terrified but excited at the same time. I remember thinking that this baby was probably destined to be an adrenaline junkie, since I'd already been on every roller-coaster ride in Disneyland, skied in the BC Winter Games, flown to Oklahoma, and lived through a tornado within the first trimester of being pregnant! I had no idea how accurate that premonition would turn out to be.

The leg, affectionately dubbed "Peggy Two," was amazing. It weighed less than nine pounds and had a pliable, adjustable, and expandable silicone waistline that allowed room for growth as the pregnancy progressed. I did an interview while I was in Oklahoma which is now posted on You Tube—Glenda talks about her prosthesis. Within three weeks, I was ready to go home. I arrived at the airport amid a jumble of news cameras and an excited mob of family waiting to see if I was actually able to walk on the leg. The TV cameras captured the joy on my face as I used one simple cane to help me walk for the first time in over two years; I danced in the airport with my father who held me as we both cried tears of joy; I walked, holding hands with my husband; I scooped my little boy into my arms and held him as I balanced on two legs again. It was like a miracle. I couldn't stop smiling.

I wore the leg practically every day, and in September 1990 when

Holding Kevin in my arms when I
returned from Oklahoma wearing
"Peggy Two."

I was about six months pregnant, Kevin started kindergarten at Little Mountain Elementary School. I think I was more nervous than he was. He had been to pre-school and was more than ready to go to kindergarten. He loved learning and made friends easily but I was afraid that the kids would make fun of the boy who had a one-legged mom. We walked into the classroom, and sure enough, the kids stared, but not for long. They were too excited to pay much attention to me and maybe they didn't really notice that one of my legs wasn't real. All the moms were supposed to stay for the first few minutes to help their children settle in, and that was when I noticed the tall blonde lady with the big welcoming smile.

Our eyes met and I liked her instantly. She didn't look away. Her smile was like a beacon and it drew me towards her. I stood beside her as we watched our children interact. She had a beautiful blonde baby boy in a stroller beside her. Her oldest son, Jon, a tall, thin boy with glasses was happily mingling with the other kids in the class. Her name was Bonnie, and she just lived down the road from the school. She asked me if I would like to come over for coffee and visit while our kids were in class, and I began another friendship with a very wonderful woman.

We spent many hours together chatting over coffee and forging a strong friendship while our boys were in kindergarten. Bonnie's sense of humor was like mine. One day towards the end of my pregnancy, I was feeling quite emotional and a little overwhelmed with the thought of having another baby. I confided in Bonnie who reassured me with "Oh well, I think it's too late to change your mind now anyway." We both laughed and Bonnie's catch phrase for every difficulty we would face over the coming years became, "Oh well...." (More of Bonnie's story is told in the Foreword and Prologue).

Kevin adjusted beautifully to school. His first week, his teacher tentatively asked if I would be willing to explain to the kids why I only had one leg. Apparently they had been asking questions that she felt would be best answered by me. Of course I agreed and, with Kevin again lugging old "Peggy" into the classroom, I explained as simply as I could. "My leg was very sick and the doctors couldn't make it better. They had to cut it off or it would have made the rest of me sick. I would have died if they hadn't cut it off." They all figured I made the right choice but I soon discovered that kids have a lot of questions that needed good answers.

"Were you awake?"

"No, they gave me medicine to make me sleep."

"Did it hurt?"

"No, not while I was sleeping but it hurt when I woke up."

"What kind of saw did they use?"

"Good question. I was asleep when they brought out the saw."

"I bet it was a Husqvarna chain saw!"

"Maybe." Obviously *his* daddy was a logger.

"Can I see where your leg came off?"

"No. I don't think I better show you that. It's kind of private."

"Hey, Mrs. Standeven, do you want to see my scar from when I fell off my bike?"

Having one leg was teaching me all sorts of life lessons. It was incredibly difficult for me to go from the able-bodied person who held doors open for others to the person who suddenly had doors being held for them. As a new amputee, my initial instinct when someone held the door for me was to snap, "I'm perfectly capable of opening a door for myself!" It was somewhat of an epiphany when I realized that, by allowing people to help me, I was allowing them to do an act of kindness. I know how good it feels when I am able to help someone, both before and after becoming an amputee. I decided that it would be gracious to allow people to "help" me even though I was perfectly — or somewhat — capable of doing the job myself. It sounds easy, but for someone as stubborn and determined as I am, it was a huge undertaking to learn to accept help.

That wonderful leg made in Oklahoma lasted my entire pregnancy. I wore "Peggy Two" almost every day to help support the growing weight of the baby on the side of my body that had no pelvis. I wrapped my stump with tensor bandages to support me when I didn't wear the leg. We also documented the pregnancy and delivery with a home video to share with other amputees so they could see how we managed. Kevin was excited about the prospect of having a new brother or sister to boss around. In my heart, I was sure Kevin would have a little brother, but most people thought the baby would be a girl. Our house was all set up for the new arrival. My dad modified an "Able Walker" to accommodate a baby carrier. The baby's room was done in white and blue. I truly believed our new addition would be a boy because my dream had shown me a second son but I think most of my family was hoping for a little girl. Rick and I, like all parents, just wanted the baby to be healthy.

I had been seeing a gynecologist throughout my pregnancy. He was very excited to be involved in such a unique birth. He was scheduled to go on vacation and, because the baby was a good healthy size already, he decided to induce me just prior to his leaving. I was happy to oblige because I was getting bigger every day, and I knew by the time my actual due date arrived in another three weeks I would be as big as a house, and the pregnancy leg would probably no longer fit. On Thursday, November 8, 1990, I proudly wore that amazing leg when I went to the hospital to be induced. My sister Beanie followed me to the car, the hospital, and the labor room with our video camera to document the birth. I'm glad she did. What an amazing thing to capture on film.

The doctors were all wondering what to expect from a delivery where the mother only had a pelvis on one side. Kevin's birth had been so easy. I was expecting this delivery to be a breeze, but four hours after inducing me, the baby still hadn't arrived. My specialist anticipated a long night of labor so he decided to take a supper break. I lay on the bed watching the baby inside my bulging belly move with each contraction.

I realized suddenly that with each contraction, the baby's head was pushing into my stump. It was as if he was looking for the door but kept bashing into the wall! I decided to lie on my side and push really hard on my stump every time I felt a contraction coming. Basically, my hands took the place of my missing pelvis and within a few short contractions I had guided the baby's head into the birth canal.

"Where's the doctor! Get a doctor quick! The baby is coming!" The nurses called my family doctor and the specialist, but the baby wasn't going to wait for them to arrive, so a young resident stepped into the room. Dr. S. looked like a deer in the headlights. I'm sure he'd never imagined he'd come on shift that night to deliver a baby to a lady with no hip or pelvis on her right side. Yet, here he was, gloved and gowned, doing just that.

My family doctor arrived but there was no time for them to switch places. There was no time for an episiotomy. The baby was crowning. I told my sister not to take any video of my bare bottom, but to wait until after the birth in order to preserve my modesty. Thankfully, she ignored me and the camera went directly to where the action was. As our beautiful baby came into this world the miraculous image of his birth is captured on film. He entered through an amazing ring of white light. You can't see any of my private parts at all; just this beautiful, perfect child emerging through the light. It still gives me shivers when I watch the images. At 7:12 PM, our little boy, Andrew Jeffrey Standeven, named in memory of my friend Andrea Jeffries' beautiful little child, Andrew, was delivered into our waiting arms. He weighed a healthy 7 pounds 14 ounces. Everyone was ecstatic. I was now a 35 year old mother of two healthy boys and I was also an amputee. There was nothing wrong with that. It would just take some getting used to. I stayed in the hospital for five days because I wanted to make sure I could handle nursing the baby, and I practiced different ways of carrying him while using my crutches. My Oklahoma leg didn't fit well anymore, because the shape of the stump had changed drastically after the delivery. There was so much soft tissue that the leg seemed like a piston when I walked on it which caused me to limp badly. I decided to learn to get by using just my crutches and only wear Peggy when and if I needed to look *normal.*

Caring for Andrew would be a challenge. My dad's invention of the baby carrier attached to the Able-Walker worked perfectly so I could hop and maneuver around the main floor of our house safely and easily. I used a baby sling to cradle Andrew when I needed to take him up and down the stairs leading to the bedrooms. I held the sling

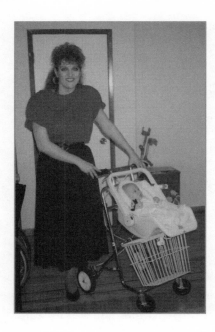

Dad's Able Walker Stroller invention.
Andrew at 2 months old.

closed using my teeth so he wouldn't fall out or bounce against my crutches on the stairs. It looked stupid but it worked. Thank God for my strong choppers!

I've always believed that where there's a will, there's a way. But I also had lots of help. My sister Lorrie and my mom would often come in to do housework for me. Kevin adapted wonderfully to being a big brother. He would "be my legs" for me and get diapers or run errands without complaint. I was very proud of him. At six and half years old Kevin was so independent, he could go into the corner store to buy a loaf of bread and a jug of milk while I sat in the car waiting with the baby. I would park in front of the store entrance and watch as he walked confidently to the bread and dairy sections, read the expiry dates, pick out the freshest loaf and jug of milk, and make his purchase. His little blonde head barely reached the top of the counter. The clerk knew us and would always make a fuss over my special little man and ask him how his new baby brother was doing. Kevin felt very grown up and I appreciated not having to load and unload Andrew from his car seat just to make a quick grocery stop. The simple things normal people took for granted took planning and effort for me to accomplish. Bathing the baby, changing diapers, getting up for midnight feedings, all had to be relearned as a one-legged mother. It took a lot more effort and energy than I remembered needing when Kevin was born. One night, I was so tired I actually forgot that I only had one leg. I was sound asleep when the baby started fussing. I got out of bed and, only half awake, headed for the crying baby. Of course, I fell flat on my face and started to laugh when I realized what I'd done. Rick didn't see the humour in it but he was glad I wasn't hurt.

Kevin was flourishing in school. The students grew accustomed to seeing the lady on crutches and, part way through kindergarten, to seeing the one-legged lady with a baby. I was blessed that Kevin was independent and made friends easily. Maybe he felt he had no choice because my hands were kept pretty busy caring for his new brother.

The president of our local Canadian Cancer Society unit called me one day. Would I be willing to help them with a fundraiser called Jail n Bail? After they had so graciously helped me, I was more than willing to volunteer for them. What I hadn't realized was that I was supposed to coordinate the event! It came off wonderfully well and I helped raise considerably more than the $300 they had given me to go to Oklahoma in 1990.

Out of the blue in January 1991, the phone rang. A woman said, "Hello, my name is Michelle. I got your name and number from the president of the Cancer Society. He said you might be interested in starting a support group for cancer patients." There was a soft vulnerability in her voice and I sensed that it had taken a lot of courage for her to call me. We chatted for a long while and agreed to get together to discuss our plans for the group.

I had no recollection of telling the president about my interest in running a support group, yet here I was being asked by a complete stranger if I was willing to do just that, under the respected umbrella of the Canadian Cancer Society. It seems "someone" was determined to keep my support group running. When we met, we instantly clicked. Michelle was also a cancer survivor. She was young, attractive, soft-spoken and intelligent, and we were both extremely motivated to help others through their cancer journey. We put our heads and our resources together. We combined our wide assortment of meditation tapes and books about self-healing to start a group lending library; we asked for and received the donation of a room at the fanciest hotel in Chilliwack to use for our meetings; we set our meeting dates for the first and third Wednesday of every month. For the next ten years, we never took a break from our routine because we both realized that cancer never took a break either.

Andrew was a very demanding baby. He didn't like me to be out of his sight for too long. It was a struggle just to get away twice a month for my cancer support group meetings. We very rarely left him and Kevin with a baby sitter. I worked at home so there was no need to have daycare. As cautious as Kevin had been as a child, Andrew was the complete opposite. He seemed to be born with a daredevil gene. My premonition that he would be an adrenalin junkie because of all the adventures I had while I was pregnant wasn't too far off the mark. Before he was a year old he had gone down the basement stairs in his walker; taken a nosedive off the bathroom counter out of his bath-tub, and badly burned the palm of his hand on the glass doors of the gas fireplace when he attempted to stand and run at 9 months. I was afraid the staff at the emergency room would think we were abusing him! I'd like to stress that I was not alone with Andrew for any of these incidents so his accidents had little to do with being supervised by a

Up, up and away . . . Parasailing on my 36th birthday.

one-legged mom who was too slow to catch him. It was obvious that he was too fast for even two-legged caregivers to keep up!

That summer, I turned 36 and Rick decided to give me something special for my birthday, but what could possibly beat skydivers landing in the back yard to deliver your birthday gift? Resourceful Rick booked a parasailing session for me off Granville Island in Vancouver. It was amazing. The operators had never had a one-legged lady up in the harness before, but if I was game to try, then so were they. I held my breath as they strapped me in and released the chute. I felt myself lifting off the deck of the boat and rising into the air like some giant, majestic, slightly lopsided bird. It was both exhilarating and scary at the same time.

The winch unwound as I continued to rise higher into the sky above the water. I felt myself exhale and suddenly realized that it was incredibly peaceful up there. I could barely see the people on the boat below me. It felt as if I were miles away from anyone and my heart filled with the pure joy of simply being alive to experience this magic moment. The adventure ended too soon but my birthday wasn't over

Thumbs up for a ride in a biplane!

yet. My sister Beanie had one more surprise for me. On the way home from Vancouver, my sister directed us to a small airport. I had no idea what we were doing but I was always game for an adventure. At the airport, I was escorted onto the runway by my sister, Rick and the boys. An old-fashioned biplane sat on the runway and the pilot handed me a scarf and a pair of goggles. As he helped me into the plane I thought, "Wow, what a great picture this will make! Here I am sitting inside an old-style plane wearing a scarf and goggles and pretending to be taking off." Then he said, "Are you ready to do a little birthday barnstorming?"

It was every bit as thrilling as my very recent parasailing experience. I couldn't stop smiling as he swooped and dove and turned in that amazing little plane. My scarf flew out behind me just like in the old movies and I was in heaven riding the best roller-coaster ride in the world up in the sky. My 36th birthday had to go down in history as the most exciting I would likely ever have. When the ride ended, I promised myself that I would do it all again someday, hopefully celebrating the milestone birthday when I turn 80. I blessed my sister and my husband for knowing that 'living' doesn't stop just because you have cancer or a disability and I was grateful to them for giving me such an amazing day.

I was very grateful when Tony van der Waarde, the wonderful prosthetist from Oklahoma, moved to Vancouver in 1991 to work for the same company that had sent one of their prosthetists to Oklahoma with me in 1990. Tony now has his own business, Award Prosthetics, in Burnaby, BC. He often asks me to test drive new crutches that come onto the market. Some have shock absorbers and contoured cushion hand grips. To this day, I don't have the wrist or shoulder pains often associated with long-term crutch use. If it weren't for the expertise and concern of people like Tony who have come into my life, I'm sure I wouldn't be as active or as capable as I am today. After I wore Peggy II out, I tried to be fitted with another leg but I found it so much slower and very awkward trying to care for two kids, a husband and a house while wearing 15+ extra pounds of dead weight strapped around my waist that I would only wear the leg when I went out.

For more than four years I had tried to wear a prosthetic leg in public. It wasn't really functional, but more for cosmetic purposes. I'd gained weight with the pregnancy and my body shape had changed. I had too much soft tissue and not enough solid muscle to prevent the leg from pistoning when I walked. Unfortunately, as the thoughtless doctor in Vancouver General Hospital had predicted so long ago, I did indeed lurch awkwardly when I tried to walk without my crutches. Still, I wasn't ready to go "legless" because I worried that it made people uncomfortable to see a one-legged woman. I continued wearing the impractical, but very shapely, artificial leg until one particularly warm summer day in 1992 when I took the kids to the park to play.

I was wearing the new leg that Tony had tried to duplicate for me using the technology we had brought back to Canada from Oklahoma. My stump shape had changed since having Andrew and I was heavier than before. It was hot, and sitting inside that artificial leg while trying to keep up to my boys was almost unbearable. Another woman about my age was also in the park with her kids. She looked completely comfortable in a sleeveless white top and a pair of shorts. It was obvious that she had a mastectomy. She had chosen not to wear a prosthesis, and was obviously choosing not to wear a bra either! Ironically, her name was Glenda as well. We talked about our kids and cancer and gradually I mustered up the courage to ask her about her breast prosthesis or lack of one. She smiled and said something so profound that it changed my attitude forever.

"Aw, who am I trying to kid? I only have one boob! If people don't like it, too bad because this is how I am."

I went home, took off my leg, parked it in the crawlspace in a big plastic bag, and decided I was tired of trying to pretend. Who was I trying to kid? I had only one leg! I officially retired Peggy III in the summer of 1992, although she does comes out now and then for "show and tell" when I go to schools to speak. I can't imagine ever slowing down my pace to accommodate the dead weight of an artificial leg but new technology comes along every day so I won't say, "It'll never happen" because I just don't know...

That summer I also discovered the Optimist Club of Chilliwack. A man came up to me in the Burger King playground where the boys and I were happily playing. He said he and his wife had been sitting inside watching me smiling and playing with my boys. He handed me a card with a copy of *The Optimist Creed* written on it (adapted from a poem by Christian D. Larson) and said he hoped I could come to the next meeting as his guest. He said, "I have a feeling this creed describes you perfectly."

The Optimist Creed

(reprinted with the permission of Optimist International)

Promise yourself . . .

To be so strong that nothing can disturb your peace of mind.

To talk health, happiness, and prosperity to every person you meet.

To make all your friends feel that there is something worthwhile in them.

To look at the sunny side of everything and make your optimism come true.

To think only of the best, to work only for the best, and to expect only the best.

To be just as enthusiastic about the success of others as you are about your own.

To forget the mistakes of the past and press on to the greater achievements of the future.

To wear a cheerful countenance at all times and give every living creature you meet a smile.

To give so much time to the improvement of yourself that you have no time to criticize others.

To be too large for worry, too noble for anger, too strong for fear, and too happy to permit the presence of trouble.

I loved the Creed. It perfectly described the way I tried to live my life. Who knew there was a special club for people like me who chose to see the glass half full? I went to the meeting and was surprised to see that there were only three members. The man who had given me the card failed to tell me that the club was faltering.

They asked if I would be willing to take on the role of club president. The meetings were only twice a month and I knew I could make the time. My only other commitments were occasional school parent meetings and my twice-a-month Living With Cancer Support Group meetings. I agreed to be the president and then they told me that my first duty was to sign up ten new members. Being an optimist by nature I didn't see any difficulty to achieving this goal. The first recruit would be my husband. Next, my friend and co-facilitator of the Living With Cancer Support Group, Michelle, and close on her heels was my friend Bonnie Holmes.

Choosing to Smile

Actually, practically everyone I chose to have in my life was an Optimist already, so getting ten new members was easy. It wasn't until after the club had grown to more than twenty members that I was told that I had done the impossible. Very few people build a club up from the brink of closing to become one of the most successful clubs in the district. As I said before, if no one tells you that something is *impossible* then anything is *possible*. Although no longer the president of the Optimist Club, I am still an active member doing my best to live by the Creed. Generally speaking, the Creed is a lot tougher to follow than the Ten Commandments! It isn't always easy to be an optimist when real life adversities interfere.

It was Valentine's Day, February 14, 1992. Andrew had had his first birthday three months earlier and Kevin was about to turn eight in March. I stood waiting in the driveway for my mom and dad. Dad had been having some health issues and the doctor had done a biopsy of his prostate. I remembered telling him about my reflexology findings, back in 1983. He hadn't pursued the notion back then. The doctor had asked mom and dad to come in today to go over the results. I made them promise to come over as soon as they came back. My stomach was in knots all morning as I waited for them to arrive. Finally mom and dad pulled into the driveway. Dad stepped out of the car and our eyes met. The look on his face told me everything. He just shook his head and didn't say a word. I threw myself into his arms and we cried. The doctor had said that if he was lucky, he might live for another year.

It was heartbreaking. Dad and mom tried so hard to beat the disease as a team. Dad voluntarily changed his diet. I don't think he even knew what tofu was until his diagnosis and mom certainly had no idea how to cook it, but they learned together. In some ways, they grew closer than they'd ever been in that last year of his life. He quit drinking. He lost weight; too much weight. His passion had always been fishing and I knew he wasn't going to make it when he gave away his fishing rods. Dad came to the cancer support group meetings with me. He wanted so badly to live. I wanted so badly for him to live. Why do some cancer patients survive while others don't? I don't know the answer. I only know that life isn't fair and anyone who says it is has never lost someone they love to cancer.

Being on the other end of the cancer stick was tough. In some ways I realized that it was easier to be a patient than it was to be a support person. As a support person, I felt hopeless and helpless to help my dad through his cancer journey. I wanted to make him better but I couldn't. Some people said that we just had to believe, and trust in God to make him well. Bullshit. God doesn't give people cancer. God doesn't play stupid games with people's lives. He's got better things to do. The one thing God can and does do is give you, if you let Him, the strength to get through the tough times. I heard people say that God was just a crutch. So what? I use crutches every day and they really come in handy. If God is a crutch then use it if you need to. That's what crutches are for — to make things easier.

Dad got through that entire year, staying at home, some days better than others, until the middle of February, 1993. Shortly after Valentine's Day, dad was admitted to the hospital for hospice care. One afternoon, Kevin and I went to the hospital for a daytime visit with dad. I stopped to talk to the nurses but Kevin went on ahead to see his grampa. After talking with the nurses, I walked down the hallway to his room. I heard Kevin's sweet voice singing a song that dad had taught him five years earlier when I was at GF Strong. I couldn't believe that he still remembered the words: "Where have you been Billy boy, Billy boy? Where have you been charming Billy..." I peeked into dad's room and tears filled my eyes. Kevin had climbed onto the bed beside his weak and frail grampa. He'd pulled dad's thin arm around his little shoulders and snuggled in under his arm like he used to do when they would read books together. His voice filled the room and dad smiled. It was the best gift Kevin could give.

Watching my big strong dad go from 250 pounds to 100 pounds was heartwrenching. Watching him suffer was even worse, but I am so grateful for the time we had together. My sisters and I made sure that one of us was with him around the clock during his last month in the hospital. I took the graveyard shift because I liked nights. Dad would always wake up around 3:00 am and we had long wonderful talks. We talked about his life and mine. What he did right, and what he felt he did wrong. I told him how much I loved him and how much I appreciated the faith he had in me to do what I thought was right. One night he gave a big sigh and he said, "My girl, I think I've spent enough time with my girls; it's time for me to go see my boys." He hadn't forgotten Sylvan after all. He asked me if I would be able to speak at his funeral, so I wrote a poem one night and read it to him. He said, "Oh my girl, you know you're going to make everyone cry." Maybe I did; I don't remember. I remember the tears were streaming down both our faces in his hospital room just like they are now when I write this. Dad was so brave throughout his ordeal with prostate cancer. I thank him for holding onto life as long as he did because the memories he gave to each of his four daughters and his wife during that last painful year are treasured by all of us.

We knew dad's time was coming. His breathing pattern had changed to ragged uneven breaths. Kevin didn't want to leave his grampa and had made himself a little bed under the sink in dad's private room. Mom was exhausted and went home to rest. She knew dad was in good hands. Dad's four daughters, Kevin, Sylvia's two kids, and Lorrie's husband held vigil through the night around dad's hospital bed. He was no longer conscious but we each whispered "I love you" into his ear and shared our favorite dad stories. The nurses couldn't believe how strongly he was clinging to life. Maybe it was because we

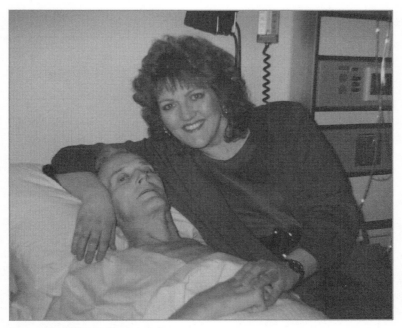

Dad and I cuddling in the hospital.

so desperately wanted him to stay. At 5:45 am I woke Kevin and we left the hospital. Kevin didn't want to leave but Rick had to go to work and I needed to be at home with Andrew. Sylvia and her exhausted kids left to go home too. We kissed dad one last time and said "I love you. See you soon." We were hoping he would still be there when we came back later in the day.

It had been several hours since dad had moved or even blinked his open eyes. At 6:00 AM, just as the sun was rising, Beanie leaned over and said, "Dad, the sun is coming up. It's time to go fishing. It's okay, dad. You can go now." He slowly turned his head to look at her, he blinked his eyes and he was gone. On March 19, 1993, at 6 o'clock in the morning, dad passed away with Beanie and Lorrie and her husband by his side. He was 3 months away from his 66th birthday. It was almost as if he had waited for Sylvia, me and his grandchildren to leave, maybe it was our desperation to keep him with us that had held him back. Rick hadn't even left the house when the phone rang to tell me the news that dad had passed. He held me close and we cried. Rick called in and said he wouldn't make it to work. Dad was gone.

The loss of our dad hit us hard. Lorrie's second marriage dissolved amicably and soon after she met and fell in love with Marcus, a wonderful man from St. Lucia. It was a shock to all of us when she found out she was pregnant. Until she met Marcus, she had no children and had felt no desire to have any. Oh, how dad would have laughed, and how he would have loved his grandson, Nathan. Lorrie decided she was going to keep her maiden name and, since all our brothers were gone, it just felt right to have a boy in the family to carry on the Bobroske name. Baby Faydra was born just 13 months after Nathan, and she was followed by Lateesha two years later. Lorrie and I often talk about how much dad would have loved his grandkids and how unfair it is that they never had the pleasure of knowing him. Nathan inherited his grampa's passion for the outdoors, however, and dad's fishing legacy lives on through his youngest grandson.

Sylvia and her husband Ray separated as well. She went to work in the BC corrections department. It seemed dad had been the glue that had held their marriage together. It was a difficult time for their kids. They missed their grampa. They lived right next door and spent lots of time together. And now their lives were changing again. Sylvia and the kids moved to a townhouse twenty minutes away. Ray stayed on in the house beside my mom and dad's home.

Beanie and her husband would eventually divorce as well but Rick and I clung to each other through it all. Both of us cried together when my dad died. Rick hadn't shed a tear when his own father passed away a few years earlier but my dad had taken Rick under his wing and they really enjoyed each other's company. We grieved his loss together. Maybe that's what made our marriage stronger. Still,

Kevin deeply missed his grampa, and every night I would tell both my boys bedtime stories about their big Grampa Barney to help keep his memory alive. Andrew was only 2 when dad died, but I created memories for him of wonderful fishing trips they took together through bedtime stories I made up. He swears to this day he remembers going fishing with his grampa even though he never did.

By the time Andrew was three years old we were frequent visitors to the park near our house in attempts to tire him out. Andrew would want to go higher on the swing while Kevin was content to swing slowly and sensibly; Andrew would scramble to the top of the monkey bars while Kevin planned each move carefully; Andrew would demand to be pushed faster on the merry-go-round long after his big brother had jumped off; Kevin would be content to watch his brother play on the slide that he still deemed to be too dangerous even five years after he first examined it. We should have listened to Kevin.

On this particular trip to the park, Andrew decided he wanted to scoot up the slide on his bum rather than take the stairs. I thought it would be safer than climbing the steep stairs that had always made me cringe. I was wrong. Andrew started off doing a great job of scooting backwards on his bum and pushing himself to the top platform of the slide but for some reason he decided to keep on going and he ignored my screams to "Stop!" I had waited at the bottom of the slide to catch him from shooting off the end and never in my wildest dreams did I imagine I should have been standing at the bottom of the stairs. What kid doesn't stop at the top of the slide and instead decides to keep scooting over the edge? Apparently, Andrew! He fell seven feet to the ground below tumbling backwards down the steep steps as his brother and I both screamed. I didn't know a one-legged lady could move so fast — unfortunately it wasn't fast enough to catch him before he hit the ground with a sickening thud. There was a horrible few seconds of silence where Kevin and I both thought Andrew was dead.

I screamed for Kevin to run home and get his dad while I prayed that Andrew would live. Fortunately, he just had the wind knocked out of him and, as soon as he caught his breath, he let me know in no uncertain terms that he was not a happy child. He screamed at the top of his lungs which brought his daddy running double-time back to the park. It was only another one of many trips we would make to the emergency room over the years with our fearless Andrew. After dad died, I often felt that he was watching over Andrew and making sure that his daredevil ways wouldn't kill him. For the next two years, as my mom and my sisters' lives changed, ours stayed the same as we happily watched our boys growing up and I became more and more involved with volunteering in our community.

I decided to take a refresher course in reflexology and, in 1994, I opened my own business, The Sole Connection Reflexology Studio. I remember feeling very proud of myself when I realized that I had finally found a career I could do on one leg. I couldn't stand for hours at a time doing hair any more, but I had no problem sitting. I also couldn't expect an employer to let me pick and choose when and how long I would work but I could certainly set my own schedule when I was the boss. I could work at home doing something I loved! What a novel idea! I still did the books for Rick's trucking business but now I felt like I was contributing even more to our household income. We had exchange students living with us on a regular basis from all parts of the world. My kids' horizons were expanding and I was quite content with the way our lives were progressing.

Oh my gosh! The phone was ringing. It was my new business phone; my first call was coming through on my new line! I was excited but I couldn't believe it would be ringing already, as I'd just had it connected that day. I wasn't even sure how to answer the call. I think I probably managed a nervous, "Hello?" The voice on the other end was sweet and melodious. I love English accents and this lady was most definitely English. She explained that she was looking for a reflexologist and "'would that be me?'" We chatted easily, like old friends, and she booked an appointment. Her name was Julie.

When Julie, my very first client, arrived at the door she may have been surprised that I only had one leg but she didn't show it. She was lovely and I immediately liked her. She was very petite and I noticed she was pale. She had not been feeling well at all, and was suffering from colitis. I worked on her feet for well over an hour. The time flew and at the end of the session I think she felt a little better. Julie came to my house for a few more reflexology sessions which helped her relax but ultimately didn't cure her. Immediately following our last session together it was as though a light bulb had gone off over her head and she said, "I know what I need to do!" I'm not sure how she figured it out — maybe the solution came to her because she was so deeply relaxed but somehow she had managed to find a cure for her colitis. Julie was very special to me; my first client.

The second call that came through on my business line went something like this:

"Hello, Sole Connection Reflexology Studio. Can I help you?"

A man's voice answered, "Uh, yes, hello. I'd like to book some time with you."

"When would you like to come?"

"Well, I can come after work."

"Great. I enjoy working evenings so that would be fine."

"My wife doesn't understand these things."

"Well, she's more than welcome to come and watch. I could explain what I'm doing so she understands it better. I'd be more than happy to show her a few techniques that she can use on you at home."

Dead silence. Then, "Um, is this really a reflexology studio?"

"Yes, I just opened for business. Have you had reflexology before?"

"Um, are you connected to the place in Abbotsford that closed last week?"

"No, sorry. I'm on my own. Would you like to book an appointment now?" More silence. So, thinking he may need to be reassured, I added, "Please feel free to invite your wife along. It's really very interesting and I don't mind an audience."

"Uh, I think I'll have to get back to you." Click. He hung up.

It wasn't until the newspaper arrived that night and I read about a reflexology studio being shut down in Abbotsford because it was a front for prostitution that the humour behind the odd phone call hit me. I laughed till my sides ached. I could just imagine the man's shock when I suggested he invite his wife to 'come and watch' our session. I wrote a letter to the editor of both local papers to assure people that the new reflexology studio in Chilliwack was in no way affiliated with the one recently closed in Abbotsford. The only body part getting rubbed at The Sole Connection Reflexology Studio would be feet! Talk about impeccable timing.

Julie was feeling better and no longer needed reflexology. She had kindly referred another friend of hers to me. Her friend, Patricia, loved the deep sense of relaxation that she got from reflexology. She became a member of the Optimist Club, too. She continued to come faithfully at least once or twice a month until she moved away.

And then along came 1995, the year I turned 40. I remember as a kid thinking anyone in their forties was practically dead, yet here I was, still feeling pretty good. It's very weird when you realize how fast the time goes as you get older. I always thought that it was just a myth that all old people believed, but now that I was forty I realized how true it was.

My family had a wonderful surprise birthday party for me in August at my sister's house. We sang songs around the campfire and had a lovely time. It was one of the only times in my life that I can say I got completely and foolishly drunk.

Yes, I'd been drunk many times before by legal standards but that night I was definitely off the chart. It was a wonderful night just sitting around the campfire with all my old friends, singing, and reminiscing into the wee hours and drinking — a lot! Well, of course eventually I had to get up to go pee and, wouldn't you know it, I was so drunk I completely forgot that I only had one leg! I hadn't forgotten about my amputation since the time Andrew was a baby and I was half asleep.

I'm sure I took two full steps before I realized I only had one leg and fell into my friend Kathy's lap! (Yes, the same Kathy from elementary school!) There was a collective horrified gasp until I said, "Well, where the hell did my leg go?" There was a split second of silence and then we all burst into gales of laughter. I love my friends.

Andrew was scheduled to start kindergarten in September, 1995. He was only four but would be five in November so he was technically old enough to start school. He was a clever little boy. At two years old, he could sing the entire alphabet song. He could print his name but would often turn his letters around. I found it odd that Kevin had been able to read quite well by the time he was in kindergarten but Andrew could only manage simple words like *mom* or *dad*. He would, however, memorize entire books, so it would sometimes seem as if he was reading them but, if I covered the picture, and just left the words he would be stumped. I chalked it up to being a November baby. He was the youngest in his class whereas Kevin, born in March, had been one of the oldest. Those extra nine months mattered at that age. In so many ways, Andrew was still my baby. He still liked to be held and cuddled and he still liked to nap. His kindergarten teacher and I discussed the fact that Andrew often fell asleep in class around naptime and we decided that keeping him home for another year would be a good thing. Secretly, I was very happy because I wasn't ready to have him be a "big boy" just yet.

Kevin, however, was a big boy. He had moved to a private school when he was in grade four on the recommendation of one of his public school teachers. He was so brilliant that the teacher suggested he attend a private Catholic school where they focused on academics. I had been raised Catholic and both Kevin and Andrew had been baptized in the Catholic faith, so it didn't bother me to put him in a religious school. Kevin blossomed there. He was intelligent, handsome and popular both with the students and the staff. He would bring home top marks every year without even trying. School was easy. He had a photographic memory and would simply study for an exam the night before the test and be able to recount the answers almost word for word from the book. I'm sure it drove his friends crazy because learning came so easy to him. Rick and I examined our budget and decided that we could afford to put both boys in private school the following year. We had agreed to teach the boys to be open-minded about all religions. Andrew would then be the oldest rather than the youngest in his kindergarten class and Kevin would be a senior in grade seven at the same school. It seemed like a good plan.

Christmas 1995 would be our third one without dad. Somehow, celebrating Christmas without him sitting in his big chair with his glasses perched on the end of his nose handing out presents, didn't seem quite right. We all missed him and the big house just felt empty; Mom was looking forward to having her entire brood home to fill it. She had the house completely decorated two weeks ahead of time. The cookies were made. The freezer was full. The turkey was bought. She was ready.

On December 15, my sister Sylvia's birthday, mom went to bed completely prepared for the holidays. She woke up around midnight with numbing chest pains. She knew immediately that she was having a heart attack. With more calm than she probably felt inside, she called Sylvia, who lived closest. Sylvia had just arrived home from a birthday dinner date with her new boyfriend when the phone rang. She was expecting birthday wishes, not "Hello, Sylvia, I think I'm having a heart attack." Luckily her new beau was a police officer, because he and Sylvia broke every speed law on their way to mom's house. By the time they got there, mom was vomiting from the severe pain. They rushed her to the hospital where they discovered that she had blown a hole through one of the chambers of her heart. If she hadn't been in such good physical condition she very likely would have died that night. She was 72 years old.

Christmas that year felt forced to me. I missed dad. I missed Granny, my mom's mom, who had passed away at age 95 just four months after dad. And now mom was missing too. She was lying in a hospital bed in the intensive care unit attached to all sorts of monitors while the rest of our family was gathered around the huge table at her house to celebrate Christmas. Even though the house was full of family, it still felt empty. How would mom ever be able to manage an acre of property and a 3,000 square-foot home in her condition? She was too feisty to live in a retirement home. She and dad had cared for Granny in their home for years before Granny moved into a retirement home. Maybe one of us kids could do the same thing for mom. It was something to think about.

New Year's came and went and I started back to work. We all wondered what changes 1996 would bring. Mom was recuperating in the hospital and we didn't know how long she'd be there. My regular client, Patricia, came for her usual session and told me about a friend who was in the hospital. She wanted to do something nice for her and, instead of sending flowers she wondered if I would go to the hospital and give her a reflexology session. Of course I would go — especially when she told me her friend was Julie Houlker, my very first client. Julie Houlker was about to come back into my life.

On a snowy day in early January, 1996, I went to the hospital to give Julie her "gift" from Patricia. She looked so tiny lying in the bed and the look of concern on her father-in-law and husband's faces tugged at my heart. I hadn't realized how much I'd missed her smile and I put all the healing I could muster into my hands that day. I hoped it would be enough but only time would tell. Somehow I knew that Julie was meant to be part of my life from then on. When she got out of the hospital she started coming for regular reflexology sessions again, and our friendship grew with each visit. We shared many wonderful and heart-wrenching moments of our lives together, both during reflexology sessions and after. Julie became another strong link in my friendship circle.

During this time, our family was trying to find the best solution for mom's living arrangements, since she wasn't well enough to manage the house and property on her own. Mom couldn't live with Sylvia. Sylvia and her kids lived in a condominium with too many stairs. Lorrie couldn't care for her; she and Marcus and the kids didn't know where they were going to settle but for now they rented an apartment in Richmond. Beanie lived in North Vancouver. Mom could never move back to the city, away from her friends and church. That left Rick and me. Could mom come and stay with us? Dad had helped us choose this house. "It has room to grow," he'd said. Maybe this was what he meant. While mom was still in the hospital, I sat down and talked it over with Rick. He agreed that mom could come live with us if she wanted, and we both agreed that she would need her own space.

Dad taught me lots of things: how to change spark plugs; wire a light; fix a flat tire; but most importantly he taught me how to draw blueprints. We had a huge corner lot. The addition of a laundry room, TV room, and bathroom on the main floor had neatly separated our back yard from our side yard. What if we built a suite in the remaining back yard space and turned our huge side yard into our new backyard? It could work. Dad must have been smiling on me because before I knew it the floor plan of a lovely little suite took shape. Now all we had to do was convince mom to move in once she got home from the hospital.

Mom was stubborn. She went back to her huge house and tried to do it on her own. The heart attack had been so massive that she had to build up scar tissue on her heart before they could patch the hole between the chambers. She had no energy and was extremely frail. In June of 1996, she had surgery to repair the hole in her heart. She had hoped the surgery would allow her to return to her pre-heart attack level of activity but recovering from the surgery took a long time. She finally realized that the house and property were too much for her.

She put a "For Sale" sign in her front yard after she saw the house plans I had drawn up for her. At the end of May 1997, one and a half years after her horrific heart attack, mom had sold her house and moved in with us. She would use some of the money from the sale of her big home to build, as she called it, her "doll house." By the end of June, 1997, her 612-square foot, one-bedroom home was complete. She moved out of our spare room and into her cozy new suite attached to our house.

All three of my sisters' marriages had crumbled after my dad died. Rick and I were the only ones who were still happily married and living in the perfect location to meet all of mom's needs. We were three minutes from the hospital and five minutes from her church — who could ask for anything better? The day she moved into her suite, I was sitting outside in our yard when I heard the distinctive call of "Jimmy's bird." To me it was a perfect sign that mom's move was simply meant to be. It's amazing how fast our lives can change.

The little blue card that arrived innocuously in the mail that year was about to throw another monkey wrench into our lives. I read the card with only passing interest. It was from Vancouver General Hospital and said something about my having received blood during my surgeries in 1987 and 1988 and that the blood may have been tainted with Hepatitis C. I'd heard of the tainted blood scandal in the news but hadn't paid much attention to it. I felt fine, but the card said I had to be tested as soon as possible, so off I went. By some coincidence, the results came back the day I was hosting a Living With Cancer Support Group meeting. As we went around the circle, I asked if anyone else had received a little blue card in the mail. Sure enough, Michelle had received one, been tested, and received the results. She said, "I'm fine."

Another woman in the group who had also had surgery in 1988, said, "I had one too, and my test results came back negative."

All eyes turned to me and I remember feeling like I'd just flunked an important exam in school, I said, "I'm not okay. My test was positive." Apparently, one of the many units of blood I'd needed during my surgeries came from a donor who didn't know he or she was sick with the Hepatitis C virus. After my diagnosis, I read that Hepatitis C kills more people than the AIDS virus, so why hadn't I heard about it before? Well, it seemed that my cross might have just got a little heavier to bear, but what the hell, I still felt pretty darn good for a one-legged, slightly overweight, cancer survivor with Hepatitis C. My doctor made an appointment for me to see a liver specialist in Vancouver.

I was one of the lucky ones who was asymptomatic. If that little card hadn't arrived in the mail I could have gone my whole life not knowing I had been infected with the Hepatitis C virus. As it was, I turned out to be one of the even luckier ones. For some reason, a small percentage of patients with Hepatitis C spontaneously clear the virus from their systems, and my body had cleared itself of the disease. I have accepted it as another one of many miracles in my life. After five years of going to see the liver specialist he told me I didn't have to come anymore. The disease was gone. I remember him saying with a big grin on his face, "I don't get to tell too many of my patients this but you're more likely to die because you got hit by a bus than from Hepatitis C." I figured that since I don't spend a lot of time around buses that the odds are pretty good that I've beaten the disease. I was pretty scared though, when I started researching the statistics about Hepatitis C. A lot of people don't survive it and I felt blessed once more.

Mom adapted to living in her small house remarkably well. We had a few bumps along the road but for the most part we got along beautifully. She had to make some adjustments and come to terms with the fact that I was a grown up now. Rick and I lived on a very flexible schedule with our boys. If we weren't hungry, we ate late; if we were tired on a weekend, we'd sleep in; if I didn't feel like doing laundry it would wait; dishes in the sink never bothered me. I had hated housework ever since I was a little girl and, after having cancer, I appreciated the importance of doing what really mattered even more. I would rather read a book to the kids and help them build a fort than tell them, "Mommy can't play right now. I have to clean the house." When mom came over from her suite to visit, she would occasionally comment on the dirty dishes in the sink or the growing pile of laundry waiting to be done. I never let her nagging get to me. Instead, I would put my arm around her shoulder and say, "You know what I love most about being a grown up mom? I get to do what I want!" We'd both laugh and I was grateful that, thanks to my experiences with my friend Shelly, I'd learned long ago not to let her criticism of me upset me.

Andrew and Kevin were like night and day in many ways but they were both spiritual and kind-hearted. Kevin spent more years studying the doctrine in a private Catholic school than Andrew did, so he developed a deeper appreciation for the Bible than Andrew, but both boys have good souls. For example, while driving downtown one day after a light rain a huge rainbow appeared in the sky. Kevin sucked in his breath and said, "Wow! Thank you God!" I loved that about him. He saw God in everything. Once, as he was playing outside, he took a stick and ran it through a spider's web without thinking. I saw what he did and called him over to the spot where he had torn the web. Although I don't particularly like spiders I recognized an opportunity to share a magical moment with my son. Together we watched as that spider slowly and carefully repaired its web. He became acutely aware of all the living creatures around him and I often joked that both he and Andrew had the souls of Buddhists, because Andrew also had a gentle heart.

Every night, I asked the boys to tell me about the worst thing that happened that day and also the best. One night, Andrew lay in bed and I could see he was struggling with his worst thing, but he couldn't bring himself to talk about it. I encouraged him to tell me what was bothering him and he started to cry. "Mom, I did something really bad today. I killed a fly. I didn't mean to. It was an accident. I didn't think I would hit it." Apparently, he had been swinging his belt at an annoying fly and he surprised himself by hitting it. I hugged him hard and told him how much I loved him and that I was happy he cared about all living things — even flies. The next day, however, I saw something miraculous happen.

It was such a little thing, yet it meant so much to Andrew. Another fly was buzzing around in the hallway. I was in the kitchen and watched as Andrew came and silently stood watching as it zigged and zagged. I watched in amazement as he held out his hand and the fly landed on his open palm. I held my breath. Andrew walked slowly to the front door with the fly sitting in the palm of his hand. He opened the door and walked out onto the step. The fly sat for a second or two and then flew away. If I hadn't seen it with my own eyes I wouldn't have believed it. Andrew turned towards me and asked solemnly, "Mom, do you think that fly forgave me for killing it yesterday?" Obviously somebody had.

Glenda's Story

One afternoon Andrew was sitting quietly at the kitchen table coloring. He struck up a conversation with me as I was doing dishes. "Mom, do you know why I picked you to be my mom?"

He was only about four years old then. I'd never discussed my belief with him that children choose their parents, so I was intrigued by his question. I stopped what I was doing and said, "No, I don't. Why did you pick me to be your mom?"

He took a deep breath and sighed, "Well, before I was borned, I was in heaven. I saw you only had one leg and I knew that someday you'd need me to push you in your wheelchair." He quietly kept on coloring as if that explained everything. Andrew had never seen me in a wheelchair. I had only used crutches since his birth. His explanation left me with goosebumps running up and down my arms and a deep sense of gratitude I couldn't really explain.

About this time, I started to cough. I couldn't seem to shake the bronchitis that had settled in my chest. I went for an x-ray and it showed a shadow on my lung. Dr. B.'s words came back to haunt me, "This type of cancer moves quickly to the lungs . . ." I thought of other cancer patients. I was nobody special. If they could die, so could I. Rick and I clung together again. His strength gave me strength and then I remembered my dream. I hadn't seen this event in my dream, and I found my optimism again. I was scheduled for my annual CAT scan and chest x-ray so I headed to Vancouver. Dr. B. had moved away to work in Arizona at the Mayo Clinic but the results would be sent to my family doctor. They injected the contrast dye into my vein as they had so many times before but this time I felt a tickle in the back of my throat and then my eyes started to itch and swell. By the time the scan was finished, I had broken out in hives, my face and neck were swollen, and I was having trouble breathing. I was having a severe allergic reaction to the contrast medium. They quickly gave me a shot of epinephrine and I felt myself starting to breathe a little easier almost immediately, but I would never be able to have that contrast dye again. For some reason, I had become terribly allergic to it. The CAT scan revealed that the shadow on my lung was scar tissue from coughing so long and so hard from the bronchitis. We were flooded with relief and eventually the cough went away. I felt as if I'd dodged another bullet.

Andrew and Kevin kept us hopping. Well, they kept me hopping and Rick running. Kevin had transferred out of private school and into public school in grade 10. The public schools offered better electives and an amazing computer program that Kevin was excited to take. He also discovered the joy of socializing in grade 10 and his grades dropped. His provincial exam marks continued to be extremely high however, because he would simply study the course material before the exam and be able to recall virtually everything he read. He refused to spend hours on homework. He was a math whiz and would do one assigned question for homework, to show that he knew the process, and refuse to "waste time doing the same question using different numbers" as he put it. I'm sure he drove his teachers crazy. At one parent-teacher interview, we walked into Kevin's physics class and the instructor said, "Oh, you're Kevin Standeven's parents. You have to be more strict with that boy!" Maybe we should have been, but we trusted Kevin to do what needed to be done. He actually chose physics and electronics as his elective classes when most kids chose woodwork or gym to lighten their academic load. Still, I was frustrated that he didn't do better in school because I knew he was more than capable. When given the choice between three hours of homework a night or hanging out with his friends, Kevin's motto was, "Do as little as possible to pass and maintain a wonderful social life." It seemed to work for him.

Andrew struggled with school from the very beginning. Starting a year later than he could have didn't seem to help him to catch up to his peers. Every morning I fought to get Andrew dressed and out the door in time for kindergarten. Every morning he reluctantly put on his school uniform—stiff blue pants, dark socks, and crisp white shirt. Every morning he would start off to school with a scowl on his normally sweet face but this morning was different. He decided he wasn't going to go to school anymore and he wasn't going to wear a stupid uniform. He ran out the door in his underwear.

Well, what's a one-legged mom on crutches supposed to do? Wishing him "bon-voyage" seemed inappropriate, so I grabbed his uniform and Kevin and I jumped in the van to chase him down. We must have looked ridiculous as I drove down the alley chasing a near-naked little boy with Kevin riding shotgun at the sliding side door. As we pulled up alongside the streaking Andrew, Kevin reached out the van door and hauled his kicking and screaming little brother inside the van. I felt like a kidnapper and was just grateful that none of the neighbours had called 911. I flipped the automatic door locks and held my finger on the button so Andrew couldn't jump from the van as we drove to school.

Andrew screamed during the whole five minute drive, "I don't want to go! You can't make me go! I hate school! I'm just stupid!" The last remark cut me like a knife. He was far from stupid, but I was exasperated. I didn't know what to do with this child who was throwing the worst temper tantrum of his entire six years of life.

I'd had enough fighting and drove him to school in his underwear. Kevin jumped out when we got to school and ran to get Andrew's teacher. He explained our situation and without hesitation, she came to the rescue. She was a no-nonsense woman, and I was happy to have her take this wild child off my hands. I had no idea what she would do but when she came out to the car and opened the door. She said, "Good morning, Andrew. You have two choices. You can come to school with your uniform on or you can come to school in your underwear. You decide." He stopped screaming and looked at her.

He could tell she was dead serious. He hesitated for a second to mull over his options, and muttered, "Fine. I'll put on my stupid uniform." He paused for effect and then declared, "But I'm NOT wearin' any socks!" His teacher and I both fought back grins. She was willing to compromise and said, "Fine. No socks today." He strutted into the school, defiant, and proud of the fact that he wasn't wearing any socks although everyone else was. Andrew hated kindergarten, and he never liked wearing socks much either. Stubborn beyond words, he didn't wear socks for the rest of the school year, and both his teacher and I decided to choose our battles carefully and let the sock rule slide. I was more than a little worried. If he disliked a half day of kindergarten so much, what was this child going to think of grade one when he had to spend a whole day cooped up in a classroom? Fortunately for me, he loved both his grade one and two teachers and he even learned to wear socks, but something was very wrong academically. It was a challenge for him to read even simple books.

In grade three, Andrew was diagnosed with "written output disability" which explained why he struggled so much with reading and comprehension. But, thanks to two years of help from an amazing tutor, he eventually learned to read but would never have the love of learning his brother had.

Kevin was practical. When he was 15 and Andrew was 9, they applied for a paper route. After the first day on the job, Kevin calculated how much time it took to deliver the papers and determined that he was making about 25 cents an hour. He quit the next day, but his brother was happy to have the extra income and worked that paper route for three years. Andrew learned how to roller-blade, and did the route in half the time. I have to admit that on rainy days I drove the van as he jumped in and out the side door so I probably ended up spending three times what he earned in a month on gas for my car! It was an expensive attempt to teach him work ethics and responsibility. Meanwhile, Kevin took a job at a computer call centre and planned to earn enough in two years to pay for his first year at trade school learning to be a geomantic engineer.

Glenda's Story

On September 11, 2001, Kevin was in Newfoundland. He was just starting grade 12 and had been chosen to go on a two-week youth exchange program. I had just pulled into the parking lot at Andrew's elementary school to drop him off when one of the other mothers met me and asked if I'd heard the news about the Twin Towers in New York city. I rushed home and turned on the TV. All airports across Canada and the United States were shut down. Kevin was supposed to be on a flight home that day but now he was stranded all the way across the country following the worst terrorist attack in U.S. history. I was terrified because I couldn't reach my "little boy," but Kevin, at 17, was practically a man. He called to reassure us that he was okay and would be home as soon as flights could be cleared for takeoff. I couldn't sleep until he was safe at home, but I realized I had to let go and let my oldest son live his life and make his own choices. I couldn't keep him wrapped in cotton anymore.

My friend Julie, whose son had gone through a bit of a rebellious stage, helped me to learn to let go and trust that Kevin had been taught the basics of common sense. I don't know what I would have done if she hadn't been there to assure me that Kevin would be okay and that he would get through all the drama of high school. I wanted him to get scholarships to go to university, but Kevin just wanted to have fun and graduate from high school. He planned on working for another year at the call centre and saving enough to go to BCIT (British Columbia Institute of Technology). When Kevin makes a plan he seldom deviates.

Rick had bought a logging truck back in 1987, just before I started having health problems, and we were making a good living. We considered moving from our split level home, but we loved the old neighborhood. In 1988, we had added an extra bathroom, TV room, and laundry area on the main floor to make it easier for me after I lost my leg. We were comfortable living on Rick's wages. At

GF Strong, they suggested I go on a disability pension but I felt that I was too young and there still had to be some job I could manage. Rick suggested that I do his business books for him. Keeping my own hours was perfect for me because sometimes the phantom pain would be so intense I couldn't get out of bed and bad weather made navigating on my crutches so unappealing I would choose to stay home. Eleven years later in 1998, the bottom fell out of the logging industry and Rick sold his business for a fraction of what it had been worth just a few years earlier. He started driving a gravel truck working for a friend, and even though he earned far less money, he didn't have the headache of searching for jobs and worrying about maintenance and repair expenses. He felt better just "packing a lunch bucket" and leaving the work worries for someone else for a change.

Rick and I spent time together working on the house, but our interests were very different. I loved doing volunteer work and Rick loved staying home. I enjoyed facilitating the support group with my friend Michelle twice a month. But it was time to let some of it go. We had devoted more than 10 years to helping cancer patients through their illnesses and I was tired of cancer; tired of saying goodbye. Many people survive cancer but there are always some who don't. Many people had no idea what had caused their illness. It just seemed to be an unfortunate coin toss that many of us were diagnosed with some type of cancer such as lymphoma, Hodgkin's, bone, thyroid, breast, or brain. Unfortunately, there were also people who came to the group who knew how they got cancer. They smoked. They had lung cancer or mouth or throat cancer all because of a bad habit and it seemed like an incredible waste of life. I decided maybe it was time to focus on prevention; to try and reach people before they became addicted to a habit that could kill them.

I started going to schools to talk to kids about the effects of smoking. I always threw in some advice about staying healthy through diet, exercise, and sun sense as well, but my main focus was on smoking awareness. I tried presenting a program that involved a lot of statistics that was offered through the Cancer Society, but kids didn't want to hear the numbers. They wanted to hear the stories. I developed my own Smoking Awareness Program for Teens using tools and techniques I garnered from various workshops, courses, and seminars plus an abundance of real life stories about the people I'd lost to cigarettes over the years. The kids loved it; the teachers loved it; I loved it.

How wonderful that volunteering for the Canadian Cancer Society all those years allowed me to find my passion. It never dawned on me to charge for presenting my program until years later, but all the times I had volunteered to speak in the past helped me to hone my program into the success it is today. I continued to volunteer for the Cancer Society whenever they needed a speaker, and it felt so much better to be working with kids and making a difference before they needed a cancer support group.

Volunteering seemed to be in my blood. Rick and I both enjoyed the Optimist Club. Their focus is to help kids in the community through all sorts of wonderful programs. We hosted the meetings at our home for two years until the club grew too large to accommodate all the members.

Terry Fox was a young man who had been diagnosed with cancer at an early age. He lost a leg to cancer, but he mounted a marathon run (with only one leg) across Canada to raise awareness about cancer. He died before completing his run, but in the process, Terry Fox became a figure of hope for many people. Fundraisers on behalf of cancer are named after him, including Terry's Team, and local runs. I became a member of Terry's Team and loved speaking at the Terry Fox Runs, held at local schools. Terry Fox was my hero before I lost my leg and I thought he was so brave to do what he did. I used to watch him on TV, thinking that if I were ever to lose my leg, I'd want to stay in bed with the covers over my head. It was just a little ironic that I should end up losing my leg to bone cancer too, and the last thing I wanted to do was stay in bed feeling sorry for myself.

I was involved with the school PAC's (Parent Advisory Committee) and made sure that the teachers knew who Rick and I were so they could call if there was ever any trouble with grades or skipping classes. I don't think we ever got a call regarding Kevin.

I can't say the same for Andrew. When Andrew entered high school he was so happy. He joined the band and learned to play the trombone. He couldn't read music, but he would get someone to show him the positions and he would memorize each song. He couldn't track the notes on the page fast enough to actually read the music but he was determined to keep playing. At the end of grade seven, he asked the band teacher to give him the next year's song list so he could learn it at home during the summer. Andrew hired a trombone instructor to teach him all the songs and paid for the lessons out of his paper-route money. In September he was so excited to start band again and show the teacher that he knew all the songs. I don't think I'll ever forgive that teacher, because he told Andrew that any student who couldn't read music could not be in band, and he had changed the song list. None of the songs Andrew learned over the summer were on it. Andrew was devastated and I was mad. I pulled Andrew out of band class. We traded his trombone for a set of drums and enrolled him in drum lessons with a teacher who felt music wasn't all about reading notes. The drums allowed Andrew to beat out his frustrations and filled his need to play music. We bought him a guitar and hired a teacher to show him how to play simple chords. Our garage looked like a band room, and he couldn't have been happier. I think one of the biggest sins someone can commit is to squash another person's dreams.

In 2002, Kevin graduated from Chilliwack Secondary School. He had been dating a lovely girl, Kimberly, throughout their senior year. She was going to attend university in Edmonton. They were quite serious about their relationship, but we thought they'd forget about each other after a year apart. They didn't. When she moved back to attend university in Chilliwack, their relationship picked up where it left off. Kevin started a course in geomatic engineering at BCIT and, with a huge sense of pride, I realized my little boy had grown up to be a wonderful, focused, and determined man. Only time would tell how high school would unfold for his little brother Andrew.

When Andrew started high school in 2003, his big brother had already graduated. I felt a sense of relief mixed with trepidation when Andrew entered high school. He had struggled so hard in the elementary grades. I was relieved to have those challenges behind him but I was afraid that he would get himself into trouble if school was too frustrating. I needn't have worried. He would generally get all 'G's on his report card for attitude and effort even when he only brought home a 'C' letter grade. As his grade 11 English teacher commented during a parent-teacher interview, "Andrew is a man of few words. He doesn't see any reason to use more words if one will do." He is direct and to the point because he doesn't know how to be anything else and that's not a bad way to be. His teachers liked him, he had an abundance of friends and wonderful social skills but I worked constantly with him encouraging him to do his best and get through school. Homework was always a struggle and we spent hours together studying, working on projects, and trying to make sense out of words that were foreign to him. I had never been happier to see a school year end than I was his last year. His graduation in June 2009, would mark the beginning of a new life of independence not only for Andrew but for me as well.

Stewart, the president of the local Canadian Cancer Society office called me one day in the spring of 2003. He wanted to meet me for lunch. I figured he had another project he wanted me to work on and was just buttering me up over a good meal so I wouldn't say no. When we met for lunch, I nodded and smiled at a group of women sitting at one of the tables and headed over to where Stuart was sitting. We chatted for a few minutes and suddenly I realized that the women were circling our table and holding flowers and balloons. At first I thought maybe it was Stewart's birthday but for some reason they were congratulating me! Apparently Stuart had nominated me to receive the Soroptimist Club's Woman of the Year award and I had won.

It was a huge honor to be Chilliwack's Soroptimist Woman of the Year and the dinner banquet in April was attended by friends and family members from near and far. As they took turns at the podium to share stories of how my life had touched theirs, I felt a little awkward; it was as if I was sitting at my own wake. It is a very strange and humbling experience to hear people sing your praises and some talked about events I could barely recall, but that had somehow impacted them. Time and time again, as people stood to talk about me, they commented on my smile. It showed me again that choosing to smile through adversity is so very rewarding.

At my family table sat a young man from China. He was dressed in a smart suit and his name was Ma Yuan. Ma had come to live with us a few months earlier as an international student who was attending our local university. He quickly became like one of our own children, and was thrilled to come to the banquet that night and sit at the family table. When I asked all the people to stand up who had known me for more than twenty years he stood up with the rest of my long-time friends and family. I laughed but, after the night had ended and we were at home, I asked him why he had stood up when we had only known each other a few months. He had a big grin on his face as he explained, "It's because

I think in another life you were my mother and I have known you for a very long time." It seemed that way for me too.

The first day he came into our lives, Ma was dropped off at our house by one of the international program directors in January 2003, and introduced to us as Ma Yuan. We liked him immediately. He was polite and kind. His face radiated a gentleness and honesty that was mirrored in his actions. I couldn't walk down the steps without him holding out his hand to touch my elbow. He stood ready to catch me in case I should fall. I couldn't get in and out of my car without that same hand holding my arm to support me. I felt like a queen!

Everyone loved Ma. When my husband would take on a renovation project, Ma was there to learn how to do the job, and help if he could. He fit into our home life as if he'd always been part of our family. After dinner one day, we sat around the table talking about our different cultures. Ma explained to us that in China, the last name is always spoken first so his given name was actually Yuan. We were embarrassed, but we'd never had a Chinese student before, so we had no idea, and no one had told us. Ma laughed and said, "You can still call me Ma. I'm used to it now and it would seem strange for you to call me Yuan." To this day, we still think of Ma Yuan as our son, and we still call him Ma even though he's now a successful business owner, and a married man living in Vancouver, BC. Rick and I can hardly wait for our first international grandchild to be born!

I had joined Toastmasters in 2003, and was learning more speaking skills which helped a lot with both my professional and my volunteer speaking engagements. I really wanted to become a paid motivational/inspirational speaker. I decided it was time to get paid for doing what I loved. After that announcement that I was Chilliwack's newest Woman of the Year, I received an invitation to attend a Rotary Club dinner function. I had been told that the coordinators of many local events would be asking me to attend their functions and, as Woman of the Year, it was hoped that I would accept the invitations. Of course, Rick and I loved going out for dinner, so when the Rotary Club invited us to attend a gala event at Minter Gardens I gladly accepted.

It was a wonderful night. The dinner, the venue, and the company were lovely and we settled comfortably into our chairs as the award and recognition speeches began. They awarded a Paul Harris Fellows Award to one of their members, and the work she'd done within the club and the community was amazing. I heartily applauded her efforts along with everyone else. As they described the next person who was going to receive the highest honor the Rotary Club can bestow, I listened in impressed amazement as they recounted the many contributions this person had made over the years to our community. Apparently, we both had volunteered for the same organizations, and I looked around the room to see if I could recognized who it would be. My husband sat with a grin on his face, since he had realized that I had no clue that they were talking about me. Even when they called my name I was still thinking they wanted me to give the award to another fellow volunteer. I whispered to my husband, "Gee, I wish they had warned me that I was going to be handing out this award. I'd like to have had a few words prepared."

Rick leaned over and whispered back with a smile, "Honey, they're giving the award to you."

Normally I pride myself on ferreting out surprises, and figuring out what presents are in which boxes at Christmas, but this award came as a complete surprise. I was an accomplished speaker and I found myself at a loss for words as I approached the podium. A simple "thank you for this great honor" didn't seem appropriate but I'm sure that's all I mustered, along with recounting the above story much to the audience's delight. So, in case I didn't thank the Rotary Club of Chilliwack enough, I'd like to say once more, "Thank you so much for bestowing your club's highest honor on me." I really do love surprises and this was a big one!

I also loved speaking, and our Toastmasters club was filled with a diverse mix of people I enjoyed spending time with. In 2005, after being in the club for only seven months, I found myself participating in the International Speech Contest. I made it to the provincial level where I had a lot of fun, but I was completely out of my league. The level of competition was far above my capabilities, but it made me more determined to keep trying. The following year I placed second in the province. I lost to a minister but I figured that he likely had more powerful connections than I did so I didn't mind. After that contest, I realized I didn't particularly like competing. It was nerve-wracking and I didn't like being "judged." I decided to remain a member of the club, but not focus on competing. It was much less stressful for me, and I discovered I enjoyed socializing much more than competing.

I can't believe it. How the hell did I get to be fifty in barely the blink of an eye? My girlfriend Paula-Marie was planning a big party for me. She didn't want me to do any of the preparation work, which practically killed me because she says I'm "a bit of a control freak." She rented a hall, sent out invitations, hired a band, and recruited my mom, friends, and family to help with food and decorating. Old friends and new filled the building. We laughed, danced, and reminisced all night long. I had another epiphany: Things would get done with or without me. I decided maybe it was okay to let a few things go.

Stewart, who was now the Regional President of the Chilliwack Canadian Cancer Society, pulled another fast one on me in 2005. He had sent my paperwork from the Woman of the Year award to the nominating committee for the Governor General's Caring Canadian Award committee, and I was one of eight British Columbia residents chosen to receive the award that year. It's presented to a person who voluntarily provides extraordinary care to individuals or groups in the community. Apparently they thought I qualified and Rick, Andrew, and I attended a lovely ceremony at Government House in Victoria, BC. It was the last time Canada's Governor General Adrienne Clarkson presented the Awards prior to her retirement in September 2005. It was an incredibly wonderful experience to be invited to Government House and to share a luncheon with Ms. Clarkson and other dignitaries. The local TV station interviewed Andrew, and he was very poised on camera. I think we were all very impressed with the degree of pomp and ceremony focused on a bunch of BC volunteers who never expected anything like this to ever happen to them.

In January 2006, a young boy from Japan came to live with us. His name was Taichi, and he was in grade 11. He fit in perfectly with our family. He started calling us mom and dad; he loved his room; he loved my cooking; he loved Rick's jokes; he loved to sing; he loved our family. He came back in September to finish grade 12 and we were thrilled when he graduated with honours from the same school that both Kevin and I had graduated from. We've had many students over the years but Taichi and Andrew really hit it off. They were constantly trying to scare each other. Well, Andrew was usually the perpetrator, and poor Taichi the victim. Andrew would wait patiently inside a closet, waiting for Taichi to walk by, and jump out. Taichi found it hysterical that Andrew would wait outside his room with a Halloween mask on until Taichi eventually opened his door for something. They became like brothers, and when Taichi went back to Japan in 2007, Andrew was thrilled to be invited to join him for a three-week vacation. What an amazing experience those two boys had exchanging their cultures and meeting new friends. Taichi came back to live with us in 2008 for his first year of university and again in 2009 for his second year. I think he can well and truly say he has two families — one in Japan and his adopted one here in Canada. If you've never considered being a home-stay family, I highly recommend it. We started doing homestay before people got paid to do it. I always asked myself, "If my child were travelling in a foreign country, what kind of experiences would I like him to have?" This question has been our inspiration to always do our best to provide every homestay student sent to us with a truly remarkable Canadian experience. Hopefully we've succeeded.

August 19, 2006, was a very special day for us. Kevin married his high school sweetheart, Kimberly. Andrew was his best man. It was a lovely wedding, and they were surrounded by the people who love them the most. They bought a house, Kevin started his own survey company and Kimberly is an elementary school teacher. They are the epitome of every parent's dream for their children: happy, successful, healthy, and in love. We are so blessed that I hate to ask them when we can expect to be grandparents, but I'm sure that day will come soon.

I was prepared to relax a little once I hit fifty, but someone upstairs had other plans. Rick and I were sitting on the couch together one night just watching TV. I was absent-mindedly stroking his arm when I felt a rough spot that I didn't remember feeling before. I looked at his deeply tanned arm and noticed an odd-shaped spot that was two-toned and scaly. I'd handed out enough skin cancer book-marks to students over the years to recognize that this spot had all the classic symptoms of skin cancer. Of course, Rick told me to quit poking it and he said those words I've heard far too often from too many people, "I'm sure it's nothing."

He had a doctor's appointment to have a painful bunion looked at, but I called the doctor's office the next day and left instructions for her to check out the mole on his arm as top priority. When Rick walked in, she said, "Okay, let's have a look at that mole." Knowing I was a bit of a worrier when it came to lumps and bumps, she took a punch biopsy right away and sent it off to the lab with instructions for us not to worry because she was sure it was nothing. There were those dreaded words again.

October 3, 2006 was a Tuesday. Funny how some dates stick in your mind. I'd had the day from hell. Mom hadn't been feeling well. She was having heart pains so I took her to the hospital at 3:00 PM and I came home at 3:30 PM I left her in the emergency room; hooked up to all the machines because they thought she was having a heart attack. They kicked me out and sent me home to wait by the phone. It was a good thing they sent me home, because there was a message waiting for me from Rick's doctor's office: could we please come in as soon as possible to go over the results of Rick's biopsy. I called Rick at work, and we made it there by 4:30 PM I knew it wasn't going to be good news when they asked us to come into the office. If it's good news they tell you over the phone.

I knew enough about skin cancer from all my cancer awareness talks and from almost 11 years of facilitating the cancer support group to be worried. As we waited for the doctor to see us, I told Rick, "I'm sure she'll tell us it's squamous cell carcinoma, or basal cell cancer, but I just hope they don't say it's melanoma."

I shouldn't have said anything. As soon as the doctor opened the door she sighed, "Well, it's not good news. It's melanoma skin cancer." Rick went pale and I almost fell off my chair. In the time it took to exhale our lives were changing again.

We went to see a surgeon on Thursday who looked over the results and assured us that because we caught it so early, very likely it had not penetrated into the deeper layers of skin. It was *in situ,* which means that the tumor cells are still confined to the site where they originated and they have neither invaded neighboring tissues nor metastasized. The surgeon scheduled Rick to have it removed the following week. Mom was still in the hospital, but with a change in medication, she was feeling better. She would be home the next day. We hadn't told her about Rick's diagnosis. We didn't want to upset her any more than we had to. I found an old email that I'd sent to my friend Julie at 2:09 AM on October 5. I'm so glad I don't remember all these details. It exhausts me just to read them now:

> Hi, Julie—I have the best news possible! Rick's tumor is
> 100% curable! That's what the surgeon said anyway. He
> says we caught it very early and it has not penetrated into
> the deeper layers of skin — it's *in situ.* YAHOO! He goes in
> to have it removed next Wednesday. I am so happy I could
> bust. Just had to let you know before I hit the sack—I have
> been up to the hospital visiting mom till 8:00, shopping
> with Taichi till 9:00, and rescuing one of Andrew's friends
> who, apparently, has been locked out of his house by an irate
> father (he missed his curfew so apparently his punishment
> was to find his own place to sleep!). Taichi needed help with
> his Socials project and we just finished—I'm beat but want-
> ed to share the good news with you. I think Rick is still in
> shock—he was prepared for the worst, but I think he forgot
> the part about expecting the best! I am so relieved—thanks
> for being there for us, Julie—I love you! Thanks for the
> prayers and positive thoughts—it worked! Love love love ya!
> Glenda

One of the mottos we had at the Living With Cancer Support Group was "Prepare for the worst but expect the best." I was getting awfully good at it. When Rick had his surgery the following week, I watched as the surgeon neatly excised the offending spot from Rick's left arm; I watched as he put the shrivelled piece of already dead-looking flesh into a small plastic biopsy bottle and snapped the lid shut with finality; I watched as he stitched up my husband's arm neatly and quickly. I felt a sense of awe and relief flood through me as the realization hit me that if I hadn't had cancer, if I hadn't volunteered for the Canadian Cancer Society, if I hadn't gone to hear the skin cancer speaker, if I hadn't handed out the skin cancer bookmarks every time I gave a speech about cancer, my husband could easily have died from a simple, harmless-looking rough spot on his arm that most people would say they were sure was nothing. I'm happy to say Rick made a full recovery from his skin cancer. He never had to have radiation or chemotherapy. It truly was an ironic twist of fate that saved his life; my cancer saved him from his. Ain't life strange?

One of the nice things that came out of Rick's cancer was that now, every year when the Cancer Society's Relay for Life comes along, I don't get to walk the track during the Survivor's Lap with just my cancer survivor friends, but my husband too. He tends to forget that he is indeed a survivor.

My friend, Michelle, has also been an important part of my life. One day she mentioned that her daughter was putting together a school project and needed to build a web site. She wanted to do one for me. I had a lot of newspaper clippings and plenty of accomplishments to list and it would be kind of fun to see what she came up with. The web site her daughter built for me was so impressive and I began to believe that perhaps I could be a successful speaker. With Michelle's encouragement, the ball began to roll. Before I knew it, I'd asked Michelle if she would be my manager to help launch my speaking business. I needed someone with focus and someone who knew me and what I loved to do. Happily, she agreed and we

Rick, Glenda, Bonnie, and Julie in the Survivor Lap of the Cancer Society's *Relay for Life.*

became a team again but without any ties to cancer. My business web site, www.glendastandeven.com was officially launched in November 2007, and we haven't looked back since.

Being involved in so many different clubs, groups, and friendships means that my husband has had to be incredibly supportive over the years. He has been content to let me fly and be the man behind the scenes. In 2007, I took on the role of entertainment chair for the provincial Toastmasters conference scheduled for November at the Harrison Hotel Resort. I was so busy with meetings, hiring the musicians, organizing the decorating committee and a million other things that I admit I wasn't paying much attention on the home front. Something was brewing but I was totally oblivious to it all.

The final day of the conference was Sunday, November 3. I was looking forward to the keynote speaker and the wrapup party afterwards, so I was a little annoyed when my friend and business manager, Michelle, called on Saturday to tell me she had scheduled a photo shoot and interview with the press to promote my new speaking business. I couldn't believe I'd have to miss my breakfast — which I'd already paid for — and the keynote speaker as well, but Michelle said that Jenna, my favourite photographer, was only available on Sunday morning and would be taking off for two weeks as soon as she finished the shoot. I reluctantly agreed to stay home for the interview the next morning. My fellow conference committee members seemed disappointed that I wouldn't be there for the breakfast, but I assured them I'd do all I could to be back in time for the wrapup party.

I was dressed with my hair and makeup done early the next morning and sat on the couch, impatiently waiting, for Michelle and Jenna to show up. I sat tapping my foot and kept watching the clock. Rick was getting more and more flustered and kept telling me that they'd be here soon. Finally I said, "Look, if they're not here in ten minutes, I'm leaving for the convention. I can still make the keynote speaker if I hurry." In retrospect, I should have been more suspicious because Andrew and our newest Japanese exchange student, Masaya, were already awake, and Rick looked nervous, but I was too busy being impatient to pay attention to their behaviour. Rick called Michelle and she said she was almost there and to meet her outside. It was a lovely November day and I thought it was a great idea to do an outdoor photo shoot. I didn't even hesitate; I just headed for the door. I stood on the sidewalk, watching for her car but she was nowhere in sight.

I turned to Rick and asked, "Are you sure she said she was just about here?" He nodded. I was getting more and more ticked off the longer I waited, when suddenly I heard a whooping and hollering coming down the alley. I saw a bunch of people walking in our direction and at first I thought, hmmm, must be a parade. I looked again, and saw that the people in the parade were people I knew and there was a white van rolling along with the crowd with the words, MAKEOVER WISH printed on the side. I almost fainted. My first thought was, "This can't be happening!" My second thought, was, "Oh my gosh, I didn't make my bed this morning and the laundry is on the bedroom floor! PLEASE don't let them be doing my bedroom!" I looked at Rick and he just grinned!

It was a whirlwind day. Apparently, my friends Bonnie and Julie had sent in an application for a Canadian television show called *Make-Over Wish,* asking them to give my living room a make-over. They were as sick of my 1980s furniture as I was! Because of all the volunteer work I'd done in the community, the HGTV *Make-Over Wish* Program chose me to receive a $25,000 home make-over. My two sneaky friends had Rick and everyone in the family, including my mom and all my other close friends, in on the surprise. Even my fellow Toastmasters at the conference knew about it. It seems I'd lost my *secret* radar and no longer could detect when anyone was keeping something from me! It was an amazing three-day experience, and my home not only received a living room make-over but they did the dining room and office as well. When it came time to reveal the gorgeous finished rooms, all I kept saying was, "Oh, my gosh." I think I counted eleven "oh, my gosh's" when the show aired on HGTV on Christmas Eve 2007. So much for being a professional speaker! May God bless my friends and family.

Toastmasters introduced me to so many new people and so many wonderful opportunities. One of the women I met, Nancy, encouraged me to write a monologue and submit it to a local theatre troupe. I thought to myself, nothing ventured, nothing gained. The theme was "Dreams" so I wrote about the dream I'd had before losing my leg. I wasn't sure what they were looking for, but I submitted it anyway. Sure enough, mine was one of the nine monologues chosen, them. Nancy auditioned to perform my piece, and she got the role. I had to laugh because I'm 5'9" with one leg and Nancy is 4'6" with two! How the heck was she going to pull "ME" off? I went to see the final production. I don't know why I didn't tell my friends or family about it, but I did take my mom to see the show. I have to say it was amazing. My monologue was the finale and Nancy had most of us in tears. She captured the emotions of my dream so perfectly it sent shivers down my spine. It was an experience that's hard to describe, but when you see yourself being portrayed on a stage, and someone else is speaking your words, the words you lived: it is both humbling and hugely satisfying.

Remember Mrs. Mac? The lady who gave us cookies and milk when we stole her apples? Mrs. Mac's lesson of offering friendship and forgiveness rather than punishment has served me well over the years. I've even written my own little 'handicapped parking' reminder to leave on peoples' cars when they don't have their disabled parking permit displayed:

> OOOPS!
> You forgot to hang up your handicapped sign —
> I'm sure you're not one of those rude, thoughtless,
> insensitive people who use these spaces simply for their
> own convenience . . . so please remember next time to
> hang up your handicapped sign . . .
> From one disabled person to another,
> Have a wonderful day!

I wonder how many people have had a chuckle when they receive one of my reminder notes. And I wonder how many people have felt inordinately sheepish. People who park in the handicapped spot when they're not disabled is one of my pet peeves. But sometimes I just have to laugh. One day when I went to visit Elaine, who had been my occupational therapist at GF Strong, I pulled into a handicapped parking spot at the grocery store. She was horrified and said, "Glenda, what are you doing? You can't park here. This is for handicapped people."

Glenda's Story

I looked at her to see if she was joking but I realized that she honestly didn't see me as a disabled person and for a moment she forgot that I was, indeed, handicapped. I think most of my friends and family see me the same way Elaine does and I feel very blessed.

On July 17, 2007 Rick and I celebrated our 25th anniversary. I was looking forward to having a big party and inviting all the friends and family who had attended our wedding 25 years earlier. Rick wanted to go on a cruise instead. He doesn't often get me to change my mind about things, but this time he made a good case for going on a cruise rather than having the big party I wanted. He wanted to be alone with me. How can a wife complain about a husband who would rather spend a week alone together with her on a cruise ship than share her for one night with family and friends? When I did the math I discovered it would cost about the same amount of money, I agreed to his suggestion to go on an Alaskan cruise instead of throwing a big party. We had a picture taken of ourselves, all dressed up in our evening wear, sitting with a table full of strangers as we celebrated 25 years of marriage somewhere on the ocean on our way to Alaska. We made more memories on that trip and some wonderful new friends as well. We'll have the big party when Rick turns 60.

The following year, it was my turn to plan our summer vacation. I was still trying to lose the weight I'd gained on our Alaskan cruise, so I knew exactly what I wanted to do for this one. I wanted an adventure. First, I planned a trip to Vancouver to fly on the zip line at Grouse Mountain. Rick had an appointment to see his dermatologist in Vancouver, so we decided to just stay overnight at my sister's and go to Grouse Mountain the next day. The dermatologist gave Rick a clean bill of health, which gave us even more reason to celebrate life. At Grouse Mountain, the sheer anticipation of zipping over the tree tops was exhilarating, but I have to admit I was disappointed that it didn't go faster and last longer. Afterwards, we headed through Washington state to Eugene, Oregon, to go white-water rafting on the Upper Mackenzie River. We stayed in a wonderful rustic motel and spent the next day on the river. I quickly discovered that if I sat on the left side of the boat I tipped easily into the water but a quick shuffle over to the right side kept me wedged in tight. (If there are any hip disarticulate amputees or hemi-pelvectomy amputees reading this, remember to sit on the side of the raft that matches your missing limb.) I discovered that I loved white-water rafting, and thoroughly enjoyed the thrill of paddling hard through the rapids. Rick probably would have been content to take another cruise and let the ship do the work, but he was a good sport and let me have my fun. He chose the next day's activity and, after rafting, we headed across to the Oregon Coast to ride dune buggies on the sand dunes in Florence. Much to my surprise, the dune buggies were even more exhilarating and thrilling than the rapids. Except for the sand that found its way into orifices I didn't even know I had, it was the highlight of the trip. Rick chose well! We headed home the next day and enjoyed a wonderful sun-filled drive along the gorgeous Oregon Coast. If you haven't taken this trip, I can honestly say that, in my opinion, it sure beats sitting on a cruise ship and watching the waves roll by.

Michelle has been my friend and support person since the day we met, back in the 1990s, so when she invited me to an event she was hosting at a local hotel in March 2009, I didn't hesitate to go. While we enjoyed visiting over drinks in the lounge afterwards I shared the news with her that our good friend, Bonnie, wasn't doing too well. Her cancer was back. Before I knew it Michelle had organized a wonderful retreat weekend in Bellingham, a town just across the border from us. Michelle, Julie, Bonnie and I, "The Four Musketeers," took off for a couple days of shopping and fun together. That was when the seeds for this book were first planted. It was supposed to be a book about the four of us and our wonderful amazing lives but Bonnie became too ill to write her story. I like happy endings but we don't always get them in real life. Still, it was a wonderful way to connect four strong cancer survivors over love and laughter. Making memories is what life is all about.

It has taken some time, but I've gradually dropped out of my executive volunteer roles. I'm no longer on the executive of the Canadian Cancer Society, the Optimist Club or Toastmasters and in October, 2009, I turned over the president's gavel for the Chilliwack Secondary School PAC for the last time. I still do volunteer work but am picking and choosing the tasks I want to do. I've decided to focus more on writing, speaking, and traveling — turning fifty has given me a sense of freedom to do what I want to do and not merely what I need to do. In October 2009, I completed my first children's book, "Who's Chasing Me?" and am working on two more. Writing is something I've dreamed of doing all my life and now I'm finally following my dreams.

A good friend, Alan Newby, passed away in August 2007, in an unexpected work accident. He had been the master of ceremonies at our wedding 25 years earlier and his death came as a huge shock to our entire community. When he left us so unexpectedly, I think it made all of his friends and family more appreciative of the time we have together. At his memorial service, we reconnected with old friends and made some new friends as well. I think that is what a funeral should do — bring old friends and new together. When I die I want a huge party thrown to celebrate my life. One of my pet peeves is people who say, "Oh, I don't want a funeral." What many people don't understand is that the funeral isn't really for the person who died. A funeral or a memorial service is a way for the people who are left behind to acknowledge a life well lived (or not!). It gives people a sense of closure and peace. Goodbyes are important, so if you're considering not having a funeral in order to save your family and friends the expense, then start saving your money now and make plans for a wonderful send off.

In the cancer support group we always told cancer patients to clean their closets and garages, get their funerals organized and paid for, and then get busy and live without worrying about leaving a mess behind for their loved ones to clean up. Hmmm, come to think of it, it's probably time for Rick and me to clean our garage and closets again!

The one thing I've learned for sure is that life is very much like a roller coaster ride. Some people are too scared to ever get on, and some people get sick and have to get off too soon; but for those people who stay on and experience all the highs, the lows, the twists, and the turns, then the ride can be a hell of a lot of fun. I know just how quickly it can end. You can choose to be afraid and spend the entire time wishing it were over or you can choose to enjoy the ride and smile through it all. For myself, I know that I'm choosing to smile.

Family photo (clockwise from top left): Andrew, Rick, Kevin, Kimberly, Grandma Carol, and Glenda.

Michelle's
Story

In the spring of 1949, my dad, Howie, came to British Columbia from Aberdeen, Saskatchewan, where he was born and raised. Dad had a job lined up in Alberta and his parents were travelling to British Columbia, when his father got sick with the flu. Since my dad was twenty-one and the only boy old enough to drive, he was asked to drive the family to BC. Instead of going to the job in Alberta, he drove his seven family members to BC in a 1941 Ford. Once he arrived in BC, he loved it and never went back to the Prairies, except for short visits.

Dad got a job at the post office in Abbotsford in 1952. This was steady work and a good paying job. Shortly after he started working at the post office, he set his eyes on a particular young lady named Ada Mae, who came in to pick up her mail. One day she came in to pick up her mail and there was a check in it. He suggested that she could buy him lunch. They went on a date, but he said he never did get that lunch. But they did get married. That's how my mom and dad met. He was twenty-three years old and she was seventeen. Not long after they were married, my sister Bonnie was born, and two years later, brother Jim came along.

In December 1959, Howie and Ada Mae had their third child, Michelle. That's me. I wasn't really a planned child; mom had already been working towards a career. She was a writer for the local newspaper and also worked as an announcer at the radio station. With mom being involved in community and local events, we sometimes were able to get behind the scenes for some exciting experiences. I have early memories of being able to go into the radio station to see the

Howie and Ada Mae's kids: Jim, Bonnie, and Michelle.

announcer's booth with all the buttons. Mom had a beautiful voice, when she wasn't yelling at us kids for getting into some kind of trouble. She sang in the choir and we all sang in the car on long drives.

We were a hard-working family living in a modest neighborhood without frills. We had to be creative to make fun out of pretty much nothing. Our Sunday outing was a game called "getting lost." We all piled in the car, dad at the wheel and mom riding shotgun, kids in the back, taking turns giving dad directions. He followed our directions to the letter. Turn left, turn right, drive straight ahead, and stop—everyone out, on and on. We kids also had to get the car back home unless we tired of the game and dad took over. One thing my sister remembers is that we kids would try to let litter fly out of the car window without letting mom see it, or stop us. She was totally against littering and I am too, today, but back then, it was fun to try and outwit mom. I regret that I didn't listen to her much earlier in my life.

Since mom worked for the radio station she got to cover community events. In a small town of twenty thousand people, we had a great fall fair, one with rides, animals, carnival food, and games. This was a huge event, and everyone in town was involved, including the children who rode their decorated bikes in the parade. In the sixties, our neigh-

Michelle's winning tricycle.

borhood was full of kids and bikes. To get ready for the parade, we brought our bikes into the centre of our street and began with a bike wash. From tricycles to two-wheelers, every bike was scrubbed and shined before we added the colorful crepe paper, winding it through the spokes and around the handlebars. After we paraded our decorated bikes through town, we ended at the fairground in the bike judging area where everyone received a ribbon. I had entered my tricycle and was very proud to win a big blue ribbon for my decorated bike!

There were the usual carnival rides like the Ferris wheel, Scrambler, and Tilt-a-Whirl, and a ride called the Salt-and-Pepper Shakers or Bullet. There were two arms with a cage at one end of a catapult that would swing around in circles while spinning the occupants of the cage. During one summer fair, the Salt-and-Pepper ride broke while there were kids in it. There were a couple of kids in the pod that was stuck in the air. Everyone looked on while we waited for the fire truck to come and pluck the kids out of the pod. The kids were frightened and the crowd was holding its breath with worry. My mom talked to the kids and kept them as calm as she could until help arrived. The kids and the onlookers watching were shaken but everyone was okay. I don't think mom ever had training to do that, but instinctively she was wonderful at it.

Disneyland opened in 1955 and all kids wanted to go. The family talked and talked about going, but it was going to be a financial stretch. Whenever we were left in the car, one kid leapt into the driver's seat and said, "Where do you want to go?" The chorus from the backseat was always "Disneyland!" The "driver" then turned the wheel left and right to get us to the mythical Disneyland. We finally did go to Disneyland in 1967, in a rented truck and camper. Bonnie was the carsick child, and she got to ride in the front. Jim and I rode in the camper with our faces pasted against the camper window peering into the cab. We didn't like riding in the back but I think maybe we had much more fun than Bonnie did with mom and dad in the front of the truck.

Dad had relatives in California who we could visit, and mom and dad had friends in Pasadena. We visited the Epplers, and parked our truck and camper in their yard. The Epplers had three kids too, and their oldest daughter Lois, was my age and we got along well. I was so amazed that in the Epplers' back yard they were growing lemons and oranges. California was quite an adventure for us, but it was so hot we had to be careful of sunburns and heat stroke. I had red hair and freckles so I would be the one likely to burn the worst.

We had a great vacation visiting with our new friends and got to go to Disneyland, Knott's Berry Farm, and Marineland. Seeing the Disney characters and going on the rides was a kid's dream come true, and one of my fondest memories of childhood.

In the early days, mom's job with the radio station was to assist the announcers at the Abbotsford International Airshow. The first air show was in 1962 and there were fifteen thousand people in attendance. That was a big crowd for our little town. The air show is always held in August and it usually ends up being the hottest weekend of the summer. At least it always felt like that on the concrete tarmac without any shade. Mom and dad got to know the announcer, Toby Trowbridge, who was brought in to emcee the show. Toby was a real character. He would arrive on the weekend of the air show, from somewhere I never knew, to stay at our house and spend the three days of the air show with us. Since mom and dad were his friends, we would host him at our house along with some of the other pilots. We'd give up our beds and sleep on the floor in sleeping bags to free our beds for guests to use. The air show was always an exciting weekend for us.

Mom was also a part of the Abbotsford Band festival which included a parade of high school marching bands. That was a really busy time for our family, as we'd host out of town students at our house. There'd be a flurry of excitement and activity before they came, as we'd watch for the big bus to turn down our street. Then it would stop at our house and let some of the young teens out. These were our guests, and we'd wait anxiously to see who was going to stay with us. While they stayed over the weekend we were busy keeping them fed and their uniforms pressed for their competitions. As with the air show visitors, we'd pull out the sleeping bags and sleep on the floor, while our guests took the beds. It was like a camping weekend.

Abbotsford also had a beauty pageant. The contestants had been competing in various events for the title of Miss Abbotsford. I must have been around five or six the year I was chosen to be the flower girl for the newly crowned Miss Abbotsford. I was to give her the congratulatory bouquet of roses. I practiced and practiced my curtsey as if I was going to meet the Queen of England. The pageant was in the local church and the pews were filled with mostly women. I was waiting in the wings with the most beautiful bouquet of red roses in my arms. As the announcement was made, and all the contestants shrieked with happiness and relief, the crown was put on the new Miss Abbotsford. That was my moment to walk up the aisle of the church, ever so carefully, with her bouquet. I nervously made my way up the aisle and everyone went quiet while they waited for me to make it to the queen. Once I reached the young lady, she graciously accepted her

Michelle as the Miss Abbotsford Pageant flower girl.

flowers, and I made my perfect curtsey. Then everyone laughed and clapped. I thought they were laughing at me and I wanted to cry, but then Miss Abbotsford put her arm around me and we had our pictures taken together. That was my moment of fame.

Dad had a good government job at Canada Customs working at the U.S.-Canada border crossing that was just minutes from our home. Dad worked shift work and kept busy fixing and building things around our house. Both my parents were well known in our small town and had many friends. We lived on a dead-end street with lots of ponds, fields, and bushes nearby. Our street was a great place to grow up, exploring the critters and bugs in the fields. In our neighborhood there were always kids to play with. We'd play in the street since only residents drove there, and they were always someone's parents.

In the summer, we'd go out and play until it was dark. We'd climb trees, collect tadpoles from the ponds, and play baseball in the fields. In the winter, we'd skate on the frozen ponds and drag our sleds to the highest hills we could find to slide down.

In the spring, I remember hearing the sounds of the birds in the daytime, and the frogs croaking in the evening. There was a corner store two blocks away, and a small town centre about six blocks away, but we were quite content on our little street. My brother Jim played with the slimy creatures, and had a pet snake that he would carry around with him all the time. We lost a babysitter because of Jim and this snake. One day Jim was in a hurry to get to the bathroom and came running into the house. He handed his snake to the babysitter and said, "Here, hold this for me. I'll be right back." She took it, thinking it was a stick. But that was the end of that babysitter. She never came back.

Every family on our street had something different in their yard or at their house, so it was really interesting to take turns playing at each place. I had a playhouse that was a converted work shed where kids could play at my house. It had a wooden kitchen with knobs made of empty thread spools. The sink was a plastic bowl with make-believe taps. We could create all kinds of scenarios in that little playhouse. There was a small table with two chairs that my grandpa had made for me. In our neighbor's house across the street, we played in the basement where there was a play spaceship console. It was loads of fun, with spinning dials, and pie tins that were make-believe Martian spaceship controls. That was the time of the TV shows like *My Favorite Martian, Lost in Space,* and *The Jetsons.* Those shows were the best science-fiction that we had in those days.

Girls also played with Barbie, changing her outfits, and creating various situations for her. The original Barbie had been created the same year I was born, 1959, so she was all the rage by the time I was in elementary school. Not all of us could have Barbie, and I had the Midge doll. Midge was created as Barbie's friend and introduced in 1963. She had red hair and freckles like mine. Each girl would bring her own Barbie with her clothes and make up accessories to someone's house. We would try to sew Barbie some clothes using scraps of fabric or create furniture for her. One of the neighborhood moms did a lot of sewing, so we'd go there to make patterns and dresses for Barbie. We played for hours.

My dad always liked to drink beer. At that time, beer came in stubby brown bottles. I liked to do what my dad did, and that included drinking beer. I must have been pretty young when I first started fetching beer for my dad. If he asked for a beer, I'd dutifully tootle along and get his beer. When I brought it to him he'd open it and I got the first sip. Since dad's name is Howie and that was his drink, I named it "Howie" pop. Dad told me that when I'd come walking along with my little girlfriends, if I saw he had an open beer, I'd pick it up and have my swig.

When I was born, my brother and sister were already in school. My parents needed help caring for me, because mom was a working woman, well established in her career. Mom and dad were both very close to mom's mother, Kay, and they asked her to come to stay with us to take care of me. My grandmother moved in with us when I was a year old. She took care of me during the day, and worked at night, as a cook in a restaurant. Once the kids were off to school, and my parents off to work, Kay and I would lie down to have a nap. We'd go into her room and lie down with her arm over me so I wouldn't go anywhere. If I was unlucky, and she fell asleep first, I had to stay there, pinned down, while she snored like a buzz saw.

Kay's parents, my great-grandparents, Grandma and Grandpa Tubbs, lived in the next town. When I was little, Kay and I would ride the Greyhound bus to Chilliwack to grandma and grandpa's house.

They had two bedrooms in their house, both with twin beds. Grandma and grandpa would sleep in their room and both snored loudly, and I slept in the other room with Kay and her buzz saw snoring. It's amazing I got any sleep at all. When I was about seven years old, Kay would put me on the bus alone, and send me to stay with grandma and grandpa. Kay had made me a little cloth pouch that she would pin inside my clothes with a dime in it. This was "mad money" to use for a phone call, in case my grandpa wasn't there to meet me. But he was always there. Grandma also told me that when I got older and was on a date it was important to carry "mad money" in case I wanted to leave the date on my own and call a taxi for a ride home. She taught me how to take care of myself.

We had great adventures together. Sometimes I could spend time with Grandma Tubbs in the kitchen making kolaches with homemade apple butter. Kolaches are a sweet bun that is rolled into squares with the corners pinched to make space for a spoonful of apple butter or apricot jam placed in the middle before they are baked.

One day Grandma saw a little green budgie (parakeet) in a tree in her back yard. She put out a cage with some food and talked to the bird each day, until one day, the bird finally flew into the cage. They gave that bird the same name as my nickname, Mickey, and it was part of the family for many years. Grandma taught Mickey to say a few words. I'd never heard a talking bird before. He would say "Pretty boy, Mickey." He was allowed to come out of his cage and would sit on the edge of Grandpa's dinner plate and pick away at his food.

There were no other kids in the neighborhood where grandma and grandpa lived, so we had to make our own fun. They had an attic where all kinds of treasures were stored, mostly old containers, and boxes of old clothes. That generation had all gone through the Great Depression on the Prairies. In those days, people didn't have money for frivolous things, and what they did have in that attic, though, were wonderful colored glass bottles, and other interesting things that we could use. Grandma had an old straw hat that I used to play with. I found long white gloves for dress-up, to go with the hat. When I was outside, I would pick fragrant flowers from grandma's garden, soak the petals in water and pour that into a bottle, to make perfume to wear for my make-believe grown-up parties. It was a wonderful attic of make believe. Even the shadows we cast on the walls turned into imaginary friends. My imaginary friend's name was Casper. He would show up when I was in the kitchen and dance around on the wall.

I always felt that I came from a line of strong, independent, and hard-working women. I always understood that women could do anything. There never seemed to be a division between men and women. During the 60s, women's liberation was an important movement in North America, but I had never known about limitations for women. My great grandma Tubbs wanted to be a teacher and finished her high school education. She was a schoolteacher in a one-room schoolhouse on the Prairie. She taught in a number of schools from 1911 to 1937. Grandma never drove a car, so she either rode her horse to school, or lived in the town where she was teaching. Grandpa Tubbs was a railroad conductor on the Canadian Pacific Railway from 1918 to 1957. They were homesteaders in Saskatchewan, had lived through the Depression, and the second World War, and came west to BC to retire.

In my family, I saw men and women work in the house, garden, cook, and I know my dad can even sew. When both husbands and wives worked outside the home, the house and families were taken care of, and fed by, whoever came home first. I never remember having a babysitter when I was young; we relied on family. My family was working-class and community-minded. In 1966, a women's prison opened in our town. This became an important employer, and provided good paying government jobs. My mom worked in the office, in the steno pool, and Kay also got a job there, as a guard.

I thought things seemed to be going along pretty well in my life until I was in grade three, about eight years old. But things weren't going all that well for mom and dad. One day, mom called me into the kitchen and told me that she and my dad couldn't live together any more. She was going to leave, and Bonnie was going with her. I can remember the day my mom told me that news. It was as if someone had knocked the air out of me. I cried and cried until I was out of breath, sobbing, but that didn't help. I thought that I'd been bad and that made her want to leave, but that wasn't true. Mom and Bonnie packed up, and Kay, my grandma, also moved out. They left my dad, my brother Jim, and me living in our family home. We three stayed in the house so that Jim and I could remain in the same school and live where our friends were. Our house changed from a home bustling with people to the three of us, alone, in the house.

In 1968, this was a highly unusual family structure. There weren't that many single-parent families in our community, none that I knew, and especially not a single father with two kids. Dad had custody of us, and we didn't see mom at all for the first year, and not too often after that, either. Kay went to live with her parents, Grandma and Grandpa Tubbs, and I didn't see them too often at first. My dad worked shift work at his job and did his best to take care of us. His sewing and cooking skills came in real handy. Dad's cooking wasn't the best, actually, it was kind of gross to a kid. I took a lot of peanut butter sandwiches to school. I'd look at the other kids' lunches that their mothers had packed. Mine was never the best lunch, but I'll always admire my dad for how well he did with the difficult job he had, raising two kids as a single father.

Dad worked the midnight to 8 AM shift to give himself time to manage the house the best he could. He would phone my brother to wake us up for school at 7:30 AM, come home after his shift ended at 8 am, in time to get us off to school, and then he'd lay down to sleep.

He'd get up just before we came home after school, and make dinner. Of course, he also had the maintenance jobs of cleaning, cutting the grass, washing clothes, etc. Once we finished dinner, we'd do our homework, and get ready for the next school day. After we went to sleep, he'd go to work at midnight. On the weekends, he worked as a bartender at the local Legion to make some extra money.

We were lucky to stay in our house near the same neighborhood families where we had grown up. I'm sure the other moms were keeping their eyes on us to make sure we were okay. I spent most weekends at my dad's parents. They were retired, and lived nearby in a house that grandpa had built. They came to the Canadian Prairies from Germany and Russia, and retired in Abbotsford.

Grandma and grandpa had raised six children and had done a lot of farming. Their retirement home had a great big garden in the back yard, and a kitchen custom-made for my short little grandma. Grandma cooked all the meals and baked fresh breads and goodies. These grandparents were Mennonites, and went regularly to church. When I spent weekends with them, I went to church, too. After church, we would get together with other families to have a traditional meal. All their friends were old and there weren't any other kids around. I got to go to Sunday school with lots of kids, though. I slept in the most comfortable bed in Grandma's guest room. It had the softest mattress, and the fluffiest, sweet-smelling comforter. It was really good for me to be with my grandparents, but I was still an alien being from a broken home, with no mom.

Aunt Marge was my dad's sister, and my favorite aunt. Sometimes I got to stay over at her house. She was married to Uncle George, who wasn't nearly as nice. They didn't have any kids, but they had two really big dogs, and a cat. They lived in a house in Vancouver, and had a cabin on Sakinaw Lake on the Sunshine Coast. When I stayed with Aunty Marge and Uncle George, I got to go with them to the cabin. We'd load up the station wagon with food, supplies, and animals, and take a ferry to the Sunshine Coast, a region close to Vancouver. From the ferry landing, we'd drive another fifty miles along a winding road to the lake. When we got to the lake, we unloaded the car, loaded up a small boat, and went across the lake to the cabin for the weekend. That cabin was so neat for a kid. There was no power, so the cabin was heated from a wood cook stove and all the cooking was done on the fire in the stove. Our light was coal-oil lanterns, and the bathroom was an outhouse down the path behind the cabin.

I had so much fun at the cabin. I could swim right off the end of the dock in the summer. The cabin was on a bay that had three cabins, but usually the other cabins were empty. There was a huge rock in the middle of the bay, and I would swim or float to the rock and stand on it. Aunty Marge let me take the rowboat out by myself. I guess she figured I couldn't row far enough to get into trouble. Ever since I was a pre-teen, she had told me that by rowing, I could develop a bust. I rowed and rowed but nothing happened. I suppose it did keep me occupied and out of her hair.

At night for entertainment, we'd play card and board games by lantern light. Aunty Marge's animals were so funny. They loved to ride in the boat and knew exactly when it was time to go home. I always felt safe when they were around. The bigger of the two dogs looked like a small black bear and I was certain he could protect me from any wild animals.

I know my dad worked really hard to take care of Jim and me. He tried to have a life, too. Dad and I would go down to the local restaurant, the Milk Bar. I'd get to sit on the stools at the counter and could choose whatever ice cream I wanted. It was a real treat for me. I also think I was date bait for dad. I was contented and cute, eating my ice cream while some of the waitresses talked to me. In the meantime, dad talked to the other waitresses. They were real nice to me, so I was fine with that.

Choosing to Smile

My dad and I always had a special bond. I know it must have been hard on him, raising two kids, and later, having another family to look after. I always knew he would take care of me and I always knew he was proud of me. We still laugh about his horrible cooking. Jim didn't mind it as much as I did. Both of them liked their steak blue-rare, making jokes about the meat hitting the pan only for a quick sizzle on each side. I was the difficult one to feed. Dad said the only thing I would eat was "man on a raft." He would cut a hole in the centre of a piece of bread, put it into the frying pan, and cook an egg in the hole. Years later as an adult, I made the decision to stop eating red meat and pork. Apparently, I was always meant to be a vegetarian, but in those days, I didn't know how to do that.

Dad remarried when I was twelve. His new wife, Jessie, had two boys. They were younger than me, so I was an older sibling for the first time. Jessie had a huge house on three acres, so we moved to her house. It was a very special house in the neighborhood and in the town. The Abbotsford Lumber Company built this house in 1920 for a BC timber baron. It was built from the finest fir lumber that came from the local sawmill. I'd seen the house before, but I thought it looked creepy, because it was old, set back from the road, and hidden behind huge old trees. It had been a majestic old home at one time, but was in need of help. When I actually got to go into the house, it was fascinating. It had high ceilings in the large rooms with beautiful wood paneling and old wood floors. The hallways were long, as was the staircase to the second floor. There were two wood-burning fireplaces to heat the house, and they had beautiful brick chimneys and wooden mantles. On my first visit to Jessie's house, I was shown what was about to become my bedroom. It was a huge room at the front of the house with a French Provincial, canopied, double bed with a matching nine-drawer dresser and mirror! It was a very cool room for a young girl but I really didn't have any choice in the matter. I wasn't too keen on having two new brothers. But my opinion didn't count, and I had to do the best I could in the situation.

Dad and Jessie were married in 1972, and we all moved into her house. Dad sold our home and started to work on this new, old house. There was much work to do. Jessie was a widow and had lived with her two boys in the house alone for a few years. Many things needed fixing and upgrading. I got to move into my new room, and we painted it pink. It had high ceilings and fancy wooden trim that we painted white. Jim lived with us for a short while, and then left to live with our mom on Vancouver Island.

I had grown up in the same house and in the same neighborhood my whole life, even after my parents split up. Now I had to move for the first time, be part of a new family, leave behind the close childhood friends I had, and start at a new school. It was a big change for me, but it had new opportunities. I started grade six in the new school and was able to make friends. After all, I was the new girl who lived in the house that everyone wanted to see. Dad started to work on the property. There were buildings that had to be torn down and fences to be fixed. He also had unsafe trees cut down and he dug up the entire yard to put in a new lawn.

Dad built a new barn and bought us a horse (I named her Duchess), and two cows that I named Amelia and Amanda. I made pets out of all of them, even the cows. The horse was primarily for dad and me. He had owned horses when he was a boy on the Prairies and wanted to teach me about horses. And what teenaged girl didn't want her own horse?

Dad tried to teach me the ins and outs of farming in our little barnyard. One day, I was in the barn wearing flip-flop sandals. I was between one of the cows and the barn wall when the cow stepped sideways, onto my foot. Then she leaned all her weight on my foot, pinning me against the wall. I was hollering and pushing her as hard as

I could, trying to get her off my foot. Finally she moved, and I jumped away. I had a hurt foot and wounded pride. I went to tell my dad and to look for sympathy. Dad said if I hadn't have been in there in the first place, I wouldn't have gotten stepped on. That was my dad's style. When I was little, if I fell down and cried, he'd say, "Come here and I'll pick you up."

Duchess was a beautiful chestnut quarterhorse. Once she and I understood each other, I could take her off the property for rides. Since our house was the only acreage in town, I'd have to ride on the city street to get to Centennial Park. After we'd spent the afternoon riding, we'd head home. Near our house was a corner store, Bev Way Grocer, where all the kids hung out.

I'd stop at the store, tie Duchess' reins to the fencepost, and go in to get my favorite kind of pop, RC Cola. There was a long wooden bench along the driveway where kids could sit to eat their chips and candy. When I was drinking my cola, I'd offer Duchess some, and she would tip her head back to get a drink. It was pretty funny to watch. We always said that she thought she was human. Dad tried to take her into the house one day by walking her up the back stairs. Duchess might actually have gone into the house, but Jessie got really mad at him, and told dad to "take that horse off the back stairs!"

I made pets of the cows, Amelia and Amanda, too. I'd run around with them and try to ride on them, but they wouldn't cooperate. I wouldn't get too far before I'd fall off. But I'd still hug them and talk to them. I think they figured they were people, too. They would be at the farthest corner of the property when dad would come home. He'd walk to the barn and call "girls!" and they would stop eating, raise their heads, and run to the barn to greet dad.

Dad tried to teach all of the kids how to make our own money; to be independent. He helped the boys set up a business selling dew worms in our yard. It was a good business for quite a few years. We had a sign at the end of the driveway that read "Dew worms, 50¢ dozen." We had lots of customers. Fishermen would come by every day for our big, fat dew worms. Keeping a good supply of dew worms was a job for my stepbrothers and all their guy friends. Dad installed an irrigation pump in the lake that was just past the end of our property. He'd pump the lake water onto our lawn in the late afternoons and early evenings, soaking the ground. When it was dark, the boys would go out with their flashlights and catch the dew worms that would be lying on the soaked night grass. They had to be fast to catch them once they shone their light on them. Some nights were better than others, too. Dad had a double cement sink at the side of the barn where they kept the worms. If I was the only one at home when a fisherman came to buy worms, he'd have to pick them out himself. I wasn't about to be touching worms.

I started my own working career at twelve. The first job I had was babysitting the neighborhood kids. From that first job, I quickly got more jobs and was quite busy in the evenings. I made really good money from those jobs and saved to buy my school clothes. We also went raspberry picking in the summer time. That job started early in the morning. We'd get up, pack our lunches, and wait at the end of the driveway for the bus to come and take us to the fields. In the mornings, the fields would be wet and cold, soaking our clothes as the water from the bushes ran down our arms. By the time the sun got warm, and then hot, we'd peel off all our wet clothes, and try not to get sunburned.

Berry picking was hard work, but it was fun when there was someone on the other side of the row to talk to. Most of the time, one of the pickers would bring a radio, and we could listen to the latest summer music while we worked. That would make the time pass quickly. Sometimes people would get really competitive and race to see how many flats they could pick in a day. I was an average picker, just there to make some money. At the end of summer, we went shopping to buy a few new outfits for school.

Since we lived right next to Mill Lake, most of the neighborhood kids swam in the lake. We had all kinds of scary stories about underwater streams that would suck you under and whisk you away. The perimeter of the lake was filled with water lilies, and under that was bottomless silt. We'd go to a neighbor's house, John Mahony's, to use his dock to get far out into the lake past the silt. Once we got out as far as we could, we'd slide out onto our air mattresses, to get past the water lilies that we imagined would grab on to our legs and pull us into those underwater streams that might drag us away. Thankfully, that never happened because, in the end, it was just a story someone had made up. The worst that ever happened to me was that once, I fell off my air mattress and found myself panicking to get back on while stirring up the silt. I got back onto my mattress, but I had silt stuck on me, every place it could stick.

Late in that summer when I was twelve, I wanted to go to California to visit my friend Lois and her family. Dad let me go all by myself. He bought me a bus ticket for $50, and I left with $50 of my babysitting money in my pocket. The bus ride was two full days and one night of travelling. I took some magazines, a deck of cards, and a travel pillow with me on the bus. Lois and her family met me in the Los Angeles depot. I spent some time with them, visiting Disneyland and other local places that were really exciting for me. They were very involved in their church so there were lots of activities associated with the church youth groups. I was welcomed to their parties and I had a lot of fun. One of Lois's brothers played baseball, so we'd also go to the baseball games and hang out with other kids.

I spent a couple of weeks in California, and then felt that I needed to go home. I got Lois's mom to call my dad and I told him I was coming home. I thought that he had said that if I took the bus there, then I could fly home; but I found out that the bus ticket was round-trip, so Lois's parents drove me back to the bus depot a few days later. The bus stopped at various towns along the route, and we were told how much time we had to get something to eat or freshen up before the bus would leave again. Many times I wouldn't get off the bus because I was afraid that the bus would leave without me, or that I wouldn't remember what bus I was on. I had a map to follow the route we were taking, but I was in a foreign country and knew no one. If I did get off the bus, I always wrote the bus number down to be sure I got back on the right one. Amazingly enough, I made it home. Dad reminded me that he had sent me to California for the summer, but I missed him so much, I had to come home after two weeks.

During the summer of grade seven, a bunch of kids were playing around in the school field behind our elementary school. We were just goofing around, throwing water balloons at each other. I spotted a guy, Greg, standing off the edge of the field. He was tall and handsome and had a really nice green bike. I was interested in him and he in me. We started hanging out together in our group of friends. One day, one of the parents took all of us in their station wagon to go bowling. As we were piling into the seats, somehow everyone got seats except me. The only place I could sit was on Greg's knee! How was that for being subtle? Greg and I were boyfriend and girlfriend for awhile then broke up, as kids do. I had a few boyfriends during high school but later met up with Greg again.

When I was fifteen, I went to live with my mom. She lived in Victoria, and I'd never lived in a city before. But I loved the city, and the freedom to ride the bus downtown, and meeting new people. I got a job in a department store as an ice cream girl. Things didn't work out for me, living with my mom, and by the end of the summer I'd made a decision to move back to my dad's home. I went back to school for grade eleven but wasn't able to keep myself on track in high school.

By this time, my sister Bonnie had met her husband, Dave, and they were living in Nanaimo. I thought Bonnie and Dave were pretty cool. When they came to dad's for a visit, I'd come running from wherever I was playing, when I heard their motorcycle, or saw their car pull into our driveway. Dave worked as a millwright in BC and that took them all over the province. It was always a treat to have them visit us, and even better if they would stay for a little while. Bonnie and I used to write letters to each other to keep up with the news. I remember the letter I got when I was around fourteen years old, telling me that Bonnie was pregnant! I was so excited! We didn't have any babies in our family and this was such great news. They lived on Vancouver Island at the time, so I didn't get to see them as often as I wanted but eventually they came to visit, and brought baby Jenny. A couple of years later they had a son, Jeremy. I was old enough at the time to go to the island, and was allowed to take care of Jenny while Bonnie was in the hospital and Dave was at work. I had fun that week. Jenny and I got to play games and watch TV all day.

My brother Jim had been dating Margaret for a few years, and they announced that they were getting married. I was a bridesmaid for Jim and Margaret's wedding. They were a great couple just being right for each other. Jim had been hired by Corrections Services, completed his training, and started his new job. Both of them were very stable making plans for a long future together. They were very involved with both families vowing to take care of their aging parents and grandparents.

When I was fifteen years old, I was going to high school in grade ten, and got two jobs: at the local cinema at nights, and in the shopping mall at the Orange Julius stand on weekends. I wasn't paying attention to school and wasn't doing well at all, so I quit in grade eleven. Dad told me to go back to school or get a job. I left home at sixteen, got a job, and moved into a one-bedroom apartment by myself in Mission, a town about fifteen minutes away from Abbotsford. I worked as a waitress in a burger bar and a couple of other small jobs to pay the rent, and pay for my car. My apartment was really nice. I didn't have much furniture, but I did have my freedom. I worked for six months at that job, until I was laid off. I managed to get another job, also as a waitress, and moved to an apartment closer to my new job in Abbotsford.

I did a better job of settling into my second apartment in Abbotsford. I had more furniture and I bought a pet budgie. One day when I came home from work, there was a pure black cat sitting at the front of my apartment building. The next day, I saw the manager chasing the cat out of the garbage bins. I asked whose cat it was, and he said someone had moved out and abandoned it. I thought that wasn't right, and adopted it. I named my new cat Kizzy, after a character in the 1977 TV mini-series "Roots" that I had been watching.

One day, while working at the restaurant, I had a visit from Greg. He had run into one of our friends and asked where I was working. We started dating again and then he moved in with me, in my apartment. I knew his family well, since we had dated in high school. It was a nice reunion for all of us and it felt familiar and comfortable. Greg's parents and large family were a close group. His mother, Julie, was a stay-at-home mom who baked, cooked, and gardened. His father, John, worked as a mechanic and came home to hot, home-cooked meals. Greg's family liked me and made me feel welcome. I went over to their house all the time. Julie taught me to embroider and sew, and I learned to cook, bake, and all about gardening. Maybe this was the family I was looking for. Greg and I were married in 1979, when I was nineteen.

Our early married years were good. I worked at the local pharmacy, running the post office, and Greg worked at various construction jobs. We lived in a rented house with a big garden. I learned how to garden from my mother-in-law. The house we rented was owned by a Hungarian man who had designed the yard with lots of fruit trees, nut trees, and a space for a large garden. We took turns having summer potluck parties at our house or his parents' where all the family would get together.

My mother-in-law, Julie, was famous for her fantastic European cooking. She handmade cabbage rolls, perogies, pies, bread, buns, etc. It was common for anyone to arrive at their house, unannounced, for a meal. There was always enough food for everyone. Holiday meals were always at mom and dad's. Some family, usually the women, would gather at mom's a few days before a holiday to make cabbage rolls and bake pies for the dinner. Julie also made chicken soup that was always served with fresh-baked buns. Whenever we did our grocery or other shopping on Friday night or Saturday, the stop before going home was to mom and dad's. Julie would always put coffee on to go with freshly baked cookies or pastries. Their house was the place to meet up with other members of the family.

Whenever company would come visiting from out of the province they would always be welcome at mom and dad's. Cousins, aunts, and uncles would come to spend a few days. Theirs was a large family and tried to stay very close. When Greg and I were first married, his grandma was still alive. She had come to Canada from Hungary, and never learned to speak English. She was the reason that so many of the family would come to BC to visit. She was a small woman who always dressed like she was still in Hungary, wearing a knee-length flowered smock dress with big pockets in the front. I got to meet her a few times, and would smile as she chattered in Hungarian. She always had cookies at her house for visitors, too.

My mom had remarried by this time. She and her new husband, George, moved from Vancouver Island back to Abbotsford. Mom continued to work at her government job. George was a retired RCMP officer and had also served in the Navy during the second World War.

George was a very tall and big man, whose size hid a heart of gold. I learned that, before he met mom, he would save his pennies all year long and bundle them up in little pouches. He'd visit the Children's Hospital dressed as Santa, to deliver these gifts to the kids. He really looked like Santa. He had children from a previous marriage, but was estranged from them. We were his family, and he became very close to Jim and Margaret, and to me.

If I had a day off from work, George would come over to my house for coffee. We'd talk for hours. We'd drink a pot of coffee and smoke cigarettes. George smoked a lot, I smoked a bit. He said with all the times he was near death, or should've died, surely smoking wouldn't kill him. He was a funny guy too. Whenever we'd have people over, young or older, George would be there. He'd join in, tell jokes, and even smoke pot if someone lit up a joint. At that time, in the 80s, it was only young people who smoked pot, the adults were usually very much against it, but George would surprise us and join in. He liked to drink a lot and could certainly hold his own, being a retired Navy guy.

During the early 80s we went through an economic recession. It was hard on many of us. My job didn't pay much but it was steady. Even though I'd quit school in grade 11, I was always taking night classes to learn more. I couldn't even think of trying for another job with only having a grade ten education so I wrote my GED (grade twelve equivalency). I bought the textbook and studied for it on my own. I went to the local college on a rainy Saturday and wrote the test. I waited a few weeks for the result to come in the mail, and I passed! I got my high school graduation equivalent!

Choosing to Smile

There weren't many jobs available then, and it was too risky to try to make a change, so I stayed at the pharmacy for eight years. Greg was having a harder time with employment. He had graduated from high school, but the employment situation was even worse for young men. The pay was minimal and the jobs didn't last long. We talked about whether he should consider going back to school to learn a trade. It was a real risk, since he would not be able to work, and would have to go into Vancouver on the bus every day for classes. I figured after he was done with his education, I'd get to go back to school, too.

We tightened our budget, and I kept working full time while Greg finished his courses. We were lucky, and he got a great job at BC Hydro as soon as he graduated. We were adjusted to living on my wages while Greg was going to school, and with this new job, he was making great money. We kept to our minimal lifestyle, and saved our money. We started making plans for our future, and talked about the possibility of starting a family and buying a house. But the great job didn't last long, and that division of BC Hydro was shut down. Greg found another job closer to home, and we limped along.

My brother Jim worked at the local prison as a guard, and his wife Margaret was a hairdresser. By this time there were more sections in the prison. The women's unit was gone and it was now a men's prison. Jim also had a keen interest in guns and was trained as a sharpshooter. Since our mom and grandmother worked at the prison, too, they always worried if Jim was called out for an emergency situation at the prison because they knew what could happen. It was dangerous and he was always on alert.

One day at work, Jim was escorting an inmate to the local hospital. It was normal procedure to take prisoners to the hospital if they claimed they were sick enough. When they arrived at the hospital, the inmate jumped up, surprised Jim, and grabbed him, demanding that he surrender his gun. Jim was not armed, so the inmate made a run for it. He escaped from the hospital, and ran into a residential neighborhood. Jim quickly alerted the prison and the local police. Some military personnel also aided in the search. It didn't take too long before they found the inmate, and returned him to the prison. I was at work that day while all this was going on near my house! Our family got the news at the end of the day only when it was all resolved.

Jim told us his story and we read about it in the local newspaper. Jim didn't let on, but it really bothered him. The inmate he was responsible for took him by surprise and escaped. Jim was not at fault, and no one ever said that he was, but he felt that it shouldn't have happened. He started to question whether this was really what he wanted to do as a career. He was a planner and had always thought things through. He and Margaret had saved their money and had just bought their first house. They didn't spend a lot of money, entertained at home, and didn't take any trips. The job at the prison was a good paying job, and also had benefits, so for his practical side, it was the place to stay. But he was still questioning his choice of career.

He talked about the possibility of quitting his job and starting a landscaping company. This would be a big change and certainly a less-stable career. Then Jim got a cold that he couldn't shake. He had it for a few weeks and his cough kept getting worse. Margaret finally got him to go to their doctor. When he saw the doctor he was told that he had the flu and to take a week off from work. He stayed home for a week and after that week he went back to work, still not any better. His cough worsened. Jim was so sick that he collapsed and was rushed to the hospital.

I got the terrible phone call on Sunday June 28, 1981. My grandma told me that my brother was ill, and that he had cancer. I didn't know anything about cancer except that there was a young man with one leg, Terry Fox, who was running across Canada to raise awareness about cancer, and *he* had cancer. My grandma said, "Didn't you hear the news today? Terry Fox died this morning."

Choosing to Smile

Michelle's brother Jim.

Michelle's brother Jim.

Jim was a very sick man. He had stage 3a Hodgkin's lymphoma. The doctors told him that the chances of survival with Hodgkin's was 85%. They started him on chemotherapy right away. Jim got sick from the chemo, and was not improving. When the doctors told him there wasn't anything more they could do for him, he went to each relative's home to tell them. It was about the worst conversation anyone could ever have. He said that he had about two months to live. We were shocked and devastated! I said, "What about the 85% survival chances?" and he answered, "Someone has to be in the 15% that doesn't make it."

The next couple of months were awful. Jim got worse but would not stay in the hospital. He would only go there until he was stable enough to go home. He would take oxygen, but no IV fluids, as that would prolong his suffering. Mom, Kay, and Bonnie were with him as much as they could be, and Margaret stayed by his side. My dad wouldn't believe that his son was dying. He kept an optimistic attitude and thought Jim would make it. Dad offered to take him to Mexico for treatment, but Jim said no. I wouldn't believe Jim was dying either. In February that year Jim turned twenty-nine years old. He died on May 5, on Bonnie's birthday.

I was working at the pharmacy and dad came into the store to get me. Dad had a hard time choking back the tears. He took me in his truck and drove as fast as he could to Jim's house. Jim had just passed away. We couldn't do any more at Jim's house, so we went to Bonnie's house to give her the news. It was devastating for everyone. Bonnie was at home alone when we got there. It was the worst news we could have delivered. Jim had planned for his death and he didn't want any funeral service or obituary in the newspaper, I don't know why. There was a quiet and small family gathering after Jim's death and that was all. Jim always loved working at his father-in-law's farm, so Margaret spread Jim's ashes in the orchard, by herself. I talked to George when Jim died and about going to the gathering. He said he wasn't going. I was shocked, since they were very close. I assumed when you were close with someone that you paid your final respects by attending the funeral or gathering. George said he and Jim talked about death and they made a pact. No matter whoever died first, the other person did not have to go to the funeral. That was their deal, and they had already said their goodbyes.

The summer passed and I think everyone was just numb. One day, George and I had one of our long coffee visits at my house. When he was leaving, he stood up and gave me an especially big hug. His hugs were like bear hugs but this one was extra special. He said "goodbye," not our usual "see you later."

I told him I'd see him soon and he said that no one would miss him. I told him not to say that, I didn't understand why he would say that. I said I wouldn't know what to do without him. He replied that I'd be fine without him. I told him that I expected him to see my children and be their grandpa, but he said he'd had enough of kids and then he went home. I didn't know what that was all about.

On September 2, my mom called me at 6 am to come to her house. I asked if everyone was okay and she said no, George had died. I went to their apartment and Kay was there with mom. My gentle giant, George, was laying silent, dead in his bed. Mom said I could go in the room to see him. I went into their bedroom to see him, but what I saw wasn't the George I knew. I didn't want to remember him that way. His life was gone and his soul had left his body. George died of a broken heart. He always said after all he went through, the War, dangerous situations in the RCMP, his own illness, smoking, drinking, and just plain being old, that it wasn't fair that Jim died first. George was cremated and there was no service or obituary.

Time passed as it will, and we got on with our work and daily lives. One day when I was at work at the pharmacy, one of the older customers who knew my family asked how Kay was. I started to say she was okay, just trying to cope with things. And he said, "No, I mean that I just saw her being taken out of her apartment on a stretcher, and put into an ambulance!"

Kay had always been very close to Jim. Jim was her favorite grandchild. She couldn't cope with losing him, and had taken an overdose of pills. At that time she was living with her mom, Grandma Tubbs, and she waited till grandma had gone out for the day. But grandma had forgotten something and came back to find Kay unconscious. She called the ambulance, and Kay was saved. She had a long recovery but was okay.

We all carried on with our lives. Greg and I had been married for four years, he had his trade, and was still working. We figured it was time to start a family. We had been saving money and an opportunity came up to purchase our first house. We did that quickly, since I wasn't pregnant at that time. As luck will have it, as soon as we signed the papers for our first house, we found out that I was pregnant! It was the summer of 1983, and we moved into our new house in the fall. I loved being pregnant. I was never sick and was growing a small baby bump. Margaret had a new friend, Bob, and we all hung out together with other couples. The guys would go out to play floor hockey, and we girls would watch nighttime soap operas. We were awaiting our new baby, the newest little one in the family.

On March 12, 1984, I went into labor and gave birth to a beautiful baby girl, Melissa Mae. I always loved being a mom, holding Melissa, feeding her, but I could've used a bit more sleep. She was a colicky baby and was up many times a night for the first year. Her grandma Julie was super with babies and tried to help me with her. She would pat her, try to burp her, and rock her to sleep. I don't think she ever had a grandchild with colic so severe, and she was a little stumped.

I wanted to stay home with Melissa but we got the unwelcome news that once again Greg had received another layoff notice. I had to go back to work because we needed the income and he stayed home with Melissa for a few months. I wanted to be a stay-at-home mom, and it was very hard for me to be back at work. Time at work dragged and there was never enough time with my daughter when I got home. I'd make supper and hold Melissa while she went to sleep. Julie would tell me to put her to bed, and I said that I didn't have enough chance to see her all day, so I just wanted to hold her.

At last, Greg got another job and it was time to have a second baby. I wanted to leave work for good so I could stay at home with the children. Our second child, Megan Beverly, was born on November 4, 1986.

By that time, Melissa was almost three years old, and was running around keeping us amused. She was thrilled to have a new baby sister. Megan was such a differently tempered baby than Melissa had been. The day I brought her home from the hospital, she slept a few hours! I was checking on her constantly to make sure she was okay.

She was a great sleeper and had no signs of colic. We had outgrown our little two-bedroom house and it was time to look for a larger home. We were enjoying the help of grandma and grandpa, and soon they would need help as they were getting older. So we bought a house with a suite for them and we all moved in together.

Our new home had a big garden, a playhouse, and a swimming pool! We had lots of family get-togethers that summer with Julie's famous food, fun in the pool, and lots of space for everyone. Greg's job took him out of town and he had a rented house there. We bought second-hand baby furniture for that house, and split our time between both places during the summer. John and Julie would drive the girls and me to the ferry and I'd walk on with them, with our belongings in a backpack. Greg would meet us at the ferry and take us to his rented house. The girls and I would spend a week or more so that we could be with Greg when he finished work at the end of the day. Those visits broke up his time away from the family. We managed to make those trips during the summer, but by fall, it was getting too difficult for me to keep up the pace of packing up and travelling.

That fall, Greg received another layoff notice, even though the job paid well and was supposed to have lasted a number of years. It was another devastating blow. I thought that with what we'd been through already, we could handle it, but Greg was very depressed and having a lot of trouble coping with this situation. He still lived away from us for a few more months, until I reassured him that we had managed in the past, and we would figure something out again. I tried to encourage him, and helped him with his job search. Christmas was coming, and we had no income. I got a part-time job in the evenings to help out, but it wasn't much. I was home with the children during the day and would go to work at night, when Greg was home. At Christmas time I tried to keep our spirits up, but I was fighting a dismal mood that year. I was so stressed, not knowing how we would manage, and Greg was getting more and more depressed, and difficult to deal with. I wasn't sleeping well, but trying my best to hold things together. We were not doing well as a couple, either.

I was busy during the day with two small children. I tried to help Greg while continuing to run our home the best I could. We were having problems with our relationship. The stress was always there, and I wasn't coping well, but tried not to show it. I was not eating right and losing weight. Melissa's fourth birthday was coming up, and I invited our friends with all their little kids to our home for a birthday party. We put together a great party on a tight budget. The children played games in the yard and made fun crafts. They made necklaces with Cheerios strung on licorice strings and ran mini relay races for prizes of small toys. I remember the ladies commenting on how thin I was getting, and how did I do it, as most women are looking for a way to stay trim. I said I was sure it was a stress diet, and not a good way to lose weight. I was thinner but I was also starting to look sick.

Then I started to itch. I was scratching all over my upper body. I was so itchy it was driving me crazy! I had never experienced anything like this before, so I was sure it was from the stress. On my evening shift at work I remember I would go into the bathroom to scratch as it was embarrassing to be seen constantly scratching. As I was scratching my neck, I felt a lump on the left side just above my collarbone. I'd never felt that before. When I got home that night I told Greg about the lump I'd found. I was concerned about it and said I'd keep an eye on it for a couple days. He told my mom, and she immediately began to worry. We tried to believe that it was an infected gland and that my body was trying to fight off some kind of infection. I was really scared and worried.

About a week passed, and I went to my regular doctor's office, but he was away. There was a young replacement doctor filling in for him. I told her about the suspicious lump and she examined me.

I think she was surprised when she felt the lump and didn't know what to make of it, but was concerned. She left the room and then came back and told me to lie down again. She then continued the examination by checking other areas. She thought I should see a surgeon immediately and asked me to wait while she made a phone call. She got me an appointment so see a surgeon just a couple of days later.

When I met the surgeon he didn't show much concern when he first talked to me. After a brief chat he asked me to get on the examining table and said, "Let's have a look at this lump," with a smile on his face.

I was really freaked out and told the surgeon that my brother died of Hodgkin's lymphoma at twenty-nine. He still didn't appear concerned until he started his examination. As he was feeling my neck, I was looking into his face and his expression changed to a serious look. He left me sitting on the examining table and told me he needed to schedule an immediate biopsy. Then I was really scared. I'd never had any procedures in a hospital except when I gave birth to the girls.

He admitted me to the hospital for surgery two days later. By this time the whole family was scared, but also not wanting to think that anything worse could happen. I checked into the day-surgery floor at the hospital. The nurses were treating me as a day-patient and didn't seem too concerned. When the nurse came with an IV, she attempted to insert the needle into a vein in my hand. She was having a difficult time but kept trying. She obviously wasn't finding the vein, and it hurt! She tried again, but then was distracted by a phone call. She left me sitting there, not knowing what she would try on me next. She told me that she would leave the IV for the doctor in the operating room to insert. That was a relief. I didn't want her to touch me again. The nurse closed the curtain and I waited. I was terrified! I couldn't hold back the tears.

I was alone and scared about the procedure, and what the outcome might be. When it was my turn, the nurse wheeled me down the hall on the bed. I was sobbing by that time, and felt completely alone. The anesthesiologist expertly put the IV into my arm in two seconds, and I didn't feel any pain. A few moments later, I was out. The incision for the biopsy on my neck was about a three inches long. When I woke up in recovery, I was lying on the stretcher and could hear the doctor asking the nurse about me. He was told I wasn't awake yet so he left. I wanted him to talk to me about the surgery, but couldn't move and felt as though I was pinned down by the pain from the incision in my neck.

When I was sent home, I was told my family doctor would get in touch with me about the biopsy results. I went home scared to death. My family came to see me and no one knew what to say. My dad came over to our house to see how I was doing. He tried to pull me to sit on his lap like he did when I was a little girl. I sat with him for a few minutes, but was in too much pain from the incision they had made on my neck. It was very difficult to sit, stand, or lay down because the slightest movement of my neck was so painful. When I needed to lay down, Greg would support my back and lower me down. Even with support, that motion was excruciatingly painful. I just cried and cried until there were no more tears left.

I waited all the next day with no phone call from the doctor's office. At the end of the day I called the doctor's office for some information. I was told it was too soon and they didn't have any word yet, but they told me I could call back the next day. I called the following day, Friday, and the receptionist said she couldn't tell me anything but told me that the doctor was in the office. I told Greg I wanted him to take me to the doctor's office and I was going to find out what the results were.

We loaded the girls into the car and went to our doctor's office. Greg and the girls waited in the car while I went inside. I told the receptionist that I was there to see my doctor. When the doctor came into the room, he sat in his chair and looked at my chart. He said, "I see you've had a biopsy on a lump in your neck."

I said that's why I came in, to see if he had the results yet. He flipped through my chart some more, and then he said "There are good lumps and bad lumps, and you had a bad lump. You've got Hodgkin's lymphoma."

Just like that. No emotion. This was my own doctor, a doctor I'd been seeing for many years. He delivered both my babies, and he had been my brother's attending doctor when he died. I was stunned with disbelief! Then he said "If you're going to get cancer, Hodgkin's is a good type to get. It has a high cure rate."

I started to cry and just sat there in his office. He and I *both* knew that Jim had been in his care, and he had signed Jim's death certificate. My heart was begging for a bit more empathy or at least a suggestion that he could bring my husband into the office, so I wouldn't have to be dealt that blow alone.

I continued to cry. I couldn't believe that this doctor didn't have anything else to say to me, except that my results were being sent to the cancer clinic, and they would get in touch with me about what would happen next. He didn't ask where Greg was, or if I was alone. That was the end of the appointment. I took some Kleenex from his office and walked straight out to the car.

How long would I have to wait to find out my fate? Greg knew something was terribly wrong but I controlled my crying and said only that we need to go home. I didn't want to upset the girls, my two precious little angels.

We went home, and Greg started to call my family to tell them the news. His mom and dad came upstairs, and were just as shocked to hear the news as I had been. We were all trying to hold it together not to scare the girls. It was pretty hard since we were all thinking

Megan and Melissa.

about my brother, and that I had just been given my death sentence. I wanted to scream. This couldn't be happening!

Greg called our friend, Larry, who was at home taking care of his two little sons while his wife was at work. Greg told Larry I had just been diagnosed with cancer, and asked if he could take care of our girls for a little while. Larry's wife had the car at work so he bundled up his boys, called a cab and came over right away. He took our girls and his boys to his home in our car for the afternoon to play, no questions asked.

Both our families came over right away, and we all just cried. We didn't know anything else except that I had Hodgkin's disease. People tried to hug me, but it hurt too much from the incision on my neck. I was so frightened and distraught. Greg couldn't even speak; he had been wrapped up in his own misery, and now we were now facing a life-and-death situation. When my dad arrived, I could see the fear in his eyes. He came to me and I grabbed his shirt collar and squeezed. He tried not to cry.

I couldn't die. I was a mother to the two most precious little girls. They needed their mother for a very long time. I was only twenty-eight years old, but that was the exact age my brother Jim had been when he was diagnosed, and he died eleven months after his diagnosis. With that realization I wondered, "How long did I have to live?" I knew we were all asking the same question. Was it my turn now?

Nobody knew what to say. What could they say? I felt that their hugs that day were ones of good-bye. My thoughts turned to how long I had left, and what could I do with the time. I wanted the girls home so I could hold them. I dried my tears and asked if Larry would please bring my girls home. I hugged them and snuggled them all I could. I held them when they slept and watched their every move. I loved to watch their pure, innocent little faces and their carefree play. They would be fine without their mother, but my heart ached as I considered that horrible possibility. I tried to think of what I could have done wrong to be in this position, fearing my own death. What could I do to fix whatever I'd done wrong? I wanted to bargain with someone, something, I didn't know what or how. I would do anything for this not to happen to me and my family.

My diagnosis was in the spring, almost Easter time, and I had just bought both girls matching pink dresses with white trim, to wear for family dinners and Sunday school. I was having a hard time sleeping because I was still in a lot of pain, and I was worried about the future of my family. One night that weekend, when I finally got to sleep, I dreamed that I saw Greg and our girls on a boat heading out to the open ocean. The girls appeared to be the same age they were now, and were wearing the pink dresses I'd just bought them for Easter. They weren't smiling or happy. I didn't know what they were doing and where was I? The boat drove along for awhile until it was in open sea and the water was relatively calm, when the captain slowed down and turned the engine off. It was a nice sunny day and the water was calm.

Once the boat came to a stop, Greg talked gently to the girls. He took out a container, and he crouched down beside the two bewildered little children. He hugged them both, then opened the container. He gave each girl a scoop of ashes and let them scatter it into the sea and wind. Those were my ashes. I was gone and they were saying their final good-byes by spreading my remains in the sea where I would find peace.

I woke up in a sweat and scared! This was too much! No more! I couldn't die! I was too young and had a family to raise. I wasn't going to accept this. Why was I waiting in fear, waiting for the doctors to tell me how long I had to live, and how and when I was going to die? How could I turn this around from being my plight to my survival? I felt so alone and only knew this cancer diagnosis as a death sentence. My parents, grandparents, aunts, uncles, and friends were all there when Jim died and I'm sure were expecting the same from me. If anyone said, "You'll be okay," I knew they didn't truly believe it.

How could I change this, turn it around? Somewhere deep inside my soul, there was a fighter and I wanted to use whatever strength I had to be there for my girls, and to live until I died of old age. I didn't want my brother's death from this terrible disease to be in vain. Jim's death was a message and had to be the reason I was going to live. No one would have paid attention to my condition if this hadn't happened to my brother, so now I saw him leading me into the fight. This wasn't going to happen to two of us in the same family!

About a year earlier, Greg and I had taken the girls to our family church to have them baptized. During that time in our lives, I wanted the girls to know the church and Sunday school as I had known it growing up. Greg and I attended a few parenting classes led by the pastor, so I knew him, and he knew who I was. Usually I'd go to the church service and the girls would run off with the other children when it was time for Sunday school. They loved their teachers and were having lots of fun with the other kids.

Mom and I hadn't been to church together since I was a child and she wanted to go with me that Sunday. The girls went off to Sunday school, and mom and I sat in the pews and looked at the program for the morning service. It was springtime during the Canadian Cancer Society's awareness campaign. On the program cover there was a picture of a daffodil, the cancer society's symbol. Seeing the picture and reading the words made me cry as the words described taking this time to remember the loved ones whom we'd lost to cancer.

The church service began and the pastor started the program describing the morning events. That morning was the monthly communion. I knew my mom was trying to be strong for me and said this was an important thing for us to do. Of course that made us both cry as she was thinking she was losing another child and I cried because I wasn't ready to die. The small stream of tears was getting hard to conceal and I couldn't contain them any longer.

We got through the communion service and went downstairs in the church where everyone went to have coffee together. Mom and I waited in the hall until the pastor came walking along. Mom stopped him, quickly introduced herself, and said "Michelle has cancer." He took one look at my face and knew that's what had been going on as we sat quietly crying during his service. He hugged me tight, with true empathy and compassion. He took me into his office to talk, although he didn't have many words to say. He did, however, give me a book that I took with me when I left his office, and went to pick up the girls from their Sunday school class.

I took the book home and read it immediately. It was *Getting Well Again,* by Dr. Carl O. Simonton. I didn't often read, other than reading children's stories to the girls, but this one was of much interest and fascination to me. It was about the power of positive thinking and how cancer patients must find inner strength to survive cancer. It was about visualizing the disease and sending in the "troops" of cleaners to rid the body of the disease. Here I was, waiting for the doctors to tell me how long I had to live. Now I learned about how I could empower myself and be a participant in my illness rather than a victim. I'd never read nor heard about his method and theory.

I read with fascination that it wasn't just up to the doctors to determine how we will live and die. They have medical guidelines and protocols that they are bound to give, but most doctors don't have the time to give patients the tools that will aid them in their own survival. We have strength and resources that, together with the right determination, can help greatly with our survival and recovery. I'd never heard of any of this before. It made sense to me while reading Dr. Simonton's theories and the stories he presented. I knew these theories were also a bit unusual, and that perhaps I'd better keep this to myself. I was already alone with my disease and didn't need people to think I was turning weird, too.

I waited for the call from the cancer clinic to tell me what they thought I should do next. In the meantime, I had more blood work and x-rays done. The call came and we were asked to go to the cancer clinic in Vancouver (a one hour drive from our home) for my first appointment. We picked up my x-rays and some lab reports. I was frightened and I'm sure Greg was too. The problems we were already having had just been compounded. I looked in the envelope of reports and lab results to see if there was anything I could understand that would give me some insight into my diagnosis. None of it made any sense to me. We had a quiet drive into Vancouver, neither of us knowing what to say. We parked the car and walked to the front door of the cancer clinic.

When we got to the door of the clinic, I stopped outside on the grounds. It was a very nice-looking building and people were bustling around, all having somewhere to go and something to do. My life was changing quickly, and I was scared shitless to go into the building.

How much more would my life change once I went to this appointment? Then I realized that I had a choice, to go in, or to walk away. What would happen if I turned and walked away? It was my choice. If I walked away and left, I knew that I would probably die, and that was not something I wanted to do. So my choice was to enter the cancer centre in hopes of a cure and a long life. I wanted to be there for my girls; to see them grow up and to help them with their journeys into womanhood. I wanted to die of old age, not cancer.

Greg and I went into the cancer clinic for the first time. The people seemed friendly and willing to help. We asked for directions to my first appointment. We took the elevator and stepped out when the doors opened. We looked in both directions and started to walk down the hall. It was very quiet and dimly lit. We saw a nurse pushing a wheelchair with a person in it who was hooked up to an IV, bald, and looking very sick. I didn't want to be rude but I was really scared. We soon realized we were on the wrong floor but that image was in my head. I didn't want that to be me. Quickly we got back in the elevator and found the floor we were supposed to be on.

We checked in and waited to see the first doctor. The nurse made all kinds of tests and asked me many questions before the doctor came in. When I met with the doctor, he looked through the reports, and said he needed more tests done before he could say how far my cancer had progressed, and what he could do to treat me. We went home and made arrangements for a friend to take care of the girls for three days the following week while I would have more tests done.

The following Wednesday, we bundled up the girls early in the morning and dropped them off at our friend's house. We went to the cancer clinic and checked in to day-surgery where I was to have a bone marrow biopsy done. I got undressed and put a hospital gown on. I was given a shot of Demerol to help me relax, but it wouldn't help with the pain of the procedure. The test doesn't take that long, but the unknown makes situations feel like they go on forever. I was prepped for the procedure and the doctor came in to aspirate bone marrow from my hip.

I was situated on the hospital bed in the fetal position and all the work was going on behind me. The doctor froze the surface of my skin, but bone can't be frozen, so they prepared me to feel the sensation as they drilled into my hip bone. I braced for the pain by thinking of the pain of childbirth. I went through that twice and I would do that again to have another child. I made it through the bone marrow biopsy. They bandaged me up and sent us home. I was instructed to keep the area dry, and was told that I would probably feel as though I'd been kicked by a horse. Well, I was surely looking forward to that! As we started to drive out of the city I started to feel like I needed to throw up. I don't know if that was because of the procedure, the Demerol, or the stress of the test, but I just wanted to go home.

The next day, it was the same thing; up early, bundle up the girls, and drive to our friend's house to drop them off. We drove to the cancer clinic and I was back in the day-surgery area and prepped for a lymphangiogram. My feet were shaved and cleaned and I was given a shot of lidocaine on the top of each foot to freeze the skin. I was really uncomfortable as my feet were strapped into a freaky looking frame, and other instruments were wheeled in for this procedure. When the lidocaine was injected into the top of my foot, the skin on my foot puffed up into a big bubble. I didn't want to look but Greg was fascinated to see what they were doing.

Next, the doctor injected a blue contrast dye between the toes on each foot. She then made an incision on the top of my foot to access to the lymph vessel. She located the lymph vessel and inserted a catheter into it to inject a liquid to send the dye up my legs to my abdomen. I had to remain completely still during this time and wait for the technician to bring in a portable scan. They watched the dye to see that it was travelling and flowing properly. Once that was done, the catheters were removed and the incisions were taped up. They sent me home and told me to limit any walking or standing, and to keep the bandages dry.

Away we went, home and picked up the girls. My feet were taped up, but you could still see the bright blue dye that seemed to be splashed on my toes. When we were home, we went downstairs to grandma's place so the girls could play, and I could sit and have a cup of tea. I sat on the couch and put my feet on a pillow on the coffee table. Little Megan (around two years old) saw my "dirty" looking feet. She was playing around me, and found grandma's dusting cloth. I guess she figured she'd better clean me up and came over to start to wipe my dirty feet off. I kind of gasped and calmly asked grandma to come over and help Megan put the dusting cloth away, without "cleaning me."

So, that day I had the bandage on my hip, and the tops of both feet were taped up. I wanted to have a bath to relax so we taped a plastic cover on my hip over the incision from the bone marrow biopsy and I managed to lay in a nice warm bath with my feet up on the edge of the tub to keep them dry. It was fairly awkward, but I wanted to try to relax a little bit.

The third day we were up early to go back to Vancouver again to meet with the doctors to see what was scheduled to happen next. During this visit, we were told that they still didn't have enough information to determine the stage of the disease. The next step was for me to have more surgery. I was told I would have a staging laparotomy and a splenectomy. As I sat in the doctor's office listening to the information about this surgery, they said I'd be in the hospital in Vancouver for at least seven days. Since it was major abdominal surgery, I wouldn't be able to lift anything heavy for at least six weeks! I think that shocked me the most, besides being freaked about the surgery. Megan was a baby and needed to be put in and out of her crib. How was I going to manage that? I told the doctors about my concerns but they regarded my comments as the last thing I should worry about.

We went home and let our families know what was going to happen next. We still didn't know how involved the cancer was or what type of treatment I'd need. I prepared to go to Vancouver General Hospital for surgery. Vancouver General is a teaching hospital so I felt very well looked after. I had more than one doctor look at me and answer my questions. There seemed to be even more staff in training willing to help out.

The laparotomy meant an incision twelve inches long, vertically down the centre of my body. During the surgery, the doctors would remove my spleen and take biopsies of other organs leaving internal staples. I was cleaned and prepped in all ways for the surgery. When they took me on the gurney to the surgical waiting area, the nurse put warm blankets on me that at least made me feel a bit comfortable. I'm sure I had been given drugs to make me drowsy as well.

I woke up from the surgery very incoherent and hallucinating. The first thing I remembered, I was in my hospital room and felt the staff transferring me into my bed. I thought the staff was taking me from the gurney that was very high, almost up to the ceiling and dropping me 6 feet to my bed! I think I was screaming or moaning loudly and trying to stop them from dropping me. In reality they were moving me from one gurney to the bed that was level with it. But in my confused state, and with the pain from my new incision I dreamed I was being dropped. I don't know how long I was unconscious, once they got me into bed. With this severe incision I was unable to move on my own. I was placed on my side and could only move when the nurses turned me over to my other side.

The next time I woke up, still very groggy, I saw my mom sitting in a chair beside my bed. I found out later that she had been at my bedside and only left when she saw that I was okay. She said I was hollering when they brought me in. I can't imagine the fear and heartache that must have caused her to hear her child in that state.

I was heavily bandaged and unable to move. The incision was deep through the centre of me, so it was too painful to move. I was on an IV and was given pain medication regularly. I was shocked that the nurses got me up to walk very soon after the surgery. I was given a shot of Demerol and I had a pillow to hold to my stomach to support myself. I'd take short walks with the nurses and student nurses. I couldn't get up by myself.

One day, dad came to visit. I was dozing on the bed, and when I woke up to see him I could tell he was really uncomfortable. He doesn't like hospitals, and this visit would've been extremely difficult for him. He's not good at sitting, but rather needs to be doing something, so I said I needed to get up, and couldn't do it by myself. He and I struggled every which way until I was finally able to sit up and get out of the bed. Then I took hold of my IV pole, and went to the bathroom.

Dad looked around the room I shared with three other women. I think I was in the gall bladder ward. He knew one of the other women from Abbotsford, and we all started talking. That helped break the ice for me so I had someone to talk to when I didn't have visitors. This woman was very funny. Once I knew her, she was always able to say something funny and make at least two of us in the room laugh. I don't remember that woman's name, but she used to make me laugh so hard I had to hold the pillow on my stomach and beg for mercy. I said it was not fair, since I had the biggest incision of the bunch of us.

My bed was the one closest to the bathroom in our ward. At night, I'd have the curtain pulled around my bed, but my IV pole was on the washroom side of my "room." One night I woke to hear one of my roommates struggling to get into the washroom. She had to let go of her IV pole to open the door, and when she went to grab it, she grabbed mine by mistake, and was going to take it with her to the bathroom. Unfortunately, it was still connected to me! Luckily I was able to stop her and keep my IV safely in my arm.

Even in the hospital, I was still having problems with my body itching. I told a nurse about it and she told me that it was a symptom of Hodgkin's. I asked if there was anything I could do about it, and she gave me an injection. It worked very quickly and I didn't feel the need to scratch. It took the itching away and left me very stoned. I was so glad about that. That was a much better feeling than the discomfort I'd been having.

By this time it was May and I was in the hospital on Mother's Day. The Sunday before Mother's Day, the girls had secretly made crafts at Sunday school for Mother's Day presents. On that Sunday, the children were to bring their mother to Sunday school for a special tea. Since I was in the hospital, they convinced their dad to come to Sunday school with them, and that he needed to shave his moustache off so he looked more like a mother. He went to the tea and got the gifts that were for me. They came to see me in the hospital and brought the gifts to me.

I was so happy to see them. I'd never been away from the girls for so long before. I was ready for them and was sitting in a chair before they got to my room. They were a little scared to see me in the hospital connected to an IV tube, but quickly gave me hugs and kisses once they realized I was still their mother. They were pretty pleased to tell me that daddy shaved his moustache and put on his good shirt to go to their Sunday school, since I couldn't be there. They gave me a vase with a little flower made out of cloth with a button at the centre, on a pipe cleaner. I was glad to be their mother, and more determined every moment to be with them for a very long time.

Shortly after the operation, my surgeon came to tell me that the operation had gone well, and he didn't see any evidence of cancer, but we had to wait for the results from pathology. After my hospital stay, I needed to go to the cancer clinic to get the results of the surgery and all the tests. For my last day in the hospital I'd asked Greg to bring my good clothes: my white pants and silk blouse with brown and tan stripes. I had lost a lot of weight by this time and there wasn't much that I could wear. I wanted to get myself cleaned up and nice looking, considering my situation. I also asked him to bring me a razor so I could shave my legs. With limited mobility, and almost no bending, even washing my hair had been a real chore. The student nurses had asked if there was anything they could do for me. I told them that I would love to have my hair washed. They set me up with great care in the bathroom, and managed to wash my hair.

So for my last day in the hospital, I got to use the shower myself, but had more tape and plastic added to cover the stomach incision. I could hardly bend. I was so happy to try to get all these things done so I could leave the hospital and feel a bit normal. I started to shave my legs, and saw that there was blood streaming into the drain. I had a new razor and was hacking away as best I could without bending, so I was cutting myself. I quickly gave that up.

Once I was finished, I dressed in my good clothes and waited. Greg and my dad came to get me. The fashion for blouses in those days was to have shoulder pads and I was quite skinny with my hair washed and a bit fluffy. My dad walked in and was happy to see me, but what he said was that I looked like a hockey stick with hair. So much for trying to look good! By the way, I think that is hilarious now. I must have been quite a funny looking sight. I was happy to be going home but anxious about the next doctor's appointment.

We went to the cancer clinic and met with the doctors. The three of us sat together to listen to what the doctors had to say. The results of the tests showed that I was a Stage 3a Hodgkin's Lymphoma patient. The cancer was in my neck (the original lump that had been biopsied), in my spleen (which had been removed), and in the lymph nodes at the top of my lungs. The doctors said I would have to have two sets of twenty radiotherapy (or radiation) treatments. This therapy would mean daily treatments at the cancer clinic. I asked if there was any way they could get rid of the cancer by surgery, to take out the affected lymph nodes, but the answer was no. With this treatment I would lose some of the hair on my head, have some skin burning, lung-function problems, and a dry throat as a result of the upper body treatments; and possibly have bowel and stomach trouble from the lower body treatments; and possibly become sterile.

We didn't have immediate plans to have another baby, but when someone tells you that you can't have more children, then it's a horrible blow. Now I was faced with a fight to survive. I didn't know what would happen next, but was glad at least, to be able to go home and be with the girls. They were very excited to have me home, too.

I was very weak and had a lot of healing to do after such major surgery. We also had to figure out how we would manage to pay to travel to Vancouver every day, and still cover daycare for our daughters. One friend took care of the girls for the first three days of my tests, but that was all she could do. We didn't have anyone else who could take care of the girls. My in-laws lived with us, but by this time John had had a stroke, was confined to a wheelchair, and they already had a homemaker coming in daily to help Julie with his care. We had been helping them out. My mom and sister both worked full time, and so did Greg's sister. Before my diagnosis, my stepmother had also been very sick, and now was dealing with breast cancer that had metastasized to her bones. Greg was out of work and had been taking care of the girls. He had taken me in for testing, but he also had to look for work and find a job.

Greg made an appointment at the social services agency to see how they could help us. They said that if he was not working, then he could take care of the kids. The Unemployment Insurance office said that he had to be actively looking for work, so he couldn't stay home and look after the girls. So where did that leave us? It was additional stress on an already stressful and scary situation. I remembered that when I first went to the cancer clinic, I was introduced to a social worker. I thought maybe she could help. I called her and told her about our situation. She was very kind and understanding.

I didn't hear directly what she had done but soon Greg had another appointment with our local social services agency. This time he had a chance to explain just how dire our situation was, and that we had exhausted all our options. They came through for us. They sent us a homemaker who would help me with housework, and take care of the girls while I was in Vancouver for my treatments. Sometimes the homemaker would prepare a meal for that night's dinner. At first, this was difficult to manage, because they sent a different person every day. While I was getting ready for the trip, Greg had to familiarize the homemaker with our house, the girls, Megan's bottles, where the diapers were, etc. Finally after a few weeks of this, they sent a woman who would stay with us until I finished all my treatments.

There was a lot of preparation to be done at the cancer clinic before the treatments began, and that meant more daily trips to Vancouver. I didn't know when the treatments would begin. I had to have a body cast made to hold me in exactly the correct position for each of the radiation treatments.

I didn't know what to expect of the appointment, only that I would be busy for most of the day. I went to the room and found that the two technicians would be making a plaster cast from the top of my head down past my torso to the top of my legs in two pieces. I let them know that I just had major surgery and was bandaged down my entire front. I didn't know what they would be doing, but I didn't want to risk anything that might give me an infection or put pressure on my incision. They said that most people they dealt with had just had surgery and that they would be careful. I laid down on the cold, hard table.

They put a layer of plastic on my body and started to build a cast from strips of gauze that they ran through loose plaster. I was laying on my back, and they put plastic over my hair, and started to build the cast around my face. I am claustrophobic, so I was quite worried about having them build this thing around my face, but they made sure I had enough space to breathe. They had to work slowly and methodically to build the cast. I just had to lay still.

It seemed like a long time went by, and they finally finished the cast on my front. They gave me a few minutes of break time, and then I had to lay face down in the first cast, while they built the cast of my back, including the back of my head. By now, I was tired, and I was getting very chilled. I thought I had never been so cold in my whole life. As they build the layers of plaster, my body was getting colder and colder. It was bone chilling. I told them I was freezing, but they explained that they had to keep the room at a certain temperature while working with the plaster. There was a fan on to circulate the air for the cast to dry, and that only made the room (and me) colder. The technicians continued to work, talking quietly to each other.

I was very thin and weak from surgery. They didn't even talk to me, and I just laid there, the inanimate surface they were building the cast on. By the time they were finished, I couldn't do enough to try to warm up. I found a couple of baby blankets in the car and wrapped them over my shoulders but still couldn't shake the chill I felt.

Since one of the sites of my cancer was in my neck, the radiation treatment was started at my jaw line, up at an angle through my ears, almost to the top of my head. The radiation would also be directed to include the area of my salivary glands. Without my salivary glands working, I was at high risk for damage to my teeth. They needed a benchmark for my saliva so I went to the cancer centre dental area for saliva tests and also a dental checkup. The saliva test was to chew on a piece of wax for a time, produce as much saliva as I could, and spit it into a tube. This had to be redone a number of times throughout my treatments. Since I wouldn't have much saliva during the treatment period, they gave me silicone trays made in the shape of my upper and lower teeth. I put a fluoride mixture in and held it on my teeth each day to try to protect them.

At another appointment, I was to be measured for the radiation treatments in the simulator. In this session, I was measured carefully, so the doctors could make precise calculations to direct the beams of radiotherapy. I was told that a customized plate would be made to allow the radiation to penetrate only certain areas of my body; other critical areas would be protected, like the top of my spine on my back, and the front of my throat. As I lay in the simulator there were a number of people in the room who were either assisting or learning about this procedure. It was a teaching situation, and I was feeling as if I wasn't even there. They tried to be nice enough, occasionally asking if I was all right, but it didn't change the fact that I was made to feel like a thing—not a person. When all the measurements and calculations were finished, everyone left the room except for one man. He was to tattoo my body with the dots that would be the guides for the radiation beams. I tell people I have tattoos, but they don't spell "Mom!"

Once the initial x-rays, blood work, dental work, body casts, and simulator measurements were completed, I was done for a while. I was sent home to wait for the call to start treatment. I was worried that as time went by, and the call to start my treatment didn't come, that my cancer was continuing to grow.

I kept myself busy with the house and the children, and tried to get some rest. It wasn't easy, because I was always on edge, waiting for that phone call. Again, all control was taken from me. I knew that I was scheduled for forty radiation treatments, and I knew what the possible side effects could be, but I had to wait for that phone call to get started. I tried to keep a positive attitude and practice relaxation and visualization as often as I could. I was trying to strengthen myself before the radiation would try to kill the cancer cells. I knew that the treatments were meant to kill the bad cells, but good cells would also be affected, and that's what could cause severe damage.

Finally, the call came. At the clinic, I checked in. I was directed to a rack of the ugliest-looking flowered sack dresses that I'd ever seen. I had to choose one that would be mine during all my treatments. It would be kept in a bag with my name on it. I went into the change room and took off all my clothes, and put the horrible dress on. Then I went into a waiting room to wait with other women wearing the same awful gowns. There were some male patients too, but they didn't have to wear the stupid, flowered dresses. I was called to the radiation room. The lights in the room were low and the technicians were ready to help me. The pairs of body casts were lined up, waiting for their patients. It was just creepy. My back cast was placed on the table. I was told to take my gown off. Dropping the gown and standing almost naked in that room was just another assault to my dignity. I felt so exposed in the middle of a room full of strangers. Once I climbed into my cast, the technicians worked to get me lined up with the light beams that connected the dots tattooed on my body. The staff were wonderful people but they have a job to do and I'm sure I was just another number.

I was so scared at that first treatment. I had no idea of what to expect. Here I was, lying in a body cast, on a table in the centre of the room, wearing only my underwear. All the people in the room were busy making necessary adjustments for my treatment. Once I was lined up, they all left the room and turned the lights down really low. Now I was really and truly alone. I had heard all kinds of horror stories about radiation treatments, the kind people tend to tell you when they think they are helping. I was scared about these great machines roaring and humming with horrible sounds during the treatments. But I will tell you, that once I was in the right place, in my cast, after the staff left and the machine came on, there was nothing to it.

I think the unknown part had been the worst. The machine came on and it wasn't scary. I didn't know if I'd heat up, or what would happen, but it was no more frightening than an x-ray, and it only lasted about 45 seconds. When the machine shut off, the lights came on, and the technicians came back to the room to help get me out of my cast. They changed the back cast for the front cast, and I climbed into that side. This cast included an opening for my face and I could look down at the floor. As I lay still in the cast, the techs left the room again, and the lights lowered. I heard the click of the machine and a whirring sound that lasted another 45 seconds. That was it. One treatment down.

Once I got used to the routine, I could use the relaxation and visualization methods that I'd been practicing at night. When I got settled in the cast for the treatment to begin, I'd close my eyes and take my mind to a quiet, warm, calm place that would help me feel relaxed. In the readings that I'd done, there was evidence that when people were opposed to the treatments they were to receive they could do themselves great harm. I *wanted* to believe that the treatments I was getting were going to do the intended job and destroy all the cancer cells in my body. I imagined the 45 seconds of radiation that were directed into my body were warming and healing powers that would save me from the cancer cells that were threatening my life.

This was my visualization for the treatments: The place I went to in my mind was a beach. I was lying on my back, on a blanket on the sand. The sand was warm and the breeze was gentle and fresh. I could hear the sound of waves gently rolling in and out. I could hear the sounds of birds, and imagined them playing in the wind over the sea. As I lay on my back in these relaxed surroundings, I could feel the warmth of the sun on my body. I welcomed the warmth as healing rays. During the first few treatments, I didn't feel or see too many effects from the radiation. I was still very thin and weak. As the treatment progressed, my hair started to fall out. The doctors told me that I'd probably lose a little hair along my hairline. That wasn't what happened. I lost a lot of the hair on the back of my head, almost from the crown. I still had hair in the front and was able to create a bit of a combover that hid the baldness (if anyone saw me from the front, or if the wind didn't blow). It was only at cancer clinics that you'd see people balded from chemo or radiation, and when you did, we looked pretty sick. It was not popular in those days to have a shaved head, or to color what hair was left with bright shades. I felt totally isolated and different-looking. I only left the house to go to the hospital for treatments, or out in my back yard to play with the girls.

One day my sister called, and said she was going to take me out. I had no idea what she had in mind. She picked me up and took me to the mall. She had made an appointment with her hairdresser for me. I was so shocked and worried. I didn't know if she had told the hairdresser anything about me before I came in. The hairdresser smiled and chatted with me. I didn't know whether to say something about the radiation first or not, so I kept quiet. She took me to the sink and gently tilted my head back to wash my hair. I think she was surprised to feel that I was mostly bald on the back of my head. Then I told her what I was going through. She was very kind, and told me what she could do to keep my hair in good condition during my treatments. I was relieved and happy to have met her. I couldn't afford to get a haircut and would have never have thought of it. What a special gift.

When I was first diagnosed, my regular doctor was away and the doctor who saw me was a *locum* (substitute) doctor. Even though my family doctor had been my brother's attending physician, and I had been seeing him through the birth of both my children, I was severely disappointed with his reaction to my cancer diagnosis. Basically, he had been no support or help and I expected more from him.

My mom was furious with him, but I thought I should give him one more chance. Mom had told her doctor about my situation and he was interested and concerned for mom and me. I made an appointment to see my doctor again, to gauge how helpful he might be during this critical time in my life. I was sitting in his office when he came in. Then he asked me, "So, what's happening with you?"

Mom was right. He was an ass. I did fill him in about my visits to the cancer centre and what was happening, but I left knowing that would be my last visit to see him.

Mom's doctor was concerned about me, and agreed to take me and my family as patients. The first time I went to see Dr. D., he knew about my condition, some of my history, and my recommended course of treatment. He had called the cancer clinic before my appointment, so he would be informed about what I was facing. I was just starting my radiation treatments and not much had happened yet, but he suggested I see him weekly so he could keep up with the effects of the radiation. The first set of 20 treatments was for the upper half of my body, from just under my breasts to my jawbone. Dr. D. said that shortly I could expect to experience burns under my arms and to be sure to come to see him the following week. I continued to go to Vancouver for my daily treatments.

I had a simple routine of getting up, getting dressed, and getting ready to go for my treatment. The homemaker would arrive and Greg would fill her in about care the girls needed that day. We'd drive to Vancouver. The ride was a bit more than an hour and we were usually pretty quiet. I'd have my treatment, and we'd stop somewhere for coffee on the way home. We were pretty broke by that time, so we'd just scrape together enough for two cups of coffee. We'd sit quietly in a coffee shop and read the newspaper. On the way back home we'd stop along the way and Greg would hand out resumes.

Dr. D. was right, and the first effect from the radiation was burns under my arms. I went to see him and he asked me to lay down on his examining table. As soon as I raised my arms, he said, "Oh, yeah, those are doozies." My armpits were burned and it was if the skin was turning itself inside out. It hurt so much. I had to hold my arms up to keep my armpits from rubbing. I was glad he was monitoring what was happening to me, but there was nothing he could do except watch for infection. It was summer, and it was hot, but while getting radiation therapy I couldn't use any deodorants or powders, except baking soda. I kept a clump of cotton balls in a bowl of baking soda to tap lightly on areas that were not burned, but needed soothing.

The next area to hurt was my throat. It started off as a dry throat, then got very sore. It was getting harder to eat and I didn't have much of an appetite anyway. Food didn't taste good at all and it was getting hard to swallow. My throat was burning on the inside. I wasn't cooking much, but thankfully, my mother-in-law was feeding the girls. She would offer me food and I'd take some dinner, only to push it around on my plate. I was worried about so many things, and getting increasingly tired from the treatments. I'd use whatever energy I had to play with the girls. I'd take them to the library and we'd bring home books to read. Our fun time was to lie in one bed and bring out all the books. We'd read them together and they would be scattered all over the floor. Part of the strategy was to get the girls to sleep, and inevitably we'd all be fast asleep before too long, all snuggled in a pile.

I was getting more and more tired but my doctor had suggested that I get out and try walking. That was a good idea but I couldn't make it much farther than to the mailbox which was pretty close to our house. One day I walked with the girls to the playground which was three houses away. The girls played on the jungle gym and I sat and watched. They tried their little girlish daredevil stunts and were satisfied when they called out, "Mommy! Watch me!" and I'd see everything they were doing. We'd been there for awhile and it was time to go home, so I called both of them to go. Melissa came but little Megan was still playing on the swings. Melissa was quite grown up at four and a half, and a little mother hen to two-year-old Megan. Megan loved to play and didn't want to go home. I tried to coax Megan but she didn't want to budge and I didn't have the strength to pick her up or to drag her, even a little bit. So I was stuck at the park, and not able to take my girls home. There was no one else around, and I couldn't see any people outside in their yards either. I knew Julie was at home and she could help me get Megan. Megan wasn't being bad, and I wasn't mad, but I was scared that I wouldn't be able to get the kids back to the house.

I stood at the end of the playground at the street and told Melissa to walk back to the house. I told her to let Grandma Julie know I was stuck, and could she please come to help me. Melissa started walking towards our house, and I watched her. I could also keep an eye on Megan happily playing in the park. I felt bad about sending my little four-year-old to walk home by herself, but it wasn't far and she didn't know it was a problem. I felt powerless and helpless. I thought I had changed from a vibrant, energetic, young mother to a vulnerable and weak woman. It was only a few minutes later that I saw Julie come out of the house with Melissa. They walked down to the park, and as soon as Megan saw Grandma, she was happy to come along. We went home and had some tea and cookies. I didn't think I would try that alone again for awhile.

I had an established routine now at the cancer centre. I'd have blood drawn twice a week, have chest x-rays taken, and visit the dental lab for saliva tests while I was coming for daily treatments. The hair on the back of my head had all fallen out. I had no appetite and was losing more weight. I really think my family found it terribly difficult to deal with my being sick. It was too close on the heels of Jim's death, and I wasn't looking very well. We had a few friends who would still visit, but it was really hard for most people to face someone their age with cancer.

One of our friends stopped coming over. He thought that he might "catch" cancer. Others didn't know what to say. One day a family friend was visiting John and Julie. He came upstairs to say hello and asked Greg how I was doing. They were talking outside on the patio, and I was standing at the window and could see them. They were looking at me, and talking about me, as if I wasn't even there.

Near the end of the first set of radiation treatments, we finally got a piece of good news, but it created another situation to deal with. Greg got a job and was to start right away. Until then, he had driven me to Vancouver for my daily treatments. I could drive, but I needed someone to go with me because, feeling as weak as I was, it was risky for me to go alone. Greg made a schedule of family and friends who could spare a day here and there to get me through my treatments.

One amazing friend, Sach, really wanted to help out. Sach and I had worked together for a few years at the pharmacy. We had lots of laughs and he became a good friend to everyone in our family. He arranged his work schedule to have Wednesdays off so he could take me to Vancouver. I was amazed and thankful for him. He came on time in the morning and we drove in his car. It never seemed to faze him that I was battling for my life and that I was a shell of who I once had been. We'd joke and laugh on the ride in, just like we did when we were working. He'd come into the clinic with me, sit in the waiting room and still be there when I finished my treatment. Then we'd go out for lunch before driving home. He was a bit of a clown and always did goofy things to keep me laughing, lifting my spirits.

One day, I thought I felt a lump under my arm, near my breast. I was always checking and was quite paranoid about finding something else. I'd never found another lump after the initial one on my neck. I was so scared by this discovery. It was very small but I wasn't going to take any chances. When I went to the clinic, I asked to see an oncologist about my concern. I told him about the lump I felt. I showed him the area I was concerned with, and he examined me, probing deeply into my armpit. He said he couldn't feel anything. I told him I figured I'd be pretreated for breast cancer with the radiation treatments I was already getting for the Hodgkin's. He replied, "Actually, you'll be at greater risk for breast cancer *because* of the radiation treatments for the Hodgkin's." Shit! Can I ever get a break?

My dad came with me to the clinic once a week. At that time his second wife, Jessie, my stepmother, was facing her own battle with breast cancer and was not doing well at all. Her cancer had metastasized and spread to her bones. She was a frail woman to begin with, and she had broken her hip while just sitting on the couch. She was also angry about many things, and had left my dad. But dad continued to support her, and tried to provide her with whatever she needed. Jessie was getting palliative radiation treatments and she needed a ride when I was going in. Dad and I took Jessie with us on my treatment day.

I drove my car and Jessie rode in the front while dad sat in the backseat. She was really sick and was carrying a bucket in case she had to throw up. And she needed it. I was navigating through traffic, and she was vomiting in the bucket. All I could do was focus on my driving and try not to get too distracted by the gasping and choking. That was quite a ride. We got to the clinic and we each went in for our own treatments. Dad had wandered off and Jessie spent a lot of time complaining to me about my dad.

When we got back to Abbotsford I had an appointment with Dr. D. I told him about that experience and he said "Don't ever do that again." It was far too upsetting for me. I didn't know what to do. Dr. D. didn't know Jessie, but from what I described, he said she was probably in really bad shape.

Nights, I continued to practice my visualization. I was getting physically weaker each day, but I still had a strong, determined mind. One of my favorite relaxation routines was practicing progressive muscle relaxation. I'd start by noticing my hands, then relaxing them. Next, I noticed my arms, then relaxing them, and so forth, until I'd relaxed my entire body. When my body was completely relaxed I'd let my mind wander to a peaceful place: It was a green lush forest with rolling meadows. The meadows had tall grasses and wildflowers that were gently blowing in the breeze. Wearing a pretty flowing white dress, I was walking through the meadows on a warm sunny afternoon. It was a very peaceful, serene setting.

As I walked across the field to the other side there was a rustic cabin on the hill. I walked up to the cabin and opened the door. There was no one there except me but it was a place I was supposed to be. The cabin was completely furnished and inviting. I'd go to the kitchen and make a cup of tea then go into the living room. There was a big overstuffed comfy chair in the centre of the room. The chair faced a nice, crackling fire burning in the stone fireplace. I'd sit in the chair, cover myself with a blanket, drink my tea, and watch the fire. Somehow, in this cabin was the power and the peace to heal my body. I was safe there and was getting better every time I visited the cabin. When I finished my visit, I'd leave the cabin and go outside to sit in a swing going back and forth taking in the calm and healing caress of my make-believe world. I knew it was made-up but I needed to have something for my mind to work on while I healed my body.

When I thought of my reality, it was a bit discouraging. I wasn't getting much encouragement from my family. I truly thought it was too hard for them. It was like they were afraid to believe I was going to get better, since that positive attitude hadn't helped to save my brother. One day I went to Burger King with mom and grandma. The girls loved going there to run free in the playground. The three of us were sitting and talking, and mom asked how I was doing. I was smiling and trying to keep a positive attitude, so I said "I feel good, I'm a bit tired, but feel like I'm getting better."

My grandma responded, "That's why they call cancer the silent killer. You think you're good and you're not."

That didn't help me much. I still can't believe she said that to me, although I'm sure she said it out of her dismay of losing Jim, her favorite grandchild. But, no matter what, it still didn't help *me*! That's why I felt I had to find my own way to survive. Sometimes loving people say dumb things when they are trying to be helpful.

One day I was talking to someone about having Hodgkin's Lymphoma and they said, "I know someone who had Hodgkin's Lymphoma." I had been trying to find someone with the same cancer to talk to so I said, "Wow, you know someone? Can I talk to him?" but the reply was, "He died."

I continued on to the second set of radiation treatments. I had a variety of people taking turns going with me for my treatments. My brother-in-law, who was paranoid about hospitals, went with me one day. We got there all right but he was very nervous. Of course, he also told me all kinds of terrible hospital stories that had freaked him out. I tried to counter his fear with my positive feedback but it didn't help. It was exhausting for me. I went in for my treatment, and I told him I'd just be a few minutes, and then we'd be able to leave. When I was done, he wasn't waiting for me. He had wandered away and gotten lost in the clinic. Eventually, I found him and we could go home. We could've left much sooner if I hadn't had to spend time looking for him.

My sister scheduled a day off from work to drive me in, along with her daughter Jenny. After my treatment, we went to the cafeteria for lunch. The cafeteria always seemed to be serving what looked and smelled like good food. I didn't have any appetite. Food looked good, and smelled good, but I couldn't eat. They ordered and ate a great-looking lunch. I remember enjoying watching them eat their lunch. I wondered if I'd ever be able to enjoy food again.

I tried to imagine what my future could be, but I couldn't see past my immediate circumstances. This situation seemed to be what my life would always be. The upcoming second set of twenty radiation treatments would be focused on my abdomen. I was still experiencing the effects of the first set of twenty treatments, and I felt that I was cooking in my own skin. The medical staff told me that being radiated in my abdominal region could cause problems with my stomach (vomiting and digestion problems), bowels, my menstrual cycle, and I'd most likely become sterile, among other trivial things. I wish they wouldn't have said what *might* happen. I didn't have any problems with my stomach after the second set of treatments, other than the loss of appetite I already had. What I did experience for many months after treatment was feeling very tired and weak. Otherwise, thank goodness, I never threw up. I had shortness of breath and developed post-radiation pneumonia, but those effects were from the *first* set of twenty treatments.

As I was coming to the end of the forty treatments, an appointment was scheduled with my oncologist. My mom and dad both wanted to be there to hear what the doctor had to say. I don't think my parents had been in the same room at the same time for many, many years, except at Jim's death. My doctor said that I'd managed the treatments very well. One thing though, was that the dye from the lymphangiogram was fading, and they needed to be able to observe the dye in my system for at least one year so they could monitor my abdomen. If there would be a reoccurrence, the abdomen was another common area for lymph nodes to become enlarged, so monitoring was very important. The lymphangiogram would have to be repeated approximately one year after the beginning of my treatments. That wouldn't happen for a few months but it never left my mind.

I also had told my mom that I had a really weird sensation whenever I nodded my head. She wanted me to tell the oncologist about it. When I tilted my head down, I'd get a tingling sensation all down the front of my body. I thought that it was strange but didn't want to tell the doctor about it, in case I was imagining things. Mom told the doctor about it and I was surprised, it was something real and not part of my imagination. It was called "Barber Chair Syndrome." The barber chair syndrome causes an electrical shock to run down the body with a tingling sensation when the head was tipped. It had something to do with the radiation of the spinal column. The oncologist told us that some people get it so badly that the electrical sensation could knock them off their feet. Mine wasn't that bad, but it was a very strange sensation that stayed with me for many years. There was nothing they could do about it in any case.

Mom's big question for the doctor was, "Is Michelle in remission?" The oncologist explained that they didn't like to use that term, but what he would say was that at that time "There was no evidence of cancer." He told us that I would be monitored regularly with checkups, and that the first five years would be critical. At first I'd come back to the clinic every three months, and after one year I'd come every six months, and so on. That was the best they could do, so I was to go home and carry on with my life. I had a few more treatments left, and then I was done.

My dad was going with me for the last couple of treatments. He and Greg suggested that I ask for my body casts. I thought that was crazy and I'd be embarrassed to ask, but I did. After my final treatment, I asked what they would do with my body casts and was told they would just throw them away, so I asked if I could take them home. They said, "Sure."

My dad took one side of the cast, and I took the other and we carried them out of the clinic. We looked and felt so silly, we were laughing all the way out to the parking lot. The next Halloween, Greg taped them together and suspended a flashlight in the head. He put a scary mask on the head and dressed the cast up in a jacket and pants with work boots on the end of the pants. We called the local newspaper and Melissa got her picture in the paper standing with the monster's arm around her while she was dressed as a friendly little cat.

I was done. It was the end of the summer, and I was finished with my treatments and didn't have to go back to Vancouver until my three-month check-up. To celebrate, we had a party in our backyard. We invited all of our families and all our friends with their kids. We had a big potluck dinner while we got to visit and celebrate. I made it through my treatments! I just wanted to be mom for the girls, and recover.

Melissa was five then, and we had registered her for kindergarten, so I took her to school for three hours every day. It was good for her to get out and meet more kids and just play. I would have time to rest, as Megan would always play quietly or have her nap when Melissa was in school.

My stepmother Jessie passed away early that fall from metastatic breast cancer. I was so weak at the time, that I couldn't even make it to her funeral. I never got any closure with her passing. Since I didn't show up for Jessie's funeral my Aunty Marge and Aunty Lou came to my house to see why I hadn't shown up. They took one look at me, and said I didn't look good at all. They insisted on taking me to my doctor so he could do something to perk me up.

Dr. D. didn't like the looks of me, either. He was ready to send me to the hospital for a blood transfusion. He sent me for blood work and opted to start me on regular injections of vitamin B12. I went to his office twice a week for many months for injections. Something worked because I perked up a bit, just enough to avoid the blood transfusion.

I made a routine for my shot day. I packed the girls in the car and drove across town for my shot. Then we'd go to Mahony Park (their favorite) so they could play. I'd sit on the bench and watch everything they did. It was a good way to get my shots over with a minimum of fuss.

I had a lot of recovering to do. I think I was as much depressed as weakened by the radiation. Greg and I were not getting along well, and my self-worth was really low. The joy I drew on was being with my girls. When I was at my weakest, I'd be in bed and I'd think and think and think. I was making deals with myself to try to set goals. I bargained with myself that when I got better, I'd get the girls involved in as many activities as they wanted, and that I could manage. I started taking them to swimming lessons and tumbling classes. There was a free class at the local library to teach children how to use computers. It was 1988, and computers were new, and touted as the way of the future. I also took them to story time at the library, and a mother and children's playtime. I felt out of place with the other young mothers and didn't talk about my recovery. Young people just didn't get cancer and I was afraid that it would scare people off if they found out I had had cancer.

When it was time for my first three-month checkup, I was anxious and worried. What if they find something? What if I have a reoccurrence? I drove to Vancouver, had my blood work and x-rays done and waited to see the oncologist. Everything was all clear! But I was told it was now time to repeat the lymphangiogram. The appointment was booked and Greg came with me for the procedure. I was so nervous and scared. It had been bad enough having it once, but twice?

The technicians set me up again, and when the doctor came in I must have looked really frightened. The doctor stopped the procedure, and took some time to talk to me. She didn't understand why I was so anxious. I told her that I'd known about this having to be repeated for over a year and had been dreading it the entire time. She shook her head, and said they shouldn't have told me that it needed to be repeated. At least her taking the time to talk to me helped to settle me down a bit. Then, there was trouble with the contrast dye flowing in the lymph vessel on one leg, and the doctor had to come back in and work a bit more in my foot. That was horrible, but I had to believe that this was the last time it would ever happen to me. I got through it.

My last long-term job had been working in the post office at the drugstore. My other work experience had been as a cashier and waitressing. I knew I was not going to be able to work for a long time, and wanted to be a stay-at-home mom for as long as I could. I remembered when we were struggling with the arrangements for the children when I needed to go to treatment appointments every day. I thought of the hardship it had added to an already stressful situation. But I remembered the world of difference made by the one visit I'd had with a social worker at the cancer clinic. I thought that someday I'd like to work for the Cancer Society and be the person who could help a patient or a family. I had always loved helping people, but I didn't know the best way I could help.

I checked out the local college and went to see an educational advisor. I told her about my goal and she directed me to the Social Services Diploma program. It was a two-year program, but I could take classes at my own pace and even take only one every term, until I finished the program. So I registered for my first college credit night class. I learned that my assignments had to be typed, so I went out and bought a typewriter. The first course I took was "Interpersonal Communications." This was a good start for me. I was still hiding my situation from the people I met and this class gave me a new identity and purpose but my first assignment required me to reflect on my situation.

Our home situation was complicated, so Greg and I felt we needed to start somewhere new. We put our house up for sale, and found a nice apartment for John and Julie to live in. During that time, John had another stroke and was in the hospital. We settled Julie in the apartment but John never came home. He passed away quietly. Greg and I found a house in Chilliwack, and prepared to move to a new community. Chilliwack was only thirty minutes from Abbotsford, but we didn't know anyone there. It was a fresh new start, somewhere that I could meet new people. They wouldn't know anything about my cancer.

My thirtieth birthday was coming up in December, and I was pretty anxious. Not because I felt I was getting older and was feeling bad about it, but because I was reaching thirty and was alive! Turning thirty was a milestone to me. Jim didn't make it to thirty and I was feeling very lucky. It was only about a year and a half since my diagnosis, and I felt very fortunate. I assessed any unhealthy risk factors in my life and vowed to myself to make changes so that I could continue to get healthier and stronger. I had been given a second chance and wanted to make it last.

Shortly after we moved into the new house in Chilliwack, I had the appointment for my six-month checkup in Vancouver. Now we lived even further away than when we had been in Abbotsford. Just the thought of the checkup got me all worked up. I spent the few nights leading up to the appointment going over my past experiences in my head. I was worried. What if they find something? All it takes is one test for them to find something and have to tell me that it's back. I didn't want to leave the girls for the time it would take me to drive to Vancouver, have my blood work and x-rays, see the doctor, and drive home. It was too long and something I was dreading.

I went alone so that Greg could stay with the girls, but what if they had something to tell me and I was alone again? With all these thoughts and the drive ahead of me, I set off. I was very distracted and I guess I was speeding because before too long I heard a siren behind me. I thought it must be for someone else, but it was for me. Now I was really nervous. What did I do wrong? I pulled over and the cop approached my car. I just wanted to burst out crying but I didn't. I was embarrassed and mad at myself because I couldn't afford to pay a speeding fine.

The cop gave me the ticket and drove away. I wasn't very far from home so I still had a long drive ahead of me. I tried to pay attention for the rest of the drive, while in my head was fear of what could happen to change my life again. I got to the cancer clinic on time, had my x-rays, bloodwork, and a saliva test.

I went in to the oncologist, still very nervous and scared. I had worried for days preceding the checkup, had a crappy 90-minute drive, alone, been through a bunch of lousy tests, and then waited to see the doctor. I explained a bit of my situation to the doctor when he came in to see me. He reviewed my tests and had a look at me. My checkups always include my neck and my abdomen being checked. They had found cancer in my neck but not in my abdomen, so they were still watching very closely for signs. The dye from the lymphangiogram was very strong so the lymph system in my abdomen would show up clearly in the x-rays. No matter how uncomfortable that test was, there was a purpose.

I got the "all clear" result from that checkup. I was so relieved! The doctor also recognized the added stress it was for me to make the long trip to Vancouver so he told me that there was a travelling cancer clinic, and the doctors could see patients in Chilliwack. I was happy to hear that. He told me that for the next checkup I could go to that clinic if I wanted. I could have my blood work and x-rays done in the local clinic a week before my appointment and then see the oncologist at the local public health unit. That was very good news! I knew that for five years after my diagnosis, it was critical for me and that I needed to be monitored very closely. The anxiety surrounding the checkups didn't help much, but I figured at least they were paying attention to my condition.

I was sure happy to turn thirty in 1989, and we were getting a new start as a family. Our neighborhood was great. New houses were being built and that meant new families were moving in. I met the other moms as the kids ventured out to play. Melissa was in kindergarten and I volunteered to help out in her class. Megan got to come along so it was like she was in kindergarten too. I wasn't well enough to get a job, so I would babysit for the neighbors when I could. It worked out great for the other moms who were on call with their jobs, and they would just let me know to bring their son or daughter home with me after school. All the kids were so good, and it was fun to have them all around.

The kids would play in the yard or the forest next door, or we'd bake cookies and muffins on rainy days. I still had some ongoing health issues. My immune system was compromised from my splenectomy and the radiation treatments. When my girls got chicken pox, I let the other moms know so they could decide if they wanted to send their kids to my house or not. They all said they were not worried about the exposure. If their kids did get chicken pox, I was still able to take care of them, since my girls had had them. After a week with chicken pox in the house I called a doctor's office and said I'd like to come in. The nurse asked why, and I said that the kids had chicken pox. Actually, the kids were okay, but I was concerned about my health. I had called my dad, my mom, and my grandma and asked them if I'd had the chicken pox when I was little and none of them remembered me having the chicken pox. Since my spleen had been removed, I had to be cautious of health, and this virus could be dangerous to me.

When I told the nurse the kids had chicken pox she replied, "Well, don't bring them in here!" I explained that the kids were okay but I'd had my spleen removed two years earlier and hadn't had chicken pox. Then she was concerned. She told me she would talk to the doctor and call me back as soon as possible. They really jumped into action.

The nurse called back soon and said that I probably needed to have injections of gamma globulin. They arranged for this to come from Vancouver and I needed to get to the hospital emergency room to have the injections. I was told that gamma globulin would boost my immunity temporarily to help me fight the virus. I said I could come to the hospital as soon as Greg came home from work to watch all the kids. By the time I got to the hospital, the medicine had arrived. The emergency room nurse was measuring the serum out and told me that she needed to use a big needle because the medicine was so thick. According to the dosage, I'd need to have four shots, where did I want them? I chose to have one in each thigh and one in each hip.

The nurse drew the medicine and proceeded to give me the first injection. She warned me that the shot would hurt and that the medicine was cold. I think it hurt her more than it hurt me. I won't say it wasn't uncomfortable, but with all the needles and poking I'd had I could take it. She asked if I'd like to take a break between each of them to rest, but I replied "No, let's get on with it. I have to get back home to make dinner."

I got all four shots and they threw in a flu shot for me as well. I hopped back in my car to get home in time to see the last of the kids I was babysitting off and to get dinner started. All the kids got better from their viruses, and I didn't get sick with the chicken pox.

Choosing to Smile

I had always led a cautious life and was happy with my new lease on life. One day we were walking through the shopping mall, and there was a stand where they sold tickets to a whale-watching trip off the coast of Vancouver Island, out of Tofino. I was excited by the pictures of the majestic grey whales in the wild and told Greg that I knew it would cost a bit, but I'd really love to try it. We bought four tickets. We told our new friends in the neighborhood, who had all come from other parts of Canada, and they bought tickets as well. My sister, Bonnie, her husband Dave, their daughter Jenny, and my mom all came too!

The trip was in February, which was rainy and windy, so we packed accordingly with rain coats, boots, gloves, and hats. My mom always loved the sea and was really happy to come along. We got there a day before the tour, and spent the afternoon walking on the beach in Tofino in the rain. Dressed in the right clothes, it was just as fun and interesting as beachcombing in the summer.

The next day we got up early and boarded the boat to go out to find the grey whales. On the way out to the open sea we were able to watch seals, eagles, sea lions and many types of birds. The grey whales migrate from Mexico and California up the west coast, past Tofino to the high Arctic in the Bering Sea. These grey-colored creatures are eleven to fourteen meters long and can weigh fifty tons.

The ride was exciting because we didn't know what to expect. It was a little scary, thinking about how close we might get to see these giant mammals. I love the ocean and was enjoying the gentle rocking and swaying of the boat. When we got past the protection of land, our boat headed out to the open sea, to the channel that the whales use as their migratory path. Our captain was experienced and took us to the location where we could safely see the whales. Everyone on our boat was quiet. The crew all took to the decks to watch for the whales

"There's one!" someone shouted.

Michelle's Story

We all turned our attention to the spray of sea water from a grey whale's spout. It happened fast, but then we knew what to look for. We were all watching as carefully as we could. Then we saw another plume of spray shoot from a whale's blow hole. It was very exciting. The kids were shrieking with glee. Then the captain found some calm water and turned the boat engine off. Everything went quiet. Our boat bobbed gently up and down on the sea and everyone held their breath waiting for something to happen. Then, gently and graciously, a grey whale surfaced next to our boat. There wasn't much sound as everyone was quiet and in awe of what we were seeing. The whale's body rose to the surface and we could see the barnacles on its back. It was an amazing sight. I was simply breathless. I was so thrilled to have seen such a miracle of nature and to have our friends and family with me. It was a very special moment.

Shortly after we witnessed this amazing event, the seas began to churn. Before long our boat was rocking back and forth very aggressively. The plumes of spray were still visible but one had to be very observant to see them before a wave blocked the view. Everyone was hanging on by this time and the waves were splashing up and over the boat. Our friends who were from Manitoba were hanging on for dear life, and looking a little green at this time. One of the kids was throwing up overboard. It was quite cold, very windy, and everyone was getting wet.

The captain turned the boat around and was heading to shore. It was far too rough to be out anymore. The shore looked far away as our boat chugged along to find the protection of the shore. We eventually made it to shore and everyone was relieved. Some were seasick, and said they had a good trip but would never do that again. I was very excited and we bought tickets to go out again the following year. We had witnessed a wonder of the world. What else could I find to amaze me?

Back at home, the girls enjoyed their days filled with elementary school, friends, and lessons. I tried to keep up on what they wanted and what was popular for kids their age. I took them to swimming lessons, ice skating lessons, dance lessons, Brownies, Girl Guides. Melissa started playing soccer when she was nine, and Megan practiced rhythmic gymnastics. We went to their first dance recital, and watched them dance with a group of other children, to music that they had practiced to for a few months. They were so cute, wearing their matching green and black dresses. We had flowers for them at the end, so they would feel like they were real stars. They really were stars!

My cancer was always on my mind, and I felt I was very different from other people my own age. I didn't know anyone else who had had cancer. If people talked about it, the story was usually about a parent or aunt, who had died. In the spring of 1990, I called the local office of the Canadian Cancer Society. I was given the phone number of the president. I introduced myself and asked him if there was a support group in Chilliwack. He replied that there wasn't one at that time but he knew someone I should talk to. This woman had started a support group but it had been stopped. He thought maybe it was a good time to start again. He gave me her number and said, "You'll never believe this, this woman lost her leg to cancer, and her name is 'Stand-even.'" He laughed at the irony. I didn't know him or this woman, so I wasn't sure if that was funny or not. The next day I called Glenda.

I introduced myself to Glenda on the phone and was greeted by the nicest person I'd ever talked to. We had an instant connection. We quickly found out that we both had had cancer at the same time, 1988, and our oldest children were the same age. We talked and talked for a long time. She explained that she tried to hold a support group in her home shortly after her surgery, but it didn't work out. But now, if I was interested in helping, maybe it was time to start again. Glenda had always lived in Chilliwack, and knew a lot of people. I didn't know anyone, but was willing to help out. Over the next little while, we just talked on the phone. The more we talked, the more we had in common. One day she had mentioned she had a brother named Jim. I stopped her and asked about her brother. She told me that her brother had died young, in a car accident. I told her about my brother Jim. It seemed strange that we both lost our brothers named Jim.

I always read the local newspaper to learn about our new community. In the spring of 1990, there was a story with a picture of Glenda standing with her son Kevin. The story was about Glenda's trip to Oklahoma to have a prosthetic leg made. This was a special leg for her since Glenda had lost her hip, pelvis, and leg to bone cancer, and she needed a prosthetic leg specially fitted for her. She needed only a cane to help her walk. This is how I first met Glenda. I was amazed by this young woman's spirit.

We got together to plan how we would conduct a support group. After much discussion we decided we needed a "neutral" setting—not a hospital (we'd all seen enough of those), somewhere comfortable and "safe." A local hotel's banquet room became our meeting space. When we arrived at the hotel for meetings, our group name was also on the information board in the hotel lobby, "Living with Cancer." Each meeting, we had a room set up with chairs in a circle, a table on the side of the room with jugs of fresh water, ice, and water glasses, all ready and waiting for our group.

We advertised our group in the local newspaper as well as in the Cancer Society office. Sometimes we would have a small group, and other times there was a larger crowd. I was still very quiet and just liked to be there to offer help if I could. We gathered a lot of books that we were willing to share, so I was in charge of the library. I'd carry the books and tapes to each meeting, laying them out on a table for people to sign out.

Glenda facilitated the group and she was a fantastic leader. I love to hear her speak. She gives an open and honest opinion, and genuinely listens to what people have to say. She offers hope and inspiration to everyone. To hear Glenda's story, and see what she has to give in her life is so inspirational to me that I always felt that I had no reason to complain about anything. Each visitor had a story to tell and some were truly heart-wrenching. If there were some suggestions we could offer we would, but we always gave each person a chance to talk and tell their story. Visitors would also find comfort in meeting someone who had a similar experience to theirs. It could be a good resource for them and an instant connection.

Glenda also adds a lot of humor to situations. To end each meeting, we would tell jokes. If we knew a joke we could tell it, or just share a funny situation. Many of these situations were related to our cancer. I remember Glenda telling us about her experiences. She told us before she had her prosthetic leg, she met a little girl who was fascinated by meeting the one-legged lady. She kept asking where her other leg went. Glenda explained that it was sick and was taken off. The little girl still couldn't figure it out, so to her mother's shock, the little girl went under Glenda's skirt to look for her other leg!

I'd never met anyone like Glenda. She is such an amazing woman and this was the beginning of a forever friendship. We met many people through our support group, too. We held meetings twice a month, twelve months a year. We thought of taking a month off at Christmas or for summer vacation, but figured that cancer never takes a break. Holidays can be a very critical time for someone who has just been diagnosed, or a family member who is sad at that time and just wants to have some company. We were there. We lost a few of our friends and would support their families as best we could. As many from our group as possible would attend funerals, no matter how hard it was on everyone.

To get the word out that our group was available, Glenda talk-

ed to the local media and in November 1991, Ken Goudswaard, a
reporter with the Chilliwack *Times* wrote an article headlined "Not
All Interviews Are this Inspirational." The article went on:

> I was expecting tears and I got them. But they were tears of
> laughter and they took me by surprise. When I went to inter-
> view several members of the Living with Cancer support group
> earlier this week, I went with some trepidation. I felt I was in
> for an emotional nightmare. I imagined sitting in a room filled
> with people recounting the horrors of a disease that can ravage
> and strip the life out of its victims. I was ready for just that—
> victims.
>
> But what I found were survivors. One of the members of the
> group called Living with Cancer "just another support group."
> He wasn't demeaning the group, but rather stating a fact. The
> world is full of them. And while he was saying theirs was no
> more special than any other group which helps its own kind, he
> was indeed endorsing their value.
>
> You only had to have been where I was that night to see the
> power of people helping people. There was enough positive
> energy flowing to jump start even the most hardened pessimist.
> And while I kept thinking about death, I'm sure I left a room
> that wasn't. These people are too busy living and laughing and
> loving it all.

I continued to study at the local college, taking courses towards my
Social Services diploma. I took one evening course each semester. I
had to fit my studies into my busy family life. I would take my homework along with me and study when I got the chance. It might be
while the girls were at a birthday party or when I was waiting in the car
during soccer practices or anywhere else that I could steal some time.

Choosing to Smile

As I was taking my classes, I always remembered what a difference the social worker I'd met at the cancer clinic had made in our lives. We were faced with a bad situation that could've been worse. In some of my classes we were required to make presentations to the other students. For one presentation, I told my story of how difficult it was to be a young mother facing cancer. I talked about the road blocks that a family can face in this type of situation. I challenged the students to remember this and to be the ones who could make a phone call to make the difference in a family's life, to help them out with their struggles, as the one social worker had done for us. At first, the social support system closed their doors to us until one person made a few calls to make the difference. It was within their power all along, but perhaps they just weren't able to make that effort for some particular reason. I hoped to become someone who could make that difference, and I extended this challenge to my classmates.

I had a practicum to complete, and chose to work at the college in the ESL (English as a Second Language) and international departments. Since our family had hosted Japanese study/tour students in the past, I was very familiar with different cultures. I finished my diploma and graduated in April 1994. Shortly after I graduated, I was offered a job in the international department. I was very happy to have this opportunity.

Early in 1994, my mom had an appointment for a routine mammogram. I got a call that evening from Kay to say that mom had been rushed to the hospital for urgent surgery. They had found a large mass on her breast, and performed a radical mastectomy. It all happened very fast and was extremely drastic. Mom was hopeful, though, that she would be okay and whatever treatment she needed would save her.

She started chemo treatments and lost all her hair. She wore a colorful turban when she went out. Mom attended our support group a couple times and was very optimistic. She told jokes along with Glenda, and put a very brave face on. When it was her turn for introductions she would say she lost her only son to Hodgkin's lymphoma, had a daughter who had survived Hodgkin's, and she herself was fighting breast cancer. She told the group that she was going to fight and beat it.

Mom finished her chemo and went back to work for a short while. Then she started taking sick days, but said she was okay, just fighting different common things, like a cold or flu. One Friday evening early in 1995, I was talking to her on the phone, and she was having a hard time catching her breath. I asked her what her doctor was saying about her condition, and she assured me that she had regular chest x-rays and she was fine. Shortly after this I got another call from Kay—mom was back in the hospital. I rushed to visit her and found her comfortable, with medication easing her pain. I left for a few hours but told mom I'd be back shortly.

When I got back early in the afternoon, mom was unconscious. Kay told me then that the attending doctor had taken x-rays and said that her lungs were full of cancer. She didn't have long to live. My sister Bonnie, Kay, and I took turns caring for mom as best we could. We'd alternate our times at the hospital so someone was always with her. Bonnie and I had never been told how sick mom really was. It was an agonizing process to watch our mother suffer. During the night I'd talk softly to her, hoping that she could hear me and understand. We didn't want to lose her but it was heartbreaking to see her in this condition.

On Monday morning when I woke up, I could tell that mom's breathing had changed. It was daylight and Kay had just come back. Dad had been away, but we'd sent a message to him about mom. He came into the hospital room that morning.

Bonnie, dad, and Kay were talking quietly. I was stroking mom's hand and telling her it was okay to go now. We were all there. It was time for her to go and be with Jim and George. We always joked about those two guys causing trouble in heaven, and I told her it was time she went to them. I noticed her breathing had become very shallow. I called Bonnie, dad, and Kay to mom's bedside, and we were all around her as she took her final breath. I watched her body and saw her spirit leave it. Mom was at peace. She died on February 6, 1995, at 59 years old.

Bonnie and I went together to make the arrangements. We were going to use the chapel at the church mom had attended, and the pastor organized a small luncheon. I purchased ten dozen daffodils to decorate the church. When it was almost time for the service, I walked into the foyer of the church, and to my surprise there was a lineup, well into the parking lot, of people coming to the church. The pastor recognized the chapel would be too small for the group, and moved us into the church. People who knew our mom from various jobs, the local bridge club, neighbors, and old friends all came to pay their respects. We were not expecting so many people, but it was an affirmation of our mom's wonderful life and the compassion she had showed to so many people.

Glenda and I continued to run the "Living with Cancer" support group. She got involved with another group, the Optimist Club, and urged me to join too. The Optimist club is a group of people in the community who raise funds to help support local children with education and sports needs. It was another great group of people. My girls were involved too, because it's a family-focused group. The girls grew up knowing Glenda, and being as inspired by her as I am. I watched in amazement what this woman did. I met so many wonderful and positive people by being a part of Glenda's world. I met Bonnie Holmes in the Optimist club and we've become good friends, too. I met Julie Houlker at our cancer support group. Glenda knew Julie and invited her to come to the support group when she was diagnosed with breast cancer. I remember meeting Julie and hearing her story. I was amazed at how knowledgeable she was about her condition and cancer treatments. She knew all the latest medical information and about what had been tested or proven to work the best.

Springtime was always a bit difficult for me. There had been some significant low points in my marriage during this season, as well as the yearly reminder of my cancer diagnosis, surgery, and treatment.

One Easter weekend, I was having a particularly difficult time, even though I spent happy days with the girls coloring paper bunnies and Easter eggs. We were having an Easter dinner with the family on Sunday. I woke up early that morning when the house was quiet. I made coffee and went out with the dog for a walk while the neighborhood slept. We lived in a new subdivision and there were empty fields and bush areas nearby. We walked through the mud in the fields and looked at the new grass poking up. I was going over the same things in my mind and trying to make sense of things. I didn't have cancer anymore. I was alive, but I was still struggling.

My dog and I entered the woods. We started down a trail of fallen trees and tangled vines. There were brambles of blackberries and tall old grasses from last summer. We climbed over stumps and under branches. It was dark in the forest. Some of the path closed in and then it would open up again. We slid down one muddy hill and climbed up the next one. I tried with all my thoughts to convince myself of all the good things that have happened to me, and to remind myself that I survived. But still I wandered, thinking, struggling. My dog was having a good time running down the paths and crackling the small branches as she climbed around.

I was getting closer to home and still I didn't have any answers. I was feeling discouraged but I knew that I needed to try to hold my head up and put on a happy face for everyone. We went down another dark, damp trail and turned a corner. At the end of the trail it opened up into a clearing, like a meadow. There I saw the sign. It was simple, but it had great meaning for me and my heart warmed up. It was a single daffodil. A beautiful yellow daffodil stood in the middle of this dark forest. My symbol of hope. This was the symbol I had seen in the church bulletin on the weekend I was diagnosed with the cancer that I was sure would kill me, but it didn't. It did change me though. I called my dog and we ran the rest of the way home. I had an especially warm glow in my heart that no one else needed to know about. It was all about living and life.

By 1997, I'd been working at the University College for four years and was fortunate to be sent on a recruitment trip with a colleague to Taiwan. We were sent to Taipei, and would also visit Kaohsiung. I hadn't been away from the girls except when I was in the hospital but it was only for one week. I'd never travelled outside of the country except going to Disneyland in California. I was very used to communicating with people for whom English was their second language, and this would be my first time being in an environment that was non-English speaking.

Our visit was filled with activity; everything from talking to students about studying in Canada at the education fair, to visiting an amazing night market with our hosts. It was an experience I will never forget. This trip was a real eye-opener for me. I watched people work and interact. I have always loved to hear different languages, and was very impressed when I'd turn to see a Canadian speaking perfect Mandarin! I wanted to travel more, continue in this line of work, and figure out what additional education I needed to advance in my career. When I got home I registered for the Bachelor Arts in Adult Education degree which took into account my two year diploma. As part of that program, I was able to take a certificate at the University of British Columbia for Intercultural Studies.

Michelle's Story

After mom died, Bonnie and I received a small inheritance. I thought about what I wanted to do that would have an impact on our lives, rather than just paying off bills. My fondest memories when I was small were at Aunty Marge's cabin, spending lazy summers swimming and playing around. I wanted our girls to have memories of swimming, camp fires, running around in the bushes, making forts, and pretending. We found a cabin to buy. It was on Loon Lake near Cache Creek, about a four-hour drive from home. The cabin was on the other side of the lake from the road, and could be accessed only by boat. My dad became a partner in this venture. He supplied a small boat with a motor for us to get across the lake to our cabin.

Weekends were spent at our peaceful cabin. Our days were filled with swimming, hiking, fishing, and just enjoying the nearness of nature. The kids would bring their friends along and set up their tents on the hill for a night of ghost stories and scaring each other. Often we'd hear the kids screaming, only to find out that a branch had rubbed on the tent roof, scaring everyone inside. On rainy days, we'd stay in the cabin and cook, bake, read, or make crafts. I hope my children will have lifelong memories of our times at Loon Lake.

In December of 1999 I had another turning-point birthday coming up, my fortieth. I had the same feeling of being unsettled as I had ten years earlier. I wanted to be really living a life of celebration, and I felt that I just wasn't living authentically. I was grateful to have beat cancer, but was anxious about something I couldn't quite name. My birthday approached and Greg had planned a surprise for me. He and the girls took me out to dinner so my friends could get into our house for the surprise party. I was truly surprised! Glenda brought along a joke about turning forty with things like "old ladies carry peppermints in their old-lady purses. They must also carry a Kleenex tucked into their sleeves." She had all the props including the old-lady purse.

It was too bad though, that after the guests left, Greg and I ended the evening with an argument. Greg and I had too many unresolved issues that were never going to be addressed. We had different plans for our lives, and that wasn't going to change.

One of my friends had joined a dragon boat team that practiced on Harrison Lake. She was enjoying it so much and suggested I join. I said I'll watch what happens with it the first year. It did seem like a lot of fun and a great way to meet people. I joined and started paddling on a team in 2001. It was hard work, and I wasn't really a sporting person but I wanted to try. I learned the technique at our practices twice a week.‑

In February 2002, a friend planned a trip to Hawaii. When my dad heard me talk about her upcoming trip he offered to pay for my ticket and tag along! What an opportunity for me—to spend time with my dad and visit Hawaii.

On vacation I spent a lot of time walking on the beach and watching people. Of course, it was a beautiful holiday spot, but I was always looking for couples and how they interacted. I watched the outright love and affection and the subtle connections.

One afternoon I set out for a walk by myself. I walked for miles in the Hawaiian heat in the direction of the Diamond Head crater, one of the world's most famous dead volcanoes. When I reached the visitor centre, I looked ahead to the stairs that visitors climbed to the top of the crater for the most amazing views of the open sea and the island of Oahu. I'd walked this far so there was no turning back. I could only keep going. I found a phone booth and called home. Luckily the girls answered. I told them where I was and how far I'd walked to get to that point. Melissa said, "Keep going mom, you'll get to the top, and don't be shy to ask someone to take your picture!"

Michelle at the top of the Diamond Head crater.

Boy, did she know me well. I looked up at the mountain and knew that I had no choice but to keep going up. The trail is very steep and there is no shade. Parts of the trail include two sets of stairs one with ninety-nine steps and the other with seventy-six steps. I climbed and climbed, sometimes passing other visitors. I'd heard about the tunnel that is 225-feet long and unlit. The people who told me about that tunnel couldn't go through it, and they had to abandon their climb. I hadn't brought along the flashlight that had been suggested, but I kept going, climbing, and sweating. The trail is one and three-quarters miles long and usually takes climbers one-and-a-half hours to finish.

I made it to the top! To the top of the Diamond Head crater. It was so worth the journey and I was elated. I was on the top of the mountain, but felt that this was *my* place. I was meant to keep climbing, and I deserved to be happier. I soaked up the scenery, and as Melissa had suggested, I finally got up the nerve to ask someone to take my picture. It was a beautiful moment for me, feeling the warm Hawaiian breeze blowing through my hair. I didn't want to leave.

Among the souvenirs I bought was a special wind chime made of sea shells—this would be the first thing I put into my new home! I was only gone for six days, but it was enough time to figure out what I needed to do. I flew home and I felt good, knowing what needed to be done. Greg never said a word about my trip. It was about a week later we had the talk. We were in big trouble by that time. Things had not been good for too long, and there was no hope of carrying on in a positive way; we both knew we needed to separate. It would not be a temporary separation, but a permanent split. We had been married for twenty-three years.

Melissa was graduating that year, and Megan was finishing grade ten. Both of the girls could live with me and see their dad whenever they wanted to. Megan came with me on all our house-hunting trips. She is a great little organizer, and kept track of all the places we'd seen and what else was available. We found a great townhouse. I was excited about it and was working out the details. Everything fell into place as our house was sold and I was able to purchase the new townhouse. Though there were a lot of details to manage, Greg and I were on amicable terms, and that made things easier.

I loved our new townhouse. The first thing I did was unpack the shell wind-chime I'd bought in Hawaii and hung it on my patio. I spent many evenings sitting relaxing on my patio and listening to the sound of the shells. I was at peace. I got busy and began creating a real home for my girls and me.

That summer, my daughters and I took our first "girls only" road trip. We drove the west coast of Washington and Oregon, marveling at nature's power in the crashing Pacific waves, and enjoying the quiet calm of small towns along the coast. It was a wonderful time for our new "family."

When September came, we were all back in school. I was working full-time and taking classes at night. One afternoon in October my colleague, Betty, was meeting Amy, an agent from China who was visiting Chilliwack, for lunch. They invited me to join them. We were chatting and Betty turned to me and said, "Do you want live in China and teach English?"

I was really surprised. Betty and Amy were looking at me and waiting for my response. I immediately said "No, I can't do that." Then I thought for a few minutes and said, "Well, maybe I can."

I started to ask more questions and the more I asked, the more it seemed like something I could do. Later that evening I saw my sister Bonnie, and when I told her about the opportunity, she said "I'll go with you!"

I was able to arrange a six-month leave of absence from my job, and started to make plans to go with Melissa, Megan, Bonnie, and Sheldon, Melissa's boyfriend. Melissa and Sheldon, having just graduated grade 12, were also able to teach in China. We made arrangements for Megan to do her school work by distance education.

All these travel plans were made in a real hurry. At a Christmas party, Glenda and her sister Lorrie told me about a guy they wanted me to meet. Dating was not something I had been thinking about. But Glenda and Lorrie were persistent. I needed to know more about this guy before I would think about it seriously. They told me that his name was Darren, he was 40 (a fib), and that he had had a serious accident about a year ago, and had made a miraculous recovery. They thought since I was a cancer survivor and Darren was also a survivor, that we'd have something in common. Lorrie said I had to meet him, and if I just made a new friend, then that would be great, too. They wouldn't stop trying to persuade me, so I agreed.

Lorrie set up a coffee date at a local coffee shop the following Saturday for Glenda, Lorrie, Darren, and me. I wasn't really nervous, because I didn't think much would come of it. I was having such a good time with my new life and I was preparing to leave the country for six months. What could happen? I went into the coffee shop and saw Glenda right away. Just then this guy passed me and Glenda motioned that was Darren. He was going to get our coffee. I looked at her with a shocked expression and asked "How old is he?"

Glenda replied, "We told Darren you were 40."

I said, "Glenda! You were at my fortieth birthday and that was a few years ago!" At that moment Darren came back carrying the coffee. We were all introduced to each other and sat for a nice relaxing chat. Darren was quizzed by three women, but he was a good sport through it all. Darren and I exchanged phone numbers and I think Glenda and Lorrie figured they'd done a good job. I felt like a teenager being set up on a blind date.

The next day my phone rang. I was really surprised that it was Darren. He asked if I wanted to meet him that afternoon and I said sure, so we met at a restaurant near my place. We were just talking, and then he caught me off guard, and asked how old I was. Glenda told me Darren was 40 so I asked him how old he was. We finally got around to the fact that Glenda had said that I was younger, and Darren was older, so that we would agree to meet. They figured once we'd met it wouldn't matter. We finally admitted that I was 43 and he was 35. I thought that would be a bit strange for him but he didn't mind at all.

We spent a nice afternoon taking a walk on the river, talking about everything. I brought along a picture of the girls, and he had pictures of his two sons: Curtis and Spencer. My girls were 18 and 16, and his boys were 12 and 11, and lived with their mom. Darren is a survivor too. A couple years before we met, he'd had an accident. He broke his neck and spent a long time in the hospital. Through a lot of rehabilitation and hard work he regained most of his mobility. I was amazed at what he went through.

The next day, Darren called me to see if I would come over to his house to have dinner with him. Both the girls were busy with their friends, so I agreed. This was so new for me but we were hitting it off really well. I told Darren that I had plans to go away for six months to live in China. I was busy getting myself ready to leave the country, and it was also getting close to Christmas. The next evening, he came to my house to meet the girls and my little dog, Tucker. I knew Tucker would be the hardest sell, because he was really possessive of me, but that meeting went well, too. I saw Darren every day until a few days before Christmas, when he went to his brother's home in Prince George with his family for a week.

I had all my family over for my first Christmas dinner in our new home. We all had a great time. A friend came over to help me cook, and we had a few drinks, and lots of laughs. Darren called to wish me a Merry Christmas.

I met Darren's boys on New Year's Eve, when the four of us went out to their friend's house for dinner. We had a nice dinner and played card games until midnight. We set off some fireworks at midnight, then took the boys home. My girls were coming home at 2 am and I was home when they got there.

Darren and I were seeing each other every day, and I kept preparing for my trip. I sensed that as we were getting closer to leaving, Megan wasn't feeling too comfortable about going to China, so I had a serious talk with her. I told her that she didn't have to come with us if she didn't want to. Of course I'd miss her terribly, but that the time would pass and we'd all be home soon enough. She said she didn't want to go. I talked with Greg and we made arrangements for Megan to live with him while we were away. Greg would also be taking care of Tucker. I felt better about that decision, especially once we got to China.

We were scheduled to leave for China at the end of February. I had one final appointment for travel shots on a Friday. It had been really busy for me at work, and getting all the arrangements made for my leave of absence, our medical coverage, my car, my payments, and so on. Friday afternoon before my appointment, I was sitting at my desk and rested my head in my hands. As I touched my neck I felt a lump! My heart sank. I went to the travel doctor and got my last vaccinations. I asked him if he could check something out for me and feel my neck. He did and was taking his time. He said that I should get that checked out right away. I asked him how soon, and his reply was "Go directly to the walk-in clinic when you leave my office."

I couldn't believe this was happening to me. Was there a possibility that the cancer was back? I was about to leave the country for six months. This was a once-in-a-lifetime opportunity. I drove directly to the walk-in clinic. I saw a doctor and told him my cancer history, and that I had just discovered a lump in my neck. He examined me and again, I saw the seriousness in his face. Damn it! This can't happen! That second doctor suggested that I see my family doctor right away on Monday morning. He would send his report over to my doctor.

I had to get through the weekend with these thoughts going around in my head. What if it was cancer again? I guess that would answer everything. We just wouldn't go on the trip and I'd have to deal with it. I tried not to think about the lump. I kept checking, though, and it was still there. As soon as Monday came, I called and got to see my family doctor, Dr. W., right away. He knew about my travel plans and he had confirmed that I was healthy enough to travel to China only a few weeks ago, and was helping the girls and me with the necessary medical preparations.

Dr. W examined my neck and grew concerned. He didn't know what it was, and wanted an ultrasound done at the hospital immediately. I was really scared and asked him "What about the trip?" He said "We have to see the results of the ultrasound first before we can make any decisions." The ultrasound was booked for 2:30 on Wednesday at the hospital. I told Darren about the situation and of course he knew how worried I was although I was trying to downplay it. He offered to go to the hospital with me and I said no, that wasn't necessary.

I left work and got to the hospital for the test. I was prepped and I told the technician my story, and what was weighing on this test result. She excused herself and went to get the doctor to look at what she was scanning. That could mean one of two things. That either she saw something that she wanted to confirm right away with the doctor, or she wanted to confirm that there was nothing to worry about.

The doctor came in and the technician told him a bit of my story. He took the ultrasound instrument and went over the area in my neck. He said "I came in here to see for myself, and to verify for your peace of mind, that the lump we are looking at is not cancer. I'll send my report to Dr. W. and you can see him. You don't have anything to worry about. Go to China!"

I thanked him and got up to leave. I walked out of the examining room and was walking down the hall, when relief flooded over me. I think the shock set in about how scared I really was. I was just about to cry, and turned the corner to the waiting room. The first person I saw was Darren. I choked back the tears and produced a smile. He immediately took my hand and asked if I was okay. I smiled and said, "Everything is okay."

We were all scheduled to leave at the end of February for a six-month teaching contract. We would be working until the end of July, and we planned to travel in China for a few weeks before we came home. Amy contacted Bonnie and asked if she could come to China sooner than the rest of us and she went. The city we were going to was Harbin, in Heilongjiang province in northeast China. Harbin is the tenth-largest city in China, and is well known for its cold winters with temperatures that can dip as low as −30C. The province borders on Russia and Mongolia. The city of Harbin is a well-known tourist destination, famous for its elaborate ice sculptures but it is plagued by poor air quality. Burning coal is the main source of heat and it emits constant billows of black smoke into the air.

Bonnie travelled to Harbin, and kept me up to date on what to expect, and what to bring. I continued to prepare for the trip. Valentine's Day was coming up and Julie's dragon-boat team was having a dinner and dance to fund raise for their team trip to New Zealand. Darren and I went with Rick, Glenda, Julie, Graham, Bonnie, and her husband Pete. It was two weeks before we were to leave, so it was bittersweet. Darren and I had such a good time dancing and hugging. Rick caught us kissing in the coat room. It was pretty obvious we were going to miss each other terribly.

Final preparations were made for our trip, and Darren said his goodbyes with big hugs for all of us. Our Chinese adventure had begun. It was six months of new people, places, and experiences. We flew from Vancouver to Beijing, then on to Harbin. We were met at the airport by some of the school staff and taken to our new home. We travelled in a van to our apartment, and met Bonnie when we arrived. She was really happy to see us and we were happy to see her. We settled into our teacher's quarters, a large four-bedroom apartment suite.

I was teaching in a number of schools, so I had to quickly learn how to get around. Crossing the road in any area of the city was an art. Vehicles didn't stop, and crosswalks were useless. We would link arms with any person we were with, and dash into the street, dodging cars, buses, bicycles, and motorcycles. I always thought it was like a game of "Frogger" and we were the frogs. To get to the other side of the street was a miracle.

After our day of teaching, we got back to our apartment in time for dinner. We had a cook, Winner, who made us two meals a day, lunch and dinner. If you weren't there to eat dinner when it was

Michelle's kindergarten class in China.

served, you would go without eating. We had Sunday off before we started work so we wanted to explore the area. Bonnie knew her way around a bit, so we ventured out to Walking Street, a popular shopping area. We went to a restaurant that Bonnie knew about. That was the first time I'd really experienced the cold. I was wearing jeans and I could feel the cold biting at my legs. When we got back to our apartment, I took my jeans off to discover that my legs were bright red and had been burnt by the cold. I also wore contact lenses, and when I got something in my eye, I rubbed my eye, which was a big mistake. My eye was scratched, and I was having a lot of trouble seeing. It was more than a week until it felt better.

On Monday morning, we set out to teach at our schools. Sometimes Becky, one of our school staff, would come along to introduce me to the school staff. She helped me get the books I needed to prepare lessons. I taught kids of many different ages, from kindergarten to university students. The most surprising thing was the number of students in the classes. Many times the children had never heard a native English speaker, so the school combined classes so that more kids could see and hear me. I was only allowed to teach verbal lessons, so I was talking and singing for hours at a time. I'd teach the kids a song and then ask if they could write the words in their books, only to be told no. I'd read from their text books and have them repeat the words. Many times I'd have up to 100 kids in a class! Then I'd walk to the bus stop, ride the bus, and walk to the apartment, to climb the eight flights of stairs. We'd eat dinner and go to our rooms to plan lessons for the following day. It was exhausting but I was up for the challenge!

I was making lots of friends with the Chinese teachers and the teacher's assistants. The children were delightful, and we had lots of fun in our classes. I learned how to bundle up for the cold and how to get to the many schools I was teaching in by bus, taxi, or walking. By the end, I was teaching in 20 different classes and seeing over 1,500 kids each week. What an experience!

Teaching English in China was so different from anything I had ever experienced. With classes of up to 100 students all eagerly watching every move I made, I often felt like I was on display. At one school I was greeted with flowers, and a huge welcome sign stretched across the school playground. At the end of the day, some kids were outside and wanted their picture taken with me under the banner with my name on it. There were hugs and waves goodbye. I was pretty tired but still in shock about what actually happened that day. I told Becky about the sign, the man filming my arrival, the flowers, etc., and she started calling me a "teacher star."

The staff at all the schools were very nice. Many of the places didn't have anyone who spoke English. We were always able to communicate. If I was at a school at lunchtime they would invite me to eat with the kids or the teachers. I'd be taken to a lineup with all the kids, and be given a tin plate or bowl. We'd file into a kitchen room where lunch ladies would scoop out the daily meal. It was always rice, cooked with vegetables, and sometimes chicken or fish. The food came out of big cauldrons or tin buckets. Sometimes I'd have no choice, because of the limited time I had between schools, but if there was a window of time I'd try my best to go home for lunch. Winner was a great cook. To get home, I'd have to jump in a cab or take the bus, walk as fast as I could a few blocks to our apartment, and run up the eight flights of stairs to get my lunch. Then I'd run back down the stairs, and jump into a cab to get to the next school. Winner's lunch was worth the trip.

All of us were working very hard at our schools. With our schedules and the poor air-quality, one of us was always sick. We seemed to take turns. Someone would get a cold and fever. The best we could do was to go to bed, to try to sleep it off. We rarely missed a teaching day but each of us was suffering from a variety of respiratory ailments.

We had Internet access in our apartment, and Darren and I talked on MSN every day. Megan was busy with her new living situation and school, so I didn't hear from her as much as I'd hoped. Shortly after we got there, Darren told me about a strange disease spreading throughout China. They were hearing about it on the news in Canada. I asked around a bit, but couldn't find out anything. We had a TV, but there was only one channel in English and reception wasn't very good. It was March 2003. Darren sent me an Internet link about a flu-like sickness that had begun in China, in Guangdong, in November 2002, and was starting to be of concern. I looked up Guangdong on the map, and we were hundreds and hundreds of miles away. I asked around some more, and no one knew about anything like that. There was nothing to worry about.

As March continued and we settled in, I was hearing more from people at home about this strange illness. I tried to find information online, and started to read about some really bizarre situations. What I learned was that the rest of the world was beginning to experience the effects of SARS. I couldn't find out what was happening in China. None of the Chinese people I asked could verify anything. I learned later that Chinese officials did not notify the World Health Organization until February 2003 about the situation that began in November 2002. This caused an epidemic and a near pandemic because of the lack of openness. On March 12, the WHO issued a global alert. It wasn't until early April that information started to get to the people. Even then there were accusations of undercounting in Beijing hospitals.

One day I was sick and lost my voice. I came home from class to rest in our apartment. I was sitting at the computer when one of the cleaning staff came in. She held a pan in her arm and a small broom. There was liquid in the pan, which smelled like disinfectant, that she splashed on the floor all around our apartment. I was writing to someone at home, and said that I couldn't believe what I was seeing. We were being sterilized against the SARS virus with Lysol! Of course no one knew what to do, what it was, what was causing it, or how to stop it from spreading. From what I was reading about what was going on in the rest of the world, there was wide-spread panic. I looked out my window and saw all the same daily activities going on. The people passed on the streets riding their bicycles, walking, delivering, and selling their goods. The regular people either didn't have any idea of what was happening in their country or they couldn't do anything about it even if they knew.

The first time I officially heard what was going on was from a press conference on TV. The first foreigner had died in China. I called Melissa and said "Turn on your TV to see what is going on!" The next day I turned the TV on and it was just snow. I learned later that the English station had been disconnected.

All of us kept going to work each day and I continued to read as much as I could every night. Things were getting scary—especially with the lack of information from Chinese officials. I learned in an email from my university, that they had restricted all international travel to suspect areas and if people travelled their medical coverage would be void. I was really beginning to worry, and needed to find out what support we'd have if something happened to us. Each of us had been sick at different times during our stay and any of the symptoms could be SARS. We didn't go to their doctors and tried to stay away from the hospitals or medical clinics.

Bonnie's husband, Dave arrived at the end of April. We were all really happy to see him, especially Bonnie. Dave had been hearing the news at home but that didn't stop him from coming to China. He wasn't worried, but I kept scouring the Internet every night. We had a blackboard in our apartment where we tracked the reported numbers of people who had died from SARS. It wasn't looking very good. We kept going to our various schools and teaching every day. I was feeling very emotional, since I loved being with the kids. I would go into their classrooms, sing and dance with them, and forget about everything else that was going on. Their smiles and hugs were precious. I took pictures of all the kids and they loved to pose for me. They would bring drawings and cutouts they made for me as gifts. I had prepared myself to miss my friends and family and to embrace the exotic experience we were fortunate to have in China. We knew how to make our way around the city to shop and look around on our own, without speaking the language. I wanted to embrace the time and told Melissa to look around, it was like we were living in a National Geographic film. We were in a very old part of the city with fascinating historic Russian architecture. I loved to hear the language, watch the people, and visit the shops and street vendors. It was amazing and sad to think we'd have to leave before our scheduled time.

We were getting closer to Golden Week in May when we were supposed to go travelling on our vacation. I had been reading that most of Beijing had been closed down. The schools were closed and the students were all made to stay home. Public transportation was virtually at a standstill. If any visitors travelled, the locals would shout at them to go away. The locals thought that if people stopped moving around that would help reduce the spread of SARS. They didn't want anyone to come near them who could potentially infect their families.

I went to teach at one of my schools one day and the Australian teacher was surprised to see me. He said that most of the other teachers were asked by their embassies to come home. He said the Americans were sent back, as well as the British, and the Europeans. I asked why he was still there but he wasn't concerned at all. We had not received any notification to leave. The following day I was at another school and one of my assistants said to me that I couldn't go home now. I asked her "what do you mean?" She told me, in broken English, that the teachers who hadn't left by now were not allowed to leave the country.

With this information I was really getting worried! Then everything came crashing in. I read on the Internet that Golden Week was cancelled. That was to try to stop the people from moving around geographically. The principal came to our apartment with her staff and they asked what our plans were. We said we wanted to visit Dalian, a beach destination closer than Beijing. She informed us that if we travelled, we would not be allowed to go back to our classrooms to protect the children from us!

On April 28, we learned that Harbin had its first reported deaths from SARS. Dave, Bonnie, and I said that was it, we needed to leave. It was not safe for us to be there any longer. The school principal felt very sorry about the situation but understood. They quickly began plans to change our flight tickets.

What an ordeal we had to re-enter Canada. We were greeted by airport officials at the Harbin airport who were wearing "hazmat" suits. We had to wear face masks and have our temperatures taken at various checkpoints, before boarding the planes. We made it from Harbin to the Beijing airport. There was a lot more chaos in the Beijing airport and the last people were trying to leave the country. We made arrangements for a ten-day quarantine location once we arrived in Canada. Since I had a renter in my house, I wasn't sure what to do. But Darren offered to let me stay with him, and I accepted. We all spent our ten days in quarantine. It was actually quite nice since I hadn't realized the amount of stress that the SARS situation had caused me. I was able to talk to people on the phone, and let them know that we were home safe and sound.

One day Darren and I went out for a walk in the neighborhood. There was no one else around and it was only the two of us walking, but I caught myself walking right next to Darren almost pushing him. That was how we walked in China since there were always hundreds of people wherever we went. Even though I didn't have anyone else pushing me, I was squished up against him. I was feeling the effects of re-entry shock. It took awhile to become accustomed to life at home.

After three weeks, my house was available to me again, and I was finally able to go home. Darren and I were very much in love, so he moved in with us. Melissa and Sheldon came home, and Megan followed shortly after. Darren's boys came to spend the summer with us, so we had a house full of kids. By the end of the summer, the boys went back home, Sheldon got his own place, Megan went back to her dad's, and I went back to work. I was working with about 60 international students at the university. Two young women from Korea, Rana and Trinity, asked if they could live with us. We learned so much about the Korean culture and shared everything about ours. We had a lovely time with Rana and Trinity. We had hosted many students in the past ten years, and this was so much fun. They too, became part of the family.

Choosing to Smile

I was still disappointed that we didn't get to travel in China to actually see some of the historic sites. I found an ad for a trip, through my university, to Vietnam. It was a three-week tour, all-inclusive, from Hanoi to Ho Chi Minh City. I was excited when I saw this. I asked Darren if he might be interested in going, and he said he was game to try it. This would be a completely new experience for him. We'd be travelling with a group and all the arrangements were handled for the entire trip. We booked the trip for April, 2004.

We met our group at the Vancouver airport and flew to Taiwan for a stopover and then on to Vietnam. There were 17 people in our group, some from our school and others from the local community. I felt at home in Asia. It was hot and humid and the streets were crowded with bikes, cars, and people. The breeze was hot, and filled with the smells of cooking food and burning incense. We had a guide in each city who took us to hotels, restaurants, and sightseeing. The best part of the trip in Hanoi was going sailing on a junk in Halong Bay. It was the most amazing thing to be on the water in the Gulf of Tonkin, seeing spectacular views of thousands of limestone karsts and islets. I couldn't close my eyes for a second.

But before our trip to Halong Bay, I had an unexpected surprise. On our first morning in Hanoi, Darren and I woke up early to meet our group for breakfast. I was getting my things organized for the day and was chatting with Darren. I had my back to him and noticed that he had gone very quiet. I turned around to find out what he was doing and he was down on one knee in front of me! He was holding a small white box with a ring in it. Then he asked the question, "Will you marry me? I want you to be my wife."

I had a big smile on my face and tears were streaming down my cheeks. I got him to stand up so I could hug him. "Of course, I'd love to!" I was so surprised at being proposed to, and surprised with the thought of getting married. I never dreamed that would hap-

Michelle and Darren in Halong Bay, Vietnam.

pen. When we were leaving home and saying our goodbyes, I had seen Melissa whisper something to Darren. The girls knew Darren was going to propose to me, and Melissa advised him to wait until our last day on the trip, but he couldn't wait. This was the first morning of the trip. My fingers were puffy from the heat and humidity, so the ring wouldn't fit while we were in Asia.

The rest of the trip took us to Hue, Danang, Hoi An, Dalat, Ho Chi Minh City, and the Mekong Delta. We visited artisans and bought beautifully embroidered pictures, lacquerware, hand-painted pictures, and we had custom-tailored clothing made. It was very interesting learning about the customs, culture, and the history of Vietnam. What I encountered was a country with people that have amazing resilience. I have never seen such resilience in my life. Vietnam has experienced hundreds of years of occupation, disaster, and sadness, but I never once felt unwelcome. This trip taught me much about the human spirit.

By the fall of 2004, I had two final courses to complete to finish my degree. I was still working full-time but I was so close that I wanted to get it done with, so I took both fourth-year courses at the same time. I prepared my family for a three-month period when I wouldn't be able to do anything but go to work, go to class, and come home to do homework. It was a very intense few months, but I did it. I finished all the course work to complete my Bachelor of Arts Degree in Adult Education. I was happy finally to have reached this goal. I had taken my first academic credit class in 1989 when I was still sick with cancer.

When I started my degree, I knew I wanted to make changes in my life and in my future. I needed to make positive changes, and to be a good role model for my daughters. When I finished my degree, Melissa had graduated from high school, and had started working on her diploma. Megan was due to graduate that year from high school. I was satisfied and proud that I'd accomplished such a milestone in my life. Once my courses were done I had some free time. It was time to plan a wedding: mine!

We chose April 9, 2005 for our wedding date. I had some planning to do, but the event was more for us to get together as a family to celebrate. We rented a hall and invited about 60 of our family and close friends. I wanted to have an arbor, so Darren built one for me. I spent a Sunday decorating the arbor with flowers, ivy, white lights, and flowing white fabric. It was beautiful. On the night of the rehearsal, Darren loaded the decorated arbor into his truck and took it to the hall. Almost all the family came to help us finish decorate the hall. We set up the arbor and Bonnie decorated a space outside the hall, so we could have our pictures taken after the wedding.

I bought a full-length sage-green dress to wear, and managed to keep it a complete secret from Darren. Melissa, Megan, and I went to have our hair done together the morning of the wedding. I picked

Michelle and Darren's wedding day and the new family.

up coffee and bagels, and we had a nice, relaxing morning together. When it was time to go to the hall, Megan drove us to the hall, and we stayed outside until everyone went in. I was getting nervous as I saw people were still milling around outside the hall. The girls started down the aisle, and soon it was my turn. "Sail Away" by Enya started playing. That was my entrance cue. I suddenly got nervous and teared up, but Bonnie was there to help me. I was so happy to have her with me on this magical day. We both had tears of happiness streaming from our eyes.

Bonnie nudged me to enter the hall and make my entrance down the aisle to Darren, his best men, Curtis and Spencer, and the girls, Melissa, Megan, and Macy, our flower girl. He was pleasantly surprised to see my beautiful wedding dress, and I was equally surprised to see the three guys wearing tuxedoes with the green ties and vests that matched my dress! Darren's mom knew what color my dress was and helped them get their findings to match.

Once the ceremony was completed, we all went outside to have family pictures taken. It was a beautiful day. We came back into the hall and had a wonderful dinner. Glenda was the one who set Darren and me up on that first blind date, so it was quite fitting that she was the emcee for our reception. She had a lot of tricks up her sleeves, and managed to entertain our families and friends for the entire evening.

We had a relaxing two-week honeymoon in sunny Puerto Vallarta, Mexico. Bonnie sent us off with a gift of wedding beach sandals. I had a white pair and Darren a black pair. On the bottom of each shoe a word was etched out in reverse. One shoe said "Just" and the other "Married." When we walked along the beach wearing our sandals, the words would appear in the sand: "Just Married. Just Married. Just Married."

We spent our days swimming in the ocean and resting on the deck chairs. We took the local bus into town to wander around the markets. We explored the town to find good Mexican food. One afternoon, I met Darren out at the beach and he had arranged for a one-hour massage on the beach for me. There was a massage table set up some distance away from the noise of the resort in a very private spot. I had the most peaceful, relaxing massage ever. The table was right next to the surf, and all I could hear was the soothing lapping of the waves. The breeze was blowing and the umbrella over the table was billowing. It was a lovely way to spend an afternoon.

It was time to go home. I would be graduating with my degree in June. Darren, Melissa, Megan, Bonnie, my dad, and my new in-laws, Pat and Gerry, and some of my friends were all there to see me cross the stage. People were cheering and clapping for all the grads, but I clearly heard *my* people shout "Way to go, Mom!" when it was my turn.

Late in the fall of 2005, I got an email from Rana in Korea. I was happy to hear from her. She had a new job for a company that

Melissa, Bonnie, Megan, Michelle, and Howie at Michelle's graduation in 2005.

ran English camps for kids and they were looking for teachers. She asked me if I would come to Korea to teach for a three-week winter camp in January 2006. I was always ready for an adventure, and I said yes. When I got to Seoul, I was able to stay with Trinity and her family for two days before I went to Seoju for three weeks to teach with Rana. I was happy to see the girls again, and to experience daily life in Korea.

Teaching in Korea.

Once I got home, I went right back to work. I had two weeks of holidays to use up, so I started looking for a warm destination with a cheap airfare. I found a trip to Belize. My dad hadn't travelled for quite awhile and wanted to come along, so I booked four tickets, two for Darren and me, and two for my dad and his wife Ursula. When we arrived in Belize, we took a short trip to Guatemala to visit Tikal, a UNESCO World Heritage site. After a few days there, we moved on to Caye Caulker Belize. We spent the rest of our vacation there enjoying the white sand and hot weather. Darren and I went snorkeling at Shark Ray Alley, where we swam with nurse sharks and stingrays. In the fall of 2006, Darren and I travelled to Costa Rica, where we hiked on a live volcano called Arenal. We traveled to the east coast of Costa Rica, to Puerto Viejo, and spent two weeks on the beach and in the jungle. It was the first time I'd ever seen real live sloths, and heard the cries of howler monkeys.

In the spring of 2007 Darren and I were traveling again. We traveled to Bangkok, Thailand for a few days and then moved south to Railay to complete a glorious vacation. We spent our afternoons snorkeling, and even went for a jungle ride on elephants! Another amazing adventure. I was seeing the world and things I never could have imagined I'd ever have the chance to experience.

When I got back to work I learned that the Student Life department at my university was looking for a speaker for their leadership conference. I asked Glenda if she would be interested in being the keynote speaker. She accepted, and the department was happy to have her speak to the students. Glenda had been giving motivational talks to groups of high school kids and all types of adult groups for twenty years. I started organizing the details for Glenda and as a joke she called me her manager. I said that I loved to do this type of work, and she said that was what she was looking for, someone to organize her, to start her speaking business. And another partnership was born.

Glenda had achieved so much over the years, and she hates the organizing part. She had all her clippings and notes in a box so I got that from her. Megan loves organizing and had some time to spare so I gave her an empty binder with plastic sleeves with the box of stuff. Megan was taking a web design course so she used this material for her project. Glenda was surprised at how great it looked. I suggested that we get a professional to design a web site with a logo, so we hired a web designer. We were both so pleased with the silhouette image that was created for Glenda's new company from a picture of her, www. glendastandeven.com was created.

That winter I was reminded that in 2008, I would be a 20-year survivor. It was a very important milestone for me. I thought about all the times of not knowing what my future would hold. I remembered how important reaching my five-year mark had been. I didn't know how critical the five-year survival rate for Hodgkin's was, until I heard a doctor mention it. I was feeling very fortunate and wondered if by telling my story I could help someone facing a similar situation. I told my daughters that I was going to write the story of how I discovered my cancer, and what I remembered of the treatments, as well as my feelings at the time. I wrote the story, and had it done by Christmas. I took Melissa and Megan aside separately and read the story to each of them. They were moved by my story and wanted me to share it.

I contacted three Canadian magazines who I thought might be interested in the story. I was surprised that in less than two weeks the health section editor at Canadian Living contacted me. She said they were interested in the story, so I sent the full version. Once she read the story I was contacted to work on editing the essay. We worked together, and the editor did her magic to help my words form a "ready for the magazine story." Then we waited. I didn't want to tell too many people in case it didn't get published.

We carried on with our lives, and went on a vacation to Panama in March 2008. Darren and I spent two weeks in Bocas Del Toro and a third week in Panama City. Bocas is a group of islands with fantastic beaches, and a laid-back lifestyle. Panama City is a stark contrast to the islands, but seeing the Panama Canal was breathtaking.

That spring, Darren and I felt that we had outgrown our townhouse and put it up for sale. It was on the market for quite a few months, but it sold by the fall. We looked around at houses and found a perfect one in the small rural town of Yarrow. Glenda had grown up in Yarrow. We found a house that needed some TLC, but Darren thought he could keep busy renovating the house. We have a big yard with a vegetable garden. I hadn't done any gardening since before the girls were born, and before I got sick, so I was looking forward to growing our own food.

All the kids helped when we moved in October 2008. We spent months renovating the house ourselves. Before winter set in, I was able to work in the yard to prepare the garden for spring planting. Megan had a change in her life that brought her back home to live with us.

The first Christmas in our new house we found ourselves in the middle of serious renovations. I was working hard helping Darren to get the new floors installed, painting, etc. and hadn't been able to do any preparations for Christmas. One day I came home and Melissa and Megan had brought us a tree complete with decorations and lights. They even surprised me with matching flannel Christmas pajamas for the three of us! We spent the afternoon decorating gingerbread houses and drinking hot chocolate just like when they were young.

In the spring of 2009, Darren, Megan and I took a trip to Asia together. Megan had never travelled out of the country and she was happy to accompany us. We flew to Cambodia and Malaysia for three weeks. This was a phenomenal trip for all of us. Here we found ourselves

Matchy-matchy!

Michelle and Megan with Cambodian friends.

meeting people who have lived incredible lives. I always find travelling to different countries to be an eye-opening and humbling experience. As I meet the local people and learn about their lives, it helps me put my life and appreciation into perspective. We spent a few days in Phnom Penh and visited the Angkor Kingdom in Siem Reap which is another UNESCO World Heritage site.

When we came home from Cambodia, I went back to work. The first day back, I stopped at the mailbox to find the April edition of *Canadian Living*. I held my breath as I opened it to find my article, "My Symbol of Hope." I quickly ran up the stairs at home and was choked up. Darren thought something bad happened, and asked "What's wrong?"

I came into the living room holding the magazine and gave it to him. The tears were those of joy. I couldn't believe it actually happened. I hadn't told too many people about the story, not wanting to get my hopes up. I called Melissa and Megan to say we needed to get a room booked and invite people to a reading of the story. The only person who'd seen the printed version was Darren.

Friday, March 13, 2009, twenty family and close friends got together at the Royal Hotel to hear my story. We got our drinks and

Glenda, Michelle, Julie, and Bonnie at my book reading.

went to a private room for a quiet reading. I sat on a tall chair in front of the group. I was nervous because no one had heard this story yet, but now it was in public view. I didn't know how people would receive my story. I looked out at everyone, and told them that in that room, there were only four people who knew me when I was sick. There were Melissa and Megan, who were just babies at the time, my sister Bonnie, and my friend Tammy. All the rest of the people had come into my life after my cancer. What a testament to my new life, my life after cancer!

Strategically seated in the front row was our survivor group: Glenda, Julie, and Bonnie H. I read the story and everyone was silent. I looked up a few times but really wanted to maintain my composure. Reading it to friends who were hearing it for the first time was heartwarming. When I finished, I looked up to proud and smiling faces. People came up and hugged me, some breaking down in tears. I asked people if they cried while I was reading but they told me how they held their breath so they wouldn't start crying. It was okay. If they did or when they did, the tears were a reminder of how far we've come in life.

When we finished the reading we all went into the hotel lounge to celebrate! We shared stories, had a few drinks and had a good visit.

It was a great evening, ending with the accomplishment of my first article going public.

The next day, I was talking to Glenda about how the night went. She said how good she thought Bonnie H. looked, considering that her tumors were back. I was shocked! I didn't know that. This couldn't be happening to her. Bonnie had been fighting so hard. I was sad to hear this news. Despite her situation, Bonnie had looked so happy that evening. She wasn't showing that anything was wrong. That's her personality.

I spent the weekend thinking about it. I felt what we needed to do was to make some memories, just the four of us. On Monday I sent an email to Glenda, Julie, and Bonnie H., saying "pack your bags ladies, we're going away for a fun weekend."

On a Saturday in April, we went to Bellingham, Washington. We checked into our hotel and went to town for an afternoon of shopping, manicures, dinner, and drinks. We stayed up late talking, like we were having a slumber party.

The next morning we drove to the historical town of Fairhaven. We walked around looking in all the shops. Julie remembered that she had been in a great bookstore years before. We found the store and had a look around. Glenda was looking for some angel cards and that led us on a search in the motivational and inspirational sections of the bookstore.

While we were standing waiting for Glenda, Julie said, "We should write a book." The four of us were all interested in this suggestion and talked about it over lunch and for hours afterwards.

Over the summer, responses came from people all over the country about the magazine article. If I can inspire or help anyone, that's my goal. I want to give hope to people. I thought I could show what life could look like, twenty years after cancer. I don't know if or when cancer will come back, and I don't want to hold my breath. I'm at risk for secondary cancers from my treatments, the treatments that were meant to save my life. I'm at a risk for breast cancer since my mother and my Aunty Marge both had breast cancer. The way things go we never know who will be here tomorrow and who won't.

My wish is for people to live. I mean really live. Take that step out. Try something that you've thought about but, until now, haven't had the inspiration to do it.

I don't want to die sitting at home waiting for cancer. But if something happens to me on a trip, or crossing the street, I want people to know that I've been living my life. I have a lot more dreams and many more places to see, so I think I have a lot more living to do.

My diagnosis was over twenty years ago. I think about it every day. I don't dwell on it, but I celebrate the knowledge and experience. I remember the feelings about the uncertainty of my life and I want to live each moment I have. I don't want to waste time. I certainly feel better physically and spiritually than I did twenty years ago.

I'm very blessed to have my family and friends. I'm proud of all our children. Their success will be measured by what is important to them in life; not by money, fame, level of education, or status, but by what's in their hearts. During all these years, my friendships with Glenda, Bonnie Holmes, and Julie kept crossing in so many ways. We wanted to make a point of getting together regularly so we started taking turns having dinner (with our husbands) at each other's homes. We called these our survivor dinners. Each couple would bring some food, our own drinks, and the host would make the main course. Occasionally we even have entertainment. As the evening progresses, the drinks flow and the laughter just gets better and better. It's a wonderful way to stay connected, to share support with friends. Julie is a dragonboat paddler too, so often we are at the same regattas. Sometimes I even paddle with the breast cancer team as a spare. We all keep in touch because we share a special bond.

Sometimes I grumble about doing housework but I'm fortunate

to have a house. Some days I don't want to get up to go to work but I've worked very hard to have my good job. Other days I'm too tired to cook dinner when I come home, but I'm lucky to have food and a kitchen.

How we live or celebrate our lives is all in our perspective. Sometimes we need a reminder or a wakeup call. Perhaps it's simplistic, but it's how I look at life. We can make choices. I choose to smile.

Julie's
Story

I don't know when I started to think of myself as "Little Julie Smith from Pleasington" but I am sure it was at a very early age. I was one of the Smith children who lived at the top of the hill in Pleasington. I inherited my grandmother's small physique which was why I think I was often referred to as "Little Julie Smith" and the title seemed to become a part of my identity. I was quite a serious child, not very confident, but I had a stubborn streak and once I decided on something I would not back down. This stubborn determination has been a huge strength to me over the years, but has also landed me in hot water on many occasions.

I was born in 1954 in a town in northern England called Blackburn, and was raised in a little village called Pleasington. I was the second child born to Fred and Marie Smith who went on to have another daughter and then a son. Our names were Anne, Julie, Geraldine, and John. We had a strong Irish Catholic background on both sides of the family.

Our family moved from a little terraced house in the town of Blackburn to a house in Pleasington when I was six months old. The house had been owned by my great uncle Frank and my paternal grandparents had inherited a share of it. The house was in pretty bad shape, with the outside walls made of asbestos and wooden beams. It needed rebuilding before it was truly livable, but my dad wanted to live and raise his children in Pleasington, and was determined to buy it.

Money was scarce, as were building materials in post-war England. Nevertheless, my dad set about rebuilding the house while we lived in it, and as our family grew in size.

The Smith Children, left to right: Anne, John, Geraldine and Julie.

Pleasington was indeed an idyllic place to grow up. It was a sleepy village with a beautiful church, Pleasington Priory. There was also a two-room elementary school called Pleasington Primary. The village had some fancy, large houses in it, however there was also a little row of ramshackle houses on Long Lane that were owned and lived in by working-class families. Ours was one of the houses on Long Lane. There were no house numbers on Long Lane, just house names, and ours was called "Stonecliffe." A wealthy person in the village was once quoted as saying that all the houses on Long Lane were a mess and should be torn down to build nice homes. This comment outraged my parents and our neighbors. There was an annual reunion dance at the school every winter, and a village garden party in the summer which was held on the grounds of Pleasington Lodge, one of the grandest houses in the village.

Throughout our childhood years, dad continued to work on the house. We would come home from school to find dad had knocked down a wall, and in its place were tarps to keep us dry until he had finished rebuilding the wall. One December, my sisters and I pleaded with mum to put up the Christmas tree and decorations in the living room which was at a bare brick stage of rebuilding. She could not bring herself to put up the decorations, so we pleaded with Uncle Frank, my dad's younger brother, to put them up for us while mum was out. We waited excitedly for mum to come home and see the lovely twirled crepe paper streamers and colorful balloons all hanging from the bare brick unfinished walls. When she saw them, she cried. As a child I didn't see the bare brick behind the streamers, I just saw the beautiful scene we had created, so I didn't understand why she was crying.

My dad was a hard worker, who for most of his life worked as a signal man for British Rail. He worked rotating shifts and when he was not at work he was usually working on the house or digging out the well, which provided drinking water for the houses on the hill. He was one of the few younger men who lived on the hill, so if there was a problem with the well, everyone would wait for my dad and our neighbor Jack to come home, and together they would dig out the well to get the water running. The excitement in our house was high on the day we were connected to the town water supply. We were in awe of the steady stream of water coming out of the taps instead of the trickle that was often the case with the well water.

Dad was a heavy smoker all of his life. When we were young, he smoked cigarettes, but later changed to smoking a pipe. When he was home the living room was full of smoke and the pipe smoke was very intense. The smell of pipe smoke still reminds me of my dad. After his first heart attack, he changed to smoking cigars because he thought they were better for him than the pipe.

With dad working shifts, we often didn't see much of him, but his philosophy of life had a powerful influence on me and still guides me to this day. He believed in the principle of never doing anything to anyone that you would not want done to yourself.

Choosing to Smile

I try to live by this principle and have gone on to teach it to my son. I have a strong memory of dad describing his disgust at a racist comment he heard someone make about a person of color who had been injured in a car accident. He silenced the racist by saying, "I don't care what color his skin was, his blood was red just like mine."

Dad was a gentle man who was usually quiet, unless he had something important to say. If there was something he felt strongly about, he could put forward a very powerful opinion, especially if he had a few drinks at the local pub. I never heard him swear; apparently even at work he was referred to as "the vicar" because he never used bad language. He had a humanistic attitude towards his fellow man and believed in equal opportunities for everyone. He was a strong believer in the union movement, serving as union steward for many years. Dad was also a compassionate man in his own way. As teenagers we used to joke about how dad could not even watch "Little House on the Prairie" without getting teary-eyed.

Mum was also a very hard worker who somehow managed to run the household and take care of four children almost single handed (because of my dad's long work hours), in addition to working part-time. The women in my extended family all worked outside the home out of financial necessity. Both my grandmothers worked as weavers in the cotton mill. When we were very small, mum cleaned for a lady who lived in the big house at the bottom of the hill. Later she got a part-time job at a sweet stall in the town's outdoor market, and eventually worked two part-time jobs helping out at the local post office, as well as the market stall. Mum kept our house spotlessly clean. She was also a good cook who could make three meals for six people with a single pound of ground beef or an inexpensive pot roast.

My maternal grandma was from a family of ten children. I loved to listen to her stories of growing up in a large family in Victorian England. They were a very poor but very proud family. One of my granny's frequent sayings was, "We were poor but we were happy and we always had food on the table."

My great grandfather supported his large family by having two jobs. He had a window-cleaning route, going from house-to-house, cleaning windows for a fee. His second job was to wake people up for work, by going from house to house at 5 AM and knocking on the upstairs windows with a long stick. This was before people had alarm clocks and everyone started work at the cotton mill at 6 AM so there was a need for someone to wake people up. So my great grandfather was the official "Knocker Upper."

Not all ten children in that family survived to adulthood; one died in infancy, and one died of diphtheria. The ones that did survive went to school full-time until age twelve and then worked part-time in the mill. By age fourteen, they were all working full-time in the mill. My granny was tiny and her job was to climb inside the cotton weaving looms to clean them. She went on to become a skilled weaver. It was a hard life, but she always insisted that they were happy. Granny was a very devout Catholic who had more interest in going to church than anything else in life.

Granny was also an accomplished worrier, and she could always find something to worry about. She passed this pattern on to my mum who passed it on to me. Sometimes I think it is genetic.

Granny had three sisters who never married. They were of marriageable age just after World War One, when a large number of young men had gone to war and never returned. I was very fond of my Great Aunts Agnes, Maggie, and Annie. They were a little eccentric, but were good people who instilled in me the need to be kind to everyone and to have compassion for those less fortunate.

I remember one of them asking me one day what I wanted to do when I grew up, and all three of them trying to hide their smiles as I told them I was trying to decide between being a nun or a ballet dancer. I really thought I might have a calling to be a nun but I loved to read stories about Margot Fonteyn, the famous British ballet dancer, and rather fancied the idea of dressing up in the pretty ballet dresses.

My paternal grandfather died when I was a small child, so I have very few memories of him. My paternal grandmother lived next door to us for most of our childhood, but we really did not spend much time with her. My mum would make her evening meals every day, and one of the kids would take it over to her. I don't remember her doing anything with us except for Christmas Day when we were allowed to pick a chocolate off her tree. Then our cousins would arrive, and she would shoo us off home while they all ate Christmas dinner together.

Life as a child in Pleasington was indeed very pleasant. There were only a few children living on the hill, so our playmates were mostly our siblings and three other local children: Julie and Susan, whose parents were best friends with our mum and dad, and a boy called John, who lived just down the road from us. My two sisters and I were two years apart in age, Anne the elder and Geraldine the youngest sister. After three girls, my parents had given up hope of having a son, and so were ecstatic when my brother John was born.

We walked to and from school on country roads with hardly any traffic. Our playground was the countryside with its endless fields, streams, and ponds to explore, and wildflowers like bluebells and buttercups to pick. We would make daisy chain necklaces and "roly poly" down the grassy hill, sometimes failing to see the cow poop in time!

If we found a dead hedgehog or field mouse, we would dig a hole and give it a decent burial marking the spot with a cross made of pebbles. We were good Catholics so there were always prayers for the deceased hedgehog or mouse.

In the summers, we went blackberry picking, usually arriving home with blackberry juice-stained mouths from eating as many berries as we collected in our bowls. Mum would then transform the berries into delicious blackberry pies and jam.

We had the freedom to roam and often went to places that were out of bounds. We would wander down to the golf course that was used by the wealthy villagers. They would chase us off the greens when they were trying to play their game of golf. In the winter the 7th hole was a perfect sledging hill.

There was a tiny village nearby called Houghton Bottoms that still had a working cotton mill with an old water wheel. The village consisted of a few weavers' cottages and several farms. We would often walk down there on a Sunday with my mum and her friend Jean, to buy eggs from one of the farms. But when we went without our parents we explored the old stone quarry, and that was a place where we were not supposed to go. The quarry itself was not too dangerous, but to get to it, we had to cross the viaduct over the river, and it was a railway viaduct. This route was fine as long as there were no trains coming, but on more than one occasion, we were in the middle of the bridge when we heard a train approaching and there was no room for the train and us on the bridge. As soon as we heard the train, we ran as fast as we could to get to the other side of the bridge. We could hear the train whistle screaming as the driver saw us on the track. Miraculously, we always made it in time.

Sometimes our cousins would come to visit and play with us. My favorite cousin was Ian. He was just a couple of weeks older than me and we were best friends. While the girls were all playing with dolls, Ian and I would be off on adventures together. We had vivid imaginations, and developed all kinds of make-believe games. One day we would be exploring a jungle, and another day we would pretend to be swimming in the ocean. Some days my younger sister, Geraldine, would want to play with us and mum would say we should let her tag along. But she was too young to understand our make-believe adventures. We would tell her we were playing "Hide and Seek" and she had to count to 100 and then come and look for us, but we were long gone before she got to 100.

Ian and I always said we would get married when we grew up. The other kids said we couldn't, because we were first cousins. So we decided that when we grew up we would go to Rome to ask the Pope to give us permission to marry. Ian was going to get a motor scooter and together we would ride to Rome. I don't know why, but we had it in our heads that if the Pope said we could get married, then it would be okay. However when we reached our pre-teen years our close friendship waned.

Ian became interested in fishing, and although he tried to include me in his fishing trips, it was not for me. I could not see the point of sitting in silence all day at the edge of a pond just to catch a fish. I have a vivid memory of the last fishing trip we took together. We walked to the pond in a local field with fishing rods in hand and sat down for the day's fishing. I caught a small fish and Ian said I had to take the hook out of its mouth. I thought this was the most disgusting thing, and refused to do it. He said I had to learn if I was going to continue fishing. So I decided that I would just watch him fish. From the corner of the field a group of small cows appeared and they started to move towards us. Though I had grown up in the countryside I was still afraid of cows, if there was not a fence between them and me. I got up to leave, but Ian said they would not bother us and to sit still. I was not going to take his word for it so I walked towards the gate. As I moved, the cows moved quickly towards me, so I started to run, and so did the cows. Within seconds, I was running full pelt with the cows following after me. Ian shouted for me to stop running and the cows would stop following, but by then I was in panic mode. I got to the gate and breathlessly clambered over it. I then walked home on my own. I was fuming mad and vowed I would never go fishing with

Ian again. After that, Ian and I drifted apart, both of us going through the roller coaster of the teen years in different ways, but he will always have a special place in my heart.

Pleasington Priory was a strict Catholic school and the curriculum was strongly guided by religious studies. We started the day with assembly and prayers. On Monday morning we were asked if we had attended Mass the previous day. When the head teacher suspected someone was not answering honestly, she would follow up with the question, "What color vestments was the priest wearing?" The colors varied from week to week so it was a good way to catch us lying. After assembly we divided up into the two classrooms and the first lesson of the day was religion.

Sometimes the priest would come in and teach the catechism. In my early school years it was taught in Latin, and I had no idea what I was chanting. Later on, it was in English but it still did not really make a lot of sense to me. The priest did not tolerate mistakes; he regularly threw the wooden duster at anyone who got the response wrong. If you didn't duck in time, it hurt. We would then fit in some math and reading or writing before lunch. After lunch, it was religion again and then on to the academic studies.

There were certain times when the religious studies took up more time. The May Procession was an event that took a great deal of preparation during school time. For this event, a May Queen was chosen, and she wore a beautiful, long dress which had a train along with train bearers. The May Queen's job was to lead the procession, and to climb up the ladder to place the crown of flowers on the statue of Mary while the congregation sang, "Oh Mary we crown thee with blossoms today, Queen of the Angels and Queen of the May."

To be the May Queen was every school girl's dream. The names of all the eligible girls were put into a hat. I remember the thrill of knowing that this was the year my name would be in the hat and that

May Queen for the day.

I might be the next May Queen. The head teacher shook the hat and pulled out a piece of paper.

I heard her say, "Julie Smith."

I could not believe it really was me. I was so excited and thrilled; I had visions of myself in the long dress with the train and the bouquet of flowers.

I remember handing mum the paper with my name on it when I arrived home from school. "You are the May Queen!" she said in an incredulous voice as she gave me a big hug.

From then until the day of the procession, our house was a whirl of preparation. There was a dress to be made, headdress to be bought, flowers to be ordered, and a hair dresser's appointment to be made for the day. Mom set to work, and I am quite sure she loved every minute of it, even though the expense was probably a big strain on our family finances.

When the big day arrived, I went to the hairdresser in the morning and was adamant that I did not want my long hair cut. I had waist-length hair that I usually wore in a thick braid. Mum assured me that I would only be having a trim. I was mortified when I looked in the mirror and saw my hair chopped off to shoulder length and curled. I hated it.

But, even with a haircut I hated, the Procession went well. I managed to climb the steps, place the crown without tripping, and prevented myself from giggling at the jokes made by the cushion bearer.

There was a downside to living in the village of Pleasington. Most of the children at the school came from the neighboring village of Feniscowles. I often felt left out because my school friends could all meet to play after school but I could not because it was too far to go. They could also go to the sweet shop, and have fish and chips from the chippy in Feniscowles. We often asked my mum for chips in a bag like the chippy sold, so she would make little bags out of bread wrapping paper and fill them with homemade chips. We would sprinkle them with salt and vinegar and eat them with our fingers pretending that they were from the chippy.

At age eleven, I went to the closest Catholic secondary school in a nearby town called Darwen. My time at the secondary school was a little unsettling at first, but I soon adjusted. Even though we lived only a few miles away, our accents were slightly different than the Darwen accent. Some of the girls thought we were being snobs and made fun of our accent. They would push us up against the wall and ask us to say the words that we pronounced differently, and then laugh at how we said them. We had been in the sheltered environment of the small Pleasington School and were very naive. I didn't know many swear words or the meaning of many of the adult words that the girls used. I would pretend to know what they were talking about but I really had no clue.

The small group of Pleasington girls tended to stay together. In our early teens we were all still quite devout and often went to church twice on Sundays. We would attend morning Mass and then go back again for the benediction at three PM.

Choosing to Smile

There was no time for lazing about during my teen years. There was a strong work ethic in our family. By the time I was 13, mum had found me a Saturday job at the market selling fruit and vegetables. The days were long, but I loved it and it gave me the money to buy clothes. It was right across from the stall where mum worked so she could keep an eye on me. I worked at the market stall every Saturday until I was 18.

When I was about 14 years old, the church built a new church hall in Feniscowles and we wanted to hold a weekly youth club in the new hall. The priest said he would allow it, but he expected some work in return from us. He wanted us to clean up the church grounds and cemetery and to raise some money for the church. Since we were eager to use the church hall, we enthusiastically spent several weekends cleaning up the church grounds and organizing a sponsored walk to raise money for the church.

To our delight, the youth club opened its doors every Friday evening; it was the highlight of our week. We would dress up in our mini dresses and dance to sixties music. The lights were dimmed to make it seem like a real disco.

The sponsored walk was a huge success and we proudly handed the money over to the priest. A short time later, the priest decided to come and check out the youth club. He walked into the church hall with a flash light because the lights were low. The first thing he saw was a girl sitting on a boy's knee and demanded that the lights be turned on high. That week he closed the youth club down because of the immoral behavior of girls sitting on boys' knees. I was incensed! I felt that we had been used to clean up the church grounds and raise money and then an excuse was made to close down our club. I went from being the devout Catholic "Little Julie Smith" to a non-believer. I stopped going to church and never went back. In retrospect, I think I was already having doubts about the teachings of the church and this incident confirmed my doubts.

When I was 14, I met Andy; a very handsome boy at the church youth club. He was very grown up at 17. Not only was he older than me but he had his own transportation, a trendy Lambretta 125 scooter decorated with lots of extra mirrors. This was the time of the "mods" and "rockers" in England. The mods were clean-cut boys in trendy clothes who rode on scooters and the rockers were the motor bikers who dressed in leather. The mods had the focus of my attention. My mum forbade me to ride on the back of the scooter but I did it anyway.

One wonderful day, he picked me up from school. I felt so special as I put on the helmet and climbed onto the back of his scooter. My school uniform skirt was a very short, grey mini skirt which was probably not the best choice of attire for riding on the back of a scooter. I felt so grown up and sexy as we sped away with all my friends watching enviously. I was totally in love with him but he was a bit too old for me. He was interested in more than the holding hands and kissing, but at this time I was still the devout church-going Catholic girl. As the kisses became more passionate, I had a hard time stopping his hands from wandering to forbidden places on my body. I was devastated and cried for days when he broke up with me quite suddenly. I later found out that he had gone back with his ex-girlfriend who was older than me and who I was sure allowed his hands to wander further than I did.

I had a few boyfriends between the age of 15 and 17, though none were ever serious. After one break-up I decided I did not want a steady boyfriend and just wanted to have fun with my friends. Even though we were underage, we went to the popular pubs. In England, it was not illegal to be in a pub under the legal age for drinking as long as you did not drink alcohol. One popular pub was called "The Lodestar."

The Lodestar had two pub rooms and a disco. We would go on a Saturday night with just enough money to buy one soft drink, and then we would then fill up our glasses with water, pretending we were drinking vodka. There was usually a house party to go to after the pub closed. On one particular night, we were invited to an all-night party at one of the big posh houses in Pleasington. Of course I was not allowed to stay out all night, so I told my mum I was staying at my friend's house, and she told her mum she would be staying at our house.

It was at this party that I first saw Graham. I caught sight of him across the room and was very taken with him. I asked one of my friends if she knew his name; she said everyone called him "Kez" but she thought this was just a nickname. I later found out his real name was Graham.

Over the next few weeks, as we chatted with Graham and his group of friends at the Lodestar, I became more interested in him, but I still was not interested in a serious relationship.

One evening I went to a house party in Darwen, and Graham and his friends were there. Graham immediately came over to chat with me. There was something about him that captivated me. As we chatted, he put his arm around my shoulders, I know this sounds like a cliché, but I really did feel an electric shock go through my body. I wanted him to keep his arm there forever. I had never felt like this before. We went out to sit in his little grey van where we chatted some more and then we kissed. Oh, my God! I was in heaven. It felt so good to have his arms around me and I was impressed that he was a perfect gentleman. I didn't have to fight off wandering hands as was usually the case with other boys I had dated. He drove me home that night, then asked if I wanted to go out with him the following night. I agreed but as I had already arranged to go out with my friend, we decided that he would drive us both to the Lodestar. That night I had a dream starring Graham. We were kissing deeply and passionately and getting very intimate. I think this was my first ever erotic dream.

Through April, May, and June, Graham and I dated regularly. On the way home, Graham would park his van and we would talk, laugh, cuddle, and kiss. Yes, we really did only cuddle and kiss.

Then in late July, I went on a holiday to the south of England with some friends. This trip had been arranged before I started dating Graham, and we both agreed we should keep our separate holiday arrangements, because we were not in a serious relationship. The time I spent away from him was agony for me. I missed him so much. The other girls enjoyed dancing at the disco and chatting with boys, but I was not interested. I just wanted to go home and see Graham again. These strong feelings took me by surprise. I had been looking forward to spending time with my friends, so why was I so miserable without him? Finally the holiday came to an end, but Graham had left for his holiday before I got home, so I had to wait another week before I could see him.

Our reunion was blissful, and by then I knew I was madly in love with him. I also knew that I wanted him to make love to me more than anything in the world. A few weeks later we were watching TV in his bedroom; we snuggled on his bed and once again the kisses became very passionate. I encouraged his hands to wander to all those forbidden places on my body, which he did without hesitation. We both knew without saying it that this was the night we were going to make love. I wanted him so much but he didn't rush me. Our lovemaking that night was every bit as wonderful as I had imagined it would be.

That's enough of the details, except to say that the magic has not worn off, even after 37 years together. The cynics who say that

Julie at 18.

the attraction wanes after a few years of marriage have obviously not experienced the true delights of hot monogamy.

When I was 18 years old, my life changed dramatically. In January 1973, I started my first day at nurse training school in Preston a town a few miles from Blackburn. I was to spend eight weeks in preliminary training school, and then would be working on the hospital wards. The schedule for the next three years would be eight weeks working on the wards, and then two weeks in training school. At that time, New Year's Day was not a public holiday so I was to report for the first classes at 8:30 AM on January first and I was scheduled to move into the nurse's boarding home on New Year's Eve.

On New Year's Eve, Graham drove me to Preston and helped me move my things into my room. The rules were strict:no boys allowed in your room and doors locked at 10 PM. The matron who was in charge of the nurses' home gave Graham a severe look as she said, "You may carry her belongings up to her room, but that will be the one and only time you are allowed in there."

I dropped my bags and left to bring in the New Year with Graham. I knew the doors to the nurses' home would be locked when I got back at 2 AM but I planned to go into the hospital and ask the night porter to open the door for me. I kissed Graham good night and then walked up to the hospital door that was closest to the building my room was in. To my horror, the door was locked, and Graham had already left. The hospital grounds were large and I was not yet familiar with the layout. I wandered around the grounds in the dark trying to find the main door, panicking that I might be out all night. Eventually after what seemed like *hours*, but was probably only 15 minutes, I found the main door.

One of the porters walked me back to the nurses' home to let me in, but not before giving me a lecture about how it was not a good idea to be out so late the night before my first day of training. After that night, I had a friend unlock the patio door in the common room after the porters had done their final check for the night, so I could let myself in.

The eight weeks in school were quite enjoyable, but I was nervous about working on the wards. I was right to be nervous. Over the next few months I grew up quickly. Within weeks I had seen a person die, and had helped lay out a dead body. I was seeing people who were gravely ill and in the final stages of life. Many of them had cancer. At that time no one said the word "cancer," it was referred to as CA. Even in the records the doctors wrote CA and many times the relatives were informed of the diagnosis, but the patient was not.

One day, a young man in his thirties was admitted with breathlessness. He had a build-up of fluid in his pleura (*lungs*) and the doctors prepared to drain it. I remember the nurse in charge of the ward having tears in her eyes when the young man was diagnosed with inoperable lung cancer. He was the first patient I knew who was given no hope at such a young age. I had always thought that cancer was something that happened to someone else, and in other families, but not to me or my family members.

I met Carrie the first day in the nurse's home and we became best friends. Carrie and I were placed at Sharrow Green Hospital for the first six months. We chatted after work most evenings, while munching on licorice allsorts. Our legs and feet would burn and ache after standing all day, so many times we would lie on the bed with our feet up on the cold wall to cool our feet and ease the aches. We would chat about the day's events, and about our boyfriends. We were usually exhausted and overwhelmed by the learning curve we were on, but we laughed a lot.

As student nurses, we were performing all kinds of new tasks everyday and most of the time I was terrified of doing something wrong. In the first few months I had learned to give injections, change IV bottles, do enemas, pass catheters, and lay out dead bodies, in addition to the more mundane work of bed bathing and helping patients with bedpans. We were not there just to observe, we were a large part of the work force. The wards were staffed by several student nurses at various levels in their training and a couple of qualified staff. There were times on the night shift when there was only one qualified nurse between two wards, with the student nurses left on their own for long periods of time. We would just start to feel confident with the ward routine when it was time to move to another ward. Each ward nurse had different rules about how things should be done, and some were stricter than others.

Within a few months of living in the nurses' home, we were getting tired of the restrictions. Carrie had a steady boyfriend who lived and worked in London, so they had to carry on a long-distance relationship. She would go down to London on her days off when she could afford it, but wanted him to have somewhere to stay when he came up to Preston. I was growing tired of being locked out when I got home late and wanted more freedom, as did our other friend Sally. So it was decided that the three of us would rent our own place. We were paid a very small salary as student nurses, but if we lived in the nurses' home with low rent and ate the inexpensive food at the hospital canteen, then it was possible to make ends meet. Everyone told us that we could not afford to rent our own place, but that just made us more determined to do it. We quickly found a little terraced house within walking distance to the two hospitals that we would be doing our training in. It came furnished with old, but clean, furniture and had a nice fully equipped kitchen.

Money was extremely tight and many times the money ran out before the month did. We would pool our money to buy a loaf of bread and a jar of jam to live on until we got paid. Graham drove over to see me at least four or five times a week. He was earning good money as a truck driver, so he would bring us food or take us to the chippy for a meal.

The electricity was a metered system where money was put in the meter to buy a certain amount of electricity. When the money ran out, the lights went out. The three of us contributed equally to a small collection of coins kept in a bottle beside the meter. However if you wanted to heat the water for a bath, you had to put several coins in the meter and this used up a lot of coins.

As time went on, we would forget to put the coins in the bottle and would regularly be plunged into darkness and have to scramble in the dark to find a coin.

One evening, Carrie and I decided to make a spaghetti meal, going to a great deal of trouble to produce a gourmet treat. We decided to eat it in the living room while watching TV. The minute we sat down the lights went out.

Carrie immediately said, "I have a coin in my purse, hold my plate, while I get it." She quickly had the lights on again only to find

Julie at 19.

me with two plates of spaghetti spilling down the front of my legs. In the darkness I had not realized that I did not have the plates balanced properly on my lap. Needless to say we collapsed in howls of laughter, which made this one of the most memorable meals we ever made together.

My romance with Graham continued throughout the three years of nurse training. I had worried that my moving to another town might cause our relationship to cool off but the opposite happened. By this time I was on the Pill, and there were many times we had the house to ourselves. The nights my roommates were not at home, Graham would stay with me until very late, but he still lived at home which was close to where he worked, so he had to drive home late every night. Our relationship deepened as we delighted in finding out how sexually compatible we were. I hated him having to get up and drive home every night. I dreamed of the day we could move in together and spend all night, every night, together.

In the summer of 1974, we were listening to a live band and Graham said, "Do you want to go shopping tomorrow?"

I replied, "Why? What do we need to buy?"

He smiled as he said, "A ring."

I realized he was proposing in his own sweet way, but replied, "You don't have any money to buy a ring."

"I have been saving up."

Being the practical person that I am, my next question was, "How much money do you have?"

"We will go to look in the jeweler's window and when we get to the window with rings above my price range I will tell you to stop."

At this time in England, the displays in the jeweler's windows were organized in price ranges. The next day we headed to the jewelry shops. I approached the first window that had the display of the least expensive rings and Graham immediately said, "Stop."

We both laughed out loud and went in the store to make our selection. There were plenty of beautiful rings in this price range and I selected a lovely diamond cluster in an 18 carat gold setting which cost twenty six pounds (about $55 dollars).

I had no interest in a big white wedding. I was very practical and wanted us to buy a house and not waste money on a one-day event. Also, I would not be hypocritical and get married in the Catholic Church when I no longer believed in the teachings of the church. So we decided to have a civil ceremony in the registry office. As is the case with most men, Graham was more than happy to have a small wedding.

We opened a joint bank account and started to save for a deposit on a house. By the fall of 1975, we had six hundred pounds (about $1300) which was enough for a deposit on our first house. My sister, who worked for a real estate agent, found us a tiny dormer bungalow that was only about ten years old. It needed some renovations but we fell in love with the house.

The completion date on our house purchase was set for January 1976, so our wedding date was set for February 28, 1976. This date was three weeks after my final exams. I really don't remember much about the wedding preparation, other than I wanted to keep it as simple as possible. I was scheduled to start midwifery training after qualifying as a registered nurse and this was a date that fit between finishing my finals and starting the midwifery training.

We had the keys to the house in January 1976, but I was unable to do much to help because I was studying hard for my final exams. Graham set to work and with the help of his dad and my dad he had the house all spruced up in time for our wedding.

My mum was trying to do the arrangements for the wedding without much help from me. I wanted to keep it as simple as possible while she was trying to make it a special day.

In the end, I conceded to a small reception meal after the wedding with 25 close relatives, and a party in the evening at a local cricket club. I wore a green suit for the wedding and had asked mum to order peach-colored freesia for a corsage. On the day of the wedding the flowers arrived and much to my dismay my corsage was not only huge, but it was pink and white carnations.

In a mildly hysterical state I asked mum, "Why is this so big and why is it pink and white carnations?"

Mum replied, "Well, I thought that the bride should have something a bit more special, so I ordered this more elaborate one."

My sister Geraldine's corsage was peach-colored freesia. I had my heart set on the freesia, so I did what I needed to do to get them. Much to my mother's chagrin, I broke the freesia bouquet in half. We then had two corsages in peach freesia, one each for Geraldine and me, with an extra large pink and white one. I decided to put the pink

Graham and Julie's wedding.

carnations on the top of the wedding cake. The cake looked lovely and I was happy with my flowers. Apparently the bride wearing green is considered bad luck and to make things worse, I accidentally broke my makeup mirror on the morning of the wedding. According to superstition, breaking a mirror brings seven years of bad luck. Needless to say, I don't believe in the bad luck superstition, considering we have been happily married for 33 years.

I was in the car with dad on the way to the wedding when he held my hand and said, "Whatever happens in life, always know that as long as your mum and me have a roof over our heads, you have a home to come back to at any time."

It was comforting to have that kind of unconditional support, but I knew I would not need to move back home. During the wedding ceremony, my granny sat in the front row of the seats in the registry office with her rosary beads, praying hard for my salvation. To the day she died, she believed I was living in sin because I didn't marry in the Church. The wedding day was nice but the best part for me was to be able to sleep all night, every night with Graham in our own home.

We settled into married life and it was truly wonderful. But I was taught by the masters on how to worry, so I constantly worried that things were too good and that something bad was going happen. If Graham was out in the car, I would worry about him being in an accident, I would worry about everything conceivable. Added to this was the worry that I was not good enough at my job. I completed my midwifery training and went on to work as a registered nurse on a medical ward. I loved the work but I constantly worried that I was not good enough.

We made plans for the future and although we wanted to have children we both agreed that we should have some holidays first. Our plan was to start a family in about five or six years.

In September of 1977, we went on a holiday to Ibiza, in Spain. We stayed in a hotel that had a main reception building with rooms that were in terraces on the hillside. The food was not that great, but we still were having a good time. But then the weather took a dramatic change for the worse. We were on the way back from exploring the island on rented scooters when we noticed the dark black clouds.

By that evening, we were in the middle of the worst storm I have ever seen. We were playing cards and drinking sangria in the main reception area when one of the waiters opened the back patio doors. Within a second, a deluge of water rushed through the lobby. The

Julie working as a nurse.

waiters responded by opening the doors at the front of the lobby. In a few more minutes there was a stream of water running through the lobby that was knee high. We still thought that we would be safer in the lobby than in our hillside room.

The flamboyant waiter rushed through the lobby with a tray of drinks held high above his head. He was quite a ladies' man who loved to show off his skills carrying the tray high. However, the water had made the floor slippery and his feet flew from under him and the drinks spattered around the room. This was a very funny sight, causing everyone to collapse in howls of laughter. The waiter got to his feet with an indignant look on his face, and suddenly there was a loud noise from above, and a large crack appeared on the ceiling. The laughter died down immediately, and then the lights went out.

"I think we need to get out of here," I said in a mildly panicked voice.

The crack in the ceiling was enough to send us out into the storm to try to find our rooms. As we tried to climb the small incline to our room, we were shocked at the power of the storm. The continuous yellow streaks of lightning gave the night sky the appearance of being intermittently floodlit. We started to make our way to the rooms with

Exploring Ibiza before the storm.

the thunder claps breaking all around us. The walkway to our room was a torrential river that made it very hard to progress up the hill.

"The water is so strong it's pushing me back," I gasped.

"Get down on your hands and knees it will be easier," Graham said while holding my hand tight.

We slowly clambered up the hill to our room, on our hands and knees against the fast flowing water with Graham still holding tight to one of my hands.

When we finally reached our room, it was very dark so we felt our way in and to our dismay found that the room was flooded and our suitcases were floating. We grabbed the cases and put them on one of the twin beds and then the two of us fell in to the other twin bed. Cuddled together, we drifted off to sleep as we listened to the storm still raging outside. As we lay in the bed listening to the torrential rain and loud thunder, I was almost afraid to go to sleep.

I whispered, "I hope we don't wake up floating in the sea."

"We won't, trust me," said Graham.

We were the lucky ones. The next day we discovered that the

row of rooms behind us had collapsed with the rubble from the back walls falling into the bedrooms, but luckily no one was hurt. There were tourists missing who were later found to have drowned in a taxi that had been washed away in the storm. The beach umbrellas and beach chairs were all floating in the sea and the sand on the beach had been washed away. The entire island was without electricity for a few days so the hotel staff was unable to provide anything other than bread rolls for food.

Just to make sure this was a holiday to remember, I then got very sick. I woke up feeling unwell and within a short time I was vomiting, had severe diarrhea and was writhing in pain. I lost consciousness several times and each time came around to see Graham's worried face.

On one occasion in my drowsiness I heard Graham's voice saying, "Please wake up, Julie."

I opened my eyes to see him looking at my face with tears in his eyes. He tried to find a doctor but the closest one was a four-hour drive away, so we just had to wait. Eventually the doctor arrived, and gave me a shot that eased the pain. He diagnosed food poisoning and prescribed nothing but bottled water and natural yogurt for a few days until my system could clear out the bacteria. I lived on this until we returned to England a few days later. Once back home I had tests done that showed I had had salmonella food poisoning. It took a long course of antibiotics and six weeks before I was given the all clear. The passing out episodes were later diagnosed as vagal attacks (*fainting attacks*) triggered by severe nausea.

After this disastrous holiday I started to re-think our plan of putting off having a baby so that we could have some holidays.

I soon realized that I was ready for a baby, but our plan had been to wait and Graham was not so sure about changing our plan. We talked and talked before deciding that we would try to have a baby. I was so excited but I knew I should be off the Pill for at least a couple of months before we tried to conceive. We waited until late November and then decided to start to try for our baby. It was very exciting to think that every time we made love we could be creating a new life. We did not have to wait long; within two weeks I thought I was pregnant, and by Christmas I knew for sure.

I had a wonderful pregnancy; my hair shone, my complexion glowed, and I did not have even a hint of morning sickness. I gained a minimal amount of weight with my baby bump all in front. I needed to be induced when I was a week past my due date, and after 12 hours of labor in late summer 1978 I gave birth to our wonderful son, Paul Graham Houlker.

Life as a young mum was good. I decided to stop working and be a stay-at-home mum, but that quickly changed for a couple of reasons. I loved being a mum and adored my son, but I soon realized that I needed the stimulation of a career as well. At the same time there was a sudden unexpected increase in interest rates. There was no such thing as a fixed-rate mortgage at that time. If the interest rates went up, your monthly mortgage payment went up. So I happily went back to work part time. I worked two evenings and alternate Saturday mornings so Graham could be at home to take care of Paul.

We slowly renovated our house, replacing the bathroom and the kitchen, and adding central heating. It was our first home and we loved it.

Paul was a delightful child, and everything we could have ever wanted in a son. He was eager to explore his world and was full of energy during the day, but thankfully slept all night. There were occasions when he would fall asleep standing against the couch but that was usually just a five-minute nap to restore his batteries. As many parents do, I look back and wish I had been more relaxed as a young mum. I was very tense and worried too much. I now know that I should have put less priority on the housework and career and enjoyed Paul's toddler years more. Paul was a picky eater which caused me

The arrival of Paul Graham Houlker.

great concern; being a nurse, I wanted to be sure he had all the right nutrients for healthy growth. Of course the more I fussed about what he ate, the more determined he was not to eat.

In his early years, he had a tendency to be accident prone and, in retrospect, I think I contributed to this by being so overprotective. Thankfully he had no really serious injuries and only one broken bone. One memorable event happened on the day of the Royal wedding of Prince Charles and Lady Diana Spencer. The wedding was a huge event for the British people, and the whole nation had a day off work to watch the wedding and celebrate.

Every neighborhood had a street party with royal regalia everywhere. My grandma gave Paul a Union Jack flag to wave. I was at work at the hospital when Graham arrived with Paul. Graham was ashenfaced and clearly very upset, however it was Paul who was in need of medical attention. He had been running with the flag stick in his mouth and had fallen on it. There was a gash at the back of his throat that was very near his tonsils. The emergency doctor said he had almost taken his own tonsils out. Who could have known that a little flag could be so dangerous? Poor Graham had been horrified to see blood in Paul's mouth after he fell, and of course feared the worst. No wonder he was ashen-faced and beside himself with worry when they arrived at the hospital. We were very lucky that Paul sustained no lasting damage.

Paul started school fulltime in January 1983 at the tender age of four years and four months. It was a long day for him, but he coped well even

Paul and Julie in Scotland.

though he was probably the youngest in the school. He learned quickly, and on a family outing to the park he demonstrated some new vocabulary skills in quite a dramatic way. At the time we were horrified, but we soon saw the funny side and still laugh about the event. It was a bright Sunday afternoon in spring with the park full of families. There were a few people playing ball games while others were out walking their dogs. Paul was walking between us holding our hands. We were the perfect picture of a family with mum and dad and their cute little toddler.

As we buttoned up our coats against the cold wind, Paul said in a loud voice, "Fucking hell, it's cold!"

Both Graham and I froze. The families around us who heard it had mixed reactions. Some saw the humor in it and chuckled, while others tutted in disapproval. I don't know who was more shocked, me and Graham, or Paul at our reaction. He had heard the big boys at school use this language and had no idea there was anything wrong with it, so he was totally stunned when we both responded with shock and horror and flooded him with our reprimands

"What did you just say?"
"Where did you learn those words?"
"Don't ever use those words again!"

We were very happy with our one-child family and while we thought we might have more children, we were in no hurry. My stubborn determination made me able to ignore all the comments from family, friends, and acquaintances that it was about time to have another child. We decided that we would not have another child until we both felt we wanted to, and would not get pregnant again just because everyone said we should.

Despite the disastrous holiday in Ibiza, we still yearned to see more of the world and to travel together as a family. With only one child it was possible to afford some holidays, even though it was always a tight squeeze to find the money.

We saved all year and searched for the least expensive ways to travel abroad and explore places like France, Italy, and Portugal. When we returned home we were rich with memories even if our finances needed some time to recover.

When Paul was only 13 months old, we drove with Graham's parents to the south of France. We took the ferry from England to France, and then all five of us drove down to the south in my in-laws' car. Driving was much cheaper than flying and by all going in one car, we cut the cost even more. Graham's parents helped out by covering more than their share of the fuel costs. It was a long drive to make with a baby, but we planned to stay over in a motel on the way. My father-in-law was a bit ambitious about how far we could get before stopping for the night. By the time we decided to stop, we found every motel was full. So we drove a little further and a little further and a little further.

Eventually, in the early hours of the morning my father-in-law parked the car in a restaurant parking lot where we all tried to get a couple of hours of sleep. I was in the front seat with Paul asleep across my chest. When daylight arrived, we were pleasantly surprised to see that the little café was opening for early breakfast. We were their first customers of the day, and must have looked pretty disheveled as we entered the café with a baby. They brought us warm milk for Paul's cereal and gave us steaming bowls of fresh coffee and warm, fresh-baked croissants with apricot jam. It was one of the best meals of my life. I can still taste the delicious coffee and croissants as I write.

After our wonderful breakfast, the rest of the journey to our holiday destination was easy. We stayed in the basement suite of a villa in St. Raphael on the French Riviera. This was the south of France where topless sunbathing was invented. I wasted no time in throwing off my bikini top in pursuit of an even tan. I thought I might be a bit shy but I was surprised at how easy it was to go topless. I think it helped that on the beach, all the women of all ages (and all sizes) were topless. The stores sold just the bottom halves of bikinis. So here I was, "Little Julie Smith" from Pleasington, sunbathing topless on a beach in the south of France.

We holidayed with our in-laws again in 1981. We rented a small villa on the Algarve in Portugal for two weeks. The local people were friendly and welcoming and always made a huge fuss over Paul because of his blond curly hair that is so unusual in Portugal. They would chuckle as he sat at the table in the restaurant picking up his menu as though he was reading it. They were charmed when he announced that he would have orange juice and chips.

The following year we found a company that did package camping holidays. They would transport us by bus to Italy or France, and

Julie and Paul in Venice.

provide a tent and equipment already set up for us to stay in for the holiday. The best part of this deal was that children traveled for free, the worst part was that we were on a bus for 26 hours with only the short channel ferry ride for a break. We were young and eager to explore, so we were more than happy to do the bus ride. We enjoyed the scenery as the bus trundled along with Paul asleep stretched across both of our laps.

We camped in a holiday village near Venice, Italy, and we were able to see the sights of Venice on a day trip. As I stepped from the boat into St. Marks Square, I was overcome by the beauty and history of the buildings. The hairs on the back of my neck stood on end and my eyes filled with tears. Here I was "Little Julie Smith," in Venice, Italy. Of course we could not afford to buy even a cup of coffee in the square. We sat down at a table to take a photo, but moved before the waiter came out to take our order. We wandered around the streets eventually finding a family-run café that served us the best Italian food I have ever eaten at a very reasonable price.

Graham and Julie—a romantic moment.

The finale of the day trip was a sail down the Grand Canal. By this time it was getting dark, and the water in the canal twinkled with the reflections from the candles in the restaurants that overlooked the canal. It was the moment of a lifetime that I thought could not get any better, until we came alongside a group of gondolas. In the middle one, there was gondolier standing tall and singing beautifully. It was a very romantic moment for Graham and me. My arms were full, because Paul was by now fast-asleep with his head on my shoulder, but I managed to reach out my hand to Graham who linked his fingers with mine. Our hearts touched.

All too soon, the holidays were over and we were back into our routines. I was working part-time, but I still had career goals, with my sights set on being a Health Visitor. The training would involve an intensive year in college, but I knew I would need some work experience in a community setting first.

I worked as a school nurse for a while, and in 1983 when I was 29, I was accepted for the Health Visitor training course at Preston Polytechnic College. After three intensive interviews, I was seconded (nominated) by the health authority to be sponsored for the course. This meant the course fees and my salary would be paid, on the condition that I agreed to work for them for two years after graduating.

I started the course in late September, and one evening in late October I was home alone with Paul when the phone rang. The female voice on the phone said, "Mrs. Houlker, I am from the Railway Police. I am sorry to tell you that your father died this afternoon. I am with your mother at her home now and she needs you here as soon as possible." She said all of this without stopping to take a breath.

I heard myself screaming into the phone, "No, No, No!" I was thinking, "It must be a mistake, my dad had heart problems, but he had been doing well recently." Eventually I composed myself and told her I would get to my mum's house as soon as possible. I called Graham to come home immediately. I was adamant that Graham should stay home with Paul because I did not want Paul to see the family in such distress. I drove to my mum's house, only five minutes away.

During the drive I cried out the words, "NO NO NO."

When I got to mum's the policewoman who called me was still with her because mum was in no fit state to be left alone. We cried together as she told me that he collapsed and died at his desk, but she didn't have any details.

Questions were flying around in my mind, "Was he in pain?" "Did he call out?" "Did he know he was dying?" "Did anyone try to do CPR?" "When did I last see him?"

There were no answers to any of my questions except for the last one. I remembered that I had last seen him the previous Friday when I had picked Paul up from his house. As usual, dad had stood in the window waving as we left. I remembered that he was wearing a red sweater and that he had been rubbing his left arm. I realized in retrospect that he was probably experiencing angina pain that day, but of course he had not said anything. Soon my sisters and brother arrived. We were experiencing shock and disbelief. We tried to get mum to rest, and walked her to her bedroom where we all sat on the bed, holding each other as we sobbed.

Between my dad's death and his body arriving at a funeral home in our town there was a gap of a few days. During this time, the electric kettle in mum's kitchen would turn itself on, and boil water. Anyone who knew my dad would know the significance of this mysterious occurrence. Dad loved his tea. The first thing he said when he came in the house was always, "Put the kettle on."

At first I thought this was just a coincidental malfunction of the kettle, but for three days the kettle continued to turn itself on, and every one of us witnessed it eventually. Even Graham, who is very cynical about these kinds of paranormal events, was shocked to see it happen. We were standing together in the doorway of the kitchen and there was no one in the kitchen, suddenly the kettle's "on" switch clicked itself in to place and the kettle boiled. After the day that we went to the funeral home to see dad, the kettle never turned itself on again. Maybe it had been just a coincidence, but we all believe that it was dad's spirit letting us know he was okay.

I had to get back to college and to studying, so I had no time to grieve. The course week schedule was four full days in college, and one day out on field work. The content was not too hard, but the volume of work we were expected to produce was almost impossible to do in the time available. I would leave college at 5 PM, pick Paul up from Mum's and spend the time from 5 PM to 8 PM with Paul and Graham. We would make dinner and have some play time with Paul before his bath and bedtime at 8 PM. After Paul was in bed, I would study until after midnight. On weekends, we would have a family day on Saturday, and Graham would take Paul out on Sundays while I studied all day. When I was alone, I would try to study but if I saw my dad's photo, I would start to cry. One Sunday, I had an essay to write on medical sociology. Graham had taken Paul out to the park so I could write; the essay had to be turned in the following day, so I could not procrastinate.

The subject was fascinating, but the teachings and the text books were full of academic medical jargon which often didn't make a lot of sense. The topic I had to write on was "The Sick Role Concept." I looked at dad's photo, and started to cry as I said out loud, "Oh dad, help me with this, I just can't do it today." After a few moments I picked up the pen and started to write, and wrote without stopping until the essay was completed. To my amazement I received an "A" for the essay. When I read it again a few days later I was shocked to see the words I had used and the fluency of the essay. I was sure that my dad had guided my pen and helped me write the essay.

By now, Graham and I had established a date night on Friday nights. This was the only night in the week that we could set aside for time together. Paul would have an early meal, and Graham and I would cook a meal together after Paul was in bed. We would try new recipes while we sipped wine, and chatted about our holiday plans or our dreams of seeing more of the world. We both had dreams of moving overseas; we knew we did not want to wake up at 40, and still be living in the same town. The Friday night date tradition has continued to this day, with both of us avoiding other commitments on Fridays.

Graham helped me study for exams, and I managed to complete the course. I always say that "*we*" graduated the course because I could not have done it without him. Once I had graduated, I made a decision that I was finished with studying and we were going to spend all our leisure time together as a family.

I started to work as a Health Visitor in a small health unit in Darwen. I had reached my career goal, and I enjoyed the work, but it was very demanding and stressful. I loved the child development part of the work, and I found it fascinating to watch a baby grow and develop into a toddler.

With three Nursing qualifications, you would think that I would be more confident, but I still worried constantly and took my work stress home with me. I often would think, "Is it really me, Little Julie Smith from Pleasington, who has the letters SRN (State Registered

Nurse) SCM (State Certified Midwife), RHV (Registered Health Visitor) after her name?"

In the autumn of 1984, I was busy learning my new job but was also still determined to develop family activities. So we joined the "Pendle Hill Ski Club." There were no ski hills in Lancashire, but the ski club had a dry ski surface with brush matting that could be skied on. It was not the same as real snow, but it was a good place to learn a few of the basics of skiing. The club members were a delightful mix of old and young people who were passionate about skiing. There were lessons provided for a small fee and social events, as well as an annual ski trip to Aviemore in Scotland. This was a perfect family activity for us and a way for us to try out skiing. Every Sunday we would dress warmly to brave the cold winds in order to learn the basics of standing up on skis. The brush matting was not as forgiving as snow when you fell on it, resulting in lots of scrapes and bruises, but we loved every minute of it. Paul took to skiing immediately and was a natural at it.

Our first time skiing on snow was in March of 1985, when we went with the club to Scotland. The snow conditions were not good, but we were in heaven. We stayed in a quaint hotel called "The Boat of Garten." A huge log fire warmed the lobby, where there were stuffed couches upholstered in tartan to comfort the tired skiers. We sat in front of the fire at the end of the day and recounted our adventures with the other club members.

Skiing on snow for the first time was more challenging than we had expected and the poor spring snow conditions did not help. We took the chair lift up to the top of the mountain where there was a plateau that had an easy run for beginners. We were not yet ready to do the full run down the hill, so we planned to do the beginners run a few times before riding the chair back down the hill. The first few runs went well, we skied in single file with me in front, Paul in the middle, and Graham behind. Then Paul said, "This is boring, I want to be in the front."

It was only a little hill, so we agreed that he could be the leader. We were just getting going when Paul suddenly increased his speed and headed towards the start of the difficult downhill run. Luckily, there was a flat area between the runs that slowed the skiers down. Paul was pushing hard over the flat area to get to the big hill before we could stop him. Graham knew that he could not catch him by pushing on his skis, so he threw them off and ran across the flat area as fast as could. My heart raced as I prayed that Graham would get there in time. There was no way we could ski that hill, but one of us would have to follow him if he set off on it. He managed to grab Paul by the back of his jacket just as he was about to set off down the hill. When I finally caught up with them, Graham was giving Paul a good telling off, and Paul was pouting. It was just the beginning of his daring escapades on the ski hills!

In late 1985, we sold our first house and bought a larger semi-detached house in Feniscowles. We loved it and quickly met our neighbours, Cathy and Paul. Their oldest son was three years older than Paul, but they got on well together.

We had dinner parties at each others' houses where the kids would be fed first before going off to play, while the adults enjoyed the great gourmet food and wine. We tried out new recipes and made special appetizers and desserts. We had many long evenings of fun, and would joke about who was the designated driver as we crossed the lawn to walk home.

The following year, we had our first ski holiday in the French Alps. Once again we did a package holiday, on the bus for 26 hours

Julie and Paul in the French Alps.

with Paul traveling for free. After this we were hooked on skiing, and dreamed of living in a place where we could ski anytime we wanted in the winter. We had a ski holiday in France again in 1987. We saved all year for our ski trip, and hated it when the holiday was over and we had to put our skis away for another year.

It was about this time that Graham and I started to talk about emigrating. We knew we did not want to live in Blackburn all our lives, and we wanted to give Paul the best opportunities in life. We started to look for information about Australia, New Zealand, and Canada. I ordered newspapers from all these places to try and get an idea of what life was like there. We decided that Canada would most likely offer us the life we wanted. The skiing was definitely a part of our decision.

In 1987, I wrote to Canada House in London and we filled out a preliminary application form. We quickly received a reply to say that we had the requirements to be considered as immigrants to Canada, and we should submit a full application. We learned that it was not easy for employers in Canada to hire prospective new immigrants until they arrived in Canada as landed immigrants. Although we could send resumes and make enquiries, we could not get a confirmed job until we moved there. This made us hesitate; we both had good jobs. Graham had worked for the same company for 14 years and was, by this time, Transport Manager. I was a Health Visitor, which was one of the best paying jobs in nursing. It was a hard decision to give up our secure jobs. We loved our new home and had wonderful friends living next door. In the fall of 1987, we decided to put a new carpet in the living room and put all thoughts of moving to Canada aside.

In November I went to a house party organized by a work friend. She had organized a tarot card reader to be there so we could all have our cards read. I did not really believe in all that stuff, but it was a fun night with the girls. I was the last one to have my cards read and did not take it very seriously when I walked into the room where the reader was waiting.

I shuffled the cards for the reader who studied them for a few moments before saying, "I am sorry but I can't read your cards tonight, there is something going to happen in January that will prompt you to consider going overseas. There are two paths you can take when this happens, so there are two different readings here. Come back in January when you have made your decision, and I will read your cards."

I was a little taken aback but then laughed it off, saying that we were going skiing in France in January so that must be the travel overseas.

The Friday night before we were due to leave for our ski holiday in January 1988, the life-changing event occurred as predicted by the card reader. I was busy doing last-minute vacation packing when Graham arrived home from work looking a bit stunned. He said, "I have some bad news; the company have announced that they are closing down in June this year, so I won't have a job."

It was not the kind of news anyone wants to hear on the day before a vacation, but then again, there is no good time to hear that kind of news. Surprisingly, I was not upset at all. I immediately thought about the card reader. Without hesitation I replied, "This is not bad news, it is great news. We are going to move to Canada, so let's get a bottle of wine to start off our holiday and celebrate our move to Canada."

We then had two weeks of time together to talk and plan our move. Paul was included in the discussions, and was very excited. By the time we came home from France, our minds were made up; we were going to move to Canada.

I set to work researching immigration, and nursing in Canada. I went to the library and found a large book called The Canadian Almanac, that had information and addresses for all kinds of services in Canada. We poured over books about Canada, and its different provinces. We narrowed it down to the province of British Columbia. I wrote to all the hospitals in BC that were listed in the Almanac. We decided to wait for responses to my letters before putting in the formal application to Canada House.

We didn't have to wait long; within a matter of weeks the air mail letters started to arrive. Most of them said that there were jobs available for nurses with my qualifications but that they could not hire me until I was a landed immigrant. We knew that Graham would get a job easily.

We applied for immigration to Canada in March 1988, and by June 1988 we had an interview at Canada House in London.

The weekend of our interview at Canada House, we made a weekend of it by staying a few extra days. We took Paul to the aircraft museum, the Imperial war museum, and the natural history museum. We also went to the Tower of London, and saw the crown jewels and the Beefeaters. Paul and Graham had a blast exploring the HMS

Belfast, a battleship that was moored in the Thames, and I managed to get them to spend an hour in the Tate Gallery with me, before they got bored.

Our weekend coincided with the Queen's Trooping of the Color ceremony which is a wonderful event with royal pomp and ceremony. We stood in the crowds and waved at the Queen and Princess Diana as they rode past in their carriages. (We did not buy any royal flags to wave after Paul's last escapade with a flag!) For me, it was the horses in the parade that were the stars, they were so beautiful and majestic.

We bought tickets for "The Phantom of the Opera" at Her Majesty's Theatre in the West End. Dressed up in our finery, we took a black cab to the theater, and afterwards had dinner in a quaint French restaurant. A few months before our trip, we had bought a record album of the music from the show, and for some reason Paul loved the songs, so he was thrilled to be going to see the show. It was a spectacular show, but all the excitement of the weekend proved a bit too much for Paul, and he fell asleep before the end of the performance.

The interview at Canada House went well. We came home feeling pretty confident that we would be accepted as immigrants to Canada. The whole weekend I believed it was going to happen, but at the same time I felt like we were in a movie and it was not real.

In early July, we had our medicals and by late July 1988, we had our landed immigrant visas. We had a year to use them or we would have to start the application process all over again. We had decided on Chilliwack, BC as a place that we thought we would like to live. It was a small town close to the ski hills and lakes, but it was only an hour's drive from the city of Vancouver, and the cost of housing was reasonable. I had also received a letter from the Chilliwack hospital indicating that there would be a job for me when I arrived. I had my qualifications verified by the Nursing Association, and would be able to work as a graduate nurse until I had my BC registration. We intended to stop in Chilliwack first, and then spend a couple of weeks exploring the province before we made a final decision about where we would live.

We told our families and friends of our plans, but I don't think anyone believed us until we put our house on the market. By now my stubborn determination had taken over, and I was set on following our dreams. Our house sold very quickly and we booked a flight to Canada for late October.

We wanted to have a party before we left England to celebrate our move and to say farewell to all our friends and family. We rented the room at the same cricket club where we had our wedding party, and a week before we left for Canada, had a wonderful party.

We hired a moving company who would pack up everything for us and put it into a container to be shipped across the Atlantic to Vancouver. It would arrive in early January, three months after our move. I was still in a state of disbelief that this was really happening, flipping back and forth between happy excitement and sheer terror. In my mind I was thinking, "Is this really happening? Is 'Little Julie Smith from Pleasington' really moving across the world to follow her dreams with her soul mate and her precious son?"

The farewell party was a memorable, wonderful success. It was attended by family and friends old and new. It would be an understatement to say that it became a bit emotional at the end of the night when all of our loved ones made a circle around us and sang along to the song, "You Will Never Walk Alone." I still cry every time I hear that song. After the party one of my friends told me that everyone she talked to had told her that they were sure we would not stay in Canada, and we would be back home before too long. We were given many cards and well wishes. One of the cards would turn out to be very special to my future. It was a beautiful card with a silk-embroidered daffodil on a blue background.

When he came to say goodbye, Graham's brother said with a smile, "See you in 18 months." I knew he meant that he was sure we would be back in England by then, but I quickly responded with, "It's great that you are coming out to visit us in Canada in 18 months." He laughed and left.

Our big day arrived, and we were buzzing with excitement. Various family and friends came to the airport to wish us well. As the jet was speeding down the runway we saw our family on the viewing platform waving scarves. Graham wrapped his hand around mine and said, "Well, kid, we really did it." I smiled back at him as my stomach churned. It was one of the most exciting and happy moments of my life, while at the same time being one of the most frightening moments.

It was a very daunting experience to be in a new country with no jobs and no real home. But we had confidence that we would both be working soon, and would be settling in to our new life.

We were very honored to have two kind and hospitable Canadians meet us at the airport in Vancouver. They were the cousins of a doctor I had worked with in England who was worried about us landing and knowing no one. He phoned before we left to tell us that his cousin Betty and her husband Jon would pick us up at the airport, and we could stay with them for the first night. He described Betty as "easy to spot" because she had flaming red hair, and just to be sure we would recognize them, they would both wear red carnations in their coats.

They drove us to their lovely apartment in Burnaby and offered us dinner, but I was too tired and emotional to eat, so we retired to bed early. I woke at about 5 AM and the enormity of what we had done hit me like a ton of bricks. I started to cry and couldn't stop. Nothing Graham or Paul said could console me. It was that morning that they invented a new family expression. I don't know if this happens in all families, but we have several expressions that I think are unique to our family. The one invented that day was, "Don't be a nelly." Every time I started to cry again, they would say, "Come on don't be a nelly," or Paul would look at his dad and say, "Dad, she's nellying again." Since that day, the term "nellying" has been used regularly in our family to describe my worrying.

Betty and Jon wanted us to stay and eat breakfast but I was too tense to eat. I managed to force a few spoonfuls of cereal down before Betty walked with us to the local bank so we could open an account and deposit our money.

With this done, we got on the road to Chilliwack. We had rented a car that had a bench seat in the front so all three of us sat in the front, with Paul in the middle. Our drive to Chilliwack that day will stay in my mind forever. We had never driven in such a big car. Paul was so excited to be in the front seat as we set off on our adventure, I think there were three kids on the front seat that day, not just one.

The road seemed to be very long, straight, and to go on forever. It was raining hard, so we didn't see any of the scenery, but the minute we arrived in Chilliwack it felt like home.

We checked into a Best Western, the first motel we saw. Paul delighted in the indoor pool, and it felt like we were on holiday. I cried off and on for three days, flipping from delighting in the adventure of it all, to begging Graham to call the moving company and ask them to send our furniture back to England, so we could go home. Both Graham and Paul comforted me when I cried ,and reassured me that I would love Canada once we had settled down.

The first store we went into was Kmart, to buy a new razor for Graham. A friendly assistant offered us some help. As soon as we spoke, she asked, "Where are you from?"

We said, "We have just emigrated from England."

"I know you're from England but where in England?"

"Blackburn, Lancashire."

It turned out that she was from Oswaltwistle, a town only a few miles away from Blackburn, and she had recognized our accents. She asked where we were staying before we said goodbye. That night, we had a phone call at the hotel from someone called Bill, whose wife, Pat, had spoken to us in Kmart. He wanted to welcome us to Canada and invited us to their home the following weekend, to meet some of their friends. It was just one of the amazing coincidences that I now know were guidance and messages from the universe, and of course, the law of attraction. We had set our minds that this move would work out well for us, and things would fall into place for us, and it looked like we were right.

It was only one week after we had arrived in Canada, and the three of us were sitting in Bill and Pat's family room with a group of their friends. They were eager to hear how we were doing with our job and accommodation searches and gave us information and advice about all kinds of things Canadian and Chilliwack-ian.

I had picked up a Vancouver newspaper on our first day in Canada, to look at the employment opportunities, and was stunned when I opened the employment page to see the perfect job for me. The requirements included education in either nursing or therapy, with knowledge of child development, and experience in working with families in home-based settings. I could not believe it! This advertisement could have been my resume. What were the odds that we would arrive in Canada in the same week that this job was advertised? Another "coincidence?" It was Saturday, and the closing date was on the following Tuesday so there was no time to mail in my resume, I would have to find a way of getting it in on time. Luckily, there was a mailing address on the job posting. I quickly wrote a cover letter to add to the resume that I had brought with me. We bought a map and found the place where the resumes were to be sent, the Abbotsford Health Unit. Early Monday morning, we hand-delivered my application, with the hotel phone number as my contact number.

We wasted no time looking for rental accommodation. Within five days, we had an apartment, and this was at a time when the vacancy rate was almost zero in Chilliwack. We just happened to stop to look at houses at a real estate office where the realtor "coincidentally" had a friend who was a new manager at an apartment block, and within hours we had an appointment to view the apartment that we subsequently rented.

I called a care facility about possible work and arranged an interview with the manager, who "coincidentally" was from England, and had almost the same qualifications as I did. She said she would hire me, but knew I would be offered the job at the hospital immediately, at a salary better than she could offer. She kindly gave me lots of information about nursing in Canada, and told me to call her if I didn't have a job within two weeks.

The following day, I had an interview at the hospital for a job in the maternity ward. I didn't really want to go back to shift work and hospital nursing, but I was willing to do whatever it took to get established in Canada. I was offered the job and was scheduled to start in late November 1988. I would be a hired as a graduate nurse but would need to write the Canadian exam to become a registered nurse. I set about contacting the Nursing Association and signed up to write the exam in January 1989.

We enrolled Paul in a school in the area where we thought we would eventually buy a house, and he started two weeks after our arrival. On his first day I was very nervous for him but he took it all in stride. As I dropped him off I asked him if he was nervous. He replied, "No, I am looking forward to meeting lots of new friends," and off he went; turning to give me a smile and a wave as he walked through the door. I watched him go through the door with tears in my eyes, thinking to myself, "What an amazing kid! He is so happy and confident, and so incredibly brave."

I had an interview for the Infant Development job ten days after arriving in Canada. I got the job, which had a start date of December 1, 1988. I now had to decide which job to take, the higher-paid hospital job with the 12-hour shift or the lower-paid four-days-a-week, 9-to-5 job in Infant Development. I knew I wanted the Infant Development job, but unless Graham got work quickly I would have to take the hospital job.

During our first week in Canada, we had picked up an Abbotsford newspaper and saw a job for a warehouse manager at a wheel manufacturer in Surrey. Graham had experience in warehouse supervision, but not in wheels, but he submitted a resume anyway. He was called for an interview, so once again we got the maps out to find the place. On the day of the interview, we left in good time but we got lost. When we finally found the place, it was only a couple of minutes before the interview time. I was getting stressed, but Graham kept calm, dashing into the building as I sat nervously in the car.

We didn't hear anything for over a week, and my start time at the hospital was getting closer. We set about looking for before- and after-school care for Paul on the assumption that Graham would be getting a job soon. We were delighted when Graham was offered the job. It meant I could take the Infant Development consultant job. Things were smoothly falling into place.

However, we still needed after-school care for Paul, and we had only a few days to find something. The following day I dropped Paul off at school and summoned up as much courage as I could to approach a group of young mums who were chatting after dropping off their children.

My words came out fast as I said nervously, "Hi, I am new here from England, and I am wondering if you could give me any advice about before- and after-school care in this area?"

They shook their heads and said they didn't know of anything, but took my phone number in case they thought of something. By the time I was opening the door of our apartment the phone was ringing. I picked up the receiver and heard a woman's voice saying, "Can I speak to Julie?"

"Yes, speaking," I replied.

She continued, "I was talking to you earlier at school about day care and I do know of someone, but I wanted to ask her first before I passed on her name and number. I just spoke to her; she has space and said for you to give her a call. Her name is Sandy and she lives just around the corner from the school."

I could not believe my good fortune. What were the odds that I would approach someone, who just happened to have a friend, who had a day care. Another one of those mysterious "coincidences!" I thanked her profusely and called Sandy as soon as I hung up. She seemed to be a delightful person, and we arranged a meeting that evening at her home with both our families. I think it was as much for her to interview us as it was for us to interview them. The visit went very well. There were two of Paul's classmates also in her day care with whom he could walk to and from school.

We soon came to love "Auntie Sandy." She was wise and good at her job, and gave us a wealth of information about schools in Canada, plus a lot of other things. Paul stayed in her day care until he was old enough to be home alone.

On November 28, 1988, Paul and Graham went to work and school but my job didn't start until December 1, so I had the day to do some shopping and explore the town. It was one month, to the day, since our arrival in Canada, and it was the first day since we had arrived that it was not raining. As I stepped out of the car at the store, I gasped at my first view of the mountains. The mountains had fresh snow on them and were a delicate shade of blue-grey against the high clouds. It was a breathtakingly beautiful scene. I reflected on the monumental life events that we had gone through in only one month, as I tingled with happiness. I knew that we were going to be very happy in our new life.

It was soon obvious that Graham loved his job. When the day arrived for me to do my first home visit in Canada, I nervously rang the doorbell. I had lots of experience of home visiting in England, but I wondered what Canadian families would be like. Happily I discovered that families are pretty much the same the world over. I loved working with the babies and their families. All of my work was visiting families in their own homes, so a portion of the day was spent driving from house to house. At that time, my case load covered a large area, which meant I was able to discover a lot about my new surroundings. I would drive along the highway taking in the majestic scenery of the mountains while thinking, "I can't believe I am getting paid to do this."

I had a solid knowledge of child development and was confident in that part of my job, but I had a lot of learning to do about Canadian ways of doing things. The part of the job that challenged me the most was my role in supporting the parents. Any parent will tell you that their worst nightmare is the thought that their child may have a disability or a developmental delay. All the parents I worked with had either been told that their child had a diagnosed disability or were waiting for me to assess their child's development. I found I was often very emotionally drained by the end of the day, and of course I stressed and worried about whether I had said or done the right thing.

We were eager to buy a house as soon as possible. We had a good-sized deposit from the proceeds of our house sale in England,

and were delighted at the quality of home we could afford. We spent our weekends driving around looking at houses and touring open houses. We were accustomed to brick-built houses in England and had no clue about the wood-frame houses in BC. We had to believe that the builder would do a good job. He didn't disappoint us.

While we lived in the apartment, waiting for the completion of our house, we spent all our spare time exploring the area. We soon discovered the river, the lakes and the ski hills. The beautiful scenery and the changing colors of the mountains captivated us. We could not believe how lucky we were to have found such a perfect place to live. Despite the cold weather, we walked at Cultus Lake every weekend.

In February 1989 (on our 13th wedding anniversary), we moved into our brand-new home. We loaded our things from the apartment into a rental van which Graham drove, with me following behind in our car. I turned on the radio and the song "I'm on Top of the World Looking Down on Creation" blared out. I sang along with the words at the top of my voice, and I truly felt on top of the world.

The moving company was scheduled to bring our furniture and belongings from England that day, and we were so excited to have all our own stuff at last. I got teary-eyed at the sight of the moving van as it pulled up outside our new home. It was a green-and-yellow Mayflower moving van. I still always smile and get a good feeling when I see one of these vans. We were amazed that everything was intact with only one loose leg on our coffee table.

Paul loved his new school and he was quickly losing his English accent. We settled down to life in our new home, and our new jobs, and Paul's new school. Over the next few years, we marveled at our new life, and delighted in sharing it with family and friends who visited us from England. Life was good.

"Coincidentally" our new neighbors who had recently moved to BC from Manitoba were our age, and had only one child, a boy who was just two weeks younger than Paul. The two boys became friends and soon our two families were friends. They introduced us to cross-country skiing and we introduced them to downhill skiing. We agreed that downhill was the best, and our two families went on to have many skiing holidays together. We had dinner at each others' houses and chatted over the garden fence.

In 1990, I read an inspirational newspaper article about an amazing Chilliwack woman who had battled bone cancer. She was married and had a young son and seemed determined to live life to the fullest, despite being a leg amputee. A few weeks later when I was in Safeway I saw a young woman expertly negotiating the isles on crutches. I realized it was the woman from the newspaper article. I was humbled by her bravery and determination.

To my delight, I had the opportunity to travel to a conference on child development in 1990. The conference was being held in New Mexico but the cost of air travel was outside of our budget. Three colleagues and I chose for the cheaper option of traveling by train. The downside was the two-and-a-half day journey with only a slightly reclined seat for sleeping. The upside was an opportunity to see more of the countryside. As we planned the journey, it occurred to us that we could take some vacation days and break up the journey by staying a couple of nights in Los Angeles and San Diego. With the travel time, the stopovers, and the time at the conference, we would be away for 13 days. I was thrilled at the prospect of traveling, but I was also uneasy about being away from Graham and Paul for so long. I had never been away from Graham overnight since our marriage 14 years before, except for the days in hospital when I gave birth to Paul. I missed them both terribly but it was going to be a wonderful trip.

The train journey took us through spectacular desert scenery in Arizona and New Mexico. We took a trolley bus tour for an afternoon in Tijuana Mexico; we visited the old town in San Diego. We discovered the beauty of the adobe buildings of Santa Fe and visited a Pueblo village. The four of us explored Universal Studios. In a line-up, we were approached by a staff member recruiting people to be in the audience for a recording of a show that day in Hollywood. We were to be at the gates of Universal Studios at 4 PM and we would be transported by bus to the studio. I sat in the studio awestruck, and of course, thinking "Is this really 'little Julie Smith from Pleasington,' sitting in a TV studio in Hollywood?" The show was a pilot for a new comedy that never made it past the pilot, but we had fun!

The opportunity to become Canadian citizens was important to us so we applied as soon as we were eligible. In November 1992, we proudly sang "O Canada" at our citizenship ceremony, with Graham's parents watching. By this time they knew we were not coming back to England, and were acknowledging that we had made a good move. They visited every year, sometimes twice a year. I think Paul actually spent more time with his grandparents than he would have done if we had stayed in England, because they often came to Canada for long visits of up to three months.

I had an unexpected trip to England that year. It was a warm sunny morning in August 1992 when the ringing phone woke us up early. Sleepily, I said "Hello." I heard my older sister Anne's voice and immediately knew something was wrong. She said, "Geraldine is very sick and in a coma, she collapsed yesterday from a brain aneurysm. The doctors have told us that she may not make it, we might lose her."

My heart lurched, and tears welled in my eyes but I managed to ask, "Are they going to do surgery?"

Anne replied, "They said if she makes it through the next 48 hours, then they will try to operate, but for now they are just trying to stabilize her."

I knew I had to go to England, and told Anne I was going to get the earliest flight possible. The following day, I was sitting on an airplane somewhere over the Atlantic Ocean with tears rolling down my face, praying that I would be visiting my sister in hospital and not going to her funeral. As I stepped into the arrival hall, I saw my sister Anne and my mum, and both were crying. My first words were, "Did she make it?"

Mum said, "Yes, she is scheduled for surgery tomorrow but she has to be kept sedated until then. I don't know if you can see her because they are worried that the excitement of seeing you might be dangerous for her." I knew I needed to be near her even if I couldn't see her so said I would go with them to the hospital but I would not go into the ward. When we got to the hospital mum went in to see Geraldine and I stayed at the end of the ward but the nurses came to get me, saying I should go in to see her. I was reluctant to go in because I was afraid that my visit would cause her to relapse, but the nurses insisted. Geraldine was very drowsy but was able to talk coherently. I tentatively gave her a gentle hug as her husband Alan watched over us anxiously.

She said, "Have you heard they are going to drill a hole in my head tomorrow?"

She had her surgery the following day, and miraculously made a full recovery. I was able to visit her in hospital a few times before flying back home to Canada. It was hard to leave with her still in hospital, but I was relieved to be going home. By this time I thought of Canada as home, despite the difficulty of being far away from my family.

We were on a camping trip in 1993, when I noticed that my right breast looked flatter than it usually did. I checked and checked for lumps but found nothing. On returning home, I checked again and this time I squeezed the nipple. I had a sick feeling in my stomach when I saw dark red blood ooze out of my nipple. The next day I went to the doctor, who reassured me that this kind of thing was usually benign. I was scheduled for a mammogram, and to see a surgeon within the week. The mammogram showed benign calcification, but the surgeon wanted to be sure, and scheduled surgery to biopsy the duct.

The following week, we sat across from the surgeon waiting for the verdict. We were delighted to hear that it was benign and there was no need to worry anymore. The offending duct had been excised, so I should not have any more problems.

By 1994, Graham was traveling overseas with his job and the following year he went to South Africa. He fell in love with Africa and returned home full of enthusiasm and talked about us going there for a holiday someday.

While Graham was away, I woke up in the night with a throbbing pain in my jaw. The next day I saw the dentist who diagnosed an infected wisdom tooth. He referred me to an oral surgeon who prescribed antibiotics and scheduled me for removal of all my wisdom teeth.

The surgery went well, but a week later I developed an adverse reaction to the antibiotic. The reaction was colitis, which I later discovered is a common reaction to the drugs. However, in my case it was extreme, and I went on to have three months of severe colitis symptoms. My doctor referred me to a specialist, but a few days before my appointment with him, I realized what I needed to do to heal myself. Before I left England, two of my colleagues had developed an interest in reflexology. It is an ancient healing practice that involved massaging the soles of the feet in specific areas to induce healing. I knew that I needed to see a reflexologist. I checked the phone book but there were none listed in Chilliwack, so I called directory assistance.

Directory assistance used to be provided by a human, not a recorded voice. I inquired about reflexologists in Chilliwack, and there was a short silence at the other end of the phone.

The operator then replied, "This is really strange; I just had a listing given to me for a new reflexologist in Chilliwack only an hour ago." She gave me the name and number.

The name of the business was "Sole Connections" and the reflex-ologist was Glenda Standeven. I called the number, and again there was a split second silence at the other end of the phone. "How did you get my number? I only got the line in this morning." I told her about calling directory assistance and how the operator was shocked to have an enquiry so soon after being given Glenda's new listing. I explained what had happened and we set up an appointment. When I arrived for the appointment, I realized immediately that Glenda was the woman who had lost her leg to cancer, who I had read about in the newspaper article, and seen in the grocery store.

Glenda chatted happily and soon put me at ease, and before long, I was feeling the benefits of her healing hands. I learned that she had been well since her surgery. It turned out that she had had her surgery in January 1988, at the time we had been making the decision to move to Canada. I enjoyed her company and felt a connection with her. She worked on my feet, encouraged me to breathe deeply, and to visualize a healing light moving through my body. Her technique was so much more powerful than what I had experienced in previous reflexology treatments.

I went for a few more sessions and after one of the sessions, I had another idea of what I could do to heal myself. It suddenly became so obvious to me. I went straight from Glenda's house to the health food store and bought some high potency acidophilus capsules and some pure spring water. For 48 hours I starved myself, drinking only the spring water, and taking the acidophilus capsules. At the end of the 48 hours, the colitis was gone. I don't know if it was my belief that it would work, or the acidophilus that cured me, but it worked. While this "treatment" may not work for others, (this is not an approved medical treatment and this is not intended as medical advice) I instinc-tively knew it was what my body needed to heal.

I kept the appointment with the specialist surgeon who confirmed the colitis diagnosis but agreed that I appeared to have cured myself. He gave me some medication to take if the colitis came back, but it didn't. While I was talking to him, I told him about the ductile excision I had had the previous year, and mentioned that there was a small lump behind the scar. He said it was probably scar tissue that often occurs after a biopsy, and because we know it was benign, there was no need to worry. I intended to have regular reflexology sessions with Glenda but was busy working and never got around to making the appointments. I did however refer a friend to Glenda, who saw her regularly for reflexology.

At 15 years old, Paul got a summer job working in the shipping department of the wheel manufacturer where Graham worked. He did very well and worked there the next summer. He was saving for his first car; we had promised him that if he saved $1,000, we would match it.

On Paul's sixteenth birthday, I remember saying to Graham, "What a wonderful young man we have for a son, and we should be very thankful that we have not seen any teenage rebellion."

Graham and Paul in the Rockies.

It was the wrong thing to say!

Paul could not wait to get his driving license, while I was dreading it. I knew the worrier in me would go into overtime when he was out driving. Graham taught him to drive and taught him well. I rarely went in the car with them while he was learning because I was just too nervous. He had a license within a few months of turning sixteen. This gave him the freedom that he was craving, while at the same time I was thinking wistfully of his younger years when I could put him to bed at 8 PM and know he was safe at home. It was so much easier then.

In the fall of his grade 11 year, he suddenly lost interest in school and his grades dropped. We tried to get him motivated again but he just seemed to be burned out with school. It was understandable that he felt he was done with school. He had been in school since he was four years old, almost two years longer than some of his friends. On one particular day, as I tried to motivate him to work on picking up his grades, he said something that struck a chord with me. I had said, "You were doing so well, with good grades. I don't understand what is happening?"

He replied, "Mum, those grades were for you and dad, not for me."

A light bulb went on in my head as I realized how much pressure we put on our children for good grades. I came to the conclusion that we had to let Paul find his own way, and that he needed to want to succeed for himself, not for his parents. I knew that whatever happened, he would be a success in life, and the best thing we could do is have faith in him.

His passion was driving and having fun, and by this time he was interested in girls. Graham and I had gone through our teenage years in a different country with a different culture and different norms. We had no clue what was normal for teenagers in Canada.

Fortunately, I had two work friends whose children were going through, or had gone through, the teenage rebellion stage. They became my support group. One wise work friend said to me one day, "You know, Julie, raising a teenager is a bit like reeling in a fish. If you pull on the line too hard, it will snap and you will lose the fish; but if you let the line go too loose, the fish will get away. So you just have to keep pulling the line in, and then letting it go a little, and eventually the fish will come to you." This was such a good analogy for me. I knew I had been pulling the line too hard. I had to loosen the apron strings.

Paul dropped out of school in March of grade eleven which turned out to be the best thing for him. He worked full-time until September, and then started at a new junior college that combined grades 11/12, and college-level courses. He settled in immediately; I am sure it was because he was treated as an adult, with the adult expectations. We backed off on the pressure for high grades and told him that the grades he obtained were his business, not ours. All we expected was for him to pass. He excelled and the following year placed first in a regional skills Canada drafting competition. He graduated grade 12 with honors and in February 1998 with a certificate in architectural drafting. He has been employed as a drafting technician since then, progressing quickly to the managerial position he holds today.

In the next couple of years, he did all the daredevil things that teenaged boys seem to need to do, including tubing down the river at midnight, jumping off high rocks into a lake, and driving too fast. On one particular night he came home late while Graham was away in Africa, and as usual I was getting very worried.

When he arrived home, he could see how worried I was and in frustration he said, "Mum, why can't you be like my friends' parents and just give me shit for coming home late, instead of always thinking I am dead?" Another light bulb went on in my head. I knew I had to start having faith he would be safe instead of always worrying something was wrong.

The day I turned 40, I woke up and reflected on the past six years we had lived in Canada. I felt very proud of what we had achieved and happy that we had followed our dreams.

We celebrated my fortieth birthday at the restaurant in the same Best Western hotel that we had stayed in when we first arrived. It was a romantic dinner for just Graham and me. Paul drove us and picked us up so we could enjoy a bottle of wine to celebrate. (I think he threw a party at our house while we were out, but all was well when we got home.) We chatted about our lives, both saying that without a doubt we were glad we had not woken up at age 40, still living in Blackburn and in the same jobs.

By early 1995, the lump in my breast behind the scar was bigger and my family doctor wanted it checked out, so off I went to the surgeon again. He again diagnosed scar tissue but ordered a needle biopsy just to be sure. He said I was too young to be having yearly mammograms and there was no need to do one now, because the lump was easy to feel; soft, and not at all suspicious for cancer. He said, too often doing mammograms at my age led to unnecessary biopsies and anxiety, adding that I did not have any risk factors for breast cancer so he was not worried. (75% of women diagnosed with breast cancer have none of the risk factors.)

The day of the needle biopsy arrived and the pathologist expected to get fluid because the lump was so obviously cystic. However, she only got a little blood-stained fluid and commented on how solid the lump was. An agonizing week later, I finally heard from the

surgeon that the cells obtained were all benign and there was no need
to worry.

As the months passed, the lump got bigger. In April I went back
to my doctor who checked it and recommended that we monitor it
and check again in June, considering it was only two months after
the biopsy had showed it was benign. By June the lump was slightly
bigger, but still had the appearance of scar tissue. Since I had already
had two biopsies that showed it to be benign, he recommended that
we monitor it for now and check again in September. By September
the lump was bothering me, it often felt hot and inflamed especially
when I was premenstrual. I was referred back to the surgeon and got
an appointment for October.

As he examined the lump he said, "This is scar and cystic tissue
and the fact that it changes with your cycle tells me it is probably connected to your hormone levels. We could try some medication for a
few months."

I stopped him by saying, "I can't help feeling we are missing
something here, I think we should take it out."

He replied, "Yeah, well, you want to sleep at night and so do I,
so let's schedule a date to do the surgery."

I explained that I had a flight to England in late November for
a two-week holiday and because the surgeon was not worried that this
was anything but benign, he scheduled me for a biopsy the day after
I returned in December. During the trip, I discussed the lump in my
breast and the scheduled biopsy with my family and assured them that
it was benign, but that it needed to be removed. A few days before I
was due to fly home I felt a cold coming on; I was worried I may have
to cancel the biopsy.

Thankfully, the cold was all but gone by the following day, so we
were able to go ahead with the surgery under general anesthesia. After
the biopsy, I woke up not knowing for a minute or two where I was,

but the memory of the circumstance quickly returned. I immediately felt a fierce burning in my right breast. It was a sensation I had never before experienced. It was far more intense than the tingling sensations I had when pregnant and breast feeding. It took me by surprise; I had not anticipated such discomfort from a small biopsy. It was not unbearable by any means, but it hurt. I slipped in and out of a hazy sleep and when awake, I flipped from feelings of fear when I allowed myself to think of what the biopsy might reveal, to feelings of relief that the biopsy was over. It amazed me how quickly I moved from dark thoughts of my premature death to absolute denial that this was anything but a silly mistake and there was nothing to worry about. I concluded that it must be the anesthesia playing tricks with my brain.

When Graham arrived to take me home, he told me the surgeon had phoned to tell him that the lump was cystic, exactly as he had predicted, but he would send it to pathology to be sure. Feeling very relieved, we headed home. The following day Graham went to work, and I intended to sleep late. But I was awakened by the phone. I picked it up and heard a woman's voice, "Can I speak to Julie Houlker?"

"Speaking," I replied.

"This is the receptionist from the surgeon's office. The doctor would like to see you today at 11 am, and he has asked that you bring your husband with you."

I said I would be there and hung up the phone. My mouth was dry and my hands were shaking as I phoned Graham at work and told him. We both knew that it must be bad news. Graham worked a good 45-minute drive from home. He told me a few months later that he had cried all the way home that day. He was terrified that he was going to lose me.

We went into the surgeon's office and sat in silence in the waiting room. Graham held my hand. When it was finally our turn to go into his office, we saw the surgeon sitting behind his desk. He started to talk without making eye contact with me. "I got a call from the pathologist this morning; he has found cancer in the tissue I removed during the biopsy. He said he almost missed it because most of the tissue was cystic, but there was a small cancerous area at the edge. He could only see this under the microscope which is why I had thought it was cystic yesterday. The sample looked benign without the microscope. It is small and early stage."

I asked a few questions and he talked about doing a larger excision and removing some lymph nodes because the cancer was on the margin of the specimen so there could be more cancer still in my breast. He then talked about possible treatments after surgery, and told me I would probably be put on medication or have chemotherapy to cause early menopause. At this point I stopped hearing anything he said. In my mind I was thinking, "I might never meet my grandchildren or bring in the new millennium. At best I need more surgery, possibly chemotherapy, and then will be pushed into early menopause, and I am not even 41 years old." Then the nurse in me thought, "This lump has been in me for a long time, it has probably spread to other organs by now."

We got up to leave and in a state of emotional numbness I talked to the receptionist about the date for the excision, which was set for December 27.

As we left the office I started to cry, and said to Graham, "I am so sorry."

Graham looked at me with disbelief in his eyes. "What on earth do you to have apologize for?"

"This was not meant to happen; we were supposed to grow old together and be sitting out on our deck together when we're 80."

"This is not your fault; there are no guarantees in life. Remember our wedding vows, for better, for worse, in sickness and in health."

This made me cry even more.

Then he said, "I know we will be sitting out on our deck together when we're 80."

Through my tears I replied, "But will I have one boob or two?"

He said, "Who cares?" and we both smiled.

I had to get blood tests done, so we went to the lab, as the girl prepared to take blood she looked at my birth date, and the words breast cancer on the form.

She said, "It's your birthday soon, not much of a birthday present is it?"

I just shook my head as the tears rolled down my face. I went through all the rational and irrational thoughts: Why did this happen? Was I exposed to DDT while playing in the fields in my childhood; Was it because I had been on the Pill for five years? Was it because I had smoked for a few years? Was it because I sunbathed topless and my boobs had too much sun? Was it because of the radiation that drifted over England from Chernobyl? Was it because of the stress of the move to Canada? At no time did I ever think, "Why me?" I had worked with so many children who faced such huge challenges in life that I knew I was lucky to have been so healthy until I was 41. My thought was more, "Why not me?"

Christmas came and went almost without us noticing it. On December 27, I had the surgery to do a bigger excision and remove the lymph nodes under my arm. The following day Paul arrived at the hospital to visit me with a young lady called Melanie, who he introduced as Mel. I was struck with what a nice girl she seemed to be. She gave me a single red rose, and said she hoped I was feeling better soon. Paul had friends that were girls but he had never introduced us to a "girlfriend" before so I knew Mel must be special to him.

The excision in my breast was not too bad, but the wound under my arm was uncomfortable. I knew that if cancer was found in my lymph nodes, then my chances of survival were less. Every time I saw someone approaching my bed, my heart raced because I thought they were coming to tell me the results of the lymph node pathology. On the second day the surgeon arrived on the ward, my heart thumped as he moved towards my bed. He sat down on the end of the bed and asked how I was feeling. "Fine," I replied quickly while thinking, "Oh, my god, it's bad news; he is preparing me for it."

"Do you feel okay to go home? Because we need the bed."

I let out a sigh of relief and said, "I thought you were coming to tell me the results of the lymph node pathology."

"Oh no, I haven't got the report back yet, but do you feel okay to go home?"

I told him I was fine to go home, and called Graham. The ride home was uncomfortable. Every bump felt like it tore at my wounds. Once I got home, I settled down on the couch, and Paul and a couple of his friends arrived. I must have not looked good because they all seemed a bit concerned about me, and left soon so I could rest. The following day I got a call to say the lymph nodes were all clear of cancer. What a relief!

Within a week I was back in the surgeon's office looking across the desk at him. Again he had a grave expression. He explained that when he did the surgery all the tissue in my breast appeared to be normal tissue so it was difficult to know what tissue to remove. But yet again, under microscopic scrutiny, it was found that the cancer was at the edge of the tissue sample, so he could not guarantee that all the cancer had been removed. He recommended a mastectomy to be sure that all the cancer had been removed. This time I was a bit more prepared. I had done my homework. I told him I wanted to have the new procedure of mastectomy and reconstruction in one operation. He said he would contact the plastic surgeon, but he was pretty sure this could be done as I was still at an early stage and the lymph nodes were negative. He gave me pages of information and suggested that I start to save my own blood so that if I needed a transfusion after surgery I could have my own blood transfused back to me. Apparently there had been some research that showed women who were transfused their own blood after breast cancer surgery had a better survival rate that those women who had received donor blood.

So for the next few weeks, I gave blood that was stored for me. I ate well and prepared myself for the major surgery. I had a whirl of appointments with the plastic surgeon, x-rays, and the lab for blood work.

The night before the surgery I lay in bed with Graham as he stroked my right breast, we were both saying goodbye to a part of my body that we would never see again. It was a very strange feeling to know that by the following day my right breast would be in a specimen jar in the pathology lab. I don't remember if I cried that night; I just know I was very sad.

On the morning of January 23, 1996, I was ready for the surgery. It all seemed surreal. I felt like I was in a dream. You know the kind of dream where you are in public in your underwear? I was prepped for surgery with the gown, hat, socks, and no make-up. The nurse came to take me to the operating room and we walked to the elevator together. I was hoping that I would not meet anyone I knew on the way and was wishing I could have been wheeled in on a gurney so I would not be as easily recognized.

Thankfully, I got to the operating room without meeting anyone I knew. The plastic surgeon was waiting and was quickly drawing lines all over my body. He was going to remove a major abdominal muscle and tunnel it up under my skin to the breast area and use it to form a new breast. This procedure was to be done after the general surgeon had removed my breast.

My family doctor arrived and told me that he would be assisting in the surgery. He stayed with me until the anesthesiologist arrived.

I had met the anesthesiologist the day before and had asked him to talk to me during the surgery and tell me that all would go well and that I would not have too much pain. I had been reading a book about the power of hearing these kinds of healing words during surgery. Even though the person is asleep there is evidence that what is said in the operating room affects the patient and the more positive words spoken, the better for the patient. He was quite young and I think he thought I was nuts, but he said he would talk to me during the surgery.

My memory of the next few days is hazy. I know I felt like I had been hit by a truck but the pain was not that bad. The worst part was the reaction to the morphine. I had an intravenous morphine line that was operated by a push button. The nurses told me that it gave only a small amount at a time so I should push the button regularly or the pain relief would not work. The problem was that every time I touched the button, I had instant nausea and threw up. The antinausea medication didn't work other than to make me very drowsy. That was bad enough, but ever since I was young, any severe nausea has caused me to pass out. This condition was diagnosed as vagal attacks, which are basically fainting attacks, but in my case they are triggered only by nausea. It is very frightening for anyone who is with me at the time and scary for me. So after a day of extreme nausea, and having passed out at least three times, the nurses agreed to stop the morphine. The nurses were worried that the oral medications would not control my pain, but they worked just fine. I lost quite a bit of blood so I did need to be transfused with the blood I had previously stored.

On the day after surgery, Graham's parents arrived from England. They had already planned a trip to stay with us before we knew about the surgery, and decided to stay longer to help me.

It was around 8 PM the following day, Graham and his dad were just about to leave for home when Glenda appeared at my bedside saying, "I am here to rub your feet and tuck you into bed for the night."

It turned out that the friend who I had referred to Glenda had sent her to do my feet, rather than send me flowers. Glenda had come out at night in a snowstorm to take care of me. She was so relaxed and easy to talk to, and she soon had Graham and his dad laughing.

She came back every night while I was in hospital and we became friends. I often say that Glenda is the guardian angel sent to me. In retrospect, the set of coincidences that led to our friendship were so amazing, that it is clear that it was guidance of some sort, not coincidences.

I had a flood of flowers, fruit baskets, balloons, and cards arriving at my bedside. In all the years I had worked as a nurse, I had not really understood the power of the cards and good wishes until I was the recipient. I literally felt like I was being physically lifted up and held safe by all the love coming in my direction in the form of cards and good thoughts. It still brings tears to my eyes when I think of how powerful that feeling was during such a difficult time.

My mum, sisters, and brother in England were all feeling helpless because they were so far away, but I learned that you don't have to be geographically close to someone to feel their love and support. I could feel it like they were in the same room.

I made a fast recovery and four days later, was ready to go home. The surgeon came and told me that the breast tissue all looked normal again but the microscopic studies showed that there had been some cancer in the breast. He said all the surgical margins were well clear, so he had finally got it all. The plastic surgeon took off the dressing and I saw my new breast for the first time. It was not a pretty sight. It was swollen and had large scars across it, but amazingly, it did look like a breast and I had no pain at all in the chest area. I had 56 metal staples in my abdomen and a drain still in place, as well as the sutures in the reconstructed breast, and was quite weak from the blood loss. When it was time to go home, the nurses provided a wheelchair for Graham to wheel me to the car. They gave me Tylenol with codeine to help make the car journey home more comfortable.

Graham collected all the flowers, balloons, and baskets and loaded them into the back seat of the car before coming back for me. He wheeled me to the front lobby where he left me for a couple of minutes while he went to get the car. He carefully helped me into the front seat, and fastened my seat belt. At the exact moment he turned to push the wheelchair back into the lobby, I decided to adjust my seat back, not realizing that when adjusting the seat forward, I would need to use abdominal muscles (of which none of mine were working at this time). In a split second, the seat back went down, and the next thing I knew, I was laid out almost flat with my head at the level of the back seat, with balloons and flowers all around my head. There was nothing I could do to get the seat back up, I was stuck. I saw Graham approach the car, but he couldn't see me. He had a look of absolute shock when he saw the front seat empty, and did a double-take looking around to check if I had gotten out of the car. It was so funny to watch that I started to giggle. With a look of disbelief and concern on his face, he came up to the car window to find me surrounded by the flowers and balloons.

He opened the door and said incredulously, "What are you doing?"

I think I was probably a bit high from the codeine by this time, because I was laughing so hard while trying to hold onto my stomach, that he could not get any sense out of me. Eventually I explained that I was stuck, and he gently put the seat back up and we set off on the drive home. But I couldn't stop giggling, and by this time Graham was seeing the funny side of it. Graham's parents were waiting for us at the front door, their expressions quickly turning to shocked concern as they saw me shaking and holding my abdomen with tears running down my face. It took a little time to explain that I was laughing, not crying.

I had just stopped laughing and settled in at home when Graham said with a serious expression on his face, "Now whatever you do, don't stand too close to the fridge."

I asked why and he replied with a smile on his face. "With all those metal staples in your belly, you'll stick to it like a magnet!" We both started to giggle again as I thought of how much I loved his sense of humor.

Three weeks after surgery, I had an appointment to see an oncologist at the Cancer Centre. I was unsure what to expect and was quite nervous. Graham and I sat in the consulting room waiting for the doctor. He whisked into the room with a file in his hand. He sat down and started to try and sort out all the loose papers in the file. He looked up saying, "The surgeon didn't take out any lymph nodes so I can't decide on treatment until that is done."

I replied, "I had 11 lymph nodes removed and they were all negative for cancer." He shuffled through the papers again and then said, "Are you sure, because there are no reports here."

I assured him that I had the node resection done and the results were negative. Eventually he found the report and had to acknowledge that the lymph nodes were all indeed negative for cancer. He then proceeded with the examination.

He commented on my abdominal scar and newly reconstructed breast as he examined me. "Wow, not exactly Mickey Mouse surgery, is it?"

I didn't know what he meant by that but I squirmed because I felt that he thought me foolish to have such major surgery for the sake of a breast. He shuffled through the papers again before sitting down with Graham and me to discuss his findings. He told us that because the cancer was early stage and the nodes were negative I probably would not need chemotherapy, but he would discuss it with the team and see me in another three weeks. We left feeling elated. I was so dreading the chemotherapy for many reasons, but one big reason was my vagal attacks that make me pass out when I am nauseous. I could not imagine having six months of constantly worrying about passing out.

We came home, and relayed the good news to Graham's parents and Paul.

The next time we saw the oncologist, he had changed his opinion. He now thought I should consider chemotherapy as a precaution. He said I had a 70% chance of being just fine and not need it and a 20% chance that the chemo would do me no good but it could reduce the risk of recurrence by 10% in the first five years. However there was no evidence that it would improve my overall chance of survival. He then went over the risks associated with chemotherapy.

I digested these numbers and facts and immediately thought, "He wants me to go through this toxic treatment when there is a 90% chance it will do me no good and 'maybe' give only 10% reduced risk of recurrence in the first five years." That was no better than the placebo effect. I also wondered how it was that three weeks ago I didn't need chemo, and now I did, but nothing had changed. I came to the realization that the decision was not a clear-cut one, and I needed to do more research. The stubborn determination kicked in again, I knew I was not going to be pushed into anything I was unsure of. We said we would think about it and left. He said he would set up my appointment for the first chemo session anyway.

For the next two weeks, Graham and I talked and talked and talked over what we should do. We read all the information available, and the only conclusion we could come to was that, in early stage, node-negative breast cancer, the evidence at that time was not clear on the benefits of chemotherapy. However, there was solid evidence of the permanent damage chemotherapy could do to my body, and that there was a slight risk that it would kill me. I think this was one of the hardest decisions in my life, but I was determined to make an informed decision and would not go ahead with the chemotherapy out of fear. I had to know it would be beneficial.

I was reading a book written by a doctor who had seen the connection between body and spirit, and the way this affects healing. He talked about the effect of the patient's beliefs on the effectiveness of medicines. If a patient truly believes that the treatment will do them harm, then it will, and vice versa. I knew in my soul that the chemotherapy was not right for me at that time, and I thought it would kill me.

On a bright winter day just after the appointment with the oncologist, Graham and I were walking along the trail by the river and discussing the pros and cons of chemotherapy.

As we talked, Graham said, "You know I will support you in whatever decision you make, but once that decision is made, we need to agree that no matter what happens in the future, we will not question it."

Graham held me in his arms as we watched the fast-flowing water in the river and we made a pact that no matter what happened in the future, we would never second guess our decision, and we never did. I chose not to have chemotherapy.

One of the disturbing things about being diagnosed with a life-threatening disease is the loss of control of your life. Suddenly the doctors have all the control, and you feel that your life is no longer your own. Once I made the decision about not having chemotherapy, I felt like I had the control back.

A quote I read somewhere sums it up for me: "Everything can be taken from a person but one thing: The last of the human freedoms is to choose one's own way." I had chosen my own way and it was the right way for me.

I went back to living my life, but there was a difference in my thinking. I no longer took anything for granted. Every day was a gift and I made a conscious decision to enjoy life to the fullest. In the weeks following my surgery, Glenda invited me to go along to the "Living with Cancer" support group. The group met at the Holiday Inn in Chilliwack. The first time I went to the group I was unsure if it was the place for me. I remember walking into the hotel lobby thinking, "What am I doing here? I don't have cancer anymore."

Once in the meeting I enjoyed myself. It was not the gloomy experience I had been expecting. The people were all cracking jokes and laughing as well as telling their stories. Glenda demonstrated some power of the mind activities and talked about the power of positive thinking. I met Michelle at this first meeting. She helped Glenda with the meeting and brought along a pile of books and tapes that could be borrowed. Everyone told their cancer story, and when it came time for Michelle to tell her story, she demonstrated the power of the mind and how it affects our bodies. When talking about her radiation treatments, the area of her neck that had been radiated would turn bright red with a clear-cut line at the edge of the radiated area. This happened every time she talked about her radiation.

I went to the group on a regular basis for a couple of years until I no longer felt I needed it. The group gave me a lot of insight into how to live life to the fullest. I began to understand that by having had cancer I had been given a perspective on life that made me live more joyously. In a weird way, the cancer diagnosis had brought some gifts with it.

Over the months after my surgery, I got to know Glenda and Michelle at the group and I had reflexology from Glenda on a weekly basis. Glenda invited us to join the Optimist Club. This was a service group that supported children and youth and promoted optimism as a philosophy of life. I read the creed that talked about many things including, "Be too large for worry, too noble for anger, too strong for fear, and too happy to permit the presence of trouble." This was the perfect creed for us to live by so we became members.

We met Glenda's husband, Rick, at the meetings and Michelle from the support group was also a member. The meetings were usually at Glenda's house where there was always lots of laughter. Glenda and Rick's home was so warm and welcoming and they threw the best parties. I remember at one Christmas party, Glenda did a skit with some of the guests acting out the story. Glenda dressed up a lady named Bonnie in curlers, and she acted the part superbly. Her husband, Pete, watched and giggled quietly.

In June of 1996, I had my reconstruction completed by having a nipple constructed from skin grafts. My new nipple was slightly lighter in color than my other one, but I decided against having the nipple tattooed to make it match. The plastic surgeon recommended exposing my new nipple to the sun to darken the color. Not an easy thing to do, but I came up with a way to do it. I cut a small hole in an old shirt so that my new nipple was exposed, and when possible would head into the garden with a book against my chest to hide the exposed nipple. Once I was out of sight of the neighbours, I would move the book, giggling to myself at the absurdity of sun tanning a nipple.

I was starting to plan for the future again. In the August of 1996, we went to an Optimist convention in Whistler, BC. The highlight of the weekend was a concert on a stage at the top of the mountain by the Vancouver Philharmonic Orchestra. I sat on the grassy mountainside, looking at the majestic Garibaldi mountain range as the music floated over the air. I cried not in sadness but in gratitude that I had survived to be able to enjoy this magic moment. It is only after your mortality has been threatened, that you truly can appreciate these kinds of moments.

I continued to have regular reflexology sessions with Glenda. I loved her sense of humor which was demonstrated one day when I was talking about something being expensive and said, "It costs an arm and a leg."

Glenda looked down at her one remaining leg as she laughingly said, "Well, that's definitely out of my budget."

The first part of each reflexology session we would chat and catch up on each others news before getting down to the work of deep breathing and focusing on healing. As the years went by, the healing light that we visualized became more intense and many times I would physically feel the heat of the light going through my body.

It eventually became clear that our son Paul was in love with Mel. Paul worshiped the ground Mel walked on and she obviously loved him to pieces. I knew that they were soul mates just like Graham and me. It warmed my heart to see how loving and affectionate Paul was with Mel. I have always believed that the ability to give and receive love is the key to success in life, and I knew Paul had those skills. Mel was quite shy at first, but over time she relaxed in our company and we were very happy that Paul had found such a wonderful girl.

I remember the first time Paul brought Mel home for dinner. Graham put some music on as we sat down at the table and, of course it was his favorite band, Pink Floyd. Paul looked at Mel and said, "Don't worry you soon get used to Pink Floyd."

In the fall of 1996, Graham's parents came out to stay with us again. They arrived a few days before Graham was due to arrive home from Africa. They had been with us a couple of days when I picked up the phone at work to hear my father-in-law's voice. "Julie can you come home? David has died." For a moment it didn't register. "David? Susan's David?" He went on to say that David, the husband of Graham's younger sister Susan, had collapsed and died of a heart attack at the age of 44.

My in-laws were distraught and wanted to get home to England as soon as possible to be with their daughter. I spent hours on the phone that day trying to secure them an early flight home and trying to connect with Graham to tell him to stop off in England on the way home to be with his sister.

After Graham's parents left, I was alone because Graham was en route home from Africa, and I had time to reflect on the family crisis we had experienced. It struck me as very ironic that David had died and yet I was the one with cancer.

It became clear to me that day that the diagnosis of cancer doesn't mean you are going to die; it just gives you an understanding that there are no guarantees in life. With my cancer diagnosis, everyone in our family was concerned that I would have my life shortened, and yet it was David who had only a short time to live. Life is terminal and no one knows when his time will come. As a cancer survivor, I had an advantage in that I had to consider the possibility that the cancer may shorten my life. I was given the gift of knowing that I could not waste a moment of the precious life I had left.

Susan and her daughters came to visit us the following spring. She seemed to be in good spirits, although she was obviously still grieving the loss of her husband. We took her and the girls skiing at Manning Park and had a great time.

In the summer of 1998, Paul moved out to set up house with Mel. He was twenty years old and ready to be independent. It was an emotional time for me but it was also a happy time because I truly believe that a parent's job is to prepare the child for independence.

We were waiting to hear from Susan and my in-laws as to the date they would be visiting, when Graham had a call from his mum. She explained that Susan had a lump in her leg and she had to have a biopsy. The nurse in me wanted to know more but Graham was unable to answer any of my questions.

That night I had a dream that Susan had cancer and didn't have long to live. When I woke up I quickly put aside all my worries about the dream. Susan was strong and what were the odds of something happening to her as well as David?

I told Graham about my dream and then forgot about it. Within a few days we heard that Susan had cancer and that it was already in her lungs.

I phoned Susan, and was relieved to hear that she was very positive that she could beat it. She had surgery booked to remove the lump in her leg and then would be having lung surgery to remove the spots in her lungs. I mailed her some of the inspirational books that had helped me.

This year Graham and I were planning to do our trip to South Africa. Graham had wanted to take me to South Africa ever since his first visit there. We had received a letter in the mail from British Airways to say that we had won a large number of air miles, and it turned out it was enough for my round-trip flight to South Africa. Talk about the law of attraction at work! We decided that I would use the air miles to fly to South Africa with Graham when he needed to be at a trade show in Johannesburg, and he would take vacation time after the show to travel with me.

We had to stop off en route in England, so decided to visit our families in Lancashire for a couple of days. Susan was recovering well from her surgery and was optimistic about the future. I thought that she looked a bit thin and strained but quickly put my worries aside.

A work friend of Graham's took us on a safari in Kruger National Park where we spotted and photographed the "Big Five": elephant, rhino, leopard, lion and buffalo. We stayed in round huts with thatched roofs in the park camps, and had wonderful meals in the camp restaurants. The huts had covered patios with outside kitchens with fridges and stoves. We went on a night drive and saw a lion kill, and witnessed the hyenas moving in for their share when the lions had finished.

The wonderful smells and sounds of Africa are unique and will stay with me forever. Our African adventure was an amazing journey full of things I could never experience anywhere else. I quickly saw why my husband loved this part of the world so much.

We stayed in Cape Town for five days, to have the opportunity to take a guided tour to the Cape of Good Hope, the place where the Atlantic and Indian Oceans meet. The two distinct colors of water can be seen from the viewing point.

On the last day of our visit, we wandered down to the waterfront to have an evening meal and were delighted to find out that it just happened to be the weekend of the Cape Town wine festival. We paid the $5 entrance fee which included two wine glasses to take home, and tried many lovely South African wines. We then *merrily* decided we should probably not walk home so we got a cab. It was a perfect end to our African adventure.

Living as a cancer survivor is, without doubt, a roller-coaster ride. On the one hand, there is a sense that every day is a gift and a motivation to enjoy life to fullest by living in the present moment. But when it is time for the routine check-ups, all kinds of worry, fear, and anxiety surface no matter how hard you try to "stay positive."

In April 1999, I thought everything was going well with my health when I was suddenly thrown for a loop by a routine mammogram. It was three years and five months since my diagnosis of breast cancer and three years and four months since my mastectomy and reconstruction. I was starting to believe that I would live and conquer the cancer. Maybe I was too confident. The scars were there but I hardly noticed them anymore. I was starting to plan for the future again.

Then I had my routine yearly check up. Everything looked good, I just needed the mammogram and then I could relax until next year. The x-ray technician asked me to wait for her to check the films, and then she needed to take more films. She studied a film and then marked a spot on my reconstructed breast.

My heart sank to my toes. I knew what this meant but deep down I felt I was well. I had none of the "gut feeling" of worry that I had before the cancer was diagnosed. The tech said I was okay to go but I left the x-ray lab with a heavy heart.

I tried not to dwell on it. It was Easter weekend and I had four days off from work, but the worry nagged me all weekend. I didn't tell Graham that I was concerned. I didn't even tell him about the extra films they had taken. It seemed that if I put my fears into words it would make them more real.

On Tuesday morning, I headed back to work. I had a lot to do, so my mind did not stray back to the worry. Then I went home for lunch. There was a message on the answering machine. I knew before I played it that it was from my doctor. I heard the words "mammogram," "abnormality," and "need to see the surgeon."

My legs started to tremble, my heart raced and I felt pounding in my head. I tried to stay calm as I dialed the number for my doctor's office. Thank god he was there and thank god he is the kind of doctor who cares from the heart. He came on the line immediately. He explained that the radiology report recommended further investigation. I told him that I had not noticed any changes in my breast. At this point I was still trying to tell myself that I was well and that this was a false alarm. I called the surgeon's office, his receptionist was kind and caring, and she had a cancellation for the following day so I didn't have to wait the usual two weeks for an appointment.

The surgeon was reassuring, and he told me that he did not believe that there was any cause for concern. He examined me and found nothing abnormal. He had not yet seen the films for himself, but had the radiologist's report. He decided to call the radiologist and suggested we do another mammogram in three months' time and he said he would call me when he had talked to the radiologist.

I felt my body physically relax, I started to believe in my future again and I was able to banish those nagging thoughts of wondering if I would live to meet my grandchildren and the visions of my funeral.

I looked at Graham that evening and I felt a surge of love as he held and kissed me. His deep love for me is the most wonderful gift. He told me that he was sure it would be good news. His strength and optimism had been my saving grace in the past. The strength seems to surge from him to me and gives me the ability to cope with the fear. I loved him so deeply and I wanted so much to have more time with him.

A few days later, there was a message on the answering machine from the surgeon saying that I needed a biopsy. It then took me 12 days to connect with him to find out why I needed the biopsy. He was away on holiday, and then too busy to call me. By the time I finally spoke to him, I was a nervous wreck. He said that he thought the density on the mammogram was fatty tissue but to be sure I had to have it biopsied.

Within a week, I was in x-ray watching the radiologist guide a metal wire into the edge of my reconstructed breast. This done, I waited for the surgeon to come and cut out another piece of my body. He said it looked benign and this was confirmed by the pathology report. I had my reprieve.

In the summer of 1999, Susan visited with her youngest daughter and her daughter's friend for a couple of weeks. Susan had undergone surgery to remove the cancer spots on each of her lungs and she had a couple of chemotherapy treatments. She had almost died from the chemotherapy, and it had had no effect on her cancer so it was discontinued. Graham's parents came out first and then went to collect Susan and the girls from the Seattle Airport a couple of weeks later.

When they arrived back, I was horrified at how ill Susan looked. She was taking morphine tablets for pain, but had also taken some travel sickness pills. I think the combination didn't work well together. She went straight to bed and I have to admit I went into her room several times that night to check that she was still breathing. The following day she was better, but was in constant pain. It was obvious to me that she had not been well enough to make the journey to Canada. She had done a good job of hiding how ill she was from her parents because she was determined to give the girls a good holiday.

We took them to all the local attractions, but Susan would often sit in the car and rock back and forth because the pain was so intense. The pain prevented her from sleeping, and she was unable to eat anything other than a bit of salad or piece of bread. It broke my heart to see her suffer so much and to see her parents so worried, but refusing to consider that she might not make it.

One night after everyone was in bed, Susan and I talked in the family room. She was determined to beat the cancer saying, "I have to get better because I need to be there for my two girls; I am not giving in yet."

She was determined to survive for her girls, but I knew in my heart that the battle was becoming one-sided, with the cancer getting the upper hand.

I arranged for her to have a reflexology session with Glenda, and also get acupuncture treatment to try to help ease the pain. Both of these helped a little, but she was never pain-free. After her parents had driven her and the girls to Seattle Airport, they arrived back at our house in a very tired state. My mother-in-law was distraught at having to put Susan on a plane in such pain.

As her mother, she wanted to be with her and take care of her. She started to tell me how hard it had been but she broke down in tears. I held her as she said between the sobs, "I don't want to lose her." I wished there was something I could say to reassure that all would be well but there was nothing.

After Graham's parents left for home, the strain of it all hit me. I cried for hours. It was all too much, my cancer diagnosis, and surgery, David's death, and now Susan so ill, and all within three-and-a-half years.

Susan was admitted to hospital soon after arriving back in England, and she never went home. In November while Graham was away in Africa, I got a call from Graham's older brother telling me that Susan had died. I was home alone and was overcome with sadness. I called Paul and Mel to give them the news. Mel answered. I struggled to contain the tears as I told her the sad news.

She asked if I was okay. "Do you want us to come over?"

I said, "No, I'm fine."

She asked again, "Are you're sure you're okay?"

I assured her I was fine. After I put the phone down I had the task of phoning Graham in Africa to tell him. He was very sad, but had been expecting it because she had been so ill when he visited her.

That night I cried for Susan and David and for their two girls left without parents at the tender ages of 15 and 21. I cried for my in-laws who I knew would never recover from the grief, I cried for Graham and Les, who had lost their only sister, I cried for the future grandchildren that would never know Susan and David. I cried for me, because as a cancer survivor, I knew that what had happened to Susan could also be my fate. I cried because I missed Graham so much, and I needed to be in his arms.

The irony of it all hit me again. I was the one first diagnosed with cancer and everyone had worried that my life would be cut short, and yet both Susan and David had such a short time left and didn't know it. No one knows how much time they have left, but when you have had cancer, it forces you to live every moment to the fullest. Graham went to England for the funeral on the way back from Africa, and by the time he came home, it was time to think about Christmas, and everyone was buzzing about the New millennium. We were feeling a bit subdued about all the celebrations but were looking forward to a family Christmas with Paul and Mel.

It turned out that the Christmas of 1999, was a memorable one.

Paul and Mel arrived for our usual family Christmas Eve dinner and looked a bit nervous.

Almost immediately Paul said, "We have something to tell you."

Before we could ask what, he said, "You are going to be grandparents."

I threw my arms around them both saying, "This is wonderful!"

The whole evening I had a big grin on my face as I repeated again and again, "Oh, my lord, oh my goodness!"

I now knew that I was going to meet my grandchild. Mel was so relieved she started to cry. She had thought we would be upset because they were not married yet. But to me and Graham, their being married or not was irrelevant, they were in love and happy and there was a new life on the way, what could be better? We were ecstatic.

We had planned a holiday for the four of us at Big White Ski resort to bring in the millennium. It was a very special holiday, our first grandchild was on the way, and I was alive to ring in the next millennium. At midnight everyone gathered in the center of the village to bring in the New Year. At exactly midnight, a dusting of light snow started to fall. I felt a warm glow as I looked at Paul, Mel, and Graham, all smiling with snowflakes on their hair and faces. Life was good.

We had started to have dinners with Glenda and Rick, alternating between our homes. Graham and Rick got on well together and we loved their company.

On Glenda's first visit to our home she stepped into the hallway and looked at my embroidered daffodil picture with a blue background and said, "That's a lovely picture of the Cancer Society daffodil."

I asked what she meant, because I didn't know it was the Cancer Society's logo. I got goose bumps as she told me about the daffodil symbol and the story of how she had painted the exact picture before

Paul, Graham and Mel bringing in the new millennium.

she had been diagnosed with cancer and didn't know at the time that it was the Cancer Society's symbol. I had been given this picture years before my diagnosis.

In the spring of 2000, I noticed a small lump at exactly the spot where the biopsy had been a year earlier. It was the size of a grain of rice. Off I went to the doctor again. He didn't think it was anything to worry about, but suggested we ask the surgeon to look at it.

The surgeon examined me and announced, "This is just scar tissue and we know it is benign because the biopsy we did last year proved it."

As I left his office, I couldn't help feeling that this had a familiar ring to it. Hadn't the first two biopsies missed the cancer four-and-a-half years ago? Over the next couple of weeks the "scar tissue" grew larger.

I arrived at Glenda's house one day for a reflexology session just as another of her friends was leaving. This woman was also a breast cancer survivor who had been diagnosed the same year as me, and had a mastectomy at the age of 21. Glenda mentioned to her that I was worried about the lump, and she immediately encouraged me to go back to the surgeon. A relative of hers had recently been told to wait six months before re-checking a lump, but had insisted on having a biopsy. It turned out that it was a cancer that would have been missed for six months had she not insisted on a biopsy. I decided to go back to my doctor who again referred me back to the surgeon.

I will always be grateful that Glenda's friend and I crossed paths that day because she gave me the encouragement I needed to be insistent. By the time I saw the surgeon the scar tissue had grown to the size of a pea.

In the examining room the surgeon sighed and said, "Show me where the lump is." I pointed to the spot. He felt it and said with an incredulous tone said, "That's it?"

By this time I was getting annoyed at his attitude. I replied, "Yes, that is it, and it has grown from the size of a grain of rice to the size of a pea in the last month!"

He agreed we should do a biopsy and we agreed that it be done under local anesthetic, so it was scheduled for the following week. My mum would be visiting from England, but we arranged to take her on a short trip to the Rockies, and be back in time for the biopsy. It was only one month before the expected arrival of our first grandchild.

On the day of the biopsy the surgeon came into the room and said, "I know you think I am being blasé about this, but I have seen hundreds of recurrences and this is nothing like a recurrence."

I replied, "I hope you're right."

He got to work. I felt the tugging and pulling but not much pain. He seemed to take a long time and at a certain point in the procedure I could see by the look on his face that he was perplexed.

I said, "You're not so sure about this anymore are you?"

He then did a backtracking performance that would have been quite funny if the situation had not been so serious.

He stammered, "Well, it's quite dense and white. You don't want it to be cancer and I don't want it to be cancer, but we will see what the pathology shows."

When the procedure was over and I left the doctor's office, I knew in my heart that it was a recurrence of the cancer.

I went from there to Mel's doctor's office where I had left my mum. She was waiting with Mel for her pre-natal appointment so she could hear the baby's heart beat. I arrived just in time to listen to the strong and vibrant beat of my grandchild's heart. My mum looked at me and I knew she could see from my face that something was wrong but she didn't say anything.

Within a few days, I was back in the surgeon's office hearing him say, "It is cancer, it's the same cancer as before, and the margins are not clear so we need to do another excision."

If this seems familiar, it's because it is exactly the same scenario as when my cancer was first diagnosed. I walked to the receptionist's desk in a state of resigned acceptance. This was it; I could no longer deny it. I was going to die. I had gone on my own to the surgeon's office and I knew that both Graham and my mum were at home waiting for me. I couldn't go home straight away. I needed some time to come to terms with the news I had been given.

I drove out to Cultus Lake and parked the car by the edge of the lake. The lake was so beautiful and so calming. I don't know how long I sat looking at the lake but I realized that I had to go home at some point, so I started the engine and headed for home.

Mum and Graham were in the living room when I got home. There was no easy way of giving them the news so I just said, "It's cancer." Mum started to cry and Graham just wrapped me in his arms and told me it would be okay.

That night I lay in bed with Graham crying, "I don't think I can do this again."

Graham held me tight and said, "You don't have to do it on your own; I have the strength for both of us. *We* can beat this."

I swear that I felt his strength surge through me and give me the faith that I could survive.

We were at a restaurant in Chilliwack with Paul, Mel and my mum when I had to do one of the hardest things in my life. Tell my son and future daughter-in-law who were expecting their first child in a matter of weeks that my cancer had returned.

The following day, I had a big meltdown. It was getting close to the due date of our first grandchild and I was dwelling on the thought that I might not live to get to know this baby. After dinner that night when we were home, I started to sob and cry, grieving that this baby might never know me. Graham just held me tight and reassured me that I would survive and that I would know my grandchild.

The next few days were a whirl of appointments, chest x-rays, liver and kidney ultrasounds, and a bone scan.

I was waiting for an appointment for the bone scan when the phone rang. It was Surrey Memorial Hospital calling to say they had a cancellation appointment and could I be there in an hour?

I replied, "I will be there." I then yelled upstairs to mum that we had to leave in 15 minutes.

The drive was a nightmare through heavy traffic and driving rain, but we managed to get there on time. I was feeling very depressed and sorry for myself. I told my mum that I felt like I had only chemotherapy and death to look forward to. She was distraught and doing her best to support me while I was bitchy and irritable with her.

I sat in the only vacant chair in the waiting room and to my surprise the woman who was sat next to me was the grandmother of one of the babies I had worked with years before.

I said "Hi, how are you doing?"

She smiled and said she was fine, but then went on to tell me that she had been diagnosed with thyroid cancer and that her husband had severe diabetes and kidney failure. But her face lit up as she talked about her grandchild who had a very severe disability. She ended with the statement, "We are so lucky."

She had a grandchild with a severe disability, a husband with diabetes and kidney failure, she had thyroid cancer, and yet thought she was lucky and was choosing to smile. I felt humbled and ashamed of my weakness. It made me resolve to be strong and to fight as hard as I could to beat the cancer, and to choose to smile.

I now know that it was no coincidence that I sat next to that grandmother on that day. She was there to give me a message, and I heard it loud and clear. The technologist who checked me in was helpful and cheery and thanked my mum for being with me to support me and said how lucky I was that I had my mum with me. She was right; it was meant to be that my mum was visiting at this time. Thankfully all the tests showed that there was no cancer anywhere else in my body.

Within a few weeks I was sitting in the cancer clinic waiting to see the oncologist. I was resigned to the fact that chemotherapy was my only hope now, and I was prepared for it. The oncologist was a very pleasant man with an air of optimism about him. He had reviewed my file, and after examining me, told me that he thought all I needed was another larger excisional biopsy to be sure that the margins were clear and then radiation therapy to the chest wall. He said he thought it was probably a local recurrence although there was no way of knowing for sure if it was residual cancer left over after the mastectomy, or if it had metastasized to the chest wall. I asked him about chemotherapy, and to my relief and surprise he said he didn't think I needed it. He recommended 30 radiation treatments and then five years of Tamoxifen (a drug that blocks estrogen uptake in the breast cells). I had the larger excision done but yet again the margins were not clear. The surgeon told me that all the margins with the exception of the inferior margin were clear. This was the margin that was closest to my chest wall.

I felt a shiver of fear go through me as he said, "There is nothing more I can do surgically. I went as deep as I could to the chest wall and the only other thing I could do is remove a rib, but that would be a job for a thoracic surgeon."

My thought was, "Is he is telling me I have inoperable cancer in my chest wall and there is nothing more he can do?"

The oncologist called me at home a week or so later. He had reviewed my case with the team at the cancer centre. He told me that the team recommended my reconstructed breast be removed.

He then went on to say, "The specimen from the biopsy was not well-oriented and we are concerned that there may be more cancer under the reconstruction."

I asked, "What does, 'not well-oriented' mean?"

He replied, "When a biopsy is done, the tissue removed is marked so that the pathologist knows which margins he is looking at. The markings were not clear so the team feels that there is some doubt about all the margins except the inferior one being clear."

I took a deep breath as I contemplated the prospect of what was essentially another mastectomy on the same side. I wondered how many women in the world had a mastectomy twice on the same side.

While all this was going on, Mel and Paul were waiting for the arrival of their baby. Mel was overdue so it was decided to induce her labor. The induction was done, but the labor didn't move very fast. It was 11:30 at night when Paul phoned to tell us we had a beautiful

The arrival of Abbygail.

granddaughter who had been born by Caesarean section. Both mother and baby were doing fine.

Words cannot describe the joy of knowing that our granddaughter had arrived in the world safe and sound. We were anxious to meet her, but the hospital would not allow visitors at such a late hour. The following morning I had an appointment with the oncologist at 9 am but I was determined to meet my granddaughter first. We called the hospital early in the morning and arranged to visit at 8 am. Mel looked tired but was doing well and was very proud to show us our granddaughter, Abbygail.

I held her in my arms and marveled at her perfection and beauty. I made a silent vow to her that day. I vowed that I would do everything in my power to be at her graduation and her wedding and would never miss an opportunity to spend time with her. Graham held her and smiled from ear to ear looking like a very proud grandpa.

Before long, we were sitting in the examining room at the cancer clinic waiting to see the oncologist, both of us with huge smiles on our faces. The oncologist came in and went on to explain the radiation plans. I am sure he wondered if we were both losing it because we just continued to smile while nodding in agreement. I asked him again about chemotherapy, and to my relief he said I didn't need it. I would have the radiation after the surgery, and stay on Tamoxifen for five years. I had dodged the chemotherapy bullet again.

A few weeks later I was on the way to the operating room again to have the reconstruction removed. By this time I was quite resigned to the fact that I would be flat-chested on one side and would need to wear a prosthesis. I was just weary of the surgeries and tired of being cut.

Four-and-a-half years earlier, I had a biopsy and then a larger excision only to still need a mastectomy. Here I was again having had the first and second biopsies, but still needing to have the reconstruction removed.

I knew I could not afford to allow myself any self-pity. I had a fight ahead of me which would require all my emotional energy. I had to beat the cancer a second time. The surgery went well and I was discharged to go home.

About a week later, Graham came home from work looking very pale. He had kidney stone pain again. He had suffered from kidney stones a couple of times before and had extreme pain from the renal colic before he managed to pass them. He tried pain killers and rested, but the pain intensified. By midnight, I knew I had to get him to the hospital. It was now my turn to be the caregiver as I helped him into the car and drove him to the emergency department.

I don't think we could believe it as we sat there in Emergency with Graham on IV painkillers, and me still with staples in my chest and a drain coming out of the wound. I remember hearing a conversation between a young doctor and a nurse about his holiday to South

America, where he planned to do some snorkeling, and I wondered if we would ever be well enough to have a holiday again.

Graham had a CAT scan that showed a large kidney stone, and was sent home with painkillers and given an appointment to see a specialist. This was the start of three months of pain and discomfort for him until eventually he had minor surgery to remove the stone. I hated to see him in pain and got a glimpse of how hard it is to see someone you love suffer. It helped me to understand that in some ways it's harder to watch a loved one go through illness than it is to go through it yourself.

This time coincided with my radiation treatments and I think was one of the most challenging times of our lives but we had the most wonderful help to get through it. We had our adorable baby grand-daughter who brought us pure joy at a time when we needed it most. We treasured every moment with her.

Within three weeks of my surgery, I was in the radiation department at the cancer clinic having the measurements done to prepare for the radiation treatments. This is very precise work that ensures the radiation is targeted on the cancer area and does not damage too much healthy tissue. I had to lie on my back with my whole upper body exposed with my right arm above my head and keep very still. This doesn't seem too difficult a thing to do except that it had been only three weeks since the surgery to remove the reconstruction so having my arm above my head for any length of time was very painful. After an hour of extreme pain I asked if I could move. The response from the doctor was, "If you move now we will have to start all over again."

I stayed still and tried to meditate but I was in too much pain and I was getting very cold. I felt like a piece of meat, not a person, as I lay there exposed from the waist up, while the doctors talked among themselves. They drew lines on me, measured me and then told me that they were having difficulty because my chest was concave shaped as a result of the surgeries. After two-and-a-half hours I had no feeling left in my right arm and was in so much pain it felt like my chest was being ripped apart. I heard one of the doctors say, "I think we need to do this again."

I couldn't stop the tears from falling down my face but I didn't move. One of the nurses noticed my tears and asked if I was okay. The doctors stopped and finally realized what bad shape I was in. My oncologist apologized. "Sorry, we have pushed you too far; we need to stop and reschedule you for tomorrow."

The tears then flowed even more because I couldn't bear the thought of going through the ordeal all over again. I tried to move my arm but I had no feeling or control because it had been over my head for so long. I lifted it down with my left hand and started to sit up. I was shivering with cold, and exhausted. The doctor said he needed me to have a CAT scan before I left, and the nurses guided me to a chair in the corridor and left me.

The CAT scan was another ordeal with my arm over my head but it was a shorter time. With this done, I was told I could go home and given an appointment for the following day. The nurse told me to take two painkillers and two anti-inflammatory tablets one hour before my appointment to help with the pain. The following day I took the medication as instructed before my appointment. Unfortunately, the doctors were delayed, and I sat in the waiting room almost three hours. By the time I was in the room having the measurements done, the medications had worn off. Thankfully this time it took only about an hour. This session ended with the nurse marking my body with several blue tattoos. Radiation can't be done in the same place more than once, so the area to be radiated is marked with permanent tattoos. I looked at the ugly blue spots on my chest thinking, "I always said I would never have a tattoo."

The radiation was scheduled to start in November and would be five days a week for six weeks, thirty sessions in all. It took about an hour to drive to the cancer center and then I needed to find parking. The actual radiation was over quickly but there was preparation time of at least half an hour or more, as the technologists set up the machines and positioned my body so that the radiation hit the right spot. So with the drive back and forth, the wait, and treatment time it took up a large chunk of each day. There was no way I could work, so I went on sick leave.

On the first appointment, the technologist drew black lines all over my chest and told me to try not to wash them off. They would be the reference marks for the six weeks of treatment. For the whole time of the treatment, I had black ink marks on all my clothes. I was given a blue gown and a plastic bag with PATIENT PROPERTY written on the side in big letters. The nurse told me that this would be my gown for treatments and I should take the gown home in the bag every day, and wash it as needed. On my way out, I saw several people walking in with their PATIENT PROPERTY bags, and my stubborn determination kicked in. There was no way I was going to be depersonalized by carrying the plastic bag with me every day. I went home and found a wonderful, bright purple, nylon shopping bag with a lovely floral design on it to carry my gown throughout the treatments. It was a very important act of defiance that was a way for me to stay in control. It was also a way of not allowing the cancer to have the upper hand.

I had lots of offers for people to drive me to the appointments, but I was determined to drive myself. Again it was an act of defiance against the cancer. I would not allow myself to be made dependent on others, which in my mind would be another way of letting the cancer have more control.

It was a long, hard, six weeks which stretched into seven weeks because of cancellations when the machines were out of order.

Initially, the only effect on me was the fatigue but as the weeks went by, the burns started to appear on my chest. I was radiated over the whole of my right chest area every treatment, and every other treatment my upper back was also radiated. The burns were only on the front of my chest so I could sleep lying on my back. By the fourth week, the burns were open wounds that would heal and then crack open again when I moved my arm. The nurses told me to soak the area with pads soaked in cold saline which temporarily eased the burning. I had also been started on Tamoxifen, and that had a side effect of major hot flashes. When the flashes came it felt like I was going to self-combust. The final week was a struggle to drive every day, but I was not going to give in to the cancer. I had made it this far and I was determined to drive myself. Sounds a bit stubborn, but I am sure my stubbornness is one of the reasons I am alive and writing this book.

The last treatment day was December 19, 2000—just in time for Christmas. I got to know the radiation technologists quite well and of course had shown them photos of our darling granddaughter and talked about her many times. On the second to last treatment day, Mel brought Abby to the centre to meet the technologists. They all agreed she was adorable.

By the end of February, the burns had healed and I was ready to go back to work. I had hoped to reduce my hours so that I could work four days a week but the week before I went back to work, I was told this was not possible. I was given permission to work shorter hours for the first month back, and then I was expected to go back to full time. I was allowed to flex my hours so that I could take every other Friday off. These Fridays were the highlights of my week because they were my "Abby and Nana"days, when Abby spent the day with me.

I treasured every moment with her. We had a little routine for the time we spent together; she had my complete attention for the whole day. After lunch I would lie down with her and sing little songs

Abby and Nana.

and then we would both nap. Just after I went back to work, I started having an annoying cough. Every time I talked, the cough would start. Of course I worried that the cancer had gone to my lungs, so I went to the doctor immediately. He thought it could be the allergies that had bothered me before, so decided to try an inhaler. If this didn't work then we would look further. The inhaler helped and within a couple of weeks the cough was gone.

I was back into the swing of things at work, but I was not enjoying it as much. I loved my work with the families but it was very stressful because many times there were waiting lists for the services that families needed. It was heartbreaking to know what was needed to help the parents but because of wait lists or funding shortfalls the help was unavailable.

On the days when I knew I had made a difference in someone's life I felt very fulfilled with my job, but on some days when I had been in a particularly emotionally draining situation I would say, "I wish I had a job where I didn't need to care".

Paul and Mel's wedding day.

I now realize that I was suffering from a kind of burnout. I had been supporting the families who were going through difficult times in the most caring and compassionate way that I could for many years. It was draining me of my emotional energy.

We continued to spend as much time as possible with Abby, as we delighted in watching her grow and develop. We felt so blessed to have Paul, Mel and Abby living so close to us.

In August 2002, Paul and Mel were married in a lovely garden ceremony at Mel's parents' house. It was a perfect day, with Abby as the flower girl. She carefully held the basket of rose petals as she walked past the assembled guests slowly dropping a few petals before she thought of a quicker way of getting the petals out and upturned the basket hurling all the petals out at once. Everyone chuckled. We brimmed with pride as we watched our son with his wife and daughter pose for pictures.

I treasured every moment of this special day for all the reasons the mother of the groom would treasure them, but even more so because there had been times when I had wondered if I would live to see it.

In the spring of 2002, I joined a breast cancer dragonboat team, not realizing how much a part of my life this team would become. The first race we entered was on a horrible, wet day in Vancouver, but we had a lot of fun. Michelle, who had joined a new women's dragonboat team, was also there that day. In the first year, I paddled in races across BC, and often ran into Michelle.

In September of that year, while at the Kelowna Dragon Boat Festival, I heard about the opportunity to be part of a team going to New Zealand. I listened to the team manager talk about how much it would cost and what was involved, and I decided there and then that I was going. As we walked back to our hotel, I said to one of my team mates. "I don't have the $4,000 it's probably going to cost, but I will find it somehow. I am going."

Seven of our team members signed up, and by October we had set about fund raising to help with the cost. We had a raffle, put on a dance with a silent auction, and wrote to every service club and business that we could think of, and we raised enough money to cover the cost of all of our flights.

The raffle draw was scheduled for December 14, 2002 and was to be done in a local coffee shop. As I walked in, I saw Glenda heading to a table with her sister and a man I had never seen before. I found out later that Glenda was doing some match-making that day. Darren, the young man, was single, as was Michelle (who was recently divorced) and Glenda thought they should meet. By coincidence the meeting was in the same coffee shop and at the same time as our raffle draw. Darren and Michele seemed to connect well, and they came as a couple with Glenda and Rick, and Bonnie and Pete, to our fund raising dance in February 2003. Michelle seemed very happy, and she and Darren looked so right together. Michelle was scheduled to leave

Julie Dragon boating in New Zealand.

for a temporary teaching job in China soon and we wondered if the romance would survive.

In March 2003, I was once again on an airplane, but this time it was somewhere over the Pacific Ocean, thinking "Is this really 'Little Julie Smith' on the way to a dragon boat festival in New Zealand?"

We were in New Zealand for three weeks. Graham came out to join us for the last two weeks. We had an amazing time, competing in festivals in Auckland and Wellington and touring the North Island between competitions. One of our team members was originally from New Zealand, so she arranged an incredible tour for us. We started at a cottage at Hot Water Beach where we dug a hole to make our own hot tub from the natural hot springs bubbling up through the sand. We stayed on a sheep farm and had a memorable welcoming BBQ dinner put on by several farming families. We were given a very exciting tour of the sheep farm on ATVs. We went to a Maori village and had traditional food cooked with hot stones underground. We went on a jet boat ride, and visited caves that were lit by glow worms. The hospitality extended to us was spectacular. It was a trip of a life time, during which I couldn't help thinking how ironic it was that, had I not had breast cancer, I would probably never have thought of joining a dragon boat team, and would have missed this experience. Life is so wonderful and so full of surprises.

We still had our family ski holidays and delighted in putting Abby on skis for the first time when she was still a toddler.

In the spring of 2003, I was shocked to hear from Glenda that Bonnie had been diagnosed with colon cancer and that she would need major surgery and probably a colostomy. What were the odds that another of our friends would have cancer? I went up to the hospital to see her after her surgery, and gave her an inspirational book to read. She looked very tired and pale but as usual was in good spirits.

Over the next few weeks, Glenda kept me informed of Bonnie's progress and I was saddened to hear that she was having a difficult time with a wound infection. It took a while, but Bonnie recovered and was very optimistic about the future. She was a strong woman, despite all the difficulties she had faced. Once the horrible wound infection cleared up, Bonnie endured six months of chemotherapy. I remember seeing her at Glenda's during this time and wondering how she managed to keep so upbeat about everything. She always chose to smile. Glenda also kept me informed about Michelle and Darren's romance.

Later that year we were paddling back to the dock in Victoria harbor after an exhilarating dragon boat race in which we placed second. I heard a little voice ring out from the crowd of spectators "Go, Nana, Go! Go, Nana, Go!" This was the voice of my granddaughter. I couldn't see her but I could hear her voice. I cried tears of joy.

I was feeling good, but had put on quite a bit of weight; partly, I'm sure, because of the Tamoxifen I was taking. After our ski holiday in February 2004, I decided to lose the weight. We changed our eating habits, and by August I had lost 28 pounds. It felt so good to be rid of the excess weight but I was plagued with repeated painful bladder infections. Eventually my doctor referred me to see a urologist who, in turn, referred me to a gynecologist. The gynecologist confirmed that the problem was an enlarged uterus caused by the Tamoxifen, and recommended a hysterectomy.

I had the hysterectomy in February 2005, and was very relieved to hear that there was no cancer. I am happy to say I have never had another bladder infection.

That was a great year. I felt good and started to feel confident about my future. It was a year when Graham and I did lots of hiking and canoeing while I continued with the dragon boating. My energy levels were high and so were my spirits.

On a sunny day in September 2005, we rushed from the bus to board the train at Seattle's Union Street Station. I was finally taking Graham on the wonderful train trip I had taken in the early 90s with my work colleagues, but this time we were traveling in style, with a private sleeping compartment. The trip was planned as a multiple celebration. I had turned 50 the previous December, Graham was turning 55 in the fall, it was five years since my recurrence, and almost ten years since my first cancer diagnosis. It was time to celebrate!

It was a memorable trip that took us on a train journey down the west coast from Seattle to Los Angeles. We had two days in Hollywood before taking the train to Flagstaff, Arizona, to spend three days exploring the Grand Canyon and Sedona. From Flagstaff, we reboarded the train to Albuquerque, New Mexico, where we explored the ancient cave dwellings and pueblos. From New Mexico, we traveled by car through northern New Mexico and Colorado, before taking a flight home from Denver to Vancouver.

I bubbled with excitement as the train pulled out of the station. The sleeper compartment was small, but very comfortable, with a large window. The seats faced each other and folded into bunks for sleep-

Julie and Graham enjoying the train trip.

ing. There was also an upper bunk that was folded away during the day. The tickets included all our meals which were served in a lovely dining car. Between the sleeper car and the dining car was a viewing car which had food and drinks available as well as a wine- and cheese-tasting event in the afternoons.

Graham and I were like two excited children as we ran around from ride to ride in Universal Studios and posed for pictures with Dora the Explorer, along with Shrek and Donkey. The following day, we walked along Hollywood Boulevard looking at the stars on the Walk of Fame. We spent a few hours in a movie memorabilia museum looking at souvenirs and photos of the famous stars and various movie scenes.

We arrived home with an album full of photographs and many special memories.

Julie, feeling fit, fabulous, and fifty.

It was hard to get back to work after such a special trip but before we knew it we were back in the routine. It helped that it was time to plan our next holiday, our family ski trip in the spring.

We had a great family Christmas that year, which was made even more special because my niece and her boyfriend came out to stay with us and do some skiing.

On New Year's Eve, Graham and I sat in the hot tub at midnight toasting in the New Year. I was reflecting on the year that was coming to an end and said to Graham, "I always wanted to feel fit and fabulous at fifty, and that's exactly how I have felt this last year, despite losing a few more body parts."

He replied, "You have always been fit and fabulous whatever your age and despite the missing bits and pieces."

In February 2006, we had our annual ski holiday with Paul, Mel, and Abby, and I returned to work invigorated. Within a few days, I went down with the cold virus that was circulating around the office, which quickly went to my chest. The cough persisted for weeks until my whole chest hurt. I went to the doctors who listened to my chest but said he didn't hear anything that worried him. Eventually the cough stopped, and I seemed to be fine. But I was tired all the time. The dragon boat season started up and I started paddling again. I put the pain in my chest down to muscle pain from the paddling.

Our team was entered in a women's regatta late in May, but two nights before it, I woke up with a very bad headache that made me feel nauseous. Without thinking I jumped out of bed and headed for the bathroom. I would usually wake Graham if I had nausea because of the vagal attacks, but this time I didn't. The last thing I remember is walking through the bathroom door. Graham woke when he heard the loud thud as I fell down. He rushed in to the bathroom to find me unconscious on the floor, between the toilet and the shower. The vagal attack had caused me to pass out, but this time, I had hit my head on the toilet as I fell. By morning, I had a black eye and a bump on my forehead. I still felt a bit woozy on race day, but I couldn't let the team down so I went to the dragon boat race.

In May, I went to a farewell party for one of my dear friends from the dragon boat team who was moving to Alberta. We were having a great time dancing when I noticed I was getting short of breath. I put it down to being tired and forgot about it. By June, I was feeling exhausted all the time. I was very busy at work and the politics were getting me down. I had an annoying pain in my back that would not go away. I was still sure it was nothing, but it hurt to lift anything, and I seemed to get out of breath easily.

I was in the car in early June, heading to a home visit, and felt so tired I was dragging myself through the day. I was going past my doctor's office when I decided to stop and make an appointment to see him. The receptionist told me I could come back later that morning. So I dragged myself through the home visit, and headed back for the appointment. My doctor listened to my chest and said, "I'm not liking what I hear; you need to get an x-ray today."

I was a bit concerned, but I knew my doctor always checked everything out, just to be on the safe side, because of my previous cancers. Later that day, I was surprised to have a message from the doctor on my voice mail at work, requesting I call him. When I phoned the receptionist put me through to the doctor right away. His voice sounded grave as he told me, "You have some fluid on your lung."

I immediately asked "Is it a pleural effusion?" (A collection of fluid in the lining of the lung). I knew that with my history a pleural effusion was almost certainly metastatic cancer.

"Yes."

My heart dropped to my toes as I said, "That's not good is it?"

He said, "We don't know for sure yet what has caused it but we need to get some blood work done and get the fluid drained as soon as possible." He had already arranged an appointment for me with a specialist. I put the phone down and felt a wave of cold fear sweep over me. I knew that metastases were not curable and life expectancy was not very long.

In a state of numbness, I told my co-workers about the lung fluid and said that I needed to get some tests done, so I was leaving work early. I went to the lab for the blood work and then headed straight to Glenda's house, praying that she would be home. She opened the door and greeted me with her usual big smile.

Her smile quickly disappeared when she saw the look on my face. "What's wrong?" she asked. I told her about the fluid on my lung and the implications of this. We sat on her couch and both of us cried and cursed.

Glenda kept saying, "Oh, fuck, fuck, fuck, I won't let this happen to you." I repeated the word "fuck" over and over because it felt good to swear and be angry at the cancer. I was so grateful to have Glenda as a friend and that she was home that day when I needed her.

Eventually Glenda and I stopped swearing, and I headed for

home. Graham arrived home from work to find me sitting in the living room. He stopped in his tracks when he saw my face. I blurted out the very bad news. I don't remember much else about that night other than I know we were both very upset and worried. But Graham refused to be pessimistic, he reassured me that no matter what, we would get through it.

I made a decision that day that I had to remove all stress from my life and to do that I had to stop working. I needed all my emotional energy to fight the cancer for a third time. My work with the families was emotionally draining and my reserves were empty. I couldn't do one more home visit. I had nothing left to give. I knew that if I didn't remove this stress from my life it would kill me. I called my boss and told her I was going on medical leave. Graham took me to the office that weekend and we cleared out my desk and filing cabinet and I walked out without looking back. I know that this decision is one of the major reasons I am alive and writing this today.

The specialist didn't tell me much other than the fluid needed to be drained and sent to the lab to check for cancer cells. I could tell from his demeanor that he thought it was cancer but he was not going to say so until the tests proved it.

On the day of the fluid draining, Graham held my hand as the doctor numbed the area and inserted the tube. I didn't feel any pain. We then waited for the fluid to drain. Very quickly, over a litre of fluid had come out of my lung. After an x-ray to check that my lung had not collapsed, the doctor said I was fine. Initially I felt some relief from the breathlessness but within a few days I knew the fluid was building up again.

In early July, I again woke up in the night with the worst headache I had ever had and was very nauseous. This time I woke Graham up, and he ran downstairs for a plastic bucket because I was no longer allowed in the bathroom if I had nausea, he didn't want me banging my head. I didn't pass out this time, but I was very worried that this was a sign that the cancer had spread.

In mid July, I was supposed to go to Vancouver Island with my dragon boat team for a weekend regatta. I was unsure if I could go, but made a last-minute decision to go. My team mates were amazing. They picked me up emotionally and carried me through the weekend. I was so grateful to have so many warm and loving friends in my life. This time I fully understood the value of my floating support group. I had always said I hoped our team would inspire women who are newly diagnosed with breast cancer, and let women know that there is life after breast cancer, and it's wonderful. I realized that weekend that my mission in life now was to let women know that there is life after a diagnosis of metastatic breast cancer and that it is also wonderful. I came home even more determined to survive.

I met with a new oncologist on July 19, fully expecting to be told that chemotherapy was my only option. The doctor examined me and took my history. She was a little concerned about the severe headaches and ordered a full body and head CAT scan. I was also scheduled for abdominal ultrasounds and a bone scan.

She said there were treatment options but that at this stage the cancer was not curable. (I recently read a quote that said "incurable means it is only curable from within.")

The treatment would depend on what the tests revealed. If the news was bad we might need to go to chemotherapy straight away but if the news was good, then hormonal treatment might work for awhile. I didn't want to wait for the test results so I asked to be started on the hormone treatment immediately. The doctor agreed and pre-scribed one of the aromatase inhibitor drugs, but said we might need to change to chemotherapy, depending on the test results.

As we were about to leave, she said, "We can treat it, but you are probably looking at a life expectancy of 18 months to two years."

I already knew the statistics, but I also knew that nothing was 100% sure and if there was only a 1% chance I could survive, then I would be in that 1%. The stubborn determination kicked in, so as I stood to leave, I said "I need to let you know that I do not accept the 18 months to two years. I will have much more time than that."

She smiled and shook my hand saying, "I am happy to hear that, and I hope you are right."

I started taking the medication that day and within hours I was having continuous, major hot sweats. It didn't help that the weather was very hot. For three nights, I lay on the family room floor under the ceiling fan, naked except for the cold wet towels I had over me to cool me down. I didn't sleep much, but when I was awake I visualized the cancer cells melting and pouring out of my body as sweat.

Within a couple of weeks, I knew the drug was working. My breathing improved, the annoying cough was gone, and my energy was returning.

That summer was the first time in my adult life when I had time to take life slowly and to stop and smell the roses. I had been in some kind of paid employment since starting my Saturday job in the market at the age of 13, except for the few months after Paul was born. It was also the first time since I was 18 that I could just be me, not "Student Nurse," "Midwife," "Staff Nurse," "Health Visitor," or "Infant Development Consultant." I was just me, Julie the wife, mother, and grandmother. I focused on healing, while allowing myself to take things easy. Amazingly, I was not bored at all.

At about this time, a former dragon boat team member called me. She had been living with breast cancer metastases for a few years, so was a wealth of information for me. She gave me some links to online support groups, and she talked about how women with "mets" were living much longer. I went on the sites and was heartened to read about women who had mets but were living for many years and living well. I was reassured that I could survive. Most importantly, I learned that I had to be my own case manager, because treating metastatic breast cancer is a strategy game with many different treatments. The skill of the game is to not use up too many treatments too soon, and to keep the big guns (chemotherapy) for the more serious situations. Most of the women on the site had already had chemotherapy as a precaution after their initial diagnosis, but the cancer had still metastasized. Because most women who develop metastases have already had chemotherapy, their cancers already have some resistance to the chemotherapy drugs. I quickly realized that it was to my advantage that I had not yet had chemotherapy.

There was humor in the postings, and a lot of jargon that only a person living with mets would understand. I was considered a "chemo virgin" because I had never had chemotherapy. If a treatment was keeping the cancer stable it was referred to as "hanging out with the stable boy." What everyone craved was to "dance with NED". The letters NED referred to "No evidence of disease".

Miraculously all my tests were clear, there was no sign of cancer anywhere else in my body except for the pleura of my right lung. My brain scan was clear, so the headaches must have been coincidental. The best news was that the tumor markers had dropped dramatically, which meant that the treatment was working. What a relief! I was hanging out with the stable boy, but had yet to meet NED.

I had decided not to tell my family in England about this latest cancer diagnosis because my sister Geraldine, and her husband Alan, along with my mum, were scheduled to come out for a holiday in mid-August. I was not going to put a damper on their trip. I decided I would tell them at the end of the holiday. I was excited to show Geraldine and Alan our home and province because this was to be their first visit to Canada.

We had an emotional reunion at the airport before heading

home to Chilliwack. Paul, Mel, and Abby came over to our house, and we had a wonderful, lively family dinner. Later, after mum was in bed, and the kids had gone home, the four of us sat around the kitchen table catching up on our news..

Geraldine asked about my health and I gave a noncommittal reply of, "I'm fine." But Alan, who is a retired police detective, saw through my words. "It's not really fine, is it?"

Then I had to tell them the truth, and after a long discussion, we decided that there was no point telling mum, because I was going to live a long time and all she would do is worry. I also decided there was no need for anyone else in England to know yet. I had a huge sense of relief that I didn't have to give them the news. We had a fantastic three weeks together, during which time cancer hardly entered my mind. My sister and brother-in-law went off on a short tour of the Rockies. Mum was able to spend time with us, and go to Abby's birthday party. All of us went on a trip to Whistler. Before they left, we had a BBQ at home and invited all our friends.

In early August, I was saddened to hear from Glenda that Bonnie needed to have a biopsy on a breast lump that had been found by mammogram. It seemed unfair that she should have this scare so soon after she had had such a difficult time with surgery, infections, and chemotherapy for the colon cancer. Shortly after this, Glenda told me that Bonnie was diagnosed with breast cancer, but the worst news was that the follow-up tests had found metastases in her liver and adrenal gland.

With tears in her eyes Glenda said, "She has been told she only has three to six months to live." It must have been very difficult for Glenda, having two of her close friends diagnosed with metastatic cancer within a few months of each other. What were the odds that two of us would be facing this at the same time?

It was hard for me to comprehend such terrible news. I asked

Glenda if there was anything I could do to help Bonnie. She thought she may need some information from me about breast cancer treatments.

I realized then that Bonnie and I were destined to support each other during this difficult journey and that our friendship was not coincidental.

In September, I went with Bonnie to her oncology appointment. She was feeling overwhelmed with dealing with the breast cancer and metastasis diagnosis. She was devastated by the poor prognosis given to her, but Bonnie is a very determined and strong woman who was not ready to throw in the towel. In the car, we talked about the survival times we had been given.

I remember saying, "Bonnie, I refuse to accept my expiry date, it is based on statistics that do not take into account my strength and determination. We don't have to die when the doctors say we will."

The appointment went well. I was able to take notes for her which was easy for me because of my nursing background. The oncologist explained that the treatment and prognosis was dependent on what kind of cancer had metastasized. If it was breast cancer then it was not operable, but if it was colon cancer it was potentially curable with surgery and chemotherapy. It was agreed that Bonnie would have a mastectomy, and he would refer her to a surgeon who did liver resections. In the meantime, he would also organize a liver biopsy to determine if she had colon cancer mets or breast cancer mets. As we left the clinic I marveled at Bonnie's strength and determination. She had to face a mastectomy, a liver biopsy, and then liver surgery and chemotherapy, and yet she had a big smile on her face and was elated that there was a potential for a cure, so she may well have longer than a few months. I was glad that I could be a support to Bonnie during her surgery and treatments.

Bonnie had her mastectomy in September and her liver biopsy

soon after. The biopsy showed colon cancer in the liver, so she was scheduled for liver surgery in December.

That fall we drove together to her oncology appointments, and spent many hours chatting about all kinds of things. We were united in our fight not just to stay alive but to make sure we enjoyed every moment of whatever time we had left.

In October that year, I was back in the oncologist's office feeling elated because my blood work results showed that the tumor markers were down considerably which meant the treatment was working. However the chest x-ray showed some increased density that may have been scarring from the radiation, but needed further investigations. The radiologist recommended a lung biopsy. I was not sure that I wanted to go ahead with this. It didn't make sense that this was cancer because the tumor markers were dropping rapidly.

I researched symptoms of radiation damage to lungs and discovered that the most common symptom was a dry cough that starts about a month or two after the radiation is finished. I had this symptom at exactly this time, but we had put it down to allergies.

However, the main reason I didn't want a biopsy was that I had a history of two benign biopsies that within a year had developed into lumps at the biopsy site. Both of these lumps were later diagnosed as cancer. Even though I knew there was no scientific basis for it, I was not convinced that this was not cause and effect. Also, the cancer was in my pleura, and not in my lung, and I was worried that putting a biopsy needle through the diseased pleura would introduce cancer cells into the lung.

I called the oncologist to express my concern, but she was insistent it needed to be done to be certain I was on the right treatment. If this was cancer, then I might need to be on chemotherapy.

In November, Graham and I arranged a dinner at our house for Glenda and Rick, Bonnie and Pete, and Michelle and Darren. We laughed so much that night that my jaw ached. We all agreed that we should do dinners with the eight of us on a regular basis. We called them our survivor dinners because we were all survivors of something.

On November 29, 2006, I lay on the bed under the CAT scan machine. The radiologist and the technician were trying to locate the spot of the density on my lung so they could accurately do the biopsy that I did not want to be done. They did several scans with me on my back and then a couple with me on my stomach. The radiologist then came into the room and told me, "I can't do the biopsy because the area in question is behind the clavicle and major blood vessels in the front, and behind the shoulder blade at the back." (I had my reprieve!)

He recommended a PET scan that would show any malignant cells in my body. I was eligible for this scan now because a biopsy was not possible. PET was a noninvasive scan that was not yet approved for use in Canada, but I was referred to a research project at Vancouver General to get the scan done.

In January 2007, I had the scan which showed no cancer anywhere except in the pleura. The lung density was radiation scarring. This was great news; I was hoping to have a dance with NED (no evidence of disease) but hanging out with the stable boy (stable disease) was okay for now.

Bonnie had her surgery in December 2006 which included a liver resection, removal of her adrenal gland and removal of her gall bladder. She was scheduled to start intensive chemotherapy in early January 2007.

The weather was the typically cold, snowy, and icy conditions of southern British Columbia in January. Most of Bonnie's appointments were at 8 AM which required us to be on the road by 6 am. The first task on arrival at the cancer centre was for her to have blood taken to determine if the chemo could be given. On several occasions the bloodwork was not so good, and we had to go home and try again the following week.

Bonnie would bring along sandwiches and we would have chemo room picnics. Bonnie makes the best turkey sandwiches!

I have memories of lots of laughter despite the grueling regime of toxic drugs that Bonnie was enduring. Her spirits were high and we both talked many times about our determination to outlive the expiry dates given to us by our doctors.

Because of the many times her chemo had to be delayed, it was September before Bonnie finally finished her chemotherapy.

I was still stable on the aromatase inhibitor but my tumor markers were starting to creep up a little.

In late August 2007, Graham and I set off on what we called our Northern Adventure tour. We traveled through northern British Columbia and up into Alaska. It was another amazing holiday. The scenery was spectacular and as ever-changing as the weather. Too soon it was over, and we were back into our normal routine.

In late September, I was at Bonnie's house when we had a brilliant idea. I had heard about a television program called "Make-Over Wish." Each episode featured a person who had been nominated by friends to have a home renovation done for them. Bonnie and I talked about how much Glenda did for other people, and wouldn't it be wonderful if we could get her a home make over? That day we sat at Bonnie's computer and wrote a letter to the TV program, nominating Glenda. We had an almost instant reply. The show's producer was interested in doing a show about Glenda, and would be calling back within days to confirm it.

The next few weeks were so much fun; we made secret calls to Rick on his cell phone to let him in on the big surprise. There were times set for the producers to go to the house and take photos while Glenda was out. We recruited Michelle to arrange a fake photo shoot for Glenda to promote her public speaking business, that was actually the day she would be surprised by the film crew.

On the big day, the film crew gathered at Bonnie's house to get their makeup done. I arrived at Bonnie's house and was introduced to the show presenter and the designer who would be supervising the makeover.

Once again I was thinking to myself, "Is this really 'little Julie Smith' and her friend Bonnie who are meeting with a TV crew ready to film a show about our friend?" It was one of those moments when you want to pinch yourself to make sure it's not a dream.

We assembled in a park near Glenda's house along with a host of friends and family. The look on Glenda face was priceless; she was taken totally by surprise. It was a memorable day. Three days later, the renovations were revealed and Glenda's and Rick's living room had been transformed. It was hard for us to settle into normal living after such excitement.

Both Bonnie and I were feeling well that fall. Bonnie had finished her chemo and I was still stable on the hormone treatment.

Graham and I decided it was time to visit family in England so we booked flights to go home for Christmas. I was a bit worried about flying with my lung problem, but my doctor assured me I would be fine. A few weeks before we left, my back was a bit achy so I went to have my doctor check it just in case the fluid was building up again but it wasn't and my lung sounded good.

We stayed with my sister Geraldine and her husband Alan. They had moved to a picturesque village called Ribchester. We loved our time with them. We arrived late at night and slowly drove along the narrow street lined with quaint stone-built houses. The windows were illuminated with Christmas lights and the doors were decorated with Christmas wreaths. It was just lovely. Geraldine and Alan and their daughter Katie were all waiting to welcome us into their beautiful home. We were tired and hungry but not sure that we wanted to eat. Alan made us the best egg and beans on toast supper which we washed down with a welcome glass of wine.

Spending Christmas in the village was like stepping back in time. On Christmas Eve, the streets were busy with villagers walking around hand-delivering cards and presents while calling out greetings to each other. The church bells rang out on Christmas morning as we watched the Vicar rushing down the street in his long black frock to give the Christmas Day service. The local pub was warm and welcoming as were the people. We felt like we belonged after only a day or two.

It was good to spend some time with our aging parents and with our siblings. We had planned to visit some old friends between Christmas and the New Year but we both came down with nasty chest colds. We flew home on New Year's Day, looking forward to another good year ahead.

Once home, I had a bit more discomfort in my chest so I called the oncologist who didn't feel there was any cause for concern. In February 2008, I had my check-up at the cancer clinic and my tumor markers were starting to rise.

Bonnie was also having some problems with pain in her abdomen and was scheduled for a PET scan to check it out.

By March, the fluid was building up in my lung again, so the oncologist decided to change my medication. The new medication made me mildly nauseous but not enough to cause the vagal attacks. We waited to see if the medication would work. By May the fluid build-up was increasing, so I was referred to a thoracic surgeon.

The surgeon looked at my x-ray, and recommended a procedure

called pleurodesis. This would seal the two pleural layers together to stop the fluid buildup. Just before we left the office, the surgeon mentioned that if the lung didn't inflate it might be necessary to put in a chest tube that could be drained regularly.

I immediately said, "I am not ready to live with a tube sticking out of my chest."

The response was, "Don't worry, you are not likely to need it." I learned later that month that Bonnie's news was not good; she had new tumors in her abdomen so she needed to have more treatments.

In mid-June, I felt unwell and had quite severe back pain. The doctor ordered a chest x-ray which showed that the fluid had increased. He drained 1.5 liters of fluid from my pleural space. It felt like my lung was being ripped open as it tried to re-expand. The doctor encouraged me to breathe deeply through the procedure to inflate the lung as much as possible.

We were due to leave for our annual holiday in the interior of BC the following day and I was still not going to give the cancer the upper hand, so we went as planned. It was a wonderful trip, and I was reasonably successful at not thinking about the cancer and the surgery planned for July 8.

At my pre-admission appointment, I listened to the nurse explaining in detail about the chest drain I was going to have put in. I interrupted her, "I am having pleurodesis done and the surgeon told me I would not need the tube. I am not even sure I need to have the pleurodesis done because I don't think the fluid had built up again since I had it drained three weeks ago."

She replied, "Let's call the surgeon and check." She put down the phone and told me that the surgeon recommended that I go ahead with the surgery. The x-ray showed only a small accumulation of fluid but she recommended we go ahead with the procedure to seal the pleural space.

While in a sleepy haze after the surgery, I heard the nurse in the recovery room talking on the phone. "I am sending up a patient, Julie Houlker. She has a pleurex catheter in place. The pleurodesis was not done because the lung would not inflate fully. There were only about 300 mils (10 ounces) of fluid drained during surgery."

I put my hand to my side and felt the large dressing and the outline of the drain beneath it. I was devastated. Why had this been done to me, when there were only 300 mils of fluid accumulated?

I spent the next days trying to come to terms with this painful tube in my chest. I could not understand why I should feel so ill. My chest hurt, and my lungs rattled when I breathed, and the tube felt like a red-hot poker in my side. I had been feeling good the day I entered the hospital for surgery. I asked several times, without success, to speak to the surgeon. I was seen by a junior doctor who didn't give me the answers I needed, but told me I could go home, and I would be given an appointment to see the surgeon the following week.

On the day I was scheduled to go home, a woman walked into my room and announced, "I am the nurse from the hospice and palliative care program, and I am here to give you information about follow-up care of your tube." My mind went into overdrive as I thought, "Palliative care? I don't need palliative care. What did they find when they did the surgery? Do I have only weeks to live?"

The nurse continued to talk, and I heard her say, "You will need to have it drained three times a week by the home care nurses. They will tell you what day they will visit but not a time."

By this time I was angry. "I have only needed it drained twice in two years so far, and now I have to have it drained three times a week? And this is supposed to have improved my quality of life? Not only do I have to have it drained three times a week, but I have to sit at home, waiting for the nurses to visit, because they will not give me an appointment time?" I was furious that the cancer would be in control for three days of every week of my life, but I was also not about to let that happen. I kept my composure long enough to say, "I want the tube removed," before bursting into tears.

They brought back the junior doctor who could not give me a good reason why the tube had been put in, but said if I wanted to take the risk of having it removed, I should talk to the surgeon. With some anger, I pointed out that I could not see the surgeon until the following week. Finally, I calmed down and told them that I would do the draining myself. It was agreed that the home care nurses in Chilliwack could help me to become familiar with how to do it.

I went home on Thursday, and by early Friday I had a fever, and felt extremely ill. The tube continued to feel like a burning poker in my side, and I had developed a cough. As instructed, I contacted the surgeon on call, and was admitted back to hospital for IV antibiotics to treat the infection that had been caused by the tube. Which I didn't want. And had refused. And got anyway.

Eventually on the Friday evening, the surgeon appeared at my bedside having been told by the head nurse that it was imperative that I get a full explanation as to why the tube was in place.

The surgeon explained, "Your lung would not inflate, which made it impossible to do the procedure to seal the pleura, so we put in the tube. I put it in the front of your chest so you can drain it yourself."

"I want it taken out; this has ruined my quality of life."

The surgeon replied, "Lots of people have colostomies and manage just fine; this is just a little tube. Don't tell anyone you have it, and no one will know."

I tried to explain, "It's not about people knowing or not. It's about having a painful drain in my chest that is a huge risk for infection. It's about not being able to even hug my husband without being in pain, because the tube is on the front of my chest. It is about never being able to soak in the bath or hot tub again. It is about the cancer being in control, because I have to have the tube drained three times a week. Most of all, it's about the fact that I have only needed my lung drained twice in two years, and I don't believe I needed this drain to be put in."

The surgeon asked me to agree to keep the drain in for a month and if there was not much drainage it would be removed. I was discharged home the following day even though I was still having fevers at night, which the surgeon said were probably caused by the cancer. The home care nurses in Chilliwack were wonderful; they set me up with the supplies I needed to drain the tube at home.

For the next month, I drained the tube at home but hardly any fluid came out. It still hurt and felt like a poker in my chest. I felt ill and tired, and I became increasingly depressed. I felt as though my spirit had been broken, and that the cancer had won the day. I was so exhausted it took all my energy to shower in the morning and once showered, I had to lie down and rest. I had no interest in anything and Graham was at a loss as to what to do to help me. One evening we argued about something so silly I don't remember what it was. We ended up screaming at each other, and I accused him of not loving me. Eventually Graham put on his jacket and went for a walk. When he returned he was distraught, and I could see he had been crying.

With both of us in tears, we sat down to talk. I will never forget his words that night as he tried to explain to me why he was so distressed. "I love you so much and I can cope with anything as long as you have hope. But I feel like you have given up and have decided to let the cancer win. I need you to believe that we have a future together or I can't go on." I realized he was right. I had given up hope and had allowed the cancer to be in control. I promised him I would rebuild my faith and recover my determination to survive.

The next day I talked to Bonnie and asked her, "How do I cope with the thought that I may be on chemo for the rest of my life?"

She replied, "You cope by getting up and smiling every day. You remind yourself that this is another day that you are still alive and life is good. It's one day at a time."

I knew she was right, and was so grateful to have a friend who knew exactly what I was going through because she had been through it in ways worse than mine.

After three weeks, I called the surgeon's office and requested an appointment to have the tube removed. The receptionist explained that I had an appointment to see the doctor the following week, and if the tube could be removed, I would be given an appointment.

In my most assertive voice I said, "I want the tube removed, it is not draining any fluid. I want it removed as soon as possible. I do not want to have to wait another week or two after seeing the surgeon, to get it taken out. Please schedule me for removal next week."

The receptionist gave me an appointment for the day after my appointment with the surgeon. I knew then that I was back in control, and had a chance of beating the cancer.

The day after the tube was removed was the Cultus Lake Dragon Boat Festival. I was in no fit state to be on the boat, but I went to watch in the morning and to do a short presentation during the carnation ceremony for the breast cancer survivors.

As I started to speak, I looked at my team across the water all holding their carnations. The emotions of the past month welled up inside me as I spoke into the microphone. After a few sentences, the tears were running down my face as I wondered if I would ever be on the boat again with my team mates. I cut the speech short and left for home.

It was Saturday morning and a paddle practice morning a week after having the tube removed, when I woke up feeling extremely ill. Once again I had a fever and severe pain in my back.

Graham was steersperson for the boat so I told him to go to the practice and I would take some Tylenol and try to sleep. Reluctantly he went.

By the time he came home, I knew I had to go to emergency. The triage nurse did my vital signs and took me straight to a bed. I had a fever of 38.7C (101.6 F) and a pulse rate of 140. Within minutes, I had an IV in place and was on antibiotics. I am now convinced that the reason I had felt so ill for the month while the tube was in my chest, was that I had an infection the whole time. I also found out from the specialist at the Chilliwack hospital that after the tube had been placed, the chest x-ray had shown that I had a hydro pneumothorax. This means the procedure had somehow caused air to leak into the pleural space, resulting in both air and fluid in the pleural space. Thankfully, by this time, the air had reabsorbed and the fluid had not built up since the surgery.

In the month since the surgery, I had lost 10 pounds and I left the hospital feeling weak and worn out.

My oncologist had moved away, so I was scheduled to see a different oncologist in the new Abbotsford Cancer Centre at the beginning of September. Prior to my appointment, I had an appointment for a CAT scan.

I recounted the events of the past few weeks to my new oncologist as she reviewed my blood tests. The blood work still showed the effects of the infection and my CAT scan showed some enlarged lymph nodes that were due either to the infection or to cancer spread. She talked about starting chemotherapy on a weekly basis, but said I needed to recover from the infection fully before I could start chemo. I listened in a detached way as she said, "It's your decision, but I would recommend that you have a port put in to make it easier to administer the chemo."

I said, "I was hoping to have more time on hormonal treatments before starting chemo. What about Falsodex?

"In my experience, it rarely works," she replied.

I then asked, "Can I try Tamoxifen again? It worked for almost five years before I had to stop taking it because of the uterine enlargement, but I no longer have a uterus."

She stopped to think momentarily. "There is a slim chance that Tamoxifen would work for a while, and I can't give you any chemo until you have fully recovered from the infection. so we could try it for a short time."

I knew in my soul that it would work and started taking it that day.

For the next few weeks, I had severe pain in my lung area and constant hot flashes. I knew that pain in the first few weeks of treatment was common when a treatment was working. Initially, my tumor markers went up which is another common symptom that indicates that the treatment is working and the cancer cells are dying.

The next month, I felt much better and the markers dropped. The depression lifted and I was hopeful again. My energy started to return, and slowly I regained the weight I had lost. Graham was relieved to see me returning to my normal self. He told me he was happy that, "I have my Julie back."

I was seeing the oncologist on a monthly basis and going with Bonnie to her appointments, so we both became very familiar with the newly opened hospital in nearby Abbotsford. We joked about being regulars at the Cancer Centre. We often had to show people how to use the new parking ticket machines.

In September, I went with Bonnie to her first appointment with her new oncologist. It was decided that she would have radiation to the abdominal tumors and then chemo. The radiation went well and she started chemo again that fall but it was in tablet form not IV chemo. At first Bonnie had quite bad side effects from the chemo but it seemed to be working. She had less pain and eventually the side effects eased.

By Christmas I was feeling good and hopeful again, and Bonnie seemed to be doing okay. Graham and I brought in the New Year in our hot tub. We were optimistic about the future again and were determined to enjoy every moment of every day.

Early in the new year, I heard that Michelle had a story she had written published in Canadian Living Magazine. She planned a reading for family and friends in March 2009. On the day of the reading, Glenda, Bonnie, and I sat in the front row of seats.

There was a connection among the four of us that could not be described in words. It was a loving connection of friends who knew that they had been drawn together by inexplicable forces. Our friendship formed before we had all been diagnosed with cancer but deepened by our eventual diagnosis of cancer.

In March, I went with Bonnie to her oncology appointment where she was told she now had a small pleural effusion. What were the odds that two friends who met before being diagnosed with different cancers would both eventually have metastatic cancer and pleural effusions? It was decided that a sample of the fluid would be taken to check for cancer cells. On the way home, we laughed as I joked that this was taking friendship too far. She really didn't need to get a pleural effusion just like me.

In late March, I opened my email to see a message from Michelle titled, "Pack your bags—we are going on a girl's road trip."

She wanted the four of us to go on a girl's weekend to Bellingham. We planned it for the first weekend in April. Two days before our planned trip, I went with Bonnie to get the results of the tests on the fluid. We were delighted to hear that the fluid didn't have cancer cells in it.

I lay in bed the night before we left thinking about the four of us, our lives, our cancers, and our friendships, and it occurred to me that we should write a book.

The weekend was awesome; we went shopping, had a manicure, went out for a lovely meal at a Mexican restaurant, tried on sexy shoes in the erotic lingerie/adult toy store, and laughed so much it hurt.

When it was time to go to bed, we each went into the bathroom and came out looking different. Bonnie and I had removed our breast prostheses, and we were flat-chested on one side. Glenda, who usually wore a skirt, had put on a short night dress so her missing limb was more obvious.

Michelle, who had lost her spleen to cancer but had no visible missing pieces came out of the bathroom with her hand extended and her contact lenses on her finger tips. She laughed as she said, "There, I took out my prostheses." We all collapsed in laughter.

The following day, we had breakfast and then headed to the old town area of Fairhaven. We gravitated to the three-story book store and ended up in the section of inspirational books.

I thought about my idea of us writing a book before saying, "You know we really should write a book together about our friendship, and our journeys with cancer." Everyone went quiet but then replied enthusiastically that we should do just that. We started writing in April and we continued to meet regularly to encourage each other.

It was in late April, that Bonnie and I were in the medical imaging department at the new hospital preparing for her to have the fluid drained from her lung. She had started to have symptoms of pleural effusion and needed it drained. We laughed with the nurses and talked about the book we were writing. The nurses were surprised to hear that I had already had this procedure done twice. Bonnie told the nurses our stories and chuckled as she said, "Julie is one of the few women who have had a mastectomy twice on the same side, isn't that funny?"

The nurse had a quizzical look on her face when she replied, "Not really."

I think it was hard for them to see what we had to laugh about. But we had both learned that when dealing with such a serious disease there was only one way to cope, and that was one day at a time. Also, that laughter helped us get through most things. Bonnie had a huge amount of fluid drained that day, only to have it build up again very quickly.

I was with Bonnie at her next oncology appointment when the doctor told her the tablet form of chemo was not working and she needed to start on IV chemo again. Bonnie was a bit quiet on the way home. I knew she was trying to come to terms with facing the next round of chemo.

I took her for the first chemo appointment, which went very well and seemed to go quickly as we chatted about writing the book during our chemo room picnic. We were delighted to hear that her bloodwork was good two weeks later, when she was due to have her second chemo. By this time, Bonnie had a tube in her chest to drain the fluid that continued to accumulate very quickly and caused her to have a cough and to become breathless.

Bonnie was feeling the effects of the chemo, and not feeling up to writing, so on her second chemo day in addition to having our chemo room picnic, we worked on her story. She talked while I typed on my laptop.

A week later, Bonnie told me she was having fevers at night and was feeling ill. It was Monday and I was due to go out with the dragon boat team. I made her promise that if her temperature went up again that evening, she would go to emergency. At 10:30 PM Pete called me to say Bonnie had been admitted to hospital and was on IV antibiotics. It appeared that the chest tube had become infected and once again Bonnie's experience was mirroring my experience of the year before. She was discharged from hospital after a few days but was still not well. We went to her oncology appointment the following week, and after hearing that she was still having fevers and looking at her dangerously low blood counts, the oncologist arranged to admit her to hospital again. She was in hospital for a week before the infection was under control and her blood counts were up high enough for her to be out of danger.

We were due to leave for our June holiday to the BC interior. I hated leaving when Bonnie was so ill but I knew Pete and their two sons, as well as Glenda and Michelle, would be visiting regularly so she would have lots of support. She looked frail and tired the day before we left and she was on my mind for the whole time we were away. Glenda promised me that she would call me if there was any change for the worse and if I didn't hear from her then all was well. Thankfully, my phone never rang during our holiday.

By the time I came home, Bonnie was feeling better and recuperating at home. She was referred to a thoracic surgeon to have the pleurodesis done to seal the pleura, and by coincidence, was referred to the same thoracic surgeon who had put in my chest drain. The week prior to her surgery I took her for the pre-admission appointment where she had to have tests in various parts of the hospital which required some walking. Bonnie was exhausted and breathless. The infections, the chemo, and the antibiotics had worn her out. I chatted about the book writing and all kinds of other things as we waited but Bonnie was not in the mood to chat. There was no laughter that day and I was worried about her. Her surgery went exactly as mine had. The sealing of the pleura could not be done so she came out of hospital with a pleurex catheter.

The following week, we saw her oncologist again who informed us that her bloods were back to normal so she could be scheduled to start chemo again. The date was set for the same day that I was due to leave for a dragon boat festival with my team. I was sorry I could not be with her, but I knew she had arranged for another friend to take her and would be in good hands. I prayed that this chemo will work for Bonnie and would give her a long remission.

The dragon boat festival was awesome. Graham steered and I drummed. Our team won a gold medal. I smiled for the whole weekend. During the festival there was a carnation ceremony where all the breast cancer teams assemble their boats into a raft and wave carnations in the air as a significant song is played before tossing them into the water in memory of those who have lost their battle with breast cancer.

As I sat at the front of the boat I looked at Graham who was standing at the back and our eyes locked for the entire time the song was playing. We both had big smiles on our faces. As the music faded, he blew me a kiss. We were both so happy to be on the boat for another year. I was fulfilling my mission of being an inspiration to women with metastatic breast cancer, proving that there is life after the diagnosis of metastases and it is wonderful.

It is now mid-July 2009. I am still doing well on Tamoxifen, I have not needed the fluid drained from my lung since last July, and I have my life energy back.

Life is wonderful and is made even more wonderful by the precious love of my soul mate, my family, and my dear friends. I don't know how long I have left on this earth but I do know that I will do my best to enjoy every moment of every day.

It is three years since my diagnosis of metastases, and I am still a chemo virgin. Chemo may be in my future but I am now confident that it will work well if I need it because the cancer has not yet been exposed to any chemo drugs. I take great comfort in knowing that I am now well past the "expiry date" given to me by the oncologist in 2006.

Choosing to Smile

It has been sixteen years since I first saw the blood oozing out of my right nipple, and it will be fourteen years in December since I was given the diagnosis of breast cancer. In that time, I have experienced many wonderful things in life some of which would not have happened if I had not had cancer. I don't know that I can say for sure that I wished the cancer had not happened.

I hate the anguish it has caused Graham and my family. My body is covered with scars from the surgeries and radiation and I am missing a few body parts, but there have been many blessings in my life brought about by the cancer. I now live every day to the fullest, and take nothing for granted. There have been so many highs in the past sixteen years as well as lows. Life is a journey and my life so far has been an exciting, adventurous journey, and I have not yet reached my destination. I now know that "choosing to smile" through whatever happens in life is the only option for me.

I still believe in miracles, so my long-term goals are to be named in the medical books as the longest living survivor of metastatic breast cancer, and of course, to attend my grand-daughter's graduation and wedding. My stubborn determination tells me I will survive to old age!

I visualize Graham and me sitting out on our deck in our old age reminiscing and planning the menu for our next survivor dinner with Glenda, Rick, Bonnie, Pete, Michelle, and Darren.

We have love and hope and that's all that matters!

Epilogue

In the fall of 2009, Julie started chemotherapy when tests showed that the hormonal treatment was no longer controlling the cancer. She remains very optimistic about reaching her goal of becoming the world's longest recorded survivor of metastatic breast cancer. Although Julie lost her hair she loves her sassy wig. She is looking forward to another season with her Spirit Abreast Dragonboat team and fulfilling her mission of showing the world that there is life after metastatic breast cancer. Follow Julie's blog on the "Choosing to Smile" web site at www.choosingtosmile.com Her son Paul, his wife Melanie, and their daughter live close by and Julie sees her wonderful grand-daughter Abby as often as possible.

Glenda continues to give keynote speeches and present her "Smoking Awareness Program for Teens." She has written her second children's book, *The Feather Tree,* which is in press. Visit her web site www.glendastandeven.com to book her for an event. Her mother continues to live in the suite attached to Rick and Glenda's home in Chilliwack and she will celebrate her 87th birthday in December 2010. Glenda's son, Kevin, owns a successful survey company in Chilliwack, BC, and is busy renovating his first house with his wife Kimberly who is now an elementary school teacher. Glenda's youngest son, Andrew, lives at home and is planning on attending college now that he has graduated with honours from Chilliwack Secondary school in 2009.

Michelle continues to work at the University of the Fraser Valley as an International Student Education Advisor. She is also planning to write a second book about the international travel experiences she and her husband Darren have had. The two of them are also kept busy remodeling their country home in Yarrow, BC. Michelle's two daughters, Melissa and Megan, are both working and finishing their degrees at UFV. Michelle's stepsons, Curtis and Spencer, have both graduated high school and are working locally.

Although Bonnie Holmes never completed writing her autobiography she is still very much part of the "Choosing to Smile" story. She is the fourth member of the Survivor Dinner Group and we would be remiss in not including her in the epilogue. In January 2010, Bonnie tried a new antibody treatment that showed promise. Her husband, two sons, and her many friends were very supportive, but on March 28, 2010, Bonnie passed away peacefully at Chilliwack General Hospital.

Julie Houlker never gave up her hope for a long life, but the reality of her diagnosis was evident as her health slowly declined, despite the chemotherapy treatments. With her family's support, Julie stopped treatment and passed away in hospice care on January 21, 2011, in the arms of her loving husband, Graham. Her son Paul was at her side with his wife, Mel, and Julie's much loved grand-daughter Abby. Her soul-sisters, Michelle and Glenda, were with her throughout her last night. Julie has left a legacy of love and hope in her words and she would want all who read her story to be inspired to choose to smile for however long they have. To read more of Julie's story, read her blog at www.choosingtosmile.com

These women epitomize the resilience of the human spirit. All four women understand how quickly life can change, and how important it is to accept the changes — both the good and the bad. They are ordinary women who have come to the realization that throughout our lives we are continually being faced with a simple choice — we can choose to be unhappy or we can choose to smile.

Acknowledgments

This book has taken more than 50 years to write and the list of people who contributed to its success are far too numerous to mention individually. We trust that you know who you are and you know how much you are loved. We want to thank our families and friends (some names have been changed)—especially our incredibly wonderful husbands—who have supported us over the years and always encouraged our dreams. We also want to thank each other because without each other's support and encouragement this book and the whole "Choosing to Smile" movement would never have happened.

Without the strong hands of our editors, Wendy McClelland and Detta Penna, this book would be three times the size it is now. Thank you for helping us to determine what to leave in and what to leave out. A special thanks to Detta for also working her magic in the book design; to Karen Massier for her wonderful photography on the front cover; our proof reader, Sarah Nermo, who made sure all our "i"s were dotted and our "t"s were crossed. We'd really like to thank the band, Slapjack—Trish and Gary Nichols and Fred Webber —who worked tirelessly and, more importantly, just for love, to put Glenda's words for the "Choosing to Smile" theme song into the most amazing musical production. The song inspires everyone who hears it:

> *We can choose to be blue and cry over all the things that we*
> *   have lost*
> *Or we can choose to smile and say it was oh so worth the cost!*
> *Just to be alive and share with you makes me smile; it's so*
> *   hard to be blue.*
> *So we're choosing to smile! We're all choosing to smile!*

Our wonderful logo is a silhouette of two smiling faces nose to nose and forehead to forehead, which creates the image of a lit candle in the white space between them. It's inspired by a common optical illusion but to us it means so much more. Our friendships with each other have helped to light the dark times and smiling always brings light into our lives. Our logo symbolizes the light that is found in friendship and smiles. Thanks to everyone who had a hand in designing our "Choosing to Smile" logo.

So many wonderful people helped this book to become a reality. To all our family and friends on the "Choosing to Smile" Facebook site, a huge thank you for continuing to spread this concept around the world. It is our sincere hope that we will all continue to choose to smile no matter what obstacles are put in our paths. Blessings to all!

Julie Houlker was born in northern England, U.K, where she qualified and worked as a state registered nurse, midwife, and health visitor. In 1988, along with her husband Graham and their son Paul, she moved to Chilliwack, BC, Canada. She worked in Chilliwack as an infant development consultant from 1988 to 2006.

Diagnosed in 1995, Julie is a 14-year cancer survivor who has been living with metastatic breast cancer since 2006. Despite facing breast cancer three times Julie has chosen to smile and live life to the fullest. She is determined to make every moment of every day count and has been an active member of the breast cancer survivor dragon boat team, "Spirit Abreast," since 2002.

She served as co-chair in 2008 and 2009, and is looking forward to being the team manager in 2010. When health issues stopped her from active paddling, she took over the job of team drummer and loves every minute of her time on the boat. Her husband Graham is the steersperson for the team so dragon boating is a family affair. Son Paul and his wife Melanie live close by, and Julie spends many precious hours with her much-loved granddaughter, Abbygail.

Julie believes that her mission in life now is to inspire others to choose to smile through adversity and to demonstrate to others that there is life after a diagnosis of metastatic disease. In addition to this, her goals are to be written up in the medical journals as one of the longest-living survivors of metastatic breast cancer and to attend her granddaughter's graduation and wedding.

About the Author

Michelle Rickaby was born in 1959 in Abbotsford, BC, Canada. She grew up with her two older siblings, Bonnie and Jim. Michelle married her high school boyfriend. They started a family with the birth of their first daughter, Melissa. Two years later Melissa was followed by their second daughter, Megan.

In 1988, Michelle was diagnosed with Hodgkin's lymphoma. Doctors removed her spleen and she underwent forty radiation treatments. After recovery she returned to university to complete her Bachelor of Arts degree. Hoping for a fresh start, the family moved to Chilliwack, but Michelle and her husband divorced a few years later. She has worked at the University of the Fraser Valley for the past 16 years and is currently an education advisor for international students.

Michelle married Darren Rickaby in 2005. They blended their families of Melissa and Megan and Darren's two sons, Curtis and Spencer, along with their dog, Tucker. Michelle and Darren love to travel to all parts of the world for exotic adventures, the most recent being Cambodia. It wouldn't be unusual to find them snorkeling with sharks, riding elephants, or hiking in the jungle. Besides travelling, Michelle also enjoys gardening, dragon boating, and writing. Michelle has published two travel articles and, in 2009 her personal story, "My Symbol of Hope," was published in the April issue of *Canadian Living* magazine.

Michelle has been a volunteer with the Canadian Cancer Society for over 20 years, trying to "give back" the kindness and support she received during her cancer diagnosis, treatment, and subsequent recovery. She spent too many years worrying and has learned that "choosing to smile" makes it so much easier to face all of life's many challenges.

Glenda Standeven was born in North Vancouver, BC, Canada, in 1955, and moved with her family to the small town of Yarrow, BC, in 1962. She grew up as a small-town farm girl with big ideas. She graduated from Chilliwack Secondary School in 1973, and moved to Alberta in 1975, where she lived and worked for the next three years. She met her future husband, Rick, in 1979, and they married in 1982. The couple had their first son, Kevin, two years later in their hometown, Chilliwack, BC, in 1984.

Five years into their marriage, Glenda was diagnosed with bone cancer. After a nine-month struggle, she lost her entire right leg, hip, and pelvis, to the disease in January 1988. Despite her disability, she gave birth to their second son in November, 1990, less than three years after her amputation.

"Choosing to Smile" is the attitude Glenda adopted early in her journey through the diagnosis and treatment of her cancer. She donated countless volunteer hours in her community and has received numerous awards for her efforts, including the prestigious Governor General's Caring Canadian Award in 2005.

Glenda and Rick reside in Chilliwack with their son, Andrew. Their older son, Kevin, and his wife Kimberly, live nearby. Glenda spends her free time speaking, traveling, and presenting her unique *Smoking Awareness Program for Teens* to middle school students. She has written two children's books that are in the process of being illustrated and is currently working on a third.

Choosing to Smile Book Fund

The Valley Women's Network (VWN), www.valleywomensnetwork. com Chilliwack Branch, created the Choosing to Smile Book Fund in order to spread the message of hope and inspiration to others facing adversity. The money donated to this fund is used to purchase copies of *Choosing to Smile* which are then given free of charge to patients who are undergoing treatments for cancer.

Donations can be made at any branch of the Envision Credit Union:

> The Choosing to Smile Book Fund—account #1455864
> Contact Joyce Esau: joyceesau@gmail.com, 604-858-2409

To receive a charitable tax receipt for a larger corporate or personal donation: make your cheque payable to:

> The New Page Human Services Society
> P.O. Box 998, Hope, BC, V0X 1L0
> *(Designate funds to The Choosing to Smile Book Fund)*
> Contact Arnice Asquin: arnice@telus.net, 604-793-8124

Choosing to Smile Publications gives a donation from the purchase of every book purchased through the VWN *Choosing to Smile Book Fund* back to the VWN Chilliwack Branch to support their local "Robertson School Families in Need" program. As well, Choosing to Smile Publications donates a percentage from every *Choosing to Smile* book purchased through the New Page Human Services Society back to the society for their ongoing support of literacy initiatives in the community.

It is our privilege to be connected to this wonderful circle of caring.
Choosing to Smile Publications
www.choosingtosmile.com

Order Form

For additional copies of this book

Choosing to Smile

by Julie Houlker, Michelle Rickaby, and Glenda Standeven

Please find _____ enclosed, for _____ copy(ies) of *Choosing to Smile* by Julie Houlker, Michelle Rickaby, and Glenda Standeven @ $19.95 each, plus shipping and handling. (See below.*) Please make checks payable to **Choosing to Smile Publications.**

Mail to: Choosing to Smile Publications
P. O. Box 2372
Sardis Station Main
Chilliwack, BC V2R 1A7
Canada

Send to:

Name _____

Address _____

_____

City _____ State/Province _____

Country _____

Phone (day) _____ (evening) _____

Email _____

(We will not share, sell, or rent your information.)

Or order online at

www.choosingtosmile.com

*Shipping and handling for U.S. orders is $9.00 per book.
*Shipping and handling for Canadian orders is $13.00 per book.